Elementary Mathematics and Science Methods:

Inquiry Teaching and Learning

Gerald W. Foster

DePaul University

Wadsworth Publishing Company

$I\widehat{T}P^{®}$ An International Thomson Publishing Company

Belmont, CA • Albany, NY • Boston • Cincinnati • Detroit • Johannesburg • London • Madrid • Melbourne
Mexico City • New York • Pacific Grove, CA • Scottsdale, AZ • Singapore • Tokyo • Toronto

Education Editor: Dianne Lindsay
Assistant Editor: Tangelique Williams
Marketing Manager: Becky Tollerson
Project Editor: Jennie Redwitz
Print Buyer: Barbara Britton
Permissions Editor: Susan Walters
Production: Rachel Youngman, Hockett Editorial Service

Cover and Interior Design: Lisa Mirski-Devenish
Copy Editor: Sheryl Rose
Illustrator: James Edwards
Cover Image: Stephen Simpson/© FPG International
Compositor: Fog Press
Printer: Mazer Corporation

Science Teaching Standards (A–F), Content Standards (A–G) for grades K–4 and 5–8 and Unifying Concepts and Processes, Assessment Standards (A–E), Program Standards (A–F), and Professional Development Standards (A–D), are reprinted, with permission, from *National Science Education Standards.* Copyright 1996 by the National Academy of Sciences. Courtesy of the National Academy Press, Washington, D.C.

NCTM Standards: Teaching Standards (1–6), Content Standards (11–13), Assessment Standards (1–10), Program Standards (11–14), and Professional Development Standards (1–6), are reprinted, with permission, from *Curriculum and Evaluation Standards for School Mathematics* (1989) and *Professional Standards for Teaching Mathematics* (1991). Copyright by the National Council of Teachers of Mathematics, Reston, VA.

The "Fossilized Footprints" drawings on page 106 are reprinted, with permission, from J. Abruscato and J. Hassard, *Loving and Beyond,* Santa Monica, CA: Goodyear. Copyright © 1976 by J. Abruscato and J. Hassard.

COPYRIGHT © 1999 by Wadsworth Publishing Company
A Division of International Thomson Publishing Inc.
I(T)P® The ITP logo is a registered trademark under license.

Printed in the United States of America
3 4 5 6 7 8 9 10

For more information, contact Wadsworth Publishing Company, 10 Davis Drive, Belmont, CA 94002, or electronically at
http://www.wadsworth.com/wadsworth.html

International Thomson Publishing Europe
Berkshire House 168-173
High Holborn
London, WC1V 7AA, England

Thomas Nelson Australia
102 Dodds Street
South Melbourne 3205
Victoria, Australia

Nelson Canada
1120 Birchmount Road
Scarborough, Ontario
Canada M1K 5G4

International Thomson Publishing GmbH
Königswinterer Strasse 418
53227 Bonn, Germany

International Thomson Editores
Campos Eliseos 385, Piso 7
Col. Polanco
11560 México D.F. México

International Thomson Publishing Asia
60 Albert Street
#15-01 Albert Complex
Singapore 189969

International Thomson Publishing Japan
Hirakawacho Kyowa Building, 3F
2-2-1 Hirakawacho
Chiyoda-ku, Tokyo 102, Japan

International Thomson Publishing Southern Africa
Building 18, Constantia Park
240 Old Pretoria Road
Halfway House, 1685 South Africa

Photo credits: page 1: © Will & Deni McIntyre, Photo Researchers; page 59: © Richard Hutchings, Photo Researchers; page 153: © Jill Fineberg, 1990, Photo Researchers; page 319: © Elaine Rebman, 1992, Photo Researchers.

Library of Congress Cataloging-in-Publication Data
Foster, Gerald W.
    Elementary mathematics and science methods: inquiry teaching and learning / Gerald W. Foster.
      p. cm.
    Includes bibliographical references and index.
    ISBN 0-534-51579-7
    1. Mathematics—Study and teaching (Elementary) 2. Science—Study and teaching (Elementary)
I. Title
QA135.5.F632   1999   98-38687
    372.7—dc21

 This book is printed on acid-free recycled paper.

*To the children of the world and elementary classroom teachers,
who devote their lives to nurturing children's emotional
and intellectual needs.*

BRIEF CONTENTS

CONTENTS

As a child, you may have had many questions about the world. Your curiosity and inquisitiveness created a desire to find answers to your questions. As an adult, your spirit of personal inquiry may have disappeared. Your questions may have changed from "I really want to know" to "what can I do to get a good grade or a good job?" The purpose of this book is to resurrect your feelings of inquisitiveness and raise questions about the natural processes of learning and teaching science and mathematics. This purpose is reflected in the themes of problem solving and inquiry found in the national standards for both mathematics and science. You may insist that being told what content to teach and the teaching procedures to use is more important than mentally constructing a knowledge base about teaching and learning mathematics and science. Being told what to do is far easier than learning from experience. However, various research studies indicate that "memorized" teaching is no less effective than "memorized" science and mathematics content.

Both the National Science Education Standards and the National Council of Teachers of Mathematics Standards call for *facilitating* learning rather than giving facts to children. Science and mathematics knowledge develops through active learning processes. The same is true in learning to teach mathematics and science. One has to learn about learning to teach. Otherwise, all of those given facts will be forgotten with nothing to fall back on when situations arise in the classroom that were not discussed in teacher preparation courses. Learning is highly individualized and teaching is highly individualized. What Elvin (1977) said twenty years ago is still relevant today:

> To give teachers routine training, instead of genuine professional education is now out of the question. For one thing, there is not a subject taught where methods of teaching are not matters of dispute. The teacher has to think for himself and make up his own mind. Is he for the new mathematics or not? Does he sympathize with the new emphasis on lively speech in early English teaching as distinct from emphasis on grammar and spelling? In the introduction to the sciences how far is he willing to press discovery methods? . . . One reason for his having to make up his own mind is that there is no invariable best method. Some methods in general may clearly be better than others, but some methods are better suited to some children than others and some better suited to one teacher's personal style than others. (p. 134)

Instructional methodologies cannot be given and worn like pieces of clothing. "Putting on clothes" is a passive approach to learning. Clothes change as styles change. Teaching based on trends and styles is in a constant flux. This forces teachers to make changes that are sometimes drastic, that require tearing down one frame of reference and erecting another. Learning to teach is a mental construction acquired through first-hand experiences. This construction taps into natural learning processes that are constant and do not change with styles and trends. Active learning creates knowledge foundations with a framework for the adaptation and modification of new knowledge.

Inquiry and problem solving inherently promotes questions about traditional beliefs and attitudes and creates alternative instructional strategies congruent to the nature of learning. This focus serves the purpose of developing a rationale or logic for decision making and promotes critical thinking.

As a reader you may totally disagree with statements in this book, but ask yourself: Does your disagreement stem from the traditional mind-set of wanting to know the facts or from what you know about how real learning occurs? For example, in Chapter 3 the following statement is found: "No questioning, no learning." At first glance, this may seem radical. A reaction might be: "I can learn by reading or listening. I do not need to ask questions." Rather than rejecting this statement outright, think about it and discuss its implications. Again, Elvin (1977) says,

> Only people so confident of their own belief systems that they shut their minds to evidence and people so lacking in respect for others that they are repressively intolerant will want to bring up a new generation in blinkers. This is a denial of the very postulates of education, which must be to develop responsible, critical minds. Not every question can be left without a provisional answer with children of every age, but it is one thing to pass on beliefs grounded in knowledge that is publicly verifiable and another thing to refuse to consider whether this is so. (p. 88)

We all learn from questions when we are open to answers from many sources. These sources can be direct teaching experiences with children, reading, and discussing original research.

Organization of the Book

The book is organized in four parts. Part 1, "The Foundation," is an exploration of the author's philosophy with the intent of helping you explore yours. In addition to examining images of mathematics and science, the influence of ethnic and cultural differences on learning mathematics and science is discussed. Part 2, "Constructing Learning," provides insight about the learning processes and how mathematics and science knowledge is constructed. Part 3, "The Constructed Framework," examines the mental structures necessary for understanding many mathematical and scientific ideas, which are constructed through hands-on activities. Part 4, "Building Inspection," offers assessment ideas as well as ideas for constructing a classroom environment conducive to teaching and learning mathematics and science.* Thus, there is an orderly sequence of learning in the book, beginning by examining your belief system about teaching and learning; next, discussing rationales for how science and mathematics knowledge is constructed; and finally, how to maintain the construction of knowledge that occurs in a classroom.

However, you and your instructor may choose to use this book (a road map) by taking alternate routes or side trips (using chapters out of sequence) if this makes sense for your learning journey. For example, Chapter 5 is about using the process of observation in understanding science and mathematics and Chapter 9 is about collecting data through observations about children learning science and mathematics concepts. These two chapters are in different sections of the book but there is no reason why they could not be explored consecutively.

Each chapter begins with a set of reflective questions called Journey Preparation. The purpose of these questions is to focus your thoughts about the contents of each chapter. You are asked to reflect upon your answers after completing each chapter. Write your answers to the reflective questions before and after reading each chapter in a journal. Use the journal to record other questions and thoughts that can be discussed with colleagues. The mathematics and science standards are used as a frame of reference in each chapter. They are identified as Tour Guides. Rest Stops and Scenic Views are also included to provide background information relevant to the main ideas in the chapters. Activities are designed not only to help develop your knowledge about teaching and learning mathematics and science but also to be considered for use with children.

A home page has been developed for the purpose of interacting with the author of this book. What new ideas have you learned about teaching mathematics and science by using this textbook in conjunction with your personal and professional experiences? What questions are raised that are difficult to resolve at this point? The author is interested in hearing about your teaching and learning experiences. The home page address is:

http://Condor.depaul.edu/~gfoster

No one will learn from this book alone. The instructor's knowledge about teaching and learning science and mathematics is an all-important component in enhancing the content of this book. Your reading and reflecting upon the contents of the book must be coupled with careful reflection upon your own teaching or learning experiences. If you have never taught mathematics and science, you will undoubtedly draw upon your experiences as a learner of mathematics and science. What you experienced as a learner will profoundly affect your attitude and beliefs about teaching even before you begin the learning process. This book encourages you to reflect upon your philosophy of teaching and learning mathematics and science. Questioning ideas through active learning will help you continue the journey of constructing and reconstructing a philosophical foundation for teaching and learning integrated mathematics and science. Philosophy is gained wisdom, accumulated through experience. The wisdom you gain about teaching and learning mathematics and science is just the beginning step down the long path of a teaching career.

Elvin, L. (1977). *The place of common sense in educational thought*. London: George Allen and Unwin.

ACKNOWLEDGMENTS

The author wishes to express appreciation to the following individuals who inspired and supported the completion of this textbook.

- Michaeline Dudas-Foster, my wife, who provided support and encouragement in the completion of this textbook. She also contributed many hours of proofreading the entire manuscript.

- Dr. Darrell Phillips, retired, University of Iowa at Iowa City, a mentor and a friend who provided a deep understanding of Piaget's theory of intellectual develoment.

- Faculty and staff in the School of Education at DePaul University, who provided technical assistance and advice for completing the book. A special thanks to Dr. Barbara Sizemore, Dean, and Dr. Gayle Mindes, Associate Dean, for their support through the process of completing the book. Dr. Marie Donovan spent many hours reviewing the text and providing excellent ideas to enrich the book.

- Christine, Eric, and Heidi, my children, who supported my efforts with the book endeavor.

- The following reviewers who spent many hours reading the chapters: Daryl Adams, Mankato State University; Art Atwell, University of Arkansas at Monticello; Joseph A. Baust, Sr., Murray State University; Sylven Beck, The George Washington University; Alan Buss, University of Wyoming; Frances R. Curcio, New York University; Sandra Darnell, Brescia College; Anne G. Dorsey, University of Cincinnati; Gary E. Downs, Iowa State University; Doris M. Franklin, NC Central University; Leo Garigliano, Salisbury State University; Richard W. Griffiths, California State University; C. Bobbi Hansen, University of San Diego; Harold Jones, Lander University; Rickie Miller, Boise State University; Mary Alyce Mize, MS University for Women; Jerry L. Montgomery, Marietta College; Eddie Morris, Kentucky State; Albert P. Nous, University of Pittsburgh; George Posner, Cornell University; Judy Reinhartz, University of Texas at Arlington; Lynn Stadtlander; Germaine Taggart, Ft. Hayes State; Camille Wainwright, Pacific University; Mark B. Wallin, Southern Utah University; and K. T. Willhite, Clark State College.

- Dianne Lindsay, education editor, assistant editor Valerie Morrison, and past and present staff of Wadsworth Publishing Co. for their patience and understanding throughout this process; to Rachel Youngman of Hockett Editorial Service for her production help; and James Edwards for the line illustrations.

PART 1   The Foundation

Chapter 1 presents the author's philosophy about teaching and learning mathematics and science, and sets the stage for the rest of the learning journey.

Chapter 2 asks readers to reflect upon their experiences with mathematics and science and how those experiences have affected their beliefs about learning and teaching.

Chapter 3 examines cultural and ethnic influences upon the development of scientific knowledge. It also suggests using environmental topics as a way to integrate children's cultural differences into learning mathematics and science.

CHAPTER 1 | A Road Map for a Learning Journey

Abandon the notion of subject-matter as something fixed and ready-made in itself, outside the child's experience; cease thinking of the child's Experience as also something hard and fast; see it as something fluent, embryonic, vital; and we realize that the child and the curriculum are simply two limits which define a single process.

J. Dewey, *The School and Society and the Child and the Curriculum*

JOURNEY PREPARATION

Reflective Questions

- What are your expectations about learning to teach mathematics and science?
- What mathematical and scientific knowledge should children know?
- How should children learn mathematics and science?
- Why should children learn mathematics and science?
- What motivates children to learn mathematics and science?

Changing Times

In the last half of the twentieth century, alternative views about how to teach mathematics and science in elementary schools have been spreading. These views appropriately reflect the nature of learning science and mathematics as an uncontrived process. Past mathematics and science teaching practices and models were based on the idea that children's minds are blank slates or void of knowledge. This void could be filled with knowledge from teachers, books, and other resources. Children were expected to be passive learners, mentally tuned into what teachers said and passively involved with the rest of their learning environment.

This method of teaching mathematics and science received its support from a comparison to factories, in which mass production of goods and materials was made possible through an assembly line approach. As the industrial age progressed, the quality of individual products became less important than the quantity of products produced. Education mirrored this industrial age viewpoint. Whole classrooms of children received the same instruction of facts and terminology, day after day, year after year, and grade level after grade level. Children were moved along the education conveyor belt by teachers hoping to produce scientifically and mathematically literate citizens.

Today, world economies have become inextricably interconnected because of the spread of democracy and communication innovations. In the new age of technological communication, the emphasis is shifting from producing goods and services to understanding the human processes of production. Quality is just as or more important than quantity. Businesses are beginning to understand organizations as dynamic interactions of people and ideas in a global economy. Senge (1990) refers to this new understanding as *learning organizations* or systems thinking. He uses the term *metanoia* to describe learning that involves a fundamental shift or movement of mind. Senge (1990) states:

> Real learning gets to the heart of what it means to be human. Through learning we re-create ourselves. Through learning we become able to do something we were never able to do. Through learning we perceive the world and our relationship to it. Through learning we extend our capacity to create, to be part of the generative process of life. There is within each of us a deep hunger for this type of learning. (p.14)

During the industrial age, children were educated to prepare them to work in industry. Today, industry is taking a back seat to communications. Communications-related jobs require people to be able to solve many complex problems. However, in many schools the emphasis is still on production or achievement rather than on the processes of critical thinking.

A focus on problem solving is exciting because opportunities for creating real learning environments become possible. This book is about real learning for both children and teachers. The purpose of this chapter is to present the framework and philosophy that will guide you on the journey of learning to teach integrated mathematics and science.

This book is about the *processes of learning* and the *construction of knowledge* about mathematics and science rather than a step-by-step procedure for teaching the content of mathematics and science. By placing emphasis on understanding teaching through the processes of learning, foundations can be created that allow for instructional choices. Foundations are constructed from our knowledge of how children learn and through our teaching experiences. In other words, drawing upon our knowledge about how children learn, we can create instructional strategies. This permits an infinite number of instructional strategies tailor-made for each teacher.

This book is neither a "traditional methods" book nor a "curriculum" book. It might be best described as a catalyst for the construction of knowledge about teaching and learning mathematics and science. Both graduate and undergraduate preservice teachers who embark on a journey of learning with this book will construct meaningful instructional strategies with the help of their instructors. However, these strategies must also be learned through the real teaching experiences that accompany the course. In addition, excerpts from the National Science Education Standards (National Research Council, 1996) and the Mathematics Education Standards (National Council of Teachers of Mathematics, 1989) will be used as signposts to emphasize the ideas presented in this book.

Learning to teach is a lifelong process that evolves and changes. This book draws parallels between teachers as learners and children as learners. The activities presented in the book are avenues for teachers to learn about the nature of science and mathematics and to reflect upon how they might adapt them for use in their classrooms. Teaching and learning are integrated. Reflecting upon the fact that the processes of learning to teach parallel the processes of learning will provide insights about children's construction of knowledge. Having knowledge and empathy about the learning process enables teachers to make translations to the classroom.

Making connections between how children learn and how teachers learn can be described as bringing the intellect to bear on practical matters, or *habits of mind* (Benchmarks for Science Literacy, 1993). The phrase "habits of mind" describes an attitude toward learning that makes problem solving and decision making an integral part of everyday life. "Habits of mind" is one of the characteristics of scientifically literate persons. "Habits of mind" is not only an attitude about learning science but is also appropriate to learning mathematics and to teaching.

The Driving Forces

Feelings and emotions are learning process catalysts for learners of all ages. For example, curiosity creates both the desire and the need to know. On the other hand, boredom is an emotion that stifles or diverts the desire and need to know. Emotions and feelings are also indicators of the depth and breadth of the personal investment in the learning process. "I did it myself!" and "It makes sense!" are the expressions of the positive feelings of understanding something, while "I hate this!"or "This is dumb!" are the expressions of negative feelings about particular learning experiences.

Curiosity and the desire to understand the environment around us drive the act of knowing. Sometimes we are puzzled by our own observations or by situations that require problem solving. For example, in an isolated place in northern Michigan, spheres of light are sometimes seen that change color and diameter while moving across the sky. This phenomenon seems to occur on a regular basis. Some say the phenomenon is caused by extraterrestrial life. Possibly this explanation is used in many cases where there does not seem to be any logical answer. Other explanations have been supported by different sets of data. This process of finding answers through problem solving is called *inquiry*. Inquiry cannot exist without curiosity. Hiebert et al. (1996) argue that problem solving based upon Dewey's concept of reflective inquiry can be the focus for reform in mathematics education.

> Reflective inquiry emphasizes the process of resolving problems and searching for solutions rather than manufacturing a product. Tasks are seen as problems and quandaries to be resolved rather than as skills to be mastered. Methods of solutions are as much as dependent on inventiveness as imitation. Feedback on the appropriateness of methods and solutions comes from the logic of the subject rather than from the master/teacher. (p. 19)

This is true of teaching as well and reflects a commonsense approach. Methods and solutions for teaching and learning should originate from the subject rather than the "master" (teacher, principal, or other authoritative figures). The subject is the object of study, whether it be "spheres of light" or children in a classroom.

Again let me emphasize that this book will purposely raise questions to challenge traditional ways of thinking about teaching and learning so that teachers will be motivated to pursue alternative teaching methods. "Spheres of light" about teaching and learning will be presented to you that may appear alien but in reality are couched within a logical framework. Inquiry is an important habit of mind not only for learning mathematics and science but for teaching as well. Questioning what we do as teachers allows us to develop options that are beyond the scope of traditional parameters.

It is important to understand our own feelings about mathematics and science and their origin. If we do not, negative feelings toward these two disciplines will, subconsciously, be the driving emotions that affect our teaching. They can have a stifling effect on the learning experience for both teacher and children. Negative feelings from the teacher will be transferred to children who may in turn develop negative attitudes about these two disciplines. Once we understand our feelings and why we have them, we can change established attitudes and perceptions about learning mathematics and science. Teaching children then becomes a joy and pleasure for all involved. Learning and having fun can go hand in hand. "This is fun!" is an expression I have heard over and over from both children and teachers when they are engaged in hands-on learning.

Problem solving or inquiry learning allows for the expression of feelings often hidden during traditional modes of teaching. For too long, only the cognitive side of learning mathematics and science received emphasis without recognition of the role of feelings and attitudes. Active learning invites the expression of feelings and requires teachers to interact with children individually. The emphasis on using textbooks, lectures, and demonstrations as the primary sources of knowledge has made it possible for teachers to avoid dealing with children's feelings. Passive learning provides a shield for teachers to keep feelings at bay. When a textbook is the only source of mathematics and science knowledge, it can become a barrier between learners and teachers. For example, a child might say: "I do not understand what the book is saying!" A response from the teacher might be: "Well, keep reading it until you understand!" The child's emotional needs are unrecognized and the teacher does not have to deal with the insecurity of perhaps not knowing enough about the subject matter to help the child understand the concepts. Children are naturally curious and want to learn. Creating an environment where they want to learn is the key to an exhilarating teaching career. To facilitate learning in children, educators have to understand learning from the child's point of view. This is why it is important to recognize the child within you and how that child responds to different learning experiences. What would an integrated science and mathematics curriculum look like if it were based on children's interests and curiosity? Curriculum issues are addressed in Chapter 14.

Chapter 2 explores the impact of attitudes and feelings, shaped by prior school experiences, on teaching and learning mathematics and science. Intertwined with feelings and attitudes are social and cultural parameters that affect the desire to learn. Chapter 3 will be devoted to understanding the role of these parameters in learning mathematics and science.

Constructing Knowledge

In this age of emerging communications technology, we are inundated with information. Information is not only available in textbooks, television, and movies, but also on the World Wide Web of the Internet. The explosion of science knowledge is more information than one can possibly learn in a lifetime. It is probably safe to say that this science information base will continue to grow at an unprecedented rate.

The traditional approach to teaching mathematics involved finding correct answers through one particular algorithmic procedure, usually determined by the classroom teacher. For example, a teacher might require children to find the answer to two plus two only by "mental counting" and prohibit the use of "finger counting." But the act of knowing takes into account a variety of personal processes for solving problems. Teaching science focused on the memorization of terminology and abstract facts and concepts. This approach has done little to promote the nature and characteristics of science learning, which occurs along a continuum from free exploration or play to organized data collection.

Isaac Asimov (1959) wrote a futuristic science fiction book called *Nine Tomorrows*. A chapter called "The Profession" is a story about learning. In the story, people learn a profession just by listening to audiotapes. George, the main character, does not understand that kind of learning and in the following excerpt he argues for a "different way":

> Don't think this is a joke. Tapes are actually bad. They teach too much; they're painless. A man who learns that way doesn't know how to learn any other way. He's frozen into whatever position he's been taped. Now if a person weren't given tapes but were forced to learn by hand, so to speak, from the start; why then he'd get the habit of learning, and continue to learn. (p. 63)

Textbooks, lectures, videos, and even computer programs can be "tapes." A learner is frozen into one position when the focus is on knowing information. Focusing on the processes of learning provides the learner with tools to continue to learn for a lifetime.

Learning isolated facts does not give the learner "the habit of learning." When a learner takes facts and fits them together like pieces of a puzzle, knowledge is being constructed. Pieces of related knowledge form concepts. Isolated facts or fragmented information about teaching and learning mathematics and science have little meaning unless relationships are built. Since concepts are based on related facts, they remain fairly stable despite the addition of new facts. Our understanding of "house" remains fairly stable but ways to build a house and how houses look have changed over time. In Chapters 4–7 you will not only explore the nature of science and mathematics through activities that illustrate scientific and mathematical thought and processes, but also research how children construct knowledge. Activities in Chapters 4–7 illustrate the act of doing both mathematics and science.

Constructed Framework

Chapters 8–12 provide activities to explore the major mathematics and science concepts that elementary school children can learn through concrete hands-on experiences. Classification, ordering, seriation, and spatial relations are mental structures that are needed to understand the basic mathematics and science concepts. Addition, subtraction, multiplication, and division are based on these mental structures. Understanding measurement as a concept is an extension of these mental structures. As we shall see later, the mathematics standards explicitly state that exploration of concepts is more meaningful through a contextual base. Many physical science concepts such as force and motion, related to sound, light, electricity, and magnetism, are based on these

National Council of Teachers of Mathematics (1989)

A person gathers, discovers, or creates knowledge in the course of some activity having a purpose. This active process is different from mastering concepts and procedures. We do not assert that informational knowledge has no value, only that its value lies in the extent to which it is useful in the course of some purposeful activity. . . . But instruction should persistently emphasize "doing" rather than "knowing that." (p. 7)

National Research Council (1996)

Learning science is something students do, not something that is done to them. In learning science, students describe objects and events, ask questions, acquire knowledge, construct explanations of natural phenomena, test those explanations in many different ways, and communicate their ideas to others. (p. 20)

mental structures. As you work with the activities in these chapters, imagine yourself a mathematical or scientific explorer so that you are a learner of these two disciplines. However, at the same time think about the role of a teacher who might use these activities in an elementary classroom.

The dictionary definitions of mathematics and science provide insight about the natural relationship between the two disciplines and why they can be integrated in an elementary school curriculum. Webster's Ninth New Collegiate Dictionary (1987) defines *science,* simply, as "the state of knowing," originating from the Latin word *scire.* The same dictionary defines *mathematics* as "the *science* [my italics] of numbers and their operations, interrelations, combinations, generalizations, and abstractions, and of space configurations and their structure, measurement, transformations, and generalizations." In other words, mathematics is *knowing* about the various relationships among numbers as well as the objects they represent.

These relationships are abstracted, in most cases, by processing learning through concrete experiences. Shamos (1995) asserts:

> Mathematics is the language of science, particularly those branches of science that have evolved beyond the early descriptive stages. It is the only language we have by which statements about nature can be combined according to logical rules—a language that not only allows us to describe in precise terms the world around us, but also provides us with a means of dealing with such descriptions so as to lead to new knowledge. It is an essential part of the structure and practice of science, not merely an accessory. (pp. 63–64)

The definition of science infers a processing of knowledge. Many mathematical and scientific processes are very similar. Another goal of this book is to develop your sense of scientific and mathematical literacy to give you enough confidence to teach science and mathematics.

Both sets of standards are also very similar in the way that they define literacy within their own disciplines:

TOUR GUIDE

> ### *National Council of Teachers of Mathematics (1989)*
>
> This term (literacy) denotes an individual's ability to explore, to conjecture, and to reason logically, as well as to use a variety of mathematical methods to effectively solve problems. (p. 6)
>
> ### *National Research Council (1996)*
>
> Scientific literacy means that a person can ask, find, or determine answers to questions derived from curiosity about everyday experiences. It means that a person has the ability to describe, explain, and predict natural phenomena. (p. 22)

Another way to think about integrating both disciplines is to view science as a contextual framework for the use of mathematics to construct knowledge about the natural world. Scientists use mathematics to define natural phenomena in precise measurements. Precision or mathematics helps scientists to verify, through replication, the findings of other scientists.

Intellectual Development or Knowledge Constructed

The construction of knowledge about teaching mathematics and science is a process just as learning science and mathematical concepts is a process for children. As was mentioned before, the result of learners engaged in the learning processes is the development of logical ideas or relationships among concepts. Logical ideas are constructed through hands-on, concrete experiences. Which aspects of a concept are developed depends on the timing and type of learning experiences. A learner may not understand a specific concept until adulthood because the opportunities to learn were nonexistent or presented when the learner had no interest or was not developmentally ready. Chapters 8 and 9 will discuss the necessary mental structures needed to construct scientific and mathematical ideas. These chapters will provide empirical data that explain how mathematics and science knowledge is constructed. Knowledge about these structures will help answer questions such as: What can children learn at certain ages? How do they learn? What do you do as a teacher to provide learning opportunities for each individual child? What are appropriate learning activities? When is group work appropriate? The research about knowing or cognitive development will be presented in Chapters 8 and 9.

By studying intellectual development you will further enhance your foundation for constructing knowledge about teaching and learning science and mathematics. You will focus on research that has been validated through replication studies. Learning is a building process but the plans are internal, within the learner. Culture, socioeconomic background, and personal experiences affect learning. The responsibility of a teacher is to facilitate children's understanding of their own internal building plans to create a solid structure of knowledge. A foundation for the construction of children's knowledge begins with recognizing and tapping into their own internal sense of learning.

Assessing the Journey

Chapters 13 and 14 are devoted to assessing the construction of teaching and learning mathematics and science. These chapters have activities and thoughts about the interrelationships between teaching and learning. We want to know not only what children are learning but also what impact curriculum and teaching behaviors have upon that learning.

Inquiry Teaching and Learning

The entire book reflects the construction of knowledge not only about teaching mathematics and science but also about learning the nature and characteristics of mathematics and science. "Habits of mind" is a reflective practice that weighs educational trends against the best practices for teaching and learning mathematics and science. Good teaching must be supported by research rather than only by opinions. Teaching is a dynamic process subject to children's intellectual and emotional needs and interests. Maintaining the status quo perpetuates practices based only upon opinions, making teaching stagnant and creating friction among educators and learners. An example of an opinion that maintains the status quo is the following: *There are mathematics and science facts that all children should know.*

What are these facts that all children should know? Who says they should know them? Learning about teaching requires asking questions as well as collecting and analyzing data about teaching and learning. When a teacher models the role of researcher, children become researchers too. Penick and Yager (1993) report that exemplary teachers provide an atmosphere that allows children the freedom to ask questions. Questions challenge current thinking, not only about subject content but also about teaching practices. Teaching and learning drive each other to create dynamic interactions that free teachers and children to learn together.

How do you know if children are learning and what they are learning? These questions will be reviewed in the two chapters that focus on assessment of teaching, learning, and the curriculum. Technology as it relates to learning mathematics and science is a tool to enhance the fundamental processes of learning. Learning through technology should not take the place of learning fundamental concepts through hands-on experiences. Computer software that merely helps children memorize facts is just as inappropriate as textbooks that do the same. Technology is a tool that helps extend our limitations when calculating large numbers or manipulating complex sets of data. Examples will be given for appropriate ways to use technology for learning and teaching.

Validating Meaningful Teaching and Learning

Architects have developed knowledge about the best ways to construct buildings through collective experiences. Collected, organized, analyzed data about those experiences is called research. Teachers of mathematics and science must also collect data about teaching and learning. A wealth of valid research exists about learning and teaching mathematics and science. You will be encouraged to collect data about your own teaching and learning frameworks and to challenge existing data. Personal data can be accrued by talking to peers and classroom teachers, working with children, and analyzing current literature. Doing action research will demystify many assumptions about teaching and learning mathematics and science.

A common assumption is made in our society about the relationship between teachers and children: Teachers teach and children learn. Good teachers possess knowledge that can be transferred to new generations. One teacher said: "Teachers and parents are sometimes so pressured by the high grade mentality and test scores that they sometimes lose sight of the genuine purpose of science—the understanding of the world and universe around us." Teaching and learning have been separated from each other. Teachers are not expected to learn with children and children are not expected to teach each other. Many people have accepted this perception as fact even though teaching occurs any time a person helps another person understand something. Understanding originates through learning.

Good teachers learn with students and continuously learn about teaching to further facilitate learning in children. Recognizing the child within empowers a teacher to take risks in teaching. This book will parallel the learning process of children with the learning process of teachers. Research literature about mathematics and science teaching and learning will be used as a starting point to build a foundation for empowerment of the teacher. Exemplary teachers incorporate what they learn from research in their day-to-day teaching strategies. You will be asked to become a researcher and to explore current research findings. You will also explore elementary classroom mathematics and science activities with manipulatives in order to understand what children will learn from them. Let the child within you enjoy the exploration of these hands-on activities and reflect upon how children might react to them.

You and your instructor can decide to explore the chapters as they are presented or in alternative sequences. The book's purpose remains the same: the construction of knowledge about teaching and learning mathematics and science, which occurs through a journey of inquiry.

Just as children are encouraged to use inquiry and curiosity to drive their learning, you are encouraged to use the same vehicles. You will be asked to question and challenge current beliefs and opinions about teaching and learning science and mathematics. You will be asked to build your own set of facts through the inquiry process. You will construct knowledge about learning and teaching by developing habits of mind similar to those used by scientists and mathematicians, i.e., continually asking questions. Consider yourself a researcher, collecting data about teaching and learning mathematics and science.

Logic is based on a set of facts, but teaching mathematics and science has been based traditionally on beliefs and opinions. Elementary teachers often use the following beliefs and opinions when choosing activities:

- The activities must be good because they are in the textbook.
- Other teachers use the activities.
- I enjoy the activities.
- These activities will prepare children for the state tests or the next grade level.
- The activities support the state's framework or the national standards.

For example, state legislatures might mandate that all fourth grade children should know about photosynthesis. Teachers are likely to teach it without questioning why. What research was used to suggest that photosynthesis should be taught at fourth grade? If the sixth grade textbook contains a chapter on the atomic theory, teachers assume that it should be taught at that grade level. Why? What research did the authors of the textbook use to place atomic theory in the textbook at the sixth grade? In general, what research dictates that children should know specific science content during their elementary school years? Often what state legislatures or science textbook authors support originates from opinions rather than research. This is not to say opinions have no merit, but data need to be collected to determine their validity. The selection of mathematics and science activities and content must be questioned as to whether or not they support the development of intelligence.

As you go through your journey, you will begin to see patterns and frameworks of knowledge emerge from your data, giving you an understanding of appropriate classroom instructional practices that support how and what children learn about mathematics and science. You are constructing ideas for creating an integrated science and mathematics curriculum. Children's backgrounds, learning experiences, and understanding shape a curriculum.

A curriculum is the knowledge framework that you create on your learning journey that will provide the foundation for the classroom learning structure you will provide as a teacher. From this point of view, curriculum development is dynamic and changes according to the intellectual and emotional needs of children within a given classroom. A traditional point of view is to adopt a prepared curriculum without collecting data about children's needs or interests. This is much easier than creating or adapting an existing curriculum. However, the adopting strategy implies that a curriculum is something done to children rather than shaped by children. But houses designed for Florida residents would not meet the needs of residents in Minnesota.

Children's interests provide the contextual framework for selecting specific problems and questions. The community environment also influences children's needs and interests. Curriculum building is not an easy task. If learning is to be meaningful for children, the following factors must be considered a priority:

1. Understanding the intellectual nature of the learner.
2. Understanding the nature and characteristics of science and mathematics.
3. Knowing appropriate instructional resources and activities that support factors 1 and 2.
4. Understanding the school's community and its resources that support factors 1 and 2.

These factors are embedded within the chapters of this book.

Have a wonderful journey and remember, this is just the beginning of understanding teaching and learning mathematics and science. Teaching and learning are lifelong journeys. Chapter 2 begins with the examination of your past journey with learning mathematics and science.

> **Go back to the reflective questions at the beginnning of the chapter and the answers you recorded in your journal. Add to or modify your answers based on what you learned from this chapter.**

Bibliography

American Association for the Advancement of Science. (1993). *Benchmarks for science literacy: Project 2061.* New York: Oxford University Press.

Asimov, I. (1959). *Nine tomorrows: Tales of the near future.* Greenwich, CT: Fawcett Crest.

Bacon, F. (1620). Novum organum aphorims: Concerning the interpretation of nature and the kingdom of man: First book. In R. Hutchins, et al. (1952). *Great books of the Western world: Vol. 30* (pp. 107–136). Chicago: Encyclopedia Britannica.

Dewey, J. (1990). *The school and society and the child and the curriculum.* (Introduction by Phillip W. Jackson.) Chicago: The University of Chicago Press, p. 169.

Hiebert, J., Carpenter, T., Fennema, E., Fuson, K., Human, P., Hanlie, M., Oliver, A., and Wearne, D. (1996). Problem solving as a basis for reform in curriculum and instruction: The case of mathematics. *Educational Researcher, 25*(4), 12–21.

National Council of Teachers of Mathematics. (1989). *Curriculum and evaluation standards for school mathematics.* Reston, VA: Author.

National Research Council. (1996). *National science education standards.* Washington, DC: National Academy Press.

Penick, J., and Yager, R. (1993). Learning from excellence: Some elementary exemplars. *Journal of Elementary Science Education, 5*(1), 1–9.

Senge, P. (1990). *The fifth discipline: The art and practice of the learning organization.* New York: Currency Doubleday.

Shamos, M. (1995). *The myth of scientific literacy.* New Brunswick, NJ: Rutgers University Press.

Shimahara, N., and Sakai, A. (1995). *Learning to teach in two cultures: Japan and the United States.* New York: Garland.

Webster's ninth new collegiate dictionary. (1987). Springfield, MA: Merriam-Webster.

CHAPTER 2

Journey to the Past: Mathematics and Science Images and Attitudes

Each time a philosophical construction is attempted, there is a whole world view behind it, and a personal one at that. . . . Because philosophy attempts to apply thought to all aspects of our individual and collective existence.

G. Edelman, *Bright Air, Brilliant Fire: On the Matter of the Mind*

JOURNEY PREPARATION

Reflective Questions

- What memories do you have about learning mathematics and science?

- What content did you learn?

- Do you think your peers had the same experiences?

- What images do children have of scientists and mathematicians?

- What is the best way to learn mathematics and science? Why?

- What influence will a person's mathematics and science learning experiences have upon the way he or she teaches these subjects?

Philosophical Introduction

Effective classroom teachers use reflective practices on a regular basis to assess their interactions with children and how those interactions affect the learning process. Calderhead (1992) says, ". . . A reflective teacher is one who is able to analyze their own practice and the context in which it occurs; the reflective teacher is expected to stand back from their own teaching, evaluate their situation and take responsibility for their own future action" (p. 141).

Using the art of reflective practices from the very beginning of learning to teach helps one to understand his or her initial philosophy of teaching mathematics and science. Take a few minutes to think about your views of teaching mathematics and science. What is constructed from your reflection is influenced by your knowledge, beliefs, and feelings. All of these factors together create a philosophy, as described in the above quote. Just as children arrive in classrooms with existing ideas about mathematics and science, novice teachers arrive in courses with existing ideas about teaching mathematics and science. Reflecting upon what it means to be a teacher of mathematics and science is just as important as the act of teaching itself.

Images, attitudes, and beliefs, created from past learning experiences, will leave a direct and often profound imprint on future mathematics and science classroom teaching practices regardless of the learning that takes place during teacher preparation. If negative attitudes were created, mental barriers may

block or filter essential messages from professional training
to Lindquist (1980),

> Anxious students often spend time engaged in negative self-talk, su
> stupid" or "I know I can't learn math." In learning or evaluative situati
> is reasonable that placing one's attention on such negative self-thoughts v
> interfere with attention to the task at hand and thereby reduce the level of
> performance on that task. (p. 168)

Reflection is useful in examining and analyzing one's past learning circumstances to identify any emotional "red flags" and to become conscious of their impact upon becoming a teacher of mathematics and science.

Reflection gives one an opportunity to think about feelings toward mathematics and science and the emotions associated with them. A good example of reflective practices is found in the story *A Christmas Carol,* by Charles Dickens. Mr. Scrooge, in his dreams, reflects about past experiences, which forces him to understand himself and how he treats others. In considering his present behavior, he sees a grim future. Through reflection he begins to understand his emotions and how they influence his behavior toward others.

For many preservice elementary teachers, the negative emotions associated with thoughts of teaching mathematics and science may also portray a grim future. There is a natural tendency to avoid doing things if negative feelings are evoked. Walk into any elementary school and find out when and how often children are engaged in learning science of any kind. In many cases, science is an option, scheduled for the end of the day when teachers often run out of time. Subconsciously, perhaps, teachers avoid science by hoping no time will be left for it.

Mathematics is usually a required subject that must be taught regardless of any negative feelings the teacher may have about it. Whatever the circumstances, children's attitudes toward mathematics and science will be influenced by the teacher's projected emotions. One of the most common emotions associated with mathematics and science is anxiety. Many studies lend support to this theory associated with learning and teaching mathematics (Tobias, 1991) and science (Ramey-Gassert and Shroyer, 1992). Facing, understanding, and coping with mathematics or science anxieties will facilitate beneficial learning experiences for both teachers and children. Many years ago Jersild (1955) said:

> The people who have the courage to face anxiety and who seek to explore its
> meaning accept the fact that they, like all people, are to some degree anxious.
> They recognize that many teachers and students have lived with the burden
> of anxiety day after day, scarcely knowing that the burden might be lightened.
> They realize that schools and colleges have usually offered them little in the
> way of help except academic activities that sidestep anxiety, or perhaps even
> increase it. (p. 8)

The anxiety surrounding mathematics and science often lingers long after the experiences that caused these feelings are forgotten. Thus, even in the absence of the original experiences, anxieties can be aroused just by thinking about these subjects. For example, some teachers express aversion to children bringing live animals such as insects, frogs, or worms into the classroom. Possibly the teacher had negative experiences with these animals as a child. The reaction is to the prior childhood experience. The child who is the recipient of reaction may "adopt" the same aversion and view insects, worms, or frogs bad," which may squelch any feeling of respect and wonder about insects as ng creatures. J. C., a female graduate student, said:

> I do remember, however, finding a couple of potato bugs under a rock, during recess when I was in first grade. I remember how when I picked them up, they would curl in tight little balls, so I put them in my shirt pocket. They started crawling out of my shirt pocket during class, and Sharon, who was seated next to me, squealed. I remember the teacher scolding me for bringing them to class, after I "confessed" that I had found them during recess. She made me wash them down the drain.

Parallels can be made with mathematics anxieties. For example, if a mathematics experience consisted of using abstract formulas one might feel like the following undergraduate liberal arts student:

> I like basic math and use it every day to make simple calculations. I just don't like math when you have to use a lot of formulas to get the answer.

This chapter provides exercises and anecdotal data to help you take a journey into your own past, exploring your experiences and feelings surrounding science and mathematics. Revisiting your "roots" will provide invaluable insight for you. Prior negative attitudes, once faced, can be changed. Prior positive attitudes will affirm positive experiences that promote the desire to use inquiry and learning. In both cases, you will experience growth as a prospective teacher of mathematics and science.

Concerns about Teaching Mathematics and Science

Before beginning this journey into the past, think about the types of concerns you have about mathematics and science teaching. Complete the concerns statement (Hall and Loucks, 1978) found in Appendix A at the end of this chapter.

Classroom Activity 2.1

Writing and Discussing Concerns

INSTRUCTIONS

Take a few minutes to think about your concerns and write them down on the form. Compare your statements with those of your classmates in a small group discussion (4–5 people per group).

DISCUSSION QUESTIONS

- How do your concerns compare? Look for patterns in the group's concerns.
- What seems to be the main concern for each discipline?
- Do you have similar or different concerns for each discipline? Why?

Table 2.1 shows the results for 70 preservice elementary students who completed the same concerns statements. The categories were created by grouping responses together that express the same idea. An example of a response is given in each category box. Additional responses are given in Table 2.3.

DISCUSSION QUESTIONS

- Which category best suits your response?

TABLE 2.1

Concerns about Teaching Mathematics and Science (n = 70)

# Student Responses	Percentage (%)	Type of Response Categories
22	31	I. Subject matter knowledge "How do I know which topics to choose?"
16	23	II. Motivating children to learn "I'm concerned about keeping science and math fun and exciting."
13	19	III. Math/science negative feelings "I don't like science and I feel that I am very poor in math."
10	14	IV. Science negative feelings "Science sometimes scares me and makes me feel like I'm stupid and will never learn."
9	13	V. Math negative feelings "I don't feel very confident in this area."

- What categories are represented by your group? What are the implications of these concerns statements for teaching mathematics and science?

Almost three decades ago Fuller (1969) found that preservice teachers express different levels of concerns as they progress through their teacher education program. The preteaching phase is characterized by little concern with specifics about teaching. In the beginning teaching phase, there are concerns about one's ability to teach. These are often expressed during student teaching. The last category is the experienced teacher phase, marked by concerns about students' learning and one's professional development. Table 2.1 indicates 54 percent of people surveyed have concerns related to teaching (Categories I and II), while 46 percent of people surveyed expressed concerns related to mathematics and science knowledge (Categories III–V). The concerns expressed in Categories I and II are fairly general and personal rather than relating to specific instructional techniques and student learning. Thus, according to Fuller, these concerns could fall into the preteaching phase. Despite the small sample of 70 students, the data tend to support Fuller's research. You may want to collect additional data from your peers to determine the validity of this small sample.

DISCUSSION QUESTIONS

- Reflect upon the categories of personal feelings identified in Table 2.1 and your own feelings. What feelings are being expressed? Explain.

- Are you concerned about your personal knowledge of math and science and how to motivate children to learn these subjects? What kinds of experiences have you had in learning mathematics and science?

Images of Mathematicians and Scientists

Classroom Activity 2.2

Images of Mathematicians and Scientists

INSTRUCTIONS

When thinking about scientists or mathematicians, what kinds of images do you have?

Take a sheet of paper. Draw or write a statement that illustrates your images of a scientist and a mathematician. After completing your drawings or written statements, compare them with those of your colleagues. Discuss your observations about the images.

DISCUSSION QUESTIONS

- How similar or different are your group's images?

- Discuss reasons why the images are similar or different.

- What images do you think children have of mathematicians or scientists?

Look at the data collected by Mead and Métraux (1957) in Appendix B of this chapter. What are your reactions to the descriptions of the images of scientists? Other studies (Chambers, 1983; Mason, Kahle, and Gardner, 1991) have been conducted using the Draw-a-Scientist Test (DAST) instrument in which children are asked to draw their image of a scientist. The data show few differences between images drawn by high school students in the late 1950s as compared to images drawn by children during the 1980s. In 1993, Rosenthal used the DAST instrument to compare liberal studies majors' images of scientists with biology majors' images. Rosenthal reported that the images of liberal studies majors who planned to be elementary school teachers were closer to the stereotypical images of scientists than those of biology majors but that both majors saw scientists as white males: "Almost twice as many liberal studies students drew figures wearing lab coats and more than twice as many drew figures with eyeglasses as did the biology majors" (p. 213). A man wearing a lab coat and eyeglasses appears to be the dominant image of a scientist among liberal arts majors. This image even exists among science majors.

Replication Research Activities

Scientists and mathematicians often validate the data of other researchers by repeating investigations to verify the results. This is one way to check reality and reach agreement about certain facts obtained from research investigations. The adage "seeing is believing" is an appropriate metaphor for replication studies. You will engage in two replication studies. The first involves collecting data about elementary children's images of scientists and mathematicians portrayed in their drawings, gathered with the DAST instrument. The second study involves collecting data about college liberal arts majors' images of a scientist, using questionnaires.

*Field Experience
Activity 2.1*

Replication of Children's Images of Scientists and Mathematicians

RESEARCH QUESTION

What images do elementary school children possess of scientists and/or mathematicians?

RESEARCH PREDICTION

Think about a particular age group you will study and write or draw the type of images you predict these children will have.

RESEARCH INVESTIGATION

Visit a school and have a classroom of children draw their images of a scientist and/or mathematician.

DATA AND RESULTS

Analyze your results and discuss them with your classmates in small groups. Use the Data Form for Children's Images of Scientists and Mathematicians Through Drawings, found in Appendix B of this chapter, to analyze your results.

DISCUSSION QUESTIONS

- What patterns are predominant in your data, the data summarized in Appendix B, and the data in Table 2.2?

- What are some possible reasons for the images children have of mathematicians and scientists?

- What are some implications of your data for teaching and learning mathematics and science?

- Have images of scientists and mathematicians changed since the studies discussed in this activity?

- What are some possible ways to help children have positive images of mathematicians and scientists?

Seventy-eight undergraduate liberal arts majors completed a questionnaire about their images of mathematicians and scientists. Rather than drawing images, students were asked to write down their answers to the following questions: (1) Who are scientists and mathematicians? (2) What do they look like? (3) What do they do?

Students responded to these questions once for scientists and once for mathematicians. Responses are given in Table 2.3. The descriptors given represent student responses with similar themes. Some descriptors are summaries of students' responses; others are direct quotations or words. The numbers in parentheses represent the number of times the descriptor appeared.

*Field Experience
Activity 2.2*

Replication of College Students' Images

INVESTIGATION QUESTION

What images do liberal arts majors at your university or college have of scientists and mathematicians?

TABLE 2.2
Second and Third Graders'
Images of Scientists
(N = 86; 40 boys, 43 girls,
3 unidentified)

Scientists' Characteristics	Male Scientist[c]		Female Scientist		Total[d]
	n = 45	%	n = 28	%	n = 73
Apparel					
Glasses	4	57	3	43	7
Lab coat	11	79	3	21	14
Lab setting	33	70	14	30	47
Lab equipment[a]	32	71	13	29	45
Other objects[b]	16	52	15	48	31
Chalkboard	2	66	1	34	3
Ethnic traits					
African American	2	100	0	0	2
White	35	64	20	36	55

[a] 49 pictures with test tubes/beakers

[b] Pictures of flowers

[c] 8 men with wild frizzy hair; 8 bald men

[d] 13 drawings showed unrecognizable gender; 2 drawings pictured both female and male

DATA COLLECTION

Interview five liberal arts majors (not science or mathematics majors) by asking the questions listed above.

RESEARCH PREDICTION

Write a prediction of what that you think these students will describe to you. Will your prediction be similar to the responses given in the list?

DATA RESULTS

Analyze and compare your results to those of your classmates and the results given in Table 2.2.

Discussion Questions

- What common descriptors do students use to describe both mathematicians and scientists?

- Do liberal arts majors see differences between the two professions? If so, what are they?

- Is there a main difference in appearance between mathematicians and scientists as described by students?

- Are university students' images similar to those of elementary school children's? Explain.

- What are the stereotypical images of mathematicians and scientists?

- What is the origin of these images?

TABLE 2.3
Descriptors of Undergraduate Liberal Arts and Science Majors' Images of Scientists and Mathematicians

Similarities

"They are": Thinkers (3); serious (4); explorers, informative, inquisitive, intelligent (4); analytical and logical (4); not very social/no social life (10); dull and boring (3); conservative, emotionless, and cold with no or a weird sense of humor, book smart or shy and reclusive (bookworms)

"They look like": Old (11); wear glasses (33); skinny and tall (7); in thirties and forties and look like regular people (12); men and women (7); males (12); balding (3); females (2); look like nerds (9); wear pocket protectors with pencils and pens (10)

"They do": Make discoveries (9); experiment (16); problem solve/ find answers to questions (18); arrive at solutions and explanations (3); calculate and work with formulas (12); discover answers to common questions about life (3); work on probability and motion, collect data, work with computers and calculators (6); invent and second guess (3); test hypotheses (6); put together theories (2)

Differences

"They are": Mathematicians are organized, methodical and technical, precise, and detailed; annoying, weird, exclusive, perfectionists (2), strict; do not care about their appearance; nerds/geeks (5); talk in big words; conservative; are accountants and engineers. Scientists live/work in labs (6); never sleep; are crazy, studious, and have limited personal hygiene; are neat and clean-cut, creative, practical, persistent, talkative, eccentric (2); are conservative, very secretive, vary as much as the population does; have a tendency toward math (2); work for corporations

"They look like": Mathematicians have short stubby gray hair, wear weird or ugly clothes, or are conservative in dress and mannerisms; carry calculators. Scientists' hair (12) is curly, dark, gray/white, wild, puffy, or messed-up; or bald; wear beards; look like Einstein or Madame Curie; wear white lab coats (25) and goggles

"They do": Scientists work daily in labs (4); study all kinds of science; study the physical world and its laws; know a lot about one specific thing; work with chemical equations, chemicals (2), flasks, test tubes, and microscopes (2); sometimes cause more trouble than good; read a lot and write in notebooks; find cures for diseases; work toward enhancement, well-being of our world; improve medicine and engineering; contribute to society (17). Mathematicians crunch (4) and work with numbers (4) and formulas (11); work with pencils; teach (10); work in isolated environments and at desks (2) or blackboards; sit around discussing; develop theories or theorems but do not prove them; try to explain why (research); look at things step by step and see things as true/false or black/white

- What can be done to change these stereotypical images and to encourage more students to think about careers in mathematics and science?
- Take the results shown in Table 2.3 to mathematics and science professors. Ask them their opinions of the lists. Discuss your findings.

Data indicate that children's interest in science peaks at fifth grade and declines through junior and senior high school. What was your experience? In what grade levels do you remember having an interest in science? Anecdotal data indicate that female elementary school science teachers are perceived by children to be scientists. For example, one female teacher asked her third grade children to draw scientists. The majority of the pictures were of women. The teacher asked why they drew women and the children said that they were scientists because they taught science.

Discussion Questions

- Based on your own experiences, why do you think interest in science declines?
- If interest in science declines, what are the implications for the number of students pursuing careers in science and mathematics?

The Spirit of Mathematics and Science Past

Besides television, what shapes our attitudes toward mathematics and science? An answer to this question may be found by thinking about your past school experiences with these subjects. Imagine that you take a journey into your past. Think about your mathematics and science experiences and the feelings, beliefs, and attitudes associated with these experiences. Write an autobiography about your experiences. A sample road map, autobiography, and autobiography assignment are found in Appendix C. Table 2.4 gives examples of autobiographical quotes from other preservice elementary education majors. An autobiography provides a database of what is remembered about feelings and learning experiences associated with mathematics and science. Table 2.4 expresses a mixture that is both positive and negative.

Discussion Questions

- After writing your autobiographies, discuss your journey of learning mathematics and science in small groups of four to five people.
- Which quotes in Table 2.4 conjure up images from your past? Discuss these images with others in your group.
- How are your autobiographies similar and different?
- What types of experiences shaped your feelings about mathematics and science?
- Table 2.1 showed that 19 percent of the students surveyed had negative feelings about both mathematics and science while 27 percent had negative feelings about one or the other. Discuss the kinds of experiences that would account for these percentages.

TABLE 2.4
Autobiography Quotes

M. Z. My earlier years in science are very vague. The best experiment I can remember is hatching eggs.

R. B. I remember science in the fifth grade . . . finally! I could never forget dissecting pigs. I actually liked taking part in this experiment. I also remember memorizing textbook science definitions. I did not enjoy that very much.

B. D. Science field trips were always interesting, mainly because they gave us the opportunity to get out of the classroom and away from the routine book lesson.

J. S. In kindergarten I remember that we had an incubator in our classroom and that we hatched some baby chicks.

J. M. I have no real memories of science before sixth grade. Prior to this my science in school must have been taught primarily with textbooks and worksheets.

J. B. In kindergarten, I was escorted out of the room because I was so horrified of the tarantula, which I was forced to touch.

M. P. The one experiment I remember from sixth grade was determining the blood types of the class. I liked this experiment because it was about the students. Each person was learning something important about themselves.

S. R. In fourth or fifth grade I won an award of recognition for my erupting volcano. I was quite proud of that fact because the boy who brought in a horse's tongue won nothing.

K. J. My experience with science was very limited until the seventh grade. Until then everything was book, read, and memorize.

B. T. For science I remember how to grow and take care of our plants. The experience was fun and I remember coming home and begging my mom to buy soil and seeds because I wanted to grow my own plant at home.

J. A. Our science class had a textbook, a workbook, and a lot of memorization and projects, which I never understood.

M. Z. I do not really remember math until the seventh grade. What I do remember was always being in the lowest group and wanting to be in the higher group.

R. B. I would dread going to school, because of those flash cards. I was absolutely petrified of those things.

B. D. I will never forget how I used to get so excited when the teacher would pick a certain kid to go up to the blackboard to do problems. Now that I think of it, they were really repetitive and boring.

J. S. When we got to first grade, we started to get more technical with math. I remember that our teacher used to time us to see how many questions we could complete in a minute or so—I used to feel very stressed and I did not do a thorough job.

J. M. I think a large part of my problem with math in my early years of school was that it was too abstract for me.

J. B. Math was always something that I could experiment with using manipulatives.

M. P. I was the best in multiplication of all the second grade. I wonder how the other children in the competition felt after they lost

T A B L E 2 . 4
Autobiography Quotes
(continued)

S. R. Fractions were always hard for me and remembering the basic functions were impossible.

K. J. My early mathematics experiences were very good. I have to admit that first learning the new ideas like multiplication, division, word problems, etc., was difficult.

B. T. In second grade I remember doing more complicated addition and subtraction.

J. A. The teacher put a big piece of construction paper on the wall, with all of our names. She kept track of each student's progress in memorizing the tables. It was very clear who in the class was ahead and who was behind. This created a lot of classroom pressure, which did not help me at all.

- What themes about teaching and learning seem to emerge from your autobiography discussions?
- Compare your concerns about teaching mathematics and/or science with your autobiographical experiences. Do you find similarities between your concerns and the experiences you had as a learner of mathematics and science? Explain.

Table 2.5 gives a summary of three major themes (teacher, learner, and learning) that emerged from the autobiographies of other elementary education preservice students.

Discussion Questions

- Do the same three major themes as those given in Table 2.5 emerge from your autobiographies?
- What other examples could your group add to each major theme that are not listed in Table 2.5?
- Memories of specific mathematics and/or science content receive little or no attention in student autobiographies. What accounts for this? What are the implications of these feelings for teaching mathematics and science?
- Discuss other mathematics and science teaching implications that emerge from your discussions of autobiographies.
- Optional: Read the author's autobiography (see Appendix D in this chapter). Discuss this in terms of your own experiences and whether or not images of mathematics and science have really changed over the last fifty-plus years. Possibly your instructor will share his or her mathematics and science learning experiences with you.

Gender Bias

Gender bias occurs when the majority of one gender receives preferential treatment over the other gender in a classroom. This preferential treatment may enhance the learning of one gender but it is detrimental to the other. Kantrowitz, Wingert, and Houston (1992) and Urquhart (1992) found that

TABLE 2.5
Autobiography Themes

Teacher	Learner	Learning
Encouraged/supported	Forced to work; I did not understand	Subject was not relevant
Embarrassed me	Math/science hard	Children have different needs
Made subjects interesting	Math/science boring	
Covered material	Had to complete worksheets	Children have different levels of understanding
Imparted knowledge	Read same material over each year	
Talked a lot		Children need to work at own pace
Listened to students' needs	Received high/low grades	
Made subject understandable	Hated "Star Board"	Children need to keep an open mind
Science was for boys	Learning was hands-on	
Used textbooks only		
Had favorite students	Learning was fun	
Made learning fun		
Assignment used as punishment		
Forced/pushed us to learn		
Built confidence		

teachers in American public schools call on boys more often than girls. They emphasize that the difference in treatment of boys and girls is greatest in science and mathematics. Barba and Cardinale (1991) also observed teachers questioning students in science classrooms and reported that regardless of teachers' gender, more interactions occurred with male students than female students. The research cited here echoes the feelings of a female graduate student who concluded:

> The aggressiveness of the boys in my class more than made up for my shyness. The boys in my class always had their hands up ready to answer the question. I wish I would have been more involved in science and given it more of a chance.

Many undergraduate female students have reported that they were told not to enter the field of science or perceived that they were being treated as second-class citizens. Here is what one student said:

> My eighth grade math teacher was a misogynist. He constantly said boys were better than girls in math and science. He often encouraged some of the female students not to worry if they did not understand math concepts. Girls were not expected to do well in math and he was not about to change this awful misperception. He never called on any of the girls in the classroom nor did he encourage any who attempted to participate in the classroom community.

As you read this passage you can get a sense that this student is very upset about her experience. Is it any wonder that many female students question whether they might have chosen a different career path if they had had more positive experiences in mathematics or science?

Field Experience
Activity 2.3

Classroom Observations

INTRODUCTION

The purpose of this activity is to gather your own data about whether elementary teachers treat boys and girls differently. Visit a classroom or watch a videotape of a teacher teaching mathematics or science and observe the behavior of boys and girls and how teachers respond. Keep a tally of the number of boys compared to girls who raise their hands or are called upon to answer questions. Also record the number of boys compared to girls who are out of their chairs and walking around the room.

DISCUSSION QUESTIONS

- If you observe one gender receiving preferential treatment, which is it?

- What do you think is the basis for this difference in treatment? Determine whether or not there are cultural factors that play a part in the differences in treatment.

- Does the type of activity create differences in behaviors? For example, children are going to be active during hands-on activities. Do you notice a difference in behaviors between boys and girls?

- If you find that there are no differences in the treatment of males vs. females, what does the teacher do to avoid preferential treatment?

- What are the differences in behaviors between boys and girls during hands-on activities compared with activities that promote memorization of facts?

It is important to become aware of children's behaviors as well as how we respond to them during hands-on activities. An effort must be made on a daily basis to give equal attention to all children in a classroom.

Summary

This chapter addressed some assumptions and premises about how students are taught. These premises are also expressed in both the mathematics and science national standards.

Insight about yourself as a learner should have been revealed through the examination of your past learning experiences. If you learned mathematics and science through memorization, you will likely want to use direct teaching methods to have children memorize. Both sets of standards say that children should be actively involved in learning. The change from teaching for memorization to learning through processes may be difficult. If you learned through hands-on activities, you will likely feel comfortable using them in your own class.

Discussion Questions

- What have you learned about yourself as a learner of mathematics and science?

- What images do you have of children as learners?

- At this time, what image do you have of yourself as teacher of mathematics and science?

TOUR GUIDE

> ### National Council of Teachers of Mathematics (1989)
>
> Our premise is that what a student learns depends to a great degree on how he or she learned it. (p. 5)
>
> Whether students come to view mathematics as an integrated whole instead of a fragmented collection of arbitrary topics and whether they ultimately come to value mathematics will depend largely on how the subject is taught. (p. 244)
>
> ### National Research Council (1996)
>
> What people learn is greatly influenced by how they are taught.
>
> The actions of teachers are deeply influenced by their vision of science as an enterprise and as a subject to be taught and learned in school. (p. 28)

Summary of Past Experiences Data

1. Teachers who project positive mathematics and science learning attitudes provide students with positive images.

2. Teachers who are willing to learn mathematics and science with students provide excellent role models of scientists and mathematicians.

3. Teachers who use hands-on activities and relevant learning experiences provide positive images of mathematics and science.

4. Teachers who provide support and encouragement to children engaging in the study of science and mathematics create a positive atmosphere for learning.

5. Teachers who recognize that children have different levels of understanding and emotional needs provide the nourishment for learning.

Past experience data also informs us as to what causes children to have negative images about mathematics and science. The causes of negative images about mathematics and science are the following:

1. Memorizing and drilling of isolated facts and terminology

2. Labeling and grouping children according to perceived abilities

3. Testing that focuses on memorization as achievement

4. Memorizing irrelevant content

Students rarely mention a teacher's mastery of the content and knowledge about mathematics and science as a positive influence on what they learned.

Discussion Questions

- What specific content in mathematics and science do you remember? Is it associated with particular teachers? Why?
- How much specific content do you remember?
- Do you remember how to derive the logarithm of a number?
- Do you remember the structure of a DNA molecule?

The last two questions show that *memorized content is not internalized unless it is relevant to the learner.* What makes content relevant to the learner? More than likely, if you experienced mathematics and science through hands-on activities, you have positive specific memories about such things as multiplying, predicting, adding, hypothesizing. Science content continuously changes, which creates difficult challenges when trying to stay current. However, basic mathematical operations remain relatively constant. Past mathematics teaching emphasized using these operations without really understanding them, which can produce negative feelings in children. Knowing and understanding the learning processes is one of the key ingredients of successful teaching, and leads to children enjoying mathematics and science. Cognitive research and how children construct knowledge will be the topic of Chapters 4–7.

Knowing about your experiences with mathematics and science and how they have shaped your attitudes and beliefs will give you a better understanding of your journey as a learner and teacher of mathematics and science. Elements of attitudes and beliefs cannot be ignored because of their impact on cognitive development. Piaget (1981) stated:

> Regarding the assertion that there is no cognitive mechanism without affective elements, it is obvious that affective factors are involved in even the most abstract forms of intelligence. For a student to solve an algebra problem or a mathematician to discover a theorem, there must be intrinsic interest, extrinsic interest or a need at the beginning. While working, states of pleasure, disappointment, eagerness, as well as feelings of fatigue, effort, or failure may occur; and finally, the student may experience aesthetic feelings stemming from the coherence of the solution. (p. 3)

Your past experiences will tell you whether your learning journey will consist of reconstructing or constructing appropriate ideas about mathematics and science teaching. These experiences provide you with important data. Reflecting on your mathematics and science learning experience can reveal why you have formed certain attitudes and beliefs about teaching and learning mathematics and science. Those who have had hands-on experience are more than likely to have positive attitudes compared with those who lack such experiences. Knowing this about yourself should help you understand how children learn. If negative attitudes exist, acknowledging and understanding past experiences gives you the power to change them to positive ones.

Now that you have some insight and a better understanding about your current philosophy of teaching mathematics and science, you have a foundation for the journey of learning about teaching these subjects. Throughout Chapter 1 and this chapter, references were made to the fact that socialization plays an important part in learning. Issues of culture and ethnicity will be explored in Chapter 3.

Go back to the reflective questions at the beginning of the chapter and the answers you recorded in your journal.

   Add to or modify your answers based on what you learned from this chapter.

APPENDIX A

Concerns Statements

Name _____

Date _____

Please complete the following statements. Write one paragraph for each subject.

When I think about teaching mathematics/science, I am concerned about . . .

Mathematics:

Science:

Adapted from Hall and Loucks (1978).

APPENDIX B

Data Form for Children's Images of Scientists and Mathematicians Through Drawings

Background

Name of student _____ # of drawings _____

Grade level represented _____

Number of boys _____ girls _____

Drawings

Male _____   Female _____

Glasses _____   Glasses _____

Lab coat _____   Lab coat _____

Lab setting _____   Lab setting _____

Lab equipment _____   Lab equipment _____

Other objects _____   Other objects _____

Chalkboard _____   Chalkboard _____

African American _____   African American _____

White _____   White _____

If male:

Bald _____

Wild, frizzy,
unkempt hair _____

Other categories _____

Images of Scientists

Shared Image

The scientist is a man who wears a white coat and works in a laboratory. He is elderly or middle aged and wears glasses. . . . He may be bald. He may wear a beard, may be unshaven and unkempt. He may be stooped and tired. . . . He is surrounded by equipment: test tubes, Bunsen burners, flasks and bottles; a jungle gym of blown glass tubes and weird machines with dials. . . . He spends his days doing experiments. He pours chemicals from one test tube into another. . . . He experiments with plants and animals, cutting them apart, injecting serum into animals. . . .

Positive Image

He is a very intelligent man—a genius. He has long years of extensive training. He is interested in his work and takes it seriously. He works for long hours in the laboratory, sometimes day and night, going without food and sleep. . . . He is prepared to work for years without getting results. One day he may straighten up and shout: "I've found it! I've found it!" . . . Through his work, people will be happier, healthier, and live longer, they will have new and better products to make life easier and pleasanter at home, and our country will be protected from enemies abroad.

Negative Image

The scientist is a brain. He spends his days indoors, sitting in a laboratory, pouring things from one test tube into another. His work is uninteresting, dull, monotonous, tedious, time consuming. . . . He may live in a cold-water flat. . . . His work may be dangerous. Chemicals may explode. He may be hurt by radiation and die. If he does medical research, he may bring home disease, or may use himself as a guinea pig, or may even accidentally kill someone. . . . He is so involved with his work that he doesn't know what is going on in the world. He has no other interests and neglects his body for his mind. . . . He has no social life, no other intellectual interests, no hobbies or relaxations. He bores his wife. . . . He brings home work and also bugs and creepy things.

From Mead and Métraux (1957).

APPENDIX C | ## *Sample Road Map and Autobiography*

Science and Mathematics Autobiography and Case Study

Part 1: Road Map

Think about your experiences with mathematics and science learning. Highlight and illustrate these experiences visually by creating a road map of your journey through K–12 schools. The road map is a visual aid to help you to write a more descriptive autobiographical account of your beliefs and activities in your role as a learner. Just as a road map helps us find our way to an unknown destination, a road map can also depict where we have been. Think of road maps and atlases and how they illustrate distances, locations, and geographical landmarks. Create your own road map to illustrate your journeys with mathematics and science. Be creative! There are many ways to illustrate your journey! A sample road map and autobiography are provided in Figure 2.1.

Part 2: Autobiography

Component A: Use the events illustrated on your road map to write an autobiography about your experiences, attitudes, and feelings toward science and mathematics.

Component B: Analyze your experiences. Consider how your thoughts and actions have been socially influenced and their effect on your teaching and learning practices. For example, has your gender, religious affiliation, or ethnicity influenced how you have been involved in specific learning opportunities? Do you wish things had gone differently, and if so, how? What are the lenses you wear as you look at other learners—should you change your perspective?

Component C: Look at your mathematics and science teaching and learning practices. Review your Autobiography and identify key experiences that most influence how you perceive teaching science and mathematics. Compare your science learning experiences with your mathematics learning experiences.

FIGURE 2.1

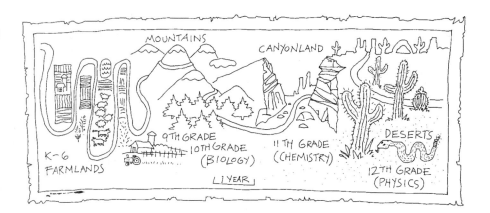

1. What images/experiences have particularly contributed to your views on teaching?
2. What does it mean to be a teacher and/or learner?
3. Are teaching and learning different for mathematics and science?
4. What is science? What is mathematics?

APPENDIX D

Author's Autobiography

Mathematics

In grade school I remember flash cards and games to help memorize basic mathematical operations: addition, subtraction, multiplication, and division. I remember doing worksheets for other mathematical operations such as fractions, percentages, and decimals that built on basics. Games, such as racing to the board to complete an operation and handing the chalk to the next person on the team, were also part of teachers' repertoires. Sometimes we would go to the front of the room and put problems and solutions on the blackboard.

Mathematics learning consisted of worksheets and reading from one textbook page to the next, year after year after year. Teachers stood before us with textbook in hand, presented directions and examples, and assigned homework from textbooks. Homework, depending on the grade level, consisted of basic mathematical operations, story problems, solving equations, or geometry proofs. We began the homework assignment in class and teachers expected us to finish it at home to bring to class the following day. The next day, the teacher again stood before us with book in hand to go over assignments. We were called upon to give answers, but I tried avoiding eye contact with teachers because I was afraid of giving the wrong answer. Pop quizzes and formal tests were routine throughout the school years. I dreaded tests because I knew I would not be able to answer all of the questions correctly. I suffered test anxiety and my mind would go blank, no matter how much I studied.

I also remember doing story problems that made little sense to me. Story problems included such activities as buying groceries, lumber, houses, grain, yards of cloth, and automobile gas. The problems would include such operations as prices per pound, cost per inch, time to complete a task or travel a given distance. Very few teachers took the time to help me understand. I was expected to follow directions and complete assignments.

I had geometry, algebra, advanced geometry, and trigonometry in high school. Again, we did mathematics through textbooks. The textbooks contained page after page of explanations, samples, and problems to solve. Tests were given at the end of chapters, units, and semesters. Teachers maintained the same routine day after day, with the only changes being chapters and topics.

Mathematics was extremely difficult for me because of the abstract topics. I sought help from peers, teachers, and my father, an engineer, who understood mathematics extremely well but lacked the patience to help me understand mathematical operations. When I struggled with problems, he would end up doing them for me because I was not "getting it."

My mathematical memories are less than pleasant because of the struggle to understand textbook explanations and follow the teachers. I also felt inferior to my peers because they understood and I did not. I feared asking or answering questions in classes. During college, I avoided taking any math classes because I did not want to have more negative experiences and feel inferior to other students.

Science

Science was also a struggle because of the negative mathematics experiences. Mathematics was a major part of science courses from upper elementary to high school. I find it intriguing that my school science experiences had very little influence on my desire to pursue a science career.

Elementary school science was also a daily ritual similar to my experience with mathematics. Science consisted of textbook readings and answering end of the chapter questions for homework. We were tested on the terminology in the chapter readings. Other parts of this ritual included teacher lectures, watching movies and filmstrips, and writing science reports. I loved the Walt Disney nature series movies but written reports were boring because they consisted of reading and copying encyclopedia information.

In high school, I remember dissecting frogs and worms in biology. We were allowed to do the dissecting by ourselves rather than watch the teacher. The dissecting experiences created a desire within me to become a medical doctor. Chemistry was boring because it consisted of book reading with cookbook labs, solving chemical equations, figuring out electron shells of atoms, and watching teacher demonstrations. If we did have labs, our experiments usually failed and we fudged the data to make sure we had the right answers. Physics was very difficult and boring because of the mathematics, textbook readings, and teacher demonstrations.

I had four years of high school science because of my desire to become a medical doctor, which also meant a college science major. Since I enjoyed biology, I decided a major in zoology would be the most beneficial for a premedical degree. Again, college science courses consisted of lectures, discussion groups, and confirmatory laboratories with substantial mathematics. I was required to take basic chemistry courses and eventually qualitative and quantitative analytical chemistry courses. The content of the two courses contained a heavy emphasis on memorization and mathematics. I was lost from the beginning.

I transferred to a teachers' college to become a biology teacher. After teaching secondary science for two years, I pursued a master's degree in secondary education with a minor in zoology. I avoided all science courses that were strictly lectures by registering for field courses in ecology and environmental sciences. Eventually I pursued a doctorate in science education with an emphasis on elementary education.

Bibliography

Barba, R., and Cardinale, L. (1991). Are female students invisible? An investigation of teacher-student questioning interactions. *School Science and Mathematics, 91*(7), 306–310.

Calderhead, J. (1992). The role of reflection in learning to teach. In L. Valli (Ed.), *Reflective teacher education: Cases and critiques.* Albany: State University of New York Press.

Chambers, D. (1983). Stereotypic images of the scientist: The draw-a-scientist test. *Science Education, 67,* 255–256.

Edelman, G. (1992). *Bright air, brilliant fire: On the matter of the mind.* New York: Basic Books.

Fuller, F. (1969). Concerns of teachers: A developmental conceptualization. *American Education Journal, 6* (2), 207–226.

Hall, G., and Loucks, S. (1978). Teacher concerns as a basis for facilitating and personalizing staff development. *Teachers College Record, 80*(1), 36–53.

Jersild, A. T. (1955). *When teachers face themselves.* New York: Teachers College Press, Columbia University.

Kantrowitz, B., Wingert, P., and Houston, P. (1992, February 24). Sexism in the schoolhouse. *Newsweek,* 62.

Lindquist, M. (1980). *Selected issues in mathematical education.* Berkeley, CA: McCutchan.

Mason, C., Kahle, J. B., and Gardner, J. (1991). Draw-a-scientist test: Future implications. *School Science and Mathematics, 91*(5), 193–198.

Mead, M., and Métraux, R. (1957). Images of the scientists among high school students. *Science, 126,* 384–390.

National Council of Teachers of Mathematics. (1989). *Curriculum and evaluations standards for school mathematics.* Reston, VA: Author.

National Research Council. (1996). *National science education standards.* Washington, DC: National Academy of Sciences.

Piaget, J. (1981). *Intelligence and affectivity: Their relationship during child development. Annual Reviews Monograph.* Palo Alto, CA: Annual Reviews, Inc.

Ramey-Gassert, L., and Shroyer, G. (1992). Enhancing science teaching self-efficacy in preservice elementary teachers. *Journal of Elementary Science Education, 4*(1), 26–34.

Rosenthal, D. (1993). Images of scientists: A comparison of biology and liberal studies majors. *School Science and Mathematics, 93*(4), 212–216.

Tobias, S. (1991). Math mental health: Going beyond math anxiety. *Journal of College Teaching, 1*(3), 91–96.

Urquhart, S. (1992, February 23). Is school unfair to girls? *Time,* 62.

CHAPTER 3

Mathematics and Science Relevancy Through Cultural and Social Issues

Facts are not pure and unsullied bits of information; culture also influences what we see and how we see it. Theories, moreover, are not inexorable inductions from facts. The most creative theories are often imaginative visions imposed upon facts; the source of imagination is also strongly cultural.

S. Gould, *The Mismeasure of Man*

JOURNEY PREPARATION

Reflective Questions

- What is the role of culture in the development of mathematics and science?

- What other social entities may affect the development of mathematics and science knowledge? Explain why.

- What countries have contributed to the development of mathematics and science knowledge?

- What are some examples of contributions made by other countries?

- How should multiculturalism be addressed in teaching mathematics and science?

How might a mathematics and science curriculum be structured to reflect a multicultural society? What kind of environment supports learning mathematics and science in a multicultural society? Revisit your autobiography and reflect upon your own experiences. Were there incidents when culture played a role in the development of your attitudes and feelings toward mathematics and science?

An Overview: Cultural Contributions to Mathematical and Scientific Knowledge

Culture plays a major role in the development of scientific and mathematical knowledge. As Gould (1981), a renowned anthropologist, points out, culture influences the way the world is viewed. Values, religion, and politics shape the development and pace of knowledge construction. Scientific and mathematical discoveries are directly influenced by social conditions and cultural perspectives. Bronowski (1973) states the following about human beings:

> His imagination, his reason, his emotional subtlety and toughness, make it possible for him not to accept the environment but to change it. And that

series of inventions, by which man from age to age has remade his environment, is a different kind of evolution—not biological but cultural evolution. (pp. 19–20)

Humankind's view of the natural world has been filtered through cultural lenses.

More than likely, if a typical citizen of the United States were asked where important scientific discoveries have been made, he or she would likely say the United States and Europe. Some might recognize Russia because of its role in space technology, but that is recent history. Throughout history important discoveries were made in Africa, China, India, and the Middle East (Hodson, 1993). Western scientists have taken credit for many of these discoveries that were made in other cultures. Hodson (1993, p. 700) gives an example of discrediting contributions made by other countries: "Despite the spectacular achievements of the civilizations of Ethiopia, Benin, and Zimbabwe, the myth is still propagated that significant African history began with the imperialist invasions."

Religion has had a great impact on scientific and mathematical discoveries. Before the spread of Christianity into Europe, pagans believed that living things had spirits and were not to be exploited. Christianity's interpretation of the Bible (humans have dominion over nature) allowed people to probe nature's secrets to find benefits for human beings. Religious viewpoints have also influenced science in other areas of the world. According to Hodson (1993, p. 703), "Islamic scientists stress the need for humility, respect for what is studied, and recognition of the limitations of science." Native American and African cultures held similar views; harmonious relationships between the natural world and people were given primary importance.

The idea of using nature for the benefit of humankind was transplanted to the Americas from western Europe. This, of course, was very destructive to the people and cultures of the Americas. This viewpoint has allowed great technological advances to be made, but at the expense of the environment and the extinction of thousands of plant and animal species. Native Americans as well as African, Indian, and Asian peoples felt respect for nature during the quest to understand it. Respect is given nature because humans are part of the environment and any destruction of the environment disrupts the harmony between humans and nature. In spite of these different views and the contributions made by other cultures, the Euro-American viewpoint dominates the study of science in classrooms.

Cultural Contexts of Mathematics and Science

Many children experience a clash of values, especially when they study science, between the viewpoints of their community, their religion, and the larger American society. Some children come from families and social groups that do not believe in evolution or modern medicine. On a larger scale whole communities in American society may consist of families that immigrated from other countries. Consider the following statistics reported by Atwater and Riley (1993):

In 1972, overall "minority" enrollment in public schools was 21.7% of the total school population; by 1981, that figure had increased to 26.7%. It has been predicted that by the year 2000 African American, Asian American,

Hispanic, and Native American students are expected to make up over 33% of school enrollment.

In the 32 largest school districts in the country, 75% of the 5,000,000 students are representatives of these groups. Florida, for example, has had an increase in its Hispanic and Asian/Pacific Islands student enrollments; southeastern states, such as Georgia, Louisiana, and Alabama, continue to experience increases in their African American populations. In the southwest, in such states as California and New Mexico, Hispanic enrollment in schools is rapidly increasing. (p. 663)

Addressing science and mathematics learning in relation to cultural diversity in the classroom is a challenge to traditional ways of teaching. In traditional ways of teaching, children are treated as a homogeneous group who, in most cases, are presented the European point of view as if other cultures had no part in the development of mathematics and science. On the other hand, addressing science and mathematics from other cultural viewpoints can be difficult because a classroom can have a global representation of countries and cultures.

How do people from different ethnic groups and cultures view the purpose of education? Science and mathematics concepts in different cultures may have different meanings. Misunderstandings can be created when certain assumptions are made. One of these assumptions is that words have the same meaning regardless of cultural differences. For example, a teacher in El Paso, Texas, said that Hispanic children do not consider chickens to be birds. Tate (1994) tells about an incident when a student teacher gave her students a problem involving two people having a certain number of pumpkin pies. She asked how many pumpkin pies there were altogether.

> The four white children were busy using manipulatives and appeared excited about the process of solving the problem. On the other hand, the African American child was not engaged in any outward activity. He was very quiet and appeared uninterested. I asked the student teacher about the African American student's behavior. She replied, "Mark does not like math. I do not understand why; he is not a bad kid." I inquired about the "pumpkin pie" math problem. The student teacher responded, "I used pumpkin pie as the object to be added because Thanksgiving is in two weeks." . . . I asked the student teacher if she thought every family ate pumpkin pie on Thanksgiving. Her response was, "Probably." I asked her to ask each of the five children in the class. She discovered that [eating] pumpkin pie was indeed a Thanksgiving ritual in the homes of the white children. For the African American child, however, sweet potato pie was the dessert of the day. Thus the background discussion that led to the problem was "foreign" to this student. (p. 480)

Differences in food, clothing, and other social amenities can create contextual problems for studying mathematics and science. Using cultural context to learn mathematics and science gives validation to learning because it becomes relevant to children's lives. In other countries, contextual or cultural-based learning is considered an integral part of children's education. Urban Russian children learn traditional dances, songs, crafts, stories, and a variety of trades. Rural children also learn about their culture through crafts, dances, songs, and stories, but learning about agriculture and gardening receives a higher priority than learning other trades. Children become cognitively aware of their own cultural heritage through these experiences, which help them to identify themselves as being "Russian."

In Russia, mathematics and science are taught within the context of the social framework and with reference to trades. Rural children learn mathematics and science by growing plants. Children learn about plants, soils, fertilizers, and animals as well as ecology through gardening. Children learn mathematics by determining the amount of vegetables grown in a certain area. Mathematics is also involved during harvesting and selling produce in the community (Foster and Easley, 1994). The cultural context places learning within the center of the child's world. Vygotsky (1987), a Russian psychologist, wrote: "Culture is in fact the product of human social life and the social activity of human beings, and therefore the very act of posing the question about cultural development of behavior already leads us directly into the social plane activity" (vol. 3, pp. 145–146). In essence, Vygotsky's theory emphasizes the importance of social interactions for children's pyschological and cognitive development (Davydov, 1995). Using a variety of cultural contexts for learning mathematics and science helps children from diverse cultures develop understandings of these disciplines from other cultural viewpoints. The value of education becomes explicit to children when they see education relating to their everyday experiences.

Discussion Questions

- When the focus is on memorizing facts and terminology, what rationale is used to engage children in learning mathematics and science?

- When memorization is used to learn mathematics and science, what messages do children receive about the value of learning mathematics and science?

Field Experience Activity 3.1

Classroom Observations of Children's Behavior

INSTRUCTIONS

Visit traditional and hands-on activities classrooms in which there are children from different cultures. Observe children during science and/or mathematics lessons. Gather some background information about the children by answering the following questions:

1. How many different languages and nationalities are there in the classroom?

2. How long have the children lived in this country?

3. How well do the children and teacher communicate with each other?

4. What are some ways the classroom teacher communicates with non-English-speaking children?

Answer the following questions by observing children:

What differences in children's behavior are noticeable between the traditional and hands-on classes? Are the differences cultural? Explain.

Discuss the differences with the classroom teacher. Does he or she think these differences are culturally based? Find library resources on behaviors that are culturally influenced to clarify your observations. Question the classroom teacher about the following from both traditional and hands-on teaching situations:

What difficulty does diversity present during mathematics and science?

Are the differences more pronounced during hands-on science and mathematics when compared to a traditional setting?

Bring your data from this class to small group discussions.

TOUR GUIDE

> *National Council of Teachers of Mathematics (1991)*
> *Standard 1: Worthwhile Mathematical Tasks*
>
> The teacher of mathematics should pose tasks that are based on sound and significant mathematics; . . . knowledge of the range of ways that diverse students learn mathematics; and that engage students' intellect; develop students' mathematical understandings and skills; stimulate students to make connections and develop a coherent framework for mathematical ideas; call for problem formulation, problem solving, and mathematical reasoning; promote communications about mathematics. . . . (p. 25)
>
> *National Research Council (1996)*
> *Content Standard G*
>
> As a result of activities, all students should develop understanding of science as a human endeavor. (pp. 141, 170)
>   In historical perspectives, science has been practiced by different individuals in different cultures. (p. 171)

Language/ Communications

Suppose you are in a classroom with thirty fourth-grade children who have recently immigrated to America from Asia, eastern Europe, India, South America, Africa, and the Middle East. They represent a diverse mix of cultures and religions.

What challenges will you face with such groups of children as you teach mathematics and science?

Obviously one of the challenges is communicating with these children, who may not understand English. English words may not have the same meaning in another language. In some cultures body language is just as important as the spoken word.

How will you communicate with children who speak different languages? What do children of different cultures interpret from body language?

The following activity not only gives insight about the nature of science but also about the difficulties of communicating with other cultures. In this case the "other cultures" are extraterrestrial.

Classroom Activity 3.1

Visit to a Distant Galaxy

INTRODUCTION

The February 5, 1996, issue of *Time* magazine devoted a major section to the question of life in outer space. The article reported the following: (1) The search for extraterrestrial intelligence has been conducted for nearly four decades using radio telescopes; (2) three planets, hundreds of light years away, have been discovered recently by land telescopes; and (3) the Hubble space telescope as well as other space telescopes will be looking for additional planets. Astronomers predict that these new telescopes will find more and more stars with planets circling them.

MATERIALS

- Pencil and paper

GUIDED FANTASY

Your instructor will read the following paragraph to you. Concentrate on the words by sitting back and relaxing with eyes closed. The instructor may dim the lights to help you concentrate.

In your mind find a quiet place. Go to that place. Become familiar with the surroundings. Imagine that you have been assigned the responsibility of writing a message to intelligent life on a planet in a distant galaxy. Think about that message. What would you say? Slowly come back to this room. Write or draw your message. You will have approximately 10–15 minutes to complete your message.

DISCUSSION QUESTIONS

In small groups (4–5), share your messages with each other.

- What themes seem to be prevalent in the messages?
- What did you think about as you composed your message?

SCENIC VIEW 3.1

A space probe was sent into space in 1972 for the sole purpose of contacting extraterrestrial life. The probe, called Pioneer 10, has a gold plaque with symbols on it (Jaroff, 1996). Inside the probe are recordings of sounds from Earth. The hope is that other intelligent beings in outer space will find the probe. A replica of the gold plaque with its symbols is located on the following Web site: http://ails.arc.nasa.gov/Images/Space/AC72-1338.html. This will facilitate the following Discussion Questions and Classroom Activity 3.2. Look at it and see if you can determine the essence of the message.

Essence of the Message

- Male and female human figures: Note the raised arm of the man (body language). Why isn't the female's arm raised?
- At the bottom the symbols represent our solar system and the position of Earth.
- The rays represent a binary code and the position of Earth within the Milky Way galaxy.
- The dumbbell-looking figure represents the hydrogen molecule. Hydrogen exists as two atoms and is the most basic element in the universe.
- The dish-shaped object represents a radio telescope and how we receive messages from outer space.
- The dots and dashes next to the human figures are a binary code representing the height of human beings.

Discussion Questions

- Why do you think so much money, time, effort, and technology are devoted to communicating with other intelligent beings?

- What do you think about using this activity with children?

- What does this activity suggest about communicating with others?

Classroom Activity 3.2

Visit to a Distant Galaxy—Elementary

By doing Classroom Activity 3.1 you became aware that curiosity drives science. The same activity can be used in the upper elementary grades to convey the difficulties of communicating with other cultures. Thus, this activity can serve a dual purpose when used with children:

PURPOSE 1

Create curiosity about elements of astronomy such as the planets, other galaxies, and the possibility of life beyond our planet. Use books, movies, videos, and the World Wide Web as resources for information.

PURPOSE 2

Develop awareness about how to communicate with those who do not have the same language or cultural background. This can be done in several ways.

- Have children create messages and exchange them with one another in their classroom. Can they interpret one another's messages?

- Extend the activity as an exercise in communication with students in other classrooms or schools.

- Have children send messages on the World Wide Web to schools across the nation or in other nations. The children can then send their interpretations of the messages they received. A written discussion can follow about the intention of the messages.

Ask the following questions when discussing with children their experiences with the activity:

- What difficulties did you experience in creating your messages?

- How does this experience relate to communicating with those who live in different countries and cultures and who speak a different language?

- What are some common universal symbols that are used for communication in foreign countries?

- What are the common languages of scientists?

Communications in Science and Mathematics

Communication, of course, is an essential element in learning mathematics (Standard 1, Mathematics Education, NCTM, 1991) and science, just as communication is important to mathematicians and scientists. Mathematics is a universal communication tool because it was developed in many different countries. The Science Education Content Standard G (National Research Council, 1996) emphasizes the importance of looking at the historical development of science in terms of contributions made by scholars from other countries and cultures. Arab scholars gave us decimal notation and Greeks such as Pythagoras and Euclid gave us basic geometrical concepts (Bronowski, 1973). One can walk into Russian schools and recognize the same mathematical symbols and formulas taught in American schools. Science formulas and symbols used in chemistry and physics are also universal. The scientific names of plants and animals are Latin words so that scientists from different countries can understand them. Both Greek and Latin symbols and words are used in mathematics and science: π (pi) is the Greek symbol for 3.14, used to find the circumference of a circle; Σ is the symbol for sum. Both are used in mathematical and chemical formulas.

Classroom Activity 3.3

Counting Systems of Other Cultures and Countries

INSTRUCTIONS

Join a group of four to five members. Each person in the group chooses a different culture or country; for example, Mexico, Japan, China, India, and Egypt. Look at their ways of counting. How far back into history do these counting systems go? Find out what symbols and methods were used for counting. Show members of the group the symbols for counting 1 through 10 and symbols for 10s to 100. During a group discussion compare the counting systems.

DISCUSSION QUESTION

■ What are the similarities and differences among the cultures you chose?

Recognizing the similarities of mathematical symbols and representations can be very helpful in communicating with children from different cultures. These symbols are useful in communicating ideas in science as well as in integrating both disciplines. According to Rosebery, Warren, and Conant (1992):

> Mathematics and language are essential tools of scientific inquiry. This stands in sharp contrast to traditional schooling, in which science is separated from mathematics and the role of language goes unacknowledged. Mathematics mediates students' scientific sense making primarily through data collection and analysis activity (e.g., measurement, statistics, and graphical analysis and representation). (p. 64)

In our schools, children who speak different languages traditionally receive the same learning experience as children who are proficient in English. They learn scientific words and definitions in English. As Rosebery, Warren, and Conant (1992) state,

> Students memorize the definition of the word hypothesis but never experience what it means to formulate or evaluate one. The emphasis is squarely on learning English vocabulary and grammar, with science as one means to that end. (p. 62)

This puts an undue burden on the classroom teacher who may be confronted by a multilingual classroom. How can children who have limited English proficiency learn terminology that may be difficult for English-proficient children? The following statistics were prepared by the Department of Education's Office of the Undersecretary in 1995:

> . . . LEP (Limited English Proficiency) students speak over a hundred languages. Spanish is spoken by more than 77 percent of these students. In low income urban schools, the proportion of Spanish speakers rises to about 90 percent of LEP students. (p. 2)
>
> Nationally, children reared in a setting in which a language other than English is commonly used comprise about 16 percent of all students in the 1st and 3rd grades. Among these language minority students, about 40 percent are classified as LEP. (p. 1)

Not only will teachers have difficulty communicating with children, but children will have difficulty communicating with each other. How much English they learn and how fast they learn it depends on their age and background. If science and mathematics textbooks emphasize memorizing terminology, learning will be frustrating for the children and teaching an overwhelming task for teachers. Teacher-directed whole-class instruction makes learning very difficult for children of diverse cultural backgrounds. An emphasis on terminology will, more than likely, require explanations in both the native language and English. Communications that rest solely on verbal and written exchanges without the context of actions will only prolong the breaking down of communication barriers. Atwater (1996) states:

> Once a message has been sent, it is irreversible. What is even more problematic is that there are two types of communication channels: verbal and nonverbal. Verbal communications uses either a written or oral language that usually reflects the thought patterns of a culture. During oral expressions, nonverbal messages are sent. These nonverbal messages also assist the receiver in making judgments and decisions. Many cultures express emotional overtones of messages with different nonverbal behaviors. Therefore, the speaker and the listener may be interpreting nonverbal messages in different ways. How one appears, how one moves the body, how one looks at the other's eyes, how one touches a person during conversation, how one has a need to sit or stand close to another, and how one uses time in conversations are only a few examples of how miscommunications occur. (p. 824)

How do we confront the challenges of teaching mathematics and science in culturally diverse classrooms? Cochran-Smith (1995) asserts that rather than trying to find universal strategies for teaching cultural diversity, the focus should be on the local community as the context for constructing pedagogies:

> Teachers who are inquirers do not have to be color blind in order to be fair to all students, teach basket making in order to "do" multicultural education, or wait for the learned authorities of teacher education institutions or school administrations to tell them the teaching strategies that are most effective for "the culturally diverse learner." Rather, these teachers are involved in intellectually vital and independent pursuits to try to answer some of the toughest questions there are about how to work effectively in the local context with learners who are like them and not like them. (p. 520)

Real-life teaching experiences will provide data about cultural diversity, which can be used to create learning environments that are built on community cultures. Inquiry becomes essential to constructing knowledge about culturally diverse classrooms.

Scientists and mathematicians create communities as well. They have common languages, they share data, and they have agreed-upon standards for accepting new data. Children can also work in communities of learners.

Just as scientists and mathematicians are influenced by social factors, children are also influenced by social factors during the learning process. Piaget (1966) said:

> Society, even more, in a sense, than the physical environment, changes the very structure of the individual, because it not only compels him to recognize facts, but also provides him with a ready-made system of signs, which modify his thought; it presents him with new values and it imposes on him an infinite series of obligations. (p. 156)

Social interactions among children as they engage in learning science and mathematics create microcommunities in which they learn through communications that science and mathematics are culturally diverse as well. Children from diverse cultures who share ideas and participate in hands-on activities in microcommunities will undoubtedly alter their own viewpoints about the nature of science and mathematics.

Environmental Education as a Contextual Framework

Cochran-Smith (1995) stated that as teachers we need to have a local context in order to be effective in culturally diverse schools. The local context for children can be the natural environment. They can all relate to it. Peter Medawar (1987) suggests:

> Like other exploratory processes, [the scientific method] can be resolved into a dialogue between fact and fancy, the actual and the possible; between what could be true and what is in fact the case. The purpose of scientific inquiry is not to compile an inventory of factual information, not to build up a totalitarian world picture of Natural Laws in which every event that is not compulsory is forbidden. We should think of it rather as a logically articulated structure justifiable beliefs about a Possible World—a story of which we invent and criticize and modify as we go along, so that it ends by being, as nearly as we can make it, a story about real life. (p. 111)

In other words, real life involves interactions with the environment. Each child brings to school a story about real life or interactions with the environment that can be told from his or her cultural perspective. Their stories provide the foundations upon which children can invent, criticize, and modify their experiences and interactions with nature without losing their cultural identity, and at the same time learn about other cultures. Children can learn mathematics and science through real-life stories and journeys that are grounded in their cultural and social contexts. Environmental education is an excellent context in which to incorporate stories about real life. The National Research Council (1996) supports the study of environmental education.

TOUR GUIDE

National Research Council (1996)
Content Standard F

As a result of activities in grades K–4, all students should develop understanding of . . .

- Changes in environments

- Science and technology in local challenges (p. 138)

Local challenges relate to real life. For example, children study the effects of pollution on the local environment. As a result of activities in grades 5–8, all students should develop understanding of

- Populations, resources, and environments
- Natural hazards
- Risks and benefits
- Science and technology in society (p. 166)

REST STOP 3.1

Defining environmental education is difficult because it can be very comprehensive. In addition to being part of science, it has also been part of the social studies curriculum because of the social issues created by technology and the destruction of the environment. The study of the environment reached its zenith in the seventies when many environmental concerns surfaced, spawned by the rapid development of technology and the gasoline shortages. The debates over global warming, the greenhouse effect, and the deterioration of the ozone layer have been around for at least two decades. Scientists voiced concerns that for every technology that is developed, there is an environmental trade-off. Despite the fact that we still have the same environmental concerns, environmental education has not played a prominent part in children's education. In many schools, environmental education may mean collecting recyclable materials, visiting nature centers, or studying units on saving whales or the rain forest. Units such as these have little relevancy to children's lives as far as developing sensitivity to the natural environment, since the majority have never seen a live whale or been to a rain forest. They become artistic exercises of making pictures and murals. Organisms may be becoming extinct within the environment in which children live, but they are ignored because they have never reached the status of the whales or the rain forest.

Environmental education can be used as one context for learning mathematics and science because it focuses on community involvement. Children can relate to the environment in which they live. Children can work together to learn about their natural environment as well as to take action on selected environmental problems.

SCENIC VIEW 3.2

Middle school children from southern Minnesota were on a biology field trip, catching frogs. They caught 22 frogs and found that 11 of them had deformed body parts (Hallowell, 1996). This finding increased awareness about the possibility of a pollutant causing the apparent genetic defects. Children from other schools in other states have also been collecting frogs to see if they also had deformed body parts. Children are learning not only about frogs but also about the environment. In addition, they probably are becoming acutely aware that pollutants can have deleterious effects on wildlife. Parents and other community members can join children in actively improving the natural environment.

Incorporating Environmental Education

The following suggestions are not intended as step-by-step procedures. They are placed here because they make sense as a sequence.

Using environmental education programs not only helps children become aware of issues but provides opportunities to study the environment through the eyes of different cultures that try to preserve the integrity of nature. Views of nature can be identified for different countries as well as for individual societies. Children can research these views and use them while studying plants and animals. For example, there may be cultures that emphasize becoming in touch with nature by meditating. Children can learn to sit quietly while observing nature. Other cultures may emphasize that harmony is destroyed if something is removed from the environment. Children can put rocks, twigs, and other things back into their original places in the environment if they happen to remove them. Children can brainstorm ideas that would help them live in harmony with the environment. That might mean planting trees, shrubbery, flowers, or even installing a birdbath. Mathematical operations might include quantifying data collected from an environment, such as keeping track of the growth of trees or how many or which kinds of birds visit a feeder or birdbath.

Find out what resources are available in the community that will support environmental education. The following questions can be used to develop a community-based environmental education curriculum:

- Does the community have a nature preserve?
- Are there woods, rivers, or lakes that can be used to study the ecology of those areas?
- Are there zoos, planetariums, and museums where students can learn about nature in other countries?
- Does the school yard have resources such as grass, trees, flowers, and other plants for studying nature?
- Are there other nearby areas in which to study nature?
- Can part of the school yard be converted for nature study?

After the assessment has been completed, activities can be selected to make use of the local environment. As part of the assessment invite naturalists, horticulturists, or park service personnel to present videos or slides about the local area and what the natural landscape originally looked like. Children can plant trees and flowers, or build bird feeders to try to restore part of the environment to its original state. Children can plant vegetable gardens and sell the produce or use it in the school lunchroom. People from the community can help with these projects.

Environmental Activity 3.1	### Examining Populations for Number and Diversity

INSTRUCTIONS

1. Rope off small areas (2 × 2 feet) of the school yard or a vacant lot and count the number of different kinds of plants. Children can work in small groups in different areas of the school yard.

2. Within these plots, examine the soil for different kinds of animals. Take a population count.

3. Place bird feeders around the school yard and keep track of the number and kinds of birds that are attracted to the feeders.

4. Collect leaves from trees; press and classify them.

5. Collect water samples from ponds, lakes, and rivers. Examine the samples with hand lenses and microscopes.

Environmental Activity 3.2	### Study of Cycles and Changes

-   Adopt a tree and learn all about it during the school year. Observe when the leaves change color and when the leaves begin to grow again. Measure the height and circumference of the tree. Learn to identify the bark texture and the shape of the leaves of the local, indigenous species.

-   Collect seeds from native plants and grow them.

-   Find out what plants Native Americans used to make dyes.

-   Find out what vegetables and fruits are indigenous to America and other countries.

Environmental Activity 3.3	### Adaptation Studies

Explore the environment around a school to see where animals such as spiders and insects live. Closely examine sidewalks, parking lots, building walls and windows, playground equipment, litter from humans, trees and shrubs, flowers, and other places.

-   How many different kinds of animals can you find?

-   What makes them easy or difficult to find?

-   Where do they live?

-   How do they use the environment to make their "homes"?

-   What kinds of "homes" do they make?

National Research Council (1996)
Content Standard E

As a result of activities in grades 5–8, all students should develop

- Abilities of technological design
- Understandings about science and technology (p. 161)

As a result of activities in grades K–4, all students should develop

- Abilities of technological design
- Understanding about science and technology
- Abilities to distinguish between natural objects and objects made by humans (p. 135)

Content Standard F

As a result of activities in grades K–4, all students should develop understanding of

- Science and technology in local challenges (p. 138)

The Relationship among Science, Technology, and Social Issues

The science standards include the study of technology and its relationship to science. The use of technology has often had a detrimental effect on the environment. Thus, the study of technology becomes relevant when children are involved in studying the natural environment. Note that the standards state that the study of science and technology should be addressed through local challenges, i.e., the environment.

Environmental
Activity 3.4

Environmental Issues

Develop investigations by choosing relevant questions.

- What can be done to protect the quality of life of animals such as deer, geese, rabbits, squirrels, and at the same time maintain the quality of life of humans who live in the same areas?
- What can be done to minimize air pollution?
- What can be done to minimize the pollution of lakes, rivers, and streams in both urban and rural areas? (Special kits can be purchased to analyze air and water pollutants.)
- What can be done to minimize the amount of throw-away items that create litter and huge garbage dumps?
- What can be done to prevent abandoned city buildings and vacant lots from becoming contaminated with toxins and other pollutants?

Activities to answer questions:

- Children can write personal stories relating to these issues (e.g., if children live where there are many wild animals, they can write stories about their experiences with them).

- Design experimental investigations to collect data on one or more questions.

- Children can write to city and state officials to express their concerns about environmental issues.

REST STOP 3.2

In Chapter 1 we defined science as the pursuit of knowledge. However, human beings are not always satisfied with just having knowledge. The application of knowledge is also important. Technology allows human beings to overcome their many limitations. Clothes were invented as protection from extreme weather conditions. We cannot fly so airplanes were invented. We cannot breathe under water but oxygen tanks were developed. We cannot run very fast for a long distance so bicycles, cars, trains, buses, and other modes of ground transportation were developed. The application of knowledge results in a culture's technology.

Every technology has consequences that can negatively affect the environment and society. The air has become polluted from automobile exhaust. Scientists say the protective ozone layer that surrounds the earth and protects us from ultraviolet waves is thinning because of certain refrigerants and other aerosol gases. Water is polluted by toxic chemicals and fertilizers that are used to make crops grow and keep yards green. Cancers and other diseases have been linked to pollutants. Technologies and their impact on the environment have created both positive and negative changes in our quality of life.

Traditionally, technology and social issues have not been part of learning mathematics and science. The emphasis was on content (knowledge) to prepare students for higher education. However, this goal is now recognized as unrealistic. Approximately 14 percent of high school graduates complete a college degree. The majority of college students take only basic mathematics and science courses. The percentage of high school graduates who actually major in science or mathematics is relatively small. Thus, the general population has a meager background in science and mathematics. Yet the goal of mathematics and science education should be to develop scientifically and mathematically literate citizens (National Council of Teachers of Mathematics, 1989; National Research Council, 1996). Eisenhart, Finkel, and Marion (1996) argue that scientific literacy is more than just knowing concepts. It involves social responsibility as well: "using science in socially responsible ways would seem to entail: (a) understanding how science-related actions impact the individuals who engage in them; (b) understanding the impact of decisions on others, the environment, and the future; (c) understanding the relevant science content and methods; and (d) understanding the advantages and limitations of a scientific approach" (p. 284). Literacy means knowing the relationship of technology to mathematics and science and the impact technology has on society and the environment.

Environmental Activity 3.5*

Billion-Dollar Being

DIRECTIONS

Part 1: The Limitations of Human Beings

Think about the limitations of human beings. Write down all limitations that come to mind (10 minutes). Share your list with others in a small group (10 minutes). Create a class list that represents all discussed limitations (10 minutes).

*Adapted from Jefferson County Public Schools (1982).

Part 2: Create a Billion-Dollar Being

Use the class list of limitations to create a Billion-Dollar Being that will overcome all of the limitations. This Billion-Dollar Being must be better than Superman or Superwoman, Batman, Million-Dollar Man, and other mythical characters. Each member of the group must contribute to the development of the Billion-Dollar Being. Here are some ways to contribute: Draw the Billion-Dollar Being; collect resources that will help develop the Billion-Dollar Being; brainstorm ideas and gather materials to make the Billion-Dollar Being.

Illustrate a model of your Billion-Dollar Being on a large sheet of butcher paper. After completing the model, explain your group's Billion-Dollar Being to the other members of the class.

DISCUSSION QUESTIONS

- What kinds of topics, questions, and issues were discussed in your group as you created the Billion-Dollar Being?
- This activity is appropriate for the upper grades. What would younger children learn from the activity?
- What limitations do you think human beings have that will never be conquered?
- What really limits what human beings can do?
- What are the relationships between science, technology, and social issues?

SCENIC VIEW 3.3

Teaching hands-on science so that it includes technology and social issues is often referred to as S/T/S (Science/Technology/Society). However, using S/T/S as a way to learn mathematics and science is more appropriate for the upper grades than the primary grades because of the complexity of the issues, technologies, and science ideas. Incorporating S/T/S into the upper elementary classroom can take three different emphases.

Emphasis 1

Begin with hands-on activities that are knowledge oriented.

Example

Children learn about the behavior and characteristics of electricity by doing experiments that explore the variables that affect the brightness of a light bulb. At the same time children can learn about the technology of light bulbs by using a magnifying lens to observe the filaments inside the bulb. They can investigate questions concerning the disposal of car batteries and dry cell batteries. What do these objects do to the environment when they are thrown away? Do chemical changes occur in old batteries which can pollute soil and water resources? The majority of science concepts can be related in some way to technology.

Emphasis 2

Choose a technology.

Example

Children can take apart old clocks and watches to examine their parts. By examining the parts, they are learning about gears and the relationships between the sizes of the gears and the amount of work that can be accomplished. They can study ratios in terms of the sizes and the number of turns each gear makes. They can look at the electricity and chemistry involved in digital watches and clocks. Social issues related to telling time and how methods of telling time have changed over the centuries can be discussed, as well as the impact on daily life and new ways of keeping time.

Emphasis 3

Begin with identifying a social issue created by technology. Children can explore solutions to help minimize the impact of the technology on the environment.

Example

An investigation may begin by studying the effects of automobile exhaust on the quality of air. What kinds of respiratory diseases are caused by air pollution? Answering this question could lead to learning about the respiratory system of the human body. Children could study the technology of cars to find out why they cause pollution. Studying car technology can lead naturally to the principles behind gasoline combustion. How is gasoline made? What are some alternatives to the gasoline engine? What happens to plants and animals when they are exposed to oil spills or exhausts from automobiles?

Studying the alternatives to gasoline energy can lead to discussions about the consequences of using alternative energy sources. What would happen if we stopped using gasoline in automobiles? What would happen if natural gas, electricity, or solar energies were used as fuel for cars?

The following guidelines are suggested when using social issues to learn about science and related technology.

1. **Choose Issues Relevant to Children's Lives:** Issues must be related to children's lives to have meaning and for real learning to occur. The following are examples: (1) litter on the playground, in the neighborhood, or in the city; (2) recycling and garbage disposal programs; (3) toxic waste dumps in the community; (4) nuclear power stations; (5) smog and air pollution; (6) lake, stream, and river pollution.

    As was mentioned before, schools often include the study of rain forests or whales as environmental issues. Typically, children paint murals, read books, watch videos, and find information on the World Wide Web about these topics. These types of activities may draw children's attention to the issues but they can do little to prevent the destruction of rain forests or the killing of whales. Besides, children may have little understanding of all of the complex political, economic, and social issues. For example, people who live in tropical rain forest areas are usually very poor and see harvesting wood as an opportunity to improve their standard of living. As the population increases, more land is needed to grow food. Rain forests are slashed and burned to make fields. Killing whales for food has been an integral part of many societies for centuries.

Children who experience involvement in local environmental issues are being prepared to be actively involved in global issues as adults.

2. **Provide Children with Resources to Search for Information about the Issue:** Use local newspapers, weekly news magazines, television documentaries, and information from the World Wide Web. Local community resources may also provide information. Resources should be as current as possible and represent different points of view. Children can read or view the original sources. Introductory paragraphs can be prepared as summaries of current information. These paragraphs can provide enough information for children to begin discussing the issues.

3. **Brainstorm Solutions:** It is not enough just to study the issues. Children can become involved in creating solutions to issues that affect the environment. Taking action demonstrates that there are solutions to environmental problems. All solutions created by children during brainstorming must be respected. Children can pursue further research about the solutions that are the results of brainstorming.

4. **For Each Solution, Brainstorm the Pros and Cons:** List the solutions that children have created. Ask children to list the consequences of each solution and discuss them.

5. **Choose the Solution That Has the Least Negative Impact on the Environment:** Give children time to examine each solution and its consequences to determine which one would have the least impact on society and the environment.

6. **Take Action to Implement Solutions:** Children can brainstorm ways to take action to implement the solution. Action may mean writing letters to companies or state and national legislators. It may mean picking up litter or stopping the use of a product. Children cannot take action on issues that are outside the realm of their influence, so keep them focused on realistic actions.

An entire class can tackle one issue or different groups of children can investigate a variety of issues. The study of issues provides a different approach to learning other than focusing on content alone. Content becomes relevant because knowing all sides of the issues requires knowing the science behind the issue. In their discussions, children are using problem solving and inquiry to reach solutions. They are also studying different points of view, which reflect their various backgrounds. Thus, children can learn about their peers and their multicultural backgrounds.

Environmental issues are complex; solutions are neither right or wrong, black or white, but fall along a continuum. Finding solutions to environmental issues involves generating many creative ideas, which requires children to work together in cohesive groups. Social settings are created in the classroom that are similar to those they will experience as adults in their community. They must wrestle not only with the issues and the scientific knowledge but also with the individual and cultural values that affect decision making.

REST STOP 3.3

The Group Process

As was mentioned before, environmental education is an excellent vehicle with which to develop a community of learners to support interactions and learning among culturally diverse groups. This is not to say that children cannot engage in group activity while doing other kinds of science and mathematics activities. But activities focusing on environmental and technological issues require collaborative work, a mirror of society. The solutions to these issues require everyone's input. Piaget (1966) identifies social transmissions as a factor that affects the development of intelligence. Thus interactions during the group process influence the development of logic. In other words, ideas communicated through verbal exchanges are mentally processed just as are ideas from action on objects. Ideas become internalized by mentally fitting them with existing ideas or rearranging ideas to create new ideas. Through the group process children become less egocentric about their ideas because their knowledge base is broadened by the perspectives of others.

Science and mathematics knowledge is created through collaborative efforts. Ideas are debated, tested, and refined, and become acceptable in scientific and mathematical communities. During group interactions, children can experience some of the same processes used by scientists and mathematicians to reach consensus.

Criteria for Creating Groups

1. **Consider Children's Age and Maturity Levels:** Children's age is a factor to consider when deciding whether to use the group process. Primary children are basically egocentric about their ideas and are still processing their own ideas through concrete experiences. This makes it difficult for them to process the ideas of other children. Young children love to talk. They want to tell everyone their thoughts but they are not necessarily interested in what their peers have to say. Piaget (1968) concludes:

   > One must, nevertheless, ask whether the child is completely aware of how to communicate his thoughts and is capable of taking the point of view of others or whether socialization has to be learned in order to achieve real cooperation. In this regard, the analysis of the functions of spontaneous language is instructive. The conversions among children remain rudimentary and linked to materials action itself. Until seven years of age children scarcely know how to have discussions among themselves and confine themselves to making contradictory affirmations. When they try to furnish explanations to others, they are not really able to put themselves in the place of the other person, who does not know what they are talking about; they speak as though they were talking to themselves. For example, while working in the same room or at the same table, each child speaks for himself, even though he thinks he is listening to and understands the others. This kind of "collective monologue" is really a mutual excitation to action rather than a real exchange of ideas. (pp. 20–21)

   The exchange of ideas is cooperation, which contributes to effective group work. Through maturity and experience, children begin to listen to and understand the ideas of others. Children can begin to work cooperatively at the primary level, but learning to cooperate takes time and children will progress at different rates.

2. **Involve Children in Goal Setting:** When children work in a function group, it is usually because they have a common goal, which they have accepted either explicitly or implicitly (Foster and Penick, 1985; Foster, 1986). A goal, other than working on a social issue, might be solving a mathematical problem that involves several steps. Each child can contribute to the various steps. Children who do not understand why they are working together may encounter difficulties in staying focused on the task at hand.

3. **Consider Children's Knowledge and Interest Levels:** In the adult world, working groups are usually made up of those who have similar expertise and interest in the same goal. This is also the case for children working in groups. Children who have similar knowledge backgrounds will have the self-confidence to contribute to the group process. Children who have neither vested interest nor the knowledge background are at a disadvantage. However, forming groups of children with a similar background knowledge may be difficult and may create disparities between groups. Choosing complex problems or issues will accommodate the interests and knowledge backgrounds of the majority of children in a classroom.

4. **Form Groups as Naturally as Possible:** Use a variety of techniques, from allowing children to form their own groups to forming groups by random methods. Forcing children to belong to certain groups may be detrimental to all members of the group. Sometimes children prefer to work by themselves and at other times they will work together. Allow children to move in and out of groups. Children can work by themselves on a problem and then rejoin the group to share their findings. Allow groups to change as the goals change. If the problem has been solved, groups may dissolve and new groups may form to solve another problem.

5. **Group Size:** The ideal group size is four to five children, especially when working on complex environmental issues. Triads may be difficult because one child may be left out of the conversations. In groups larger than five some children may sit on the sidelines and not participate.

6. **Establish Parameters for Group Interactions:** Children must respect one another's ideas, beliefs, and opinions. Children should try to reach a consensus when making decisions. Each group member should have a particular responsibility as they work toward finding solutions. Examples of responsibilities are recording data, gathering materials, finding resources, analyzing data, and writing conclusions.

Using groups as a way to manage children, though, can defeat the purpose of cooperative group learning. When used properly, group work places children in microcosms of our society, working together to solve problems. Environmental and social issues related to science and technology are appropriate for group work because many people's ideas are needed to find good solutions. Environmental issues are social problems that cannot be solved by individuals. Solutions require cultural and ethnic groups to work together, because the environment belongs to everyone.

Summary

Cultural Differences and the Processes of Learning

The development of scientific and mathematical knowledge stems from processes such as observing, measuring, classifying, and communicating natural events. In all cultures children learn to count, add, subtract, and do other mathematical operations. All children use the same basic process for learning. All children are curious about the world. Cultures create frameworks or viewpoints that guide curiosity and the desire to understand nature and the universe. Some frameworks are based on understanding nature to improve human life, even at the expense of the natural environment. Other frameworks are based on respecting nature and maintaining harmony with it. Imposing one culture's viewpoint of exploiting nature on other cultures has created conflicts and disruption. Environmental groups have adopted frameworks of other cultures to restore the balance of nature and save endangered species of plants and animals.

Emphasizing science and mathematics processes rather than terminology and content validates children as human beings regardless of their cultural and ethnic background. All children learn through exploration and curiosity. The most important thing to remember is that each child brings to school a different set of experiences and knowledge to create a framework for viewing the world. Children's views vary because of the different social factors affecting their knowledge, and as unique individuals, they do not all respond in exactly the same way to cultural parameters. Gallard (1993) says: "Each student (minority and nonminority) has a unique set of experiences from which the science teacher can draw in order to facilitate learning" (p. 171). Stereotypes of ethnic and social groups are based on generalizations. Avoid putting children in pigeonholes according to their ethnic and cultural backgrounds. Learn about the children you teach, respect their backgrounds, and understand the frame of reference they use for learning mathematics and science. If children are to learn to live with others from different cultures, each child must be shown respect.

Emphasizing the processes also provides a means for effective communication in the classroom. The meanings of words are associated with objects and actions on objects. English words can be given for objects or actions and, in turn, children can express their native language words. Thus teacher and children are sharing their languages.

Using cultural contexts adds relevancy to problem solving. For example, studying musical instruments from different cultures can add relevancy to studying the science of sound. The study of time can be explored by making sundials, sand clocks, and other timing devices used in present and past cultures. Children can find out how different cultures view science and mathematics and use these views to explore scientific ideas.

Celebrate diversity by recognizing the contributions of scientists and mathematicians from different cultures. Display their pictures. Be sure to include women scientists and mathematicians. Have children look at different resources to learn about these famous people. Children can choose a particular person to portray in plays or presentations. For example, they can create mini-plays that include famous people coming together to discuss their contributions to science.

The natural environment provides a cultural context in which to learn mathematics and science. Environmental issues affect all of us. Children can become engaged in learning about environmental issues and solutions.

These last three chapters have focused on the origins of beliefs and attitudes that have created a philosophy of mathematics and science learning as well as teaching. Not only classroom experiences but also cultural and ethnic experiences influence this philosophy. The journey continues in Chapter 4 by examining learning processes that are essential to understanding mathematics and science concepts. However, keep in mind that the extent to which these processes are used is influenced by cultural and ethnic factors.

> **Go back to the reflective questions at the beginning of the chapter and the answers you recorded in your journal.**
>   **Add to or modify your answers based on what you learned from this chapter.**

Bibliography

Atwater, M. (1996). Social constructivism: Infusion into the multicultural science education research agenda. *Journal of Research in Science Teaching, 33*(8), 821–837.

Atwater, M., and Riley, J. (1993). Multicultural science education: Perspectives, definitions, and research agenda. *Science Education, 77*(6), 661–668.

Bronowski, J. (1973). *The ascent of man.* Boston, MA: Little, Brown.

Cochran-Smith, M. (1995). Color blindness and basket making are not the answers: Confronting the dilemmas of race, culture, and language diversity in teacher education. *American Educational Research Journal, 32*(3), 493–522.

Davydov, V. V. (1995). (S. T. Kerr, Transl.). The influence of L. S. Vygotsky on education theory, research, and practice. *Educational Researcher, 12,* 12–21.

Eisenhart, M., Finkel, E., and Marion, S. (1996). Creating the conditions for scientific literacy: A re-examination. *American Educational Research Journal, 33*(2), 261–295.

Foster, G. (1986). Adolescent development and group inquiry. *Science Scope, 10*(3), 122–123.

Foster, G., and Easley, J. (1994). *The hidden curriculum is not hidden in the Talovski District.* Paper presented at the annual meeting of the National Association of Research in Science Teaching, Anaheim, CA.

Foster, G., and Penick, J. (1985). Creativity in a cooperative group setting. *Journal of Research in Science Teaching, 22*(1), 89–95.

Gallard, A. J. (1993). Learning science in multicultural environments. In K. Tobin (Ed.), *The practice of constructivism in science education.* Hillsdale, NJ: Lawrence Erlbaum Associates.

Gould, S. (1981). *The mismeasure of man.* New York: W. W. Norton.

Hallowell, C. (1996, October 28). Trouble in the lily pads. *Time,* 87.

Hodson, D. (1993). Rationale for multicultural education. *Science Education, 77*(6), 685–711.

Jaroff, L. (1996). Still ticking. *Time, 149,* 80.

Jefferson County Public Schools. (1982). *Topics in applied science: A science course for junior high school.* Jefferson County, CO: Author.

Medawar, P. (1987). *Plato's republic.* Oxford: Oxford University Press.

National Council of Teachers of Mathematics. (1989). *Curriculum and evaluation standards for school mathematics.* Reston, VA: Author.

National Council of Teachers of Mathematics. (1991). *Professional standards for teaching mathematics.* Reston, VA: Author.

National Research Council. (1996). *National science education standards.* Washington, DC: National Academy Press.

Office of the Undersecretary. (1995). *Prospects: The congressional mandated study of educational growth and opportunity.* Washington, DC: U.S. Department of Education.

Piaget, J. (1966). *Psychology of intelligence.* Totowa, NJ: Littlefield, Adams.

Piaget, J. (1968). *Six psychological studies.* New York: Vintage Books.

Rosebery, A., Warren, B., and Conant, F. (1992). Appropriating scientific discourse: Findings from language minority classrooms. *The Journal of the Learning Sciences, 2*(1), 61–94.

Tate, W. (1994). Race, retrenchment, and the reform of school mathematics. *Phi Delta Kappan, 75*(6), 477–484.

Vygotsky, L. S. (1987). The collected works of L. S. Vygotsky (R. W. Rieber and A. S. Carton, Eds.). New York: Plenum.

PART 2 Constructing Learning

When children are actively engaged in learning through hands-on, problem-solving experiences, they are using specific learning processes. These processes are identified and discussed in Chapters 4, 5, and 6. Chapter 4 is entirely devoted to the process of questioning since it is the foundation for inquiry that drives the construction of knowledge. Chapter 5 focuses solely on the process of observing since it is so fundamental to all of the other processes as well as to the construction of knowledge. Chapter 6 discusses the other learning processes and how they relate to mathematical and science ideas. Chapter 7 is devoted to a theory that explains how logic and reasoning are mentally constructed through these engaging experiences.

CHAPTER 4

Why Is the Sky Blue?

A question determines and brings about its answer just as the desired end shapes the nature of the kind of question asked. This is the way by which science synthetically creates that which it then "discovers" out there in nature.

J. C. Pearce, *The Crack in the Cosmic Egg*

Reflective Questions

- Think back to your learning experiences. When did meaningful learning occur? How did you feel when you were able to successfully answer your questions?

- What role do questions play in learning science and mathematics? In teaching science and mathematics?

- What do both sets of standards say about asking questions?

- How important are the answers children give?

- What is the role of questions within inquiry?

- What is a good question?

- What are the relationships of questioning to learning science and mathematics?

- How do you feel about answering children's science and mathematics questions?

Philosophical Background: We Want Answers!

"Why are there more brown than red M&Ms?" "Why is the baby in mother's tummy?" "Why does it snow?" "Why do birds fly?" "Why do we have winter?" "Why do children have to sleep?"

Have you ever noticed the questioning behavior of two- and three-year-old children? They seem to have nothing else on their minds but questions. They want to know about everything. Adults express exasperation with inquisitive young children because of their continuous questioning. "Questions! Questions! Why do you ask so many questions, Dennis?" asked a frustrated Mr. Wilson. Dennis the Menace replied: "I'm only five years old and there is a lot about this world that I don't know much about" (*Dennis the Menace,* Warner Brothers movie, 1993). Children like Dennis the Menace simply want to understand the world around them. Their learning journey begins long before entering school.

Human beings are unique because they do ask questions. No other animals display such inquisitive behavior. Monkeys are seen as inquisitive beings because of their ability to solve simple problems, but this behavior pales in comparison to that of humans, who have the capacity to question their world through reflective thoughts. The behavior of questioning is unique to humans and individual questions are as unique as each person.

An individual's questions, driven by curiosity, act as the internal guidance system that directs the learning journey during the construction of intelligence. A self-regulated process of learning occurs through an individual's questions and the answers received. Questions help "wire the brain" to make connections among ideas. Each individual's learning journey is singular because of their own sets of questions, shaped by culture, heredity, and experiences.

Learning through questions constructs knowledge, understanding, and meaning by finding answers. Knowledge learned through questions is knowledge hard won, making that knowledge an integral part of the learner. To put it simply: no questions, no learning. Questions lead to problem solving, which is real learning.

> "A question," says Claparède, "is the conscious realization of a problem or of the difficulty of solving it," i.e., of the direction in which to seek for its solution. To search effectually, one must know what it is one is searching for, one must have asked oneself a question. The nature of this question will determine the whole orientation of research. Thus the function of the question is quite clear: it is an incitement to mental activity, in a certain direction in view of readjustment. (Piaget, 1974, pp. 230–231)

Questions continually occur no matter the situation: listening to a teacher, watching a demonstration, or touching objects. Having questions, whether they are internally or externally driven, indicates an investment in wanting to know or understand.

TOUR GUIDES

> ### National Council of Teachers of Mathematics (1989)
> In sum, we believe that learning should be guided by the search to answer questions—first at an intuitive, empirical level; then by generalizing; and finally by justifying [proving]. (p. 10)
>
> ### National Research Council (1996)
> Scientific investigation involves asking and answering a question and comparing the answer with what scientists already know about the world. (p. 123)

Children begin their formal school years full of questions and curiosity. As school years progress, children are asked to leave their set of questions at the school door and relinquish questioning to the classroom teacher. Children no longer need to ask their own questions because textbooks and curriculum guides have a preplanned learning journey with all the questions and answers readily available. The natural learning process through questions becomes muted and stunted. If children's learning process is to continue in school, they must bring their own suitcase of questions for the journey.

Scientists and mathematicians have somehow survived the education system because they held on to their own curiosity. They continuously ask questions, which not only lead to answers but also to further questions. Mathematics and science bodies of knowledge depend upon questioning and finding answers and solutions and therefore becomes broad based and cyclical; asking questions, finding answers, asking new questions, and finding new answers. Any scientist will tell you that answering one question always leads to new questions. Learning is a continuous and active process through questioning and finding answers.

TOUR GUIDES

> ### The National Council of Teachers of Mathematics (1991) Standard 2: The Teacher's Role in Discourse
>
> The teacher of mathematics should orchestrate discourse by posing questions and tasks that elicit, engage, and challenge each student's thinking; listening carefully to students' ideas; asking students to clarify and justify their ideas orally and in writing. (p. 35)
>
> ### Standard 3: The Students' Role in Discourse
>
> The teacher of mathematics should promote classroom discourse in which students listen to, respond to, and question the teacher and one another; use a variety of tools to reason, make connections, solve problems, and communicate; initiate problems and questions; make conjectures and present solutions; explore example and counterexample to investigate a conjecture; try to convince themselves and one another of the validity of particular representations, solutions, conjectures, and answers; rely on mathematical evidence and argument to determine validity. (p. 45)
>
> ### National Research Council (1996) Teaching Standard B
>
> Teachers of science guide and facilitate learning. In doing this, teachers
>
> - Focus and support inquiries while interacting with students
> - Orchestrate discourse among students about scientific ideas
> - Encourage and model the skills of scientific inquiry, as well as the curiosity, openness to new ideas and data, and skepticism that characterize science. (p. 3)
>
> ### Content Standard A
>
> As a result of activities in grades K–4 and 5–8, all students should develop
>
> - Abilities necessary to do scientific inquiry
> - Understanding about scientific inquiry. (pp. 121, 143)

Both sets of standards advocate teaching and learning based on knowledge development through active questioning. In addition, the National Research Council (1996) defines inquiry as "the activities of students in which they develop knowledge and understanding of scientific ideas as well as an understanding of how scientists study the natural world" (p. 14). The act of *inquiry* (questioning) is the search for truth or knowledge (answers). But the truth is elusive because the knowledge raises new questions.

Teachers and children must feel safe and comfortable when asking questions on the learning journey. Teachers facilitate children's learning journeys by presenting new exploration possibilities through questions. Teachers must also raise questions about accepted and traditional mathematical and science learning practices. What practices are the best in supporting children's learning journeys? Teachers' learning journeys are also enhanced by children's questions because their inquisitiveness provides valuable insight about the learning and thinking process they are experiencing.

Identifying Questions

Analyzing and categorizing questions and answers are essential to effectively supporting the use of inquiry during teaching and learning mathematics and science. These categories identify the type of questions and answers they will elicit. Answers to questions provide indicators of understanding. Questions are assessment tools. Chapter 14 gives more details about using questions to assess children's understanding.

Many attempts have been made to place questions in categories according to their characteristics, creating systems of relationships that are both horizontal and vertical. Understanding such systems lets teachers choose questions according to the response they want. The taxonomy created by Bloom (1956) is familiar to many classroom teachers, and is a classic example of a system that classifies questions according to levels of cognitive learning. Blosser (1991) uses a category system for asking the right questions. Gilbert (1992) developed a taxonomy of questions specifically related to science. However, as in all taxonomic schemes, the categories are subject to the biases of the inventor and not necessarily user friendly to all. Questions placed in one category for a particular taxonomy could just as well be placed in another category in a different taxonomy. The number of categories and subcategories and their hierarchical relationships, all in the eyes of the beholder, can make them complex and difficult to interpret and use.

Classroom Activity 4.1

Categorizing Questions

Review Bloom's taxonomy and other systems of categorizing and organizing questions that were presented in other classes. Search current literature for others as well. In small groups of 4 to 5, discuss their similarities and differences.

DISCUSSION QUESTIONS

- Which taxonomies make sense to you?
- Which ones would be helpful in developing questioning strategies?

As an educator you will want to use those systems that make sense to you. This book offers another strategy that is simply based upon *inquiry*. Questions that elicit memorized facts are not considered as a category since they have little to do with inquiry. Four categories of inquiry questions have been developed that are based on the type of responses a question may elicit: (1) confirmation (yes, no); (2) factual (the ball is blue); (3) process (the water was weighed); and (4) conceptual (subtraction is the reverse of addition). Each category is explained with examples in the following paragraphs.

Confirmation questions ask for a simple yes or no answer and are useful indicators of reality. These questions are asking for responses that relate to actions involved in investigations rather than the recall of information provided by a teacher, textbooks, or other resources. Responses to confirmation questions give minimal evidence as to what has been learned. There is a 50-50 chance of picking the right answer without learning anything through inquiry. On many occasions, perceptions override actual data. For example, a teacher asks a child: "Did the bulb light?" A child might say no even though the teacher saw it light. This is an opportunity for a teacher to clarify the contradiction by asking questions such as: "What did you do?" or "How do you know for sure?" These questions ask children to reflect upon their actions (processes). Answers can confirm agreement of observations between persons asking the question and those being questioned. Discrepancies often occur because perceptions, opinions, and/or prior knowledge can influence observations. For example, a kindergarten child was asked, "Are squares and rhombuses different?" The child said "yes" because a rhombus is a square that has been "stretched." When differences occur between observations, consideration must be given to the type of action needed to reconcile the differences.

Questions that begin with "Can you . . . ?" "Will you . . . ?" are also confirmation questions with an invitation to a challenge. "Can you make the bulb brighter?" "Can you make a hexagon from these triangles?" "Can you divide the pie into fourths?" Children who say they cannot divide the pie into fourths confirm that additional activities are needed about fractions at a very basic level. Accepting the challenge indicates a level of understanding and invites learners to take actions leading to further exploration. Confirmation questions are catalysts asking learners to explain their thoughts to support "yes" or "no" answers. Thus, a teacher can ask process, factual, and conceptual questions based on the answer to a confirmation question.

Factual questions are those that begin with *what, when,* and *where* and require learners to give short answers beyond yes or no. Specific answers are elicited by this type of question. "What does two times two equal?" "What happened when you added more weight?" *What if* questions can challenge children to make conjectures, predictions, and hypotheses with additional creative exploration. "What if you turn the test tube upside down?" "What if you add another square?" *When* and *where* questions elicit contextual answers. "When does the bulb light?" "Where have you seen triangles?" Sometimes observational conditions need to be clarified before results can be understood. The questioner is gathering data about the factual knowledge possessed by the learner. Factual questions are indicators of the processes a child used or the level of conceptual understanding attained. Thus, factual questions can lead to process or conceptual questions.

Use factual questions to analyze knowledge children understand from data they have collected. "What happened to the weight of the cup when you added the other beans?" "Where do you see it turning color?" "When did you take it out of the freezer?" Answers to factual questions reveal children's knowledge about cause and effect relationships and patterns that are emerging from the data. Factual questions directly related to observations give both teacher and children the same frame of reference when discussing the resulting data. If discrepancies occur between observers (teacher and child), additional data can be collected either by repeating the actions or involving other children in the data collection to see if they arrive at the same results.

Process questions ask the learner to explain actions used to formulate an answer to the other types of questions. Typically they begin with the words "how" or "what." Asking learners these questions reveals the actions used to collect a given set of facts. Answers to process questions are based on some kind of action such as measuring, controlling variables, classifying, ordering, operationally defining, and communicating. "How did you get the bulb to be twice as bright as before?" "What did you do to make the ball bounce higher? the bulb light?" "How do the three triangles fit together?" Learners who can explain their actions become cognizant of how their activities influence and create new knowledge. Perceptions, opinions, and beliefs are replaced by actual data. Knowledge developed from actions leads to facts and concepts.

Use process questions to understand what children are doing to collect data. "How do you know that the inclined plane has an effect on the distance the marble rolls?" "How do you know that the area of a circle is greater than the area of a square?" "How do you know for sure how many beans are in each container?" Answering process questions provides opportunities for children to practice creating explanations. Explaining actions is much easier than explaining conceptual ideas.

Conceptual questions begin with "why." These questions require responses that explain relationships abstracted from factual information. Conceptual questions are the most difficult to ask and answer because they require learners to probe the knowledge they have internalized. The internalized knowledge is the culmination of the processes and data collected from active learning with concrete objects. Responses to "why" questions can be numerous and may place a teacher in a vulnerable position because the answer may challenge the teacher's knowledge base. For example, asking the question "Why does the bulb light?" can produce several answers. Answers could range from reference to the flow of electrons to light produced by heat. All of the answers could be partially correct, but teachers may not know whether there is any scientific accuracy in the answers.

Conceptual questions do not necessarily elicit a conceptual response. This explains the diversity of responses from learners despite the fact that they are experiencing the same learning situation. Different responses are indicators of different levels of conceptual understanding. The following answers are examples of different levels of conceptual understanding. The teacher asks the following question: "Why does the bulb light?"

Student A responds: "The bulb lights because the wires, batteries, and bulbs are touching each other."

Student B responds: "The bulb lights because the electricity, which is in the battery, travels to the bulb through the bulb's base. The electricity continues through the wires inside the bulb and out of the bulb through the copper wire that is touching the side of the bulb. The electricity continues to travel through the wire to the other battery end. This creates a complete circle for the flow of electricity."

Student C responds: "The bulb lights because a chemical reaction occurs in the battery that creates electricity. This electricity builds up and flows through the wire and bulbs in a particular sequence. The flow continues as long as the other wire is connected to the other end of the battery."

Explanation A is based on minimal data. Explanation B indicates that the child recognizes that the wires must touch certain parts of the battery and bulb and that when everything is hooked together a circle is formed. This explanation demonstrates the ability to understand the relationships between the wires, battery, and bulb needed to light a bulb. Thus explanation B indicates a higher level of understanding than explanation A. This is a higher level of thinking since the answer is based on abstracting an idea from evidence given by the data. Explanation C is based on further evidence gathered by opening a battery. A child might know this by examining and comparing the contents of a new battery and a battery that no longer lights any bulbs. Further evidence would need to be gathered to be more conclusive about answering this "why" question. The point being made here is that the more evidence is gathered, the more likely children can explain things at the conceptual level.

The question examples, used to illustrate differences between questions, have something in common. All of the questions converge on the action on objects. Answers that originate from action on objects (primary source) are more valid and believable than from secondary sources. Multiplication knowledge learned by actually manipulating objects is more valid than from secondary sources (books, media, another person).

EXCURSION 4.1

The above examples by no means indicate right or wrong answers. They are given to illustrate different levels of thinking. For example, children may have misperceptions about electricity but only in terms of making comparisons to explanations given by scientists. It is unrealistic to expect that elementary school children will arrive at the same level of understanding as scientists regardless of the type of learning situation. The purpose of questions and activities is to help children grow in their understanding of scientific concepts. Having the ability as a teacher to discriminate different levels of thinking by asking questions helps to assess what children do understand and the type of learning situations they need to further develop concepts.

Use conceptual questions to assess children's understanding about relationships derived from a given set of facts. "Why do six equilateral triangles make a hexagon?" "Why does the area of a given set of shapes always stay the same no matter how you arrange them?" "Why does the bulb get brighter when you add another battery?" Asking conceptual questions gives children opportunities to explain their conclusions about their data. Asking children to respond to conceptual questions not directly related to observable data may be misleading, however. Use the following question as an example: "Why do electrons travel in the same direction through the wire?" Using the word "electrons" assumes that children understand this terminology. Electrons and their characteristics cannot be directly observed. The only exposure children will have to understanding electrons is through secondary sources. Remember, secondary sources are those that contain explanations and conclusions developed by someone other than the learner. Therefore answers will be either conjecture or memorized from a secondary source. Thus this answer does not tell you what a child really understands. The answer may indicate what they have memorized.

Table 4.1 is a summary of the question categories and the type of responses they elicit. Answers to questions reveal levels of thinking possessed by learners but what is revealed depends on the type of question asked. *Confirmation* questions reveal little about thinking processes. Yes or no answers only indicate the next appropriate question. *Conceptual* questions ask learners to share their thinking in terms of what knowledge has been internalized. *Process* and *factual* questions require responses that are in between confirmation and conceptual questions. Thus, questions used in a discriminatory fashion elicit responses that are indicators of different levels of the learning process and understanding. The different levels of learning and understanding that develop during inquiry will be explained in further detail in Chapter 13.

The type of question asked and the answer given are indicators when making decisions to probe further for understanding. It is important to ask questions to find out what knowledge children have constructed and also to challenge what they have learned. Driver, Guesne, and Tiberghien (1985) have shown that children arrive at school with preexisting ideas that are not necessarily based on reality or logic but on perceptions or opinions. For example, children may think the value of money is determined by the size or weight of the coin, i.e., a nickel is heavier and larger than a dime, therefore it is worth much more.

Classroom Activity 4.2   *Analysis of Teachers' Questions*

INSTRUCTIONS

1. For each question determine if the response would elicit facts, processes, or concepts.

2. Discuss some possible answers children might give to the questions.

3. Discuss the source of the child's knowledge used to give a response to the question (e.g., action on objects, textbook, teacher, etc.).

4. Decide whether the questions are related to math, science, or both.

DISCUSSION QUESTIONS

- What did you do after you collected the seeds?
- How many grew?
- How many batteries did it take to light three bulbs?
- What would happen if you used a smaller jar?
- How large are the leaves?
- Why are they the same weight?
- Why did the candle go out?
- What kind of animal made the tracks?
- How many paper clips will the magnets pick up?
- When will the candle burn out?
- Which objects will produce static electricity?
- Why did the piece of wood sink?
- How many inches are in a yard?
- Why is the length times the width equal to area?
- What is ten times ten?
- What does it mean to divide?
- How many triangles does it take to make a hexagon?
- If I have 20 beans in ten different cups, how many beans do I have altogether?

TABLE 4.1
Summary of
Question Categories

Question Category	Question Root Examples	Type of Answers
Confirmation	Is . . . ? Can you . . . ? Did you . . . ?	Yes, no
Process	What did . . . ? What happened . . . ? How . . . ?	Elicit responses that describe actions
Factual	What . . . ? Where . . . ? When . . . ?	Elicit responses that describe characteristics, properties, and behaviors of objects
Conceptual	Why . . . ?	Elicit responses that express relation-ships between facts

- If I have the same amount of butter and salt, which one will weigh the most?
- Why is multiplication the opposite of division?

Questioning Strategies for Teaching Mathematics and Science

1. **Use wait time.** In 1969, Mary Budd-Rowe (1996) revealed that teachers wait an average of one second for children to answer questions. She suggested prolonging wait time to five seconds or longer. Next time you are in the classroom asking children questions, time yourself to see how long you actually wait for an answer. Waiting provides children with time to think about their answer before responding. Conceptual questions probably require the most wait time, compared to other types of questions, because children have to reflect upon thoughts rather than upon actions or facts. Waiting demonstrates willingness and sincerity about listening and hearing real answers. In other words, children can express themselves rather than repeat answers from other sources. The use of wait time validates children's self-confidence.

2. **Use questions that maintain focus on children's activities with objects.** Answers will originate from first-hand experience that children can explain at their own comfort level. The activities can be observed by the teacher. If the focus is on giving the same answers found in textbooks, other resources, and/or espoused by the teacher, children may be anxious about whether their answer is right. Teachers also may be afraid of not knowing enough content. Content arises from action on objects. Content can be discussed and questioned during interactions between children and teacher.

3. **Use questions to raise consciousness about contradictions** between children's perceptions and your own observations. When perceptions are challenged, children are likely to look at other possible explanations for a given phenomenon. For example, a child says, "I can see the different

phases of the moon on the Styrofoam ball but I still think clouds cause moon phases." Acknowledge this answer without being critical or condescending. Saying it is wrong may only damage the child's self-confidence rather than facilitate learning. It is more helpful to ask questions to clarify what the child is saying. The teacher says, "Are you saying there are no moon phases when the sky is clear? Can you prove that to me? What data do you have to support your claims?" Driver, Guesne, and Tiberghien (1985) report children do not readily give up their perceptions in favor of reality. But their perceptions are likely to be relinquished when children become cognizant of the contradictions. Rather than forcing children to give up incorrect ideas, provide experiences that offer data to contradict their ideas and lead to meaningful learning.

When children do not see the contradictions between their answers and reality, their responses to conceptual questions will be based on perceptions rather than logic. The teacher says, "I have made a square shape with this string (ends of string are tied together). Does the distance around the string stay the same, increase, or decrease when I make a rectangular shape?" Since the length of the string is the same no matter what the shape, an appropriate answer would be, "The distance around stays the same regardless of the shape." However, the child may respond with a different answer such as: "The distance decreases." This answer contradicts reality. Asking the child "Why?" will not yield a conceptual answer. The answer will likely be expressed in terms of what a child observes.

If a child responds, "The distance decreases," you might say, "I don't understand. From what I can see, the distance doesn't decrease. How do you know the distance decreases?" or "Can you show me that it decreases?" The idea is to have children gather data to support their claims. It is also possible that there are errors in their data collection and they may need help in discovering those errors. For example, "The number you have in your data table doesn't match the length of the string. Check your measurements again to make sure they are accurate." Rather than telling children they are wrong, analyze contradictions through data collection.

4. **Use stock questions** when questioning children. "Why do you think so?" "What do you think?" "What would happen if . . . ?" "What are some other ways to explain your observations?" "What are you doing?" can be used regardless of the activity. Use stock questions rather than questions that focus on terminology and recall of specific content. A child is building with blocks and a teacher asks: "What kind of house are you building?" This question assumes the child made a house and focuses the child's attention on terminology when the activity is really about developing relationships. Asking terminology questions about these kinds of activities can derail children's thought processes. Asking for terminology or recall of content does not reveal what a child knows. But asking what the child is doing allows him or her to continue working while explaining his or her actions. Further questioning can reveal the processes children understand. The teacher's credibility, as an observer of children's learning behaviors, is diminished by assuming what the child is doing without asking for clarification. Thus, inquiry is just as important to a teacher's understanding as it is to a child's understanding.

5. **Use questions to stimulate thinking about other possibilities** for solving problems. For example, children are counting beans, one by one, to find out how many are in a quart jar. The teacher says, "What are some other ways of finding out how many beans are in the jar without counting them one by one?" Without questioning, children may continue to count one by one, become bored, and quit without inventing more efficient counting methods. Through questioning, children learn that the world is full of different possibilities, which nourishes and stimulates curiosity and further investigation.

Discussion Question

Read the mathematics and science standards to support answers to the following question:

Does the nature of mathematics or science define the type of questions a teacher will ask children? For example, even if memorization is not a goal, is a teacher likely to ask more factual questions in mathematics than in science? Explain your answers.

Responding to Children's Questions

Responding to children's questions is as much of a challenge as asking the right question. The challenge originates from perceived barriers that prevent honest and natural exchanges between teachers and children. One of these perceived barriers is the preplanned curriculum, produced either locally or nationally. Traditionally curriculum guides include material that has to be covered by a given time during the school year. Children's spontaneous questions may be viewed as *getting in the way* of covering the material. The path of the learning journey is established and any side trips created by children's questions are to be prevented. Their questions are put on hold until a more convenient time.

Another barrier is the teacher's perception of a weak mathematics or science content background. The thinking behind the perception may be something like the following: "I did not learn mathematics or science in high school or college; therefore, I do not know enough to answer children's questions." These kinds of perceptions are evident from comments expressed by preservice elementary students. Children's questions may be avoided because they may resurrect teachers' feelings of insecurity. Teachers are expected to be fountains of knowledge, which makes any weaknesses in their mathematics and/or science content background even more glaring. Parents, children, administrators, and even teachers themselves may believe that giving specific content answers to children's questions means teachers have been well prepared and trained to teach. However, a teacher can teach science and mathematics effectively without having a strong content background when inquiry is the focus of teaching. When inquiry is the focus, the quality of learning improves and the quantity of material decreases.

The following are suggested options for dealing with children's questions. These options are some examples that have worked for teachers. They are intended as primers to get you started on the journey of interactions with children. Through experience, you will find other options.

Teaching Strategies for Responding to Children's Questions

Option 1: Take a Reality Check

Accept the reality that children will ask questions that challenge your mathematics and science background. No one person in any profession has all the answers. Scientists and mathematicians often specialize in a given area. A physicist may be hard pressed to answer specific questions about genetics.

When confronted with a question be honest and simply say: "I do not know the answer." Is it realistic to expect scientists and mathematicians to have answers to all of the questions they are asked? If that was true, there would be no need for further exploration and problem solving. In addition, unanswered questions keep curiosity alive. Yager and Yager (1984) found that students in the third grade had negative perceptions about science because they thought teachers knew the answers to all questions. When children understand that there are many, many unanswered questions, they will understand about humankind's limitations. If children persist in pursuing an answer to a seemingly unanswerable question, of course, support the pursuit. Unexpected learning may occur. Facilitating the process of finding an answer is more important than the answer itself. Children who are allowed to question and pursue answers on their own will gain confidence as problem solvers.

Option 2: Think Before Answering

Avoid automatically giving answers to questions to save face or time. Automatically responding supports the notion that teachers are the fountains of knowledge, which in turn creates dependency on teachers as the main providers of information. In addition, the information being given is not first-hand knowledge. The teacher may have heard the information in a lecture, read it in a book, or found it in other sources. Even if a teacher has learned the knowledge first-hand, the knowledge given to the child is second-hand. Information is processed through the knowledge bank of the giver. What comes out in words has been filtered and sorted according to the mental processes of the source. The farther away from the original source, the more likely the information will be interpreted differently.

The practice of automatically giving answers can also be challenged by the following questions: What information and how much information related to a child's question should be given? What guarantee is there that the given information is meaningful to children's understanding? What do children really need to know that will help them construct meaning of their world? Thus, "the answer" is not as important as the process of finding an answer for oneself.

Option 3: Offer Answers as Possibilities

When children ask questions that challenge your mathematics and science knowledge base, you might say, "This is what I know about the topic," or "What I know may be different from established scientific or mathematical knowledge." You can continue the dialogue by saying, "We may have to do some investigating," or finish with "Let's find out together." The point is to be honest rather than saving face and giving an answer that children accept as right but that may not be entirely correct.

EXCURSION 4.2

Elwin (1977) explains it this way: "The most familiar test of the teacher's equivalent of the Hippocratic Oath concerns his willingness to acknowledge his ignorance when he just does not know. The standard answer is the right one: that the risk to his (her) authority if he says he does not know is less dangerous than the loss to his integrity if he tries to bluff. A friend of mine, inspecting a West African class which for some reason was on the unlikely subject of seals, was surprised to hear the teacher say, when asked what seals live on, 'Bananas.' After the lesson he asked the teacher if he really thought the staple diet of seals was bananas. The teacher said he didn't know what their main food was, but had to give some answer if he was not to lose his authority with the class. I suspect it did not take long for some bright boy to find him out in any case. But what was the teacher doing to himself? Education is not at all about facts, but when facts are involved we must be honest about them" (pp. 85–86).

Keeping the door open to other explanations that can be investigated or answered through secondary sources maintains the integrity of inquiry. We are all learners. Science questions are difficult to answer because science is the process of understanding the unknown aspects of the natural world. Since mathematics uses mental operations to quantify the known natural world, mathematics questions may be easier to answer than science questions.

Option 4: Allow Children to Find Their Own Answers

You might say, "I have an answer but I would like you to see what you can find out on your own." Allow children to use problem solving to find answers to questions. Children can find answers through hands-on investigations and secondary sources. Learn to discriminate between questions to which children can find answers and those that should be given immediate teacher attention. If they do not want to search on their own for answers, analyze the situation. Are they really interested in finding answers? Do they want the answers to do well on a test?

On the other hand, withholding terminology answers serves little purpose. A child asks, "What color is that wooden block? What is the name of the shape of this wooden block?" Go ahead and answer! The answers to these questions cannot be discovered through investigation and it wastes time to have to go to a book for the answer. Give direct answers when children are asking for factual information. Children cannot learn terminology through discovery. But emphasizing terminology diverts attention away from the true purpose of learning, which is constructing conceptual understanding.

Supplying answers deprives children of opportunities to become problem solvers. Giving answers also sends a message that there is only *one* answer to a question. This can prevent following any other paths to other possible answers. Duckworth (1987) says,

> It occurred to me, then, that of all of the virtues related to intellectual functioning, the most passive is the virtue of knowing the right answer. Knowing the right answer requires no decisions, carries no risks, and makes no demands. It is automatic. It is thoughtless. (p. 64)

In traditional teaching strategies, the only criterion for making an answer "right" is whether or not children will be tested on it. In inquiry, answers are neither right or wrong. They are accepted as what is currently known and can be challenged and altered.

Facilitation is more than just telling a child, "Go look it up in the library." Without support and encouragement, children are likely to stop pursuing an answer when they have no idea how to find it. You might say to children: "How or where would you like to begin finding an answer?" Classrooms need to be rich in question-answering resources such as books, videos, computers with Internet access, telephones for speaking to experts directly, and materials and equipment to create investigations. Most cause and effect questions children ask can be answered through simple investigations.

Questions about certain science topics are difficult to answer through simple investigations. Ideas about such topics as astronomy, evolution, ecology, genetics, certain diseases, earth formations, and chemistry have been developed through inferences because the causes and effects cannot be directly observed. Sophisticated technologies are used to increase powers of observations. Scientists use drills, sound waves, and seismic waves to collect data to answer questions like "What causes volcanic eruptions?" Children are even more limited in answering such a question. They rely on creating simulations from secondary information. Provide activities and materials for questions that can be answered through direct observations and have secondary resources readily available for questions that go beyond what is observable.

Option 5: Paraphrase Children's Questions

Paraphrasing provides time before deciding the most appropriate responses to questions. Paraphrasing means repeating the question in your own words. A child asks, "If all atoms are moving, why don't I see them moving? There are millions of them in an object!" An example of a paraphrase might be the following: "What you are saying is 'How can millions of molecules be moving if we don't see them moving?' Is that right?" The child has an opportunity to respond with yes or no and the teacher an opportunity to try paraphrasing differently until understanding is reached. Paraphrasing is also a strategy used to clarify questions when children have difficulty stating them. Paraphrasing is an art that requires practice in listening to children.

Paraphrasing provides the teacher time to sort out thoughts before deciding the best way to tackle the question. Using paraphrasing provides other additional benefits such as demonstrating to children that you are listening and are sincerely interested in their questions. Then children will be encouraged to ask questions without fear of ridicule or rejection.

Option 6: Maintain a Data Bank

Keep a list of mathematics and science questions that children ask. Take time to write them down and file them so that you can analyze them later. A data bank will provide a rich resource of questions children are likely to ask and topics they want to learn. The lists of questions can be analyzed according to the following categories:

1. Most common questions

2. Most common topic questions

3. Questions requiring secondary sources for answers

	Barriers to Effective Questioning	Barrier Busters	Action to Take
TABLE 4.2 **Learning the Art** **of Questioning**	Focusing on the "right" answer	Allow children opportunities to answer their own questions	Provide activities, books, videos, and computers for finding answers
	The need to give answers	Help children find their own answers	Listen and paraphrase questions before responding
	Limited knowledge or background to answer questions	Acknowledge that children will ask unanswerable questions	Maintain a data bank of children's questions
		Acknowledge that a teacher is not the source of answers to all questions	Offer an answer as a seed to further investigation
			Discriminate between questions children can and cannot answer

4. Questions that can be answered through investigations

5. Percentage of factual, process, and conceptual questions (observable data)

After analyzing the questions, appropriate activities can be collected and organized into a unit of study, and appropriate secondary sources can be found and made available for student use. You may want to do some research and find answers to these questions if they pertain to areas in which you have little background knowledge.

Table 4.2 summarizes the six options and strategies to facilitate answering children's questions.

Capitalizing on Children's Questions

Children's questions are indicators of their interests. A curriculum can be built around their questions.

Classroom Activity 4.3

Analysis of Children's Questions

INSTRUCTIONS

The following are mathematics and science questions that children might ask. Discuss, in small groups, what you would do to help children answer the questions. What kinds of resources and experiences would you provide? Will the answers be factual, conceptual, or processed based?

- What is the plant called?

- What color is it?

- Which ones are orange?

- Why did some of the seeds grow and not the others?
- Where do birds go in the winter?
- What happens to earthworms during the winter?
- How can fish live in a frozen pond?
- Why is ice cream so cold?
- How many bones are there in the skeleton?
- When will the bulb burn out?
- How many nickels does it take to make one dollar?
- When will the ice cream be ready?
- How many oranges can I buy for two dollars?
- How many gum balls are in the jar?
- Why are bubbles always round?
- Which weighs more, apples or oranges?
- Why does water freeze?
- Which one is bigger, one-half or two-thirds?
- Where is the tallest tree?
- How many sides do snowflakes have?

Helping children answer questions is part of problem solving. Problems originate from questions.

TOUR GUIDE

> ### *Standard 1: Mathematics as Problem Solving*
>
> In grades K–4, the study of mathematics should emphasize problem solving so that students can—
> use problem-solving approaches to investigate and understand mathematical content; formulate problems from everyday and mathematical situations; develop and apply strategies to solve a wide variety of problems; verify and interpret results with respect to the original problem; acquire confidence in using mathematics meaningfully. (p. 23)
> In grades 5–8, the mathematics curriculum should include numerous and varied experiences with problem solving as a method of inquiry and application so that students can—
> use problem-solving approaches to investigate and understand mathematical content; formulate problems from situations within and outside mathematics; develop and apply a variety of strategies to solve problems, with emphasis on multistep and non-routine problems; verify and interpret results with respect to the original problem situation; generalize solutions and strategies to new problem situations; acquire confidence in using mathematics meaningfully. (p. 75)

Classroom Activity 4.4 **Analyzing Children's Questions**

RESEARCH DATA

The following list of questions comes from 125 elementary teachers who were asked to identify the most common questions children ask that are difficult to answer. The questions are grouped according to grade level.

Kindergarten

Why doesn't the sun burn out when it rains?
Where would we get light if the sun burns out?
Why does a crab walk sideways?
What does cold-blooded mean?
Why are all snowflakes different?
Why do we have bones in our bodies?

How does a fish swim?
How does the newt breathe?
How big were dinosaurs?
How does a magnet work?
Why does the wind blow
     and how?

Grade 1

How does TV work?
Are there other life forms on other planets?
How many planets are there besides the 9 we know about?
How did the planets get there in the first place?
Can dogs see at night?
Why did some of our planted seeds grow and others didn't?
Why are zebras black and white?

Grade 2

How big is the solar system?
Who (what) made dinosaurs?
How long ago did dinosaurs live?
Why do some plants have only one seed?
Does a tree grow from a seed?

How do fish breathe?
What is the sky made of?
Why did dinosaurs die?
How did dinosaurs sleep?

Grade 3

Why are there so many different types of clouds?
How do tornadoes and hurricanes start?
What is the fastest thing on earth?
Are there other creatures in space?
Will we bump into other planets?
Why are snowflakes different shapes?
Why do we have hiccups?
How do volcanoes blow up?
Who named the first planet?
How do cats have babies?

How hot is the sun?
Why are clouds white?
What is a sneeze?
Why is the moon bright?
What are goosebumps?
How do people grow?
What is the sun?
Why can't stars fall?
Why is the earth round?

Grade 4

Why do astronauts in space lose calcium in their bones?
Why does the sun stay hot if it is continually shining?
If things on earth weigh so much why don't they sink into the earth?
Why is the sky blue?
If we think all the continents might have been joined at one time, how could they
     possibly have drifted apart when they weigh so much?
Where do plants get food?

Grade 5

How does electricity get to a power plant?
Is a star cold after it disintegrates?
Is there really life on other planets?
Why can't humans regenerate limbs?
Why don't small fish regenerate in the
   Antarctic ocean?

Why do we get headaches?
Why do people dream?
Why do things have to die?
Why do some organisms
   regenerate?

Grade 6

How old is the earth?
Why are there stars in the sky?
What would happen if the sun blew up?
Why is an atom an atom?
What if stars didn't twinkle?

What if the sky wasn't blue?
Why is the moon white?
Why is there night and day?
Why is the earth round?

INSTRUCTIONS

Use the children's questions above to answer the following:

- How would you help children answer these questions?

- What topics are most prevalent among the questions?

- What are some reasons why children are interested in these particular topics?

- What topics were you interested in as a child?

---

*Field Experience
Activity 4.1*

Classroom Questions

INSTRUCTIONS

1. Visit elementary classrooms and collect data about the kinds of questions teachers and children ask during mathematics and science lessons. Use the four inquiry question categories to analyze them. Observe a teacher for a given amount of time and tally the number of questions asked.

   - What kinds of questions do teachers typically ask? Why do you think so?

2. While children are doing science and/or mathematics, listen to the kinds of questions they ask. Write them down. Categorize them using the four inquiry question categories. The type of questions children ask will also tell you about their level of understanding.

   - If children are asking mainly factual questions, what does this say about what children are learning from the activity?

   - Is there a correlation between the nature of activities and the type of questions children ask?

---

*Field Experience
Activity 4.2*

I Wonder About . . .

INSTRUCTIONS

Take time to let children respond verbally or in writing to the incomplete phrase "I wonder about . . . ." Give them enough time to generate a list of several ideas. Collect their lists for analysis. The most common question can be developed into a unit of study. Or several common questions can be selected and groups of children can choose their favorites to study. Questions can be selected about topics that are already in the curriculum or new topics can be created. For example, you may find children have questions about the probability of winning a lottery. Probability may already be part of the curriculum but now it can be studied within the context of lottery systems. The questions can be answered through a variety of probability activities and resources about lotteries, which would be made available in the classroom. The children's questions may be better than the ones found in textbooks and other curriculum materials because they are specifically relevant to the needs and interests of the children.

- What do children wonder about?
- How does your list compare to the questions given by the teachers in Classroom Activity 4.4?
- Are there similarities between questions for grade levels?

Classroom Activity 4.5   **Identifying Questions**

INSTRUCTIONS

Two activities are included in the next chapter that are appropriate for collecting data about questions. One is "Observation of a Burning Candle" and the other is "Cornstarch Mixtures." As your group is engaged in the activity write down the questions that are asked. After completing the activity, analyze the questions by category (process, confirmation, factual, or conceptual). Determine how answers may be found for each question (activity investigations, research using the media, or contacting experts).

Summary

The art of asking good questions takes practice. Questions are important to guiding the construction of knowledge along the learning journey. Elstgeest (1985) says, "A good question is the first step towards an answer; is a problem to which there is a solution. A good question is a stimulating question which is an invitation to a closer look, a new experiment or a fresh exercise" (p. 37). Good questions from teachers go beyond merely asking children to recall memorized facts and good questions from children go beyond asking, "Did I do this right?"

Human beings' natural curiosity, especially children's, provides catalysts to asking good questions. The natural curiosity of teachers can be nurtured by asking good questions about how children learn science and mathematics. Children have an insatiable desire to understand the world around them and will express their curiosity through questioning. They want to know. Both the teacher's and children's curiosity will flourish in learning environments rich with active learning experiences. Haury (1993) states,

> In its essence, then, inquiry-oriented teaching engages students in investigations to satisfy curiosities, with curiosities being satisfied when individuals have constructed mental frameworks that adequately explain their experiences. One implication is that inquiry-oriented teaching begins or at least

involves stimulating curiosity or provoking wonder. There is no authentic investigation or meaningful learning if there is no inquiring mind seeking an answer, solution, explanation, or decision. (p. 2)

Good questions are not artificial when they originate from a sense of wonder and first-hand experiences. Questions that seek right answers and originate from curriculum materials are insensitive to the needs and interests of children. Such questions can stifle curiosity.

Engaging them in activities that challenge their knowledge can stimulate children's curiosity. Children may not realize that a lemon or a potato can produce enough electricity to light a miniature lamp. Imagine the disbelief and curiosity about an experiment that uses fruits and vegetables to produce electricity, or one that questions heating water in a paper cup over an open flame. Activities such as these will raise many questions that children can answer through further exploration. Children's questions lead to curriculum development.

Stimulating curiosity begins with learning about children's needs and interests. Besides collecting a database of children's questions, teachers need to find out what really interests them by listening and asking questions that probe their curiosities. Listen to what they have to tell you about themselves, their hobbies, pets, summer vacation plans, and games.

Besides giving you information about their needs and interests, questions also tell you what children know. For example, after completing activities on multiplication, 50 percent of the children are still asking factual questions and the other 50 percent are asking process or conceptual questions. The 50 percent asking factual questions may need additional multiplication activities while the other children can explore multiplication problem-solving activities.

The emphasis in this chapter has been on questions initiated during verbal interactions with children. Informal questions, emanating from curiosity, provide seeds for organized investigations. Writing down the question is the first step, followed by creating methods for collecting, organizing, and analyzing data. Mathematical or science-based problems, developed from questions and answered through child-constructed investigations, are more exciting than passively following the steps of exercises. Observing is another important learning process, which deserves an in-depth discussion. This take places in Chapter 5.

> **Go back to the reflective questions at the beginning of the chapter and the answers you recorded in your journal.**
>
> **Add to or modify your answers based on what you learned from this chapter.**

Bibliography

Bloom, B. (1956). *Taxonomy of educational objectives*. New York: Longman, Green.

Blosser, P. (1991). *Asking the right questions*. Arlington, VA: National Science Teachers Association.

Budd-Rowe, M. (1996). Science, silence, and sanctions. *Science and Children, 34*(1), 35–37.

Driver, R., Guesne, E., and Tiberghien, A. (1985). *Children's ideas and the learning of science.* Philadelphia: Open University Press.

Duckworth, E. (1987). *The having of wonderful ideas and other essays on teaching and learning.* New York: Teachers College Press.

Elstgeest, J. (1985). The right question at the right time. In W. Harlen (Ed.), *Primary science: Taking the plunge* (pp. 9–20). Oxford, England: Heinemann Education.

Elwin, L. (1977). *The place of commonsense in educational thought.* London: George Allen and Unwin.

Gilbert, S. (1992). Systematic questioning. *The Science Teacher, 59*(9), 41–46.

Haury, D. (1993). *Teaching science through inquiry.* Columbus, OH: ERIC Clearinghouse for Science, Mathematics, and Environmental Education. (ERIC Document Reproduction Service No. ED 359 048)

National Council of Teachers of Mathematics. (1991). *Professional standards for teaching mathematics.* Reston, VA: Author.

National Research Council. (1996). *National science education standards.* Washington, DC: National Academy of Sciences.

National Research Council of Teachers of Mathematics. (1989). *Curriculum and evaluation standards for school mathematics.* Reston, VA: Author.

Pearce, J. C. (1971). *The crack in the cosmic egg: Challenging constructs of mind and reality.* New York: Washington Square Press.

Piaget, J. (1974). *The language and thought of the child.* New York: New American Library.

Yager, R., and Yager, S. (1984). Changes in perceptions in science for third, seventh, and eleventh grade students. *Journal of Research in Science Teaching, 22*(4), 347–358.

CHAPTER 5 | # Observations

Since all knowledge comes from sensory impressions and since there's no sensory impression of substance itself, it follows logically that there is no knowledge of substance. It's just something we imagine. It's entirely within our own minds. The idea that there's something out there giving off the properties we perceive is just another of those common-sense notions similar to the common-sense notion children have that the earth is flat and parallel lines never meet.

R. Pirsig, *Zen and the Art of Motorcycle Maintenance*

JOURNEY PREPARATION

Reflective Questions

- What does it mean to observe?

- How does observing relate to learning mathematics and science? To teaching mathematics and science?

- What influences what is observed?

- Why is observation the single most important process used by mathematicians and scientists?

- What do the mathematics and science standards say about the role of observation in teaching and learning?

- What is meant by a scientific or mathematical fact?

- What is a scientific or mathematical concept?

- How would you define mathematics?

- How would you define science?

The Power of Observations

Of all of the inquiry processes, observation may be the most important to scientists and mathematicians. Without observation, very few questions would be asked. Observation is the core, foundation, principle, and rationale for the existence of science and mathematics. An entire chapter is devoted to this process because it is so fundamental to the other processes. Observation is driven by curiosity and the need to find patterns and answers to questions. Inquiry depends upon observations to provide data for processes such as predicting, hypothesizing, and inferring. Unexplained events and occurrences are constructed through inquiry processes. The unexplained becomes reality by creating conclusions, theories, principles, and laws. Without special attention to observations there would be little advancement in science and mathematics.

Defining Observation

To many, observing is like the song "For Your Eyes Only." But observing is much more than the use of eyes to see. It involves the use of all senses: seeing, tasting, hearing, touching, and smelling. Campbell (1953) says:

> How do we come to have any knowledge at all of the external world of nature? The answer is obvious. We learn about the external world through our senses, the senses of sight, hearing, and touch, and, to a lesser degree, those of taste and smell. Everything we know about the external world comes to us from this source; if we could neither see, hear, nor feel, we should know nothing of what was going on around us, we should not even know that there was anything going on around us; we probably should not even form the idea that there is such a thing as the external world. (p.16)

However, it is true that the sense of sight is predominantly used to learn about the external world. To really learn basic mathematical operations (addition, subtraction, multiplication, and division), children must interact with manipulatives such as buttons, seeds, and beads. Understanding these operations requires interaction and coordination between seeing and touching physical objects. Since algebra and calculus use symbols, these processes require interaction and coordination of sight and mental constructs of the basic mathematical operations. The more ideas rest solely in the mind without relying upon objects, the less likely the senses will be involved in learning.

The same ideas apply to science as well. Basic science concepts such as classification, ordering, and seriation, which are also important in mathematics, are learned through sight and touch, but in some cases require the use of other senses as well. Science ideas such as energy, black holes, and ecology are based more on mental abstraction than observable data. These ideas are made concrete through symbols, models, diagrams, and formulas.

Basic knowledge is learned through sense observations. Observing is not unique to scientists and mathematicians; every human being uses observations, consciously or unconsciously, on a daily basis to make decisions. Bronowski (1981) says:

> In using the word observation, I am conscious still of having drawn too passive a picture of the process of science. We may be tempted still to think of the world as going its mighty way and merely impressing on the scientist in passing a glimpse from time to time of its imperturbable motion. This would be a grave misunderstanding. Indeed it would perpetuate the breach between the world and the experimenter which I have been trying to close. Science is not only rational; it is also empirical. Science is experiment, that is orderly and reasoned activity. The essence of experiment and of all science is, that it is active. It does not watch the world, it tackles it. (p.104)

People other than scientists and mathematicians are less likely to understand the significance of observations for decision making. Scientists and mathematicians are actively and consciously engaged in using observations through formal methodology. They are careful about dismissing data from observations without thoughtful consideration.

Teaching and Learning Through Observation

Consciously using observation is just as important to teachers as it is to scientists and mathematicians. Observing helps to construct reality and make sense of the classroom environment. Watching and listening to children while they are engaged in mathematics and science activities provides a wealth of data about what they are learning. Instructional strategies, curriculum content, and assessment techniques can be revised or deleted according to the set of facts collected during observations of children. Gathering data from actual teaching experiences is much more effective than exclusively trusting curriculum guides to inform teachers about the best practices. Curriculum guides typically express general viewpoints of teaching, which may have little relevance to individual classroom situations.

Learning to observe is a significant inquiry process for children to consciously use while they are engaged in mathematics and science activities. Children of all ages are continuously collecting data about the world around them, but they may not be consciously aware of their actions. By using their senses, children consciously learn to construct reality by exploring objects in the real world around them, which also includes interactions with peers and adults. Teachers can help children learn to trust their own observations, which will provide them with experiences in becoming good problem solvers and independent thinkers.

The Development of Facts from Observations

Why are observations important to scientists and mathematicians? Usually they attempt to find answers to questions by looking for patterns in nature, numbers, or controlled experiments. These patterns are detected in data collected through the use of the senses, which we will call *sense data*. Patterns are interpretations made by the observer of the collected data. Mathematics is used to quantify patterns and to describe attributes in precise terms. Use Classroom Activity 5.1 to understand how observations are used in collecting facts and forming concepts.

Classroom Activity 5.1

Observation of a Burning Candle

DISCUSSION QUESTIONS

- Do you recall watching a burning candle to introduce you to using the scientific method or to becoming skilled at making observations?
- What related experiences do you remember?
- What feelings do you associate with this activity?
- What instructions were you given?
- What was expected of you as a student?
- Were you allowed to discuss your observations with your peers?

Record these remembrances for further reference. After writing them down discuss your memories with your peers.

GOALS

- To engage in the process of collecting data through making observations.
- To record observations of a burning candle and compare them with peers' observations.

- To discuss the parallels between your own data collection processes and those used by scientists and mathematicians.
- To identify the products (facts and concepts) of observations.
- To discuss the implications of this activity for teaching mathematics and science.

GRADE LEVELS

- Upper grades

MATERIALS

- 1 wax candle (1″ × 3/4″ in diameter) per group of 4 to 5 students
- Some kind of surface protector such as a jar lid or a square piece of glass to support the candle while it is burning
- Matches to light the candle
- Paper and pencil to record data

INSTRUCTIONS

1. Have group members sit around a table. Stand the candle on the surface protector and place it in the center of the group.
2. Light the candle.
3. Have group members observe the candle from where they are sitting and write down their observations without discussion or conversation. Allow 3–5 minutes for observing and recording data.
4. Afterward, share your observations with the other members of your group.

DISCUSSION QUESTIONS

- How were your observations similar or different?
- What senses did you or others in your group use to make observations?
- What are ways to make your observations as precise and exact as possible?
- Did you expect everyone to have the same set of observations? Why or why not?
- What are the implications for science investigations/activities that require children to follow step-by-step procedures and to verify expected outcomes?
- Think back to childhood science experiences. What were your feelings when you didn't get the same answer as your peers or the answer that the teacher or book expected? Share those thoughts with your group.
- What are the "facts" about a burning candle?
- What concepts or ideas have you learned about a burning candle?
- Where is the mathematics in this activity?
- How might this activity be used in elementary school classrooms?
- What do you think would be the appropriate grade level(s) for this activity? Why?
- What safety precautions would you have to take during this activity?

SCENIC VIEW 5.1

Using Demonstrations as a Teaching Strategy

Think about the use of teacher demonstrations to learn science. Remember your science classes: You watched while your teacher used equipment and materials to demonstrate scientific concepts. This is a passive learning situation. A demonstration provides only one point of view. You can only observe from a particular angle. You do not see the demonstration from the teacher's point of view. Did you notice that while observing the burning candle you or someone else in your group was leaning over or peering around the candle to see what the candle looked like from other points of view? To learn science concepts, children must be allowed to move around and look at the experiment from all sides. This idea will be explored further in Chapter 9, which discusses spatial relations, which are important to understanding many mathematical and science concepts.

Cookbook Labs

Remember following step-by-step procedures during science class? Those experiments were really confirmation investigations. In other words, students were to follow procedures to confirm results established by the scientific community. Do you remember what happened if you did not obtain the expected results? One thing that might have happened is that you tried to fudge your results by asking other students for theirs. If you were not successful in finding the correct results, you probably received a poor grade. No wonder many of us felt intimidated or stupid in science classes. These experiences contribute to the negative image of science.

Cookbook labs leave one with the impression that experiments do have right answers. However, what each person brings to an experiment influences its outcome. Past experiences, culture, ethnic background, and other social factors can affect experimental procedures and interpretation of results. That is why scientists check each other's results to assess what may be causing differences. It is impossible and unrealistic to expect that all children will do experiments exactly the same way and learn exactly the same thing. We may all be looking at the same burning candle but learn different things about its characteristics.

Parallels to Teaching and Learning

Social and political influences can affect teaching and learning practices, especially when they are different and innovative. For instance, an elementary classroom teacher observes that children learn science and mathematics better by doing hands-on activities rather than by reading textbooks. However, for whatever reasons, the data is ignored because of certain groups that oppose the use of hands-on science teaching. These groups may be composed of fellow teachers, parents, administrators, and/or community leaders. There is resistance to change in these groups because the new ideas do not fit the current educational practices and traditions. They may be resistant to change because change is difficult. Therefore the data, which has the potential of improving the way children learn mathematics and science, lies dormant.

Likewise, children will ignore important and unexpected data from "verifiable" investigations if they are reprimanded verbally or through grades for not finding the expected results or answers. It is not in their best interest to pursue those observations if their grades and self-esteem are penalized. For example, if children are expected to observe the melting wax at the base of the wick and ignore the smoke, they will do just that, even though observing the smoke and other aspects of the candle is just as valid. A child who insists that his or her experiment is more accurate than the book's may be viewed as a troublemaker who questions authority. In the long run this may be harmful to children because they have had very few opportunities to trust their own observations.

REST STOP 5.1

Safety precautions must be used when children are working with open flames and chemicals. Children must wear safety goggles. Children can wear smocks to protect their clothing and long hair must be tied behind the head. Have fire extinguishers and/or fire blankets available in case of an unexpected fire. Children should never look into a container (e.g., a test tube) of liquid that is being heated regardless if it is over a flame or on a hot plate. Remove the container from the heat before looking or look through the sides if they are transparent. Some chemicals will produce harmful vapors either by themselves or when mixed. Never directly smell fumes from chemicals or chemical reactions. Gently waft the fumes with your hand for smelling. More safety tips are given in Chapter 14.

Extension Activity: Writing Burning Candle Content
(Optional activity; graduate level)

INTRODUCTION

Science textbooks often include important facts about scientific knowledge. This activity will give you experience in writing a section for a science textbook.

GOALS

- To collaborate on writing a textbook entry
- To understand the formation of content for science textbooks
- To understand the appropriate use of science and mathematics textbooks in elementary classrooms

INSTRUCTIONS

1. Form groups of four to five. Pretend that you are a group of scientists selected to write important facts about burning candles for a section in an elementary science textbook. Create a name for the textbook company you represent.

2. Use your combined lists of observations about a burning candle and write a paragraph that explains the "facts" or content knowledge about a burning candle. Include "facts" that you think children should know.

3. Include "quantifiable data" that will illustrate the use of mathematics in science. Remember to use only those "facts" that were collected during the observations.

4. Arrive at a group consensus to determine what should be written.

5. After completing your paragraph, let someone in your group read the paragraph to the other groups.

DISCUSSION QUESTIONS

- What were the major issues that were discussed as you formulated the paragraph's content?

- Did all groups say the same thing about what it is important to know about a burning candle? Why or why not? What are the implications for the content of science textbooks?

- As you heard other groups read their paragraphs, what thoughts went through your mind about learning science and mathematics from textbooks?

- Did you have difficulty focusing on the observable facts or did you find that prior knowledge kept creeping into your discussion? Discuss the implications of your answers to these questions.

SCENIC VIEW 5.2

The Role of Textbooks in Learning Mathematics and Science

Learning science concepts from books is not only passive, but the selection of content may vary from author to author. Textbook authors and editors have to consider children's reading abilities and comprehension. Authors also have to consider what background is needed to understand a particular concept. The selection of content is controlled by the authors. One set of authors may select certain aspects of the facts or concepts while another set of authors selects a different set. Textbooks may present the same concepts but from different points of view. And on top of that, it is highly possible that many scientific and mathematical facts or concepts found in textbooks contradict the knowledge of "experts." Textbooks should be viewed as resources to supplement and enrich hands-on activities. Their contents should be examined to compare what is said about given topics. Do textbooks A, B, and C agree on selected concepts? Are there disagreements? If so, what are the reasons for the disagreements?

Reflection Activity 5.1

Think about what was expected of you as a student in a science or mathematics class. Were you expected to duplicate the results of a mathematical or scientific problem? What if you didn't get the expected results? What did you do? How did you feel?

Preservice students who were asked to express their feelings about their past experiences in mathematics and science have said:

> I was to get "the right answer." I agreed with the rest of the class or the teacher just to say I understood. The experiment lesson proved it because the teacher wanted us to think a certain way and it was hard for me at first because I couldn't get it or understand it.

> I realized that I remember facts and a few details, but I didn't make the connection of the overall concept. I feel that this is so important in teaching and learning science and mathematics.

> The activity was pretty difficult for me and it made me remember what it was like to be asked to do something by a teacher and not know how to proceed.

Facts or Sense Data

Sense data are also called facts. An apple, for example, has specific attributes such as color and shape. The apple is red and oval shaped. It has five oval points on one end. These facts or sense data are collected through observations. Facts are meaningless by themselves. In the past, emphasis was placed on mathematical and scientific facts. What image is created by the following scene (Ford and Monod, 1966)?

> "Now, what I want is, Facts. Teach these boys and girls nothing but Facts. Facts alone are wanted in life. Plant nothing else, and root out everything else. You can only form the minds of reasoning animals upon Facts: nothing else will ever be of any service to them. This is the principle on which I bring up my own children, and this is the principle on which I bring up these children. Stick to the Facts, sir!" The scene was a plain, bare, monotonous vault of a schoolroom, and the speaker's square forefinger emphasized his observations by underscoring every sentence with a line on the schoolmaster's sleeve. . . . The speaker's obstinate carriage, square coat, square legs, square shoulders, nay, his very neckcloth, trained to take him by the throat with an unaccommodating grasp, like a stubborn fact, as it was, all helped the emphasis. "In this life, we want nothing but Facts, sir; nothing but Facts!" The speaker, and the schoolmaster, and the third grown person present, all backed a little, and swept with their eyes the inclined plane of little vessels then and there arranged in order, ready to have imperial gallons of facts poured into them until they were full to the brim. (p. 1)

Discussion Questions

- Can you relate this passage to your own experiences of learning mathematics and science?
- In a group discussion, share the images that the passage creates in your mind about learning mathematics and science.

For three centuries our image of science has stemmed from Newtonian physics. According to the Newtonian viewpoint, the universe is divided into separate parts, which exert forces on each other in a linear fashion (Wheetley, 1994). Thus, the belief, that Dickens (1866) so aptly describes above, "learning is just filling empty vessels" represents the influence the Newtonian viewpoint had upon teaching and learning practices in the last three centuries. This view of education reflected the industrial age mentality of the conveyor belt producing products. Children were treated the same way.

The Development of Concepts from Observational Facts

A new view of education is taking shape which reflects science and mathematics as understanding relationships between systems and their parts. The emphasis is on process rather than products and, through processes, relationships among facts (products) become apparent and meaningful. Returning to the apple example, observing (process) a variety of apples gives understanding about different colors (facts) of apples. The same is true in mathematics. The number 3, by itself, has little significance to a child who is learning it for the first time. It will make sense when 3 is connected to objects. Three apples or three dogs gives meaning to the concept of 3. When children explore the concepts of even and odd numbers by looking at a large pool of numbers and investigating which ones can be evenly divided into two groups, the formation patterns emerge in their minds.

The new view of science and mathematics is based on understanding patterns and relationships to form organized ideas, which are called concepts. The following is a definition of science (Medawar, 1984) that incorporates this idea. What images are created in your mind about science?

> . . . one construes "science" merely as knowledge. It is thought of rather as knowledge hard won, in which we have much more confidence than we have in opinion, hearsay and belief. The word "science" itself is used as a general name for, on the one hand, the procedures of science—adventures of thought and strategems of inquiry that go into the advancement of learning—and on the other hand, the substantive body of knowledge that is the outcome of this complex endeavor, though this latter is no mere pile of information: Science is "organized" knowledge, everyone agrees, and this organization goes much deeper than the pedagogic subdivision into the conventional "-ologies," each pigeonholed into lesser topics. (p. 3)

Medawar's "knowledge hard won" is knowledge created through mental wrestling with facts obtained through observations, abstracting and organizing ideas in relationships. Thus, as Medawar says above, concepts are organized ideas about sets of facts. The more facts gathered through observations, the more broad-based concepts become. Here is what Gleick (1987) says about mathematics: "He was studying numbers, yes, but numbers are to a mathematician what bags of coins are to an investment banker: nominally the stuff of his profession, but actually too gritty and particular to waste time on. Ideas are the real currency" (p. 178).

Reflection Activity 5.2

- Think about examples of organized ideas that you have learned in the past that represent "knowledge hard won."

- Write down examples of concepts and explain the learning situation and your feelings at the time.

- Discuss your feelings with one another about those "hard-won knowledge" experiences you have had. Are your feelings similar or different? Write down your thoughts about the discussion.

- Write down examples of concepts and explain the learning situation and your feelings at the time. Share your thoughts with a classmate.

- Discuss your feelings and experiences. Were they similar or different? Write down your thoughts about your discussions.

Returning to the apple example, one may gather data about the variety of apples grown in the United States, and then decide to study apple varieties found in other parts of the world. The concept of apple takes on additional meaning when it is studied through literature and other disciplines. For instance, there are biblical stories about apples, phrases such as "apple of my eye," a drink called applejack, and a plant called mayapple. Thus, the fundamental concept of apple is based on mental constructs created from facts, which in turn changes those mental constructs as new knowledge is added and prior knowledge is revised.

The basic, fundamental idea stays the same, but webs (relationships) of ideas and facts continue to grow as more data are gathered. Hirst (1974) says that knowledge has structure and that certain concepts are central to disciplines with particular networks of possible relationships. The more one understands a concept, the more ideas become related across disciplines. On the other hand, using different sets of facts will give each individual a different understanding of the concepts. Thus, a group of scientists can observe the same phenomenon but collect different sets of facts and reach different conclusions. The observer and the observed are integrated. What one observes depends on experiential background and knowledge, which in turn shapes points of view about the observed. No two observers are likely to have the exact same results. In other words, patterns, conclusions, laws, and theories of nature are human interpretations from observations. Scientific truths are based on how scientists interpret their data. The "truths" are influenced by past experiences and knowledge as well as the cultural, religious, and even political background of each individual. Pearce (1971) says:

> We used to believe that our perceptions, our seeing, hearing, feeling and so on, were reactions to active impingements on them by the "world out there." We thought our perceptions then sent these outside messages to the brain where we put together a reasonable facsimile of what was out there. We know now that our concepts, our notions or basic assumptions, actively direct our percepts. We see, feel, and hear according to what Bruner calls a "selective program of the mind." Our mind directs our sensory apparatus every bit as much as our sensory apparatus informs the mind. (p. 2)

Sharing, questioning, and replicating someone else's data and conclusions gives validity to agreed-upon ideas. Data that withstand this scrutiny become acceptable in scientific circles. This makes the data true. Thus theories, laws, and principles are accepted at the time, but change if new data warrant the change. Science and mathematics are dynamic.

Reflection Activity 5.3

After completing Classroom Activity 5.1, write a reaction statement in your journal to the quote above by Pearce.

Classroom Activity 5.2

Cornstarch Mixtures

INTRODUCTION

Unusual characteristics are created when cornstarch is combined with water in certain proportions. You will have a chance to explore the characteristics of this unusual mixture by using all your senses. Elementary school teachers know this activity by the names of gloob, goo, and oobleck. Some teachers read Dr. Seuss' *Ooblecks* story to accompany this activity. Possibly you are familiar with it. Return to childhood memories about science and remember whether you worked with this mixture.

REFLECTION QUESTIONS

What was required of you as a learner during this activity? What feelings did you have while doing the activity?

GOALS

- To identify the physical characteristics of cornstarch using more than one sense.

- To identify characteristics of physical changes.

- To engage in the following characteristics of inquiry: playfulness, direct observations, genesis of questions, curiosity, creating hypotheses and predictions, developing inquiry investigations, and quantifying observations and data using measurement

GRADE LEVELS

- Primary to upper

MATERIALS

- Dry cornstarch
- Water
- Cookie sheets or trays for mixing starch and water
- Cups to hold water
- Newspaper to cover surface
- Paper towels

INSTRUCTIONS

1. Spend a few minutes using your senses to observe the characteristics of dry cornstarch.

2. Put some dry cornstarch on a cookie sheet. Add water slowly and mix with your fingers. Create the right combination of cornstarch and water so that the mixture is not a liquid (more water than cornstarch) or a solid (more cornstarch than water). You may have to add more water or more cornstarch to make the right consistency. Continue to use your hands to explore the nature of the mixture.

DISCUSSION QUESTIONS

- What happens when you pick up the mixture of cornstarch and water?
- What does the mixture feel like?
- Can you keep the mixture in a ball in your hand?
- What happens when you let the ball lie in the palm of your hand?
- What happens when you pound on the mixture with your fist when it is lying on the cookie sheet?
- Write down questions that occur to you as you work with the mixture.

FURTHER INSTRUCTIONS

1. Discuss with colleagues questions about the mixture; e.g., "Does heat from hands cause the mixture to go from a solid to a liquid?"

2. With a partner, create and conduct an experiment to explore one of the questions generated during discussion.

3. Develop ways to make the outcome of your experiments as precise as possible. That is, quantify your data using mathematics.

4. Predict what will happen before you begin your investigation. For example, using the question above about heat, a prediction might be the following: The mixture will remain a liquid when it is manipulated with room-temperature objects.

5. Your instructor will provide additional materials and resources for your investigations. You can use rubbing alcohol, glycerin, or vegetable oil instead of water. Mix these, one at a time, with dry cornstarch. Substitute the following starches for cornstarch: rice, potato, tapioca, taro, and wheat. Mix them, one at a time, with either water or one of the other liquids to see what happens.

ADDITIONAL DISCUSSION QUESTIONS

■ Which of the questions developed during the discussion can be answered through investigations?

■ Which questions will have to be answered by consulting other sources such as books, bakeries, and cornstarch manufacturing companies?

■ Discuss this method of investigation as compared to science and mathematics investigations that are verification-type activities (predetermined outcomes or cookbook method).

■ Did you feel uncomfortable not having more directions or expectations as to what you were to learn from the activity?

■ Think back to your cookbook method experiences and reread the quotation from Medawar (1984).

■ Discuss the implications and purpose of "play" in learning science and mathematics. A dictionary defines play as "the spontaneous activity of children." Were you "playful" during this activity? Explain.

■ What is the relationship of play to learning?

■ As a teacher, what behavioral indicators will tell you the difference between "playful learning" and "nonplayful learning"?

■ What is the relationship of mathematics to science?

■ Compare the use of the senses in this activity and the burning candle activity.

■ What science and mathematics processes did you use as you worked with the cornstarch mixture?

■ What "facts" and "concepts" did you learn about starch?

REST STOP 5.2

Scientists are known for "playing" when working with new ideas or phenomena. Mathematicians can also be playful by manipulating number patterns and formulas as they look for new patterns. They are trying to learn through observation as much as possible about the characteristics of the phenomenon. Once their curiosity is somewhat satisfied, they may begin exploring the phenomenon by setting up controlled environments and being precise in collecting data. Thus, inquiry can range from loosely organized data collection to highly organized data collection. The cornstarch activity can be an ideal "play" situation for young children; older children can learn how to develop controlled experiments and have fun at the same time. However, remember that when children's curiosity is piqued by a new situation, no matter what their age, you can expect lots of play before getting down to business!

SCENIC VIEW 5.3

Examples of Other Direct Observation Activities

- Observe an ice cube as it melts.

- Identify your own apple when it is placed in a bowl of other apples. Other fruit such as lemons, limes, and oranges can be used instead of apples.

- Give everyone a green leaf from the same kind of tree. Identify your leaf after it has been placed in a pile with everyone else's leaves.

These activities as well as the starch activity can be adapted to all grade levels. Although primary children may focus on a few attributes, older children can work with a variety of attributes. For example, primary children may focus only on the shape of the leaf while upper-grade children can focus on its shape, edges, and veins. Measurements that are either nonstandard or standard can be used to make precise observations.

Indirect Observations

So far, the discussion about observation has been about collecting data directly through all available senses. However, many science disciplines such as biology, chemistry, and physics rely upon indirect observation. Scientists cannot directly observe the intricate inside of a living human being, the motion and structure of molecules or galaxies, or the different layers of the earth. Microscopes, telescopes, radar, and sonar are examples of technologies that help increase the ability to observe. Knowledge created through indirect observation is referred to as *inferences*. In other words, conclusions are deduced from indirect data. Knowledge bases in biology, chemistry, and physics began with direct observation, but the desire to know more has taken the knowledge to levels that must rely on technology for collecting data. Technology has become highly sophisticated for making observations.

Classroom activities 3–7 not only require collecting data through the senses but also require the understanding of spatial relations. Spatial relations are important to understanding both mathematical and science concepts. This will be further discussed in Chapter 9. This set of activities requires developing good explanations based on sound evidence to create models. NCTM Standard 12 identifies the appropriate grade levels for the following activities.

Classroom Activity 5.3

Inference Boxes

INTRODUCTION

The following activity involves collecting data or "facts" through limited use of the senses. Inferences or conclusions are created by limited direct observations. Explanations of inferences are not only verbal or written, but are often created by designing two- or three-dimensional illustrations or models. Investigating the contents of inference boxes is another activity you may have experienced in grade school or high school. This activity will allow you to experience the following inquiry ideas: inferences, scientific model, replication, points of view, and measurement.

TOUR GUIDE

National Council of Teachers of Mathematics (1989)
Standard 12: Geometry

In grades 5–8, the mathematics curriculum should include the study of the geometry of one, two, and three dimensions in a variety of situations so that students can identify, describe, compare, and classify geometric figures; visualize and represent geometric figures with special attention to developing spatial sense; develop an appreciation of geometry as a means of describing the physical world. (p. 112)

National Research Council (1996)

Scientists develop explanations using observations (evidence) and what they already know about the world (scientific knowledge). Good explanations are based on evidence from investigations. (p. 123)

GOALS

- To collect data about objects that cannot be seen directly

- To create a model that represents the inside of the box based on data collected outside the box

- To participate in the process of reaching agreements or conclusions to create principles, theories, and laws

- To devise an accurate model of a phenomenon that cannot be observed directly

GRADE LEVELS

- Middle to upper

MATERIALS

- Sealed boxes that contain objects, which will be supplied by your instructor. (Instructor: See Appendix A for directions for making the boxes.)

INSTRUCTIONS

1. Without opening the box, work by yourself to identify the object(s) within the box.

2. Be as precise as possible in identifying the number of objects, their actual dimensions and shape, and what they are made of, such as metal, plastic, wood, or paper.

3. Use the outline of the box in Appendix A to draw the objects in proportion to their actual size. Indicate whether or not the object(s) in the box move around or remain stationary.

4. Write down your data and the rationale that supports your illustrations.

5. After completing your model, return the boxes to the instructor without opening them.

DISCUSSION QUESTIONS

- Does everyone list the same box contents? Why or why not?

- What kind of evidence did everyone use to determine the content of the boxes?

- What kind of evidence provides the most valid and reliable data?

- How accurate are the illustrations or models in terms of actual size, shape, and material? How do you know?

- Which model seems to be the most accurate in representing what is in the box?

- Without opening the box, what are some techniques to increase the accuracy of your observations?

- Without opening the box or using technologies, what is the best way to know what is inside the box?

- How are spatial relations involved in this activity?

This is called *replication.* By trying to duplicate the phenomenon, you gain a good idea of what it is. This is true for such phenomena as molecular motion, the motion of planet and stars, or sap running through the trunks and stems of trees.

- What science and mathematical processes did you use to develop your model?

- How did you feel about returning your box to the instructor without opening it?

- What are the implications for learning mathematics and science?

- What happens to your curiosity if the boxes are opened?

- Discuss how you might use this activity in your future classroom.

- How could the activity be adapted for different grade levels?

REST STOP 5.3

The cornstarch activity is also a "black box" activity because we cannot directly observe the behavior of the individual starch particles without the aid of technology such as a high-powered microscope. Thus, you and the children may question why cornstarch powder behaves the way it does when mixed in a certain composition with water? How can you find answers without being given direct answers from a teacher? You might find books or search the Web. Or you might write to companies that produce cornstarch and ask them what they know. In this way you learn where to find answers rather than relying solely on the teacher. This also sustains your curiosity. Once that box is opened, curiosity dissipates!

Classroom Activity 5.4   ***Fossilized Prints***

INTRODUCTION

Archaeologists and paleontologists work with black box situations. They may have a piece of bone, a skull, or just a tooth of an animal from which they try to reconstruct the physical characteristics of the animal. They also try to reconstruct from the surrounding layers of rock and soil climatic conditions, vegetative characteristics, and the age of fossils. Sometimes, scientists have even less than an actual part of a prehistoric living being. They may have just the imprints of plants or animal parts. In this activity you will receive a paper copy of a set of prints that were found embedded in rock.

In many cases scientists will never have a complete set of facts. They will continually search for new facts, which in turn creates a new set of questions that can only be answered through observation and data collection.

GOALS

■ To create a specific set of facts that can be used to develop a theory

■ To create a theory (acceptable explanation, based on observable facts) about what created the tracks or imprints

GRADE LEVELS

■ Middle to upper

MATERIALS

■ Picture of actual fossilized imprints. (See Appendix B.)

INSTRUCTIONS

1. In a group of four to five students, develop a theory that explains how the impressions were made.

2. After reaching a consensus, designate a group spokesperson to explain your group's theory to the entire class.

3. After all groups have presented their theories, discuss as a class which group has the "best theory." Be prepared to defend your group's theory.

4. Your instructor will provide new information about the fossilized prints. Discuss the new information and its impact on your group's theory.

DISCUSSION QUESTIONS

■ Does the additional information support your theory? Explain.

■ What new insights do you have about the inquiry process?

■ What does this experience teach you about the image of scientific and mathematical facts as never unchanging or "set in stone"?

■ How does the use of mathematics make the data more valid and reliable?

■ What processes, content, and concepts did you learn and use during this activity?

ACTIVITY EXTENSIONS

■ Take a walk and try to find evidence of fossils in the concrete of sidewalks, the stones and bricks of buildings, and the rocks found around or near the playground. Children can look for "manmade" fossils.

■ Use pieces of Playdough™ or clay and push objects into them to make imprints. Have other students determine what caused the imprints.

■ Mix some plaster of paris in water and place it in glass jar lids. Make imprints by placing different objects in the plaster of paris mixture.

■ Mix plaster of paris and sand together and place it in paper cups. Put objects into the mixture. When the mixture is hard, chip away the plaster to find the objects and see if imprints were made.

Classroom Activity 5.5

Digestive System Model

INTRODUCTION

The human body is another black box. When doctors diagnose certain symptoms in the body, they make inferences about the probable causes. They may poke around with their fingers or use technological instruments such as stethoscopes and blood pressure gauges. Their observations are limited so they make logical guesses based on a set of limited facts.

GOALS

- To create a diagrammatic model of the digestive system using a limited set of observable data
- To create a representation in proportion to the body of the person who acted as a model

GRADE LEVELS

- Primary to upper grades

MATERIALS

- Butcher paper
- Colored markers
- Measuring devices: meter sticks, metric rulers, metric tape measures, string

INSTRUCTIONS

1. Form groups of four to five. In each group, one student volunteers to have his or her body outlined on butcher paper.
2. Give each group a length of butcher paper comparable to the height of the volunteer.
3. Place the butcher paper on the floor or table, or attach it to a wall.
4. Outline the person's body on the butcher paper.
5. Use colored markers to draw the organs of the digestive system without using books or other types of resources. Be as precise as possible about location and size of the organs in relation to the body.
6. After each group has completed the model, hang the sheets of paper on a wall for everyone to see.

DISCUSSION QUESTIONS

- Did every group's digestive system look the same? Why or why not?
- What does this say about the "content" of science?
- Recall how you learned about the digestive system in high school or college. What is the difference between this activity and how you learned it in the past?
- Which way is more meaningful? Why?
- What does this activity say about the use of science textbooks to learn concepts?
- During this activity, what were some inquiry processes you used to complete the placement of the digestive system organs?
- What did you notice about the group processes and interactions?

- How might you modify this activity for different grade levels?
- How could this activity be used to assess what children know about the digestive system?

Classroom Activity 5.6   ***Cupcake Geology***

INTRODUCTION

The majority of earth science concepts are developed from limited observations or inferences. Knowledge about rocks, minerals, volcanoes, earthquakes, water cycles, global weather patterns, and other earth science concepts are abstracted from data that requires the use of technology to increase their accuracy. This activity will help you understand how scientists collect data about layers of the earth's crust.

GOAL

- To draw a cross section of a cupcake to illustrate its inner composition

GRADE LEVELS

- Middle to upper

MATERIALS

- One cupcake per person. (Directions for making the cupcakes are in Appendix C.)
- One clear plastic straw per person
- Colored crayons, pencils, or pens

INSTRUCTIONS

1. Use the straw to pull out core samples of the cupcake by carefully pushing one end of the straw down into the cupcake. You may want to go all the way to the bottom of the cupcake for your sample.
2. Carefully squeeze the sample out of the straw and place it on paper. Do this especially if your straw is not transparent. Otherwise you may want to leave the sample in the straw and cut the straw.
3. Determine how many samples you will have to collect to have enough data to draw a complete cross section of the cupcake. However, keep in mind that too many samples will destroy the internal and external environment!
4. Take "core" samples at various parts of the cupcake.
5. Draw an outline of a cupcake cross section.
6. Using colored markers and drawing to scale, illustrate on your drawn cupcake cross section how you think the cupcake looks inside.
7. After completing your cross sectional diagram, cut your cupcake in half to verify what it actually looks like inside.

DISCUSSION QUESTIONS

- Compare your cupcake cross section to that of others. Is it the same or not? Why?
- What caused the layers to form as they did?
- What do you think about using this activity in a classroom?

- For which grade level(s) is this activity appropriate? Why?

- Would you make any modifications? If so, what?

- What is the minimum number of "core samples" needed to complete a cross section of the cupcake?

- Recall learning about the earth's layers. What do you remember? Diagrams are two-dimensional models. How does learning about the earth's layers this way compare to studying diagrams?

- What science and mathematics processes, content, and concepts are learned from this activity?

REST STOP 5.4

It is not important for children to make the connections between determining the cross sections of a cupcake to actual layers of the earth. What is important is the process of collecting data and creating a two-dimensional model that requires looking at the cupcake from different perspectives. Let children decide whether they want to learn more about how scientists actually determine how the earth looks inside and create models from their data.

Long-Term Observation Activities

The majority of elementary school science activities are constrained by time limits: the daily time schedules for science and mathematics classes rather than the time needed to gather data through direct or indirect observations. To understand something in depth requires collecting data over long periods of time. Scientists pursue investigations over years because it may take that long for patterns to emerge. Classroom Activity 5.7 will give you experience in collecting data for approximately two months.

Classroom Activity 5.7

Direct Moon Phase Observations and Study

INTRODUCTION

The study of moon phases is frequently found in third- and fifth-grade textbooks and junior and senior high school earth science textbooks. In these books, knowledge about moon phases is presented through pictures, diagrams, and illustrations. Activities usually consist of observing phases by shining light on a three-dimensional model. In the SCIS 3 unit, "Relative Position and Motion" (Thier and Knott, 1993), children study moon phases by using a commercially prepared three-dimensional model and system. This unit is designed for the fourth-grade level. Other moon phase activities may use objects such as a basketball to represent the earth, a baseball to represent the moon, and a light source for the sun. Understanding moon phases requires collecting data through limited use of the senses and creating models.

GOALS

- To experience collecting data over a long period of time (one to two months)

- To create an explanation for moon phases based on data from direct observations rather than textbooks or other sources

■ To identify and answer questions that arise from studying moon phases

■ To understand angles and sky directions

GRADE LEVELS

■ Primary through upper grades (noticing differences in phases may be sufficient for primary grades)

MATERIALS

■ Charts, index cards, or pocket calendars for recording changes in moon phases, angle, time, and sky directions

INSTRUCTIONS

1. Before beginning your observations, write on a sheet of paper an explanation for moon phase creation. Hand this paper to your instructor. It will be given back to you to compare what you learned at the end of the moon phase observation experience.

2. Form groups of four to five members. Choose different days and times for collecting data. You will share the data together.

3. Devise a way to record your data. For example, on an index card outline the horizon and indicate the direction you are looking. Draw the moon's shape and its angle in the sky. Place several observations on one card or use a different card for each observation. Remember to record dates and times.

4. Record the following during your moon phase study: date, time of day, moon phase, angle of moon at time of observation, and direction in sky. You may be recording data for as long as two months to insure enough data is collected to see patterns in the moon phases.

5. Try to observe the moon at the same spot at the same time. You may find you have to change location or time during this long period of observation.

6. Record questions that come to your mind. You will be given opportunities in class to discuss your findings and your questions. Distinguish between those questions that can be answered through direct observations and those that cannot.

Classroom Activity 5.8

Classroom Moon Phase Simulation

INTRODUCTION

After you have collected data for a month or two, your instructor will lead you through an activity that illustrates moon phase changes.

GOALS

■ To understand moon phases using the earth as a point of reference

■ To observe the positions of the earth, moon, and sun during each phase

■ To compare learning moon phases by direct observations and by using a model

GRADE LEVELS

■ Upper grades

MATERIALS

■ Meter stick or yardstick

- Styrofoam ball (25–30 cm/10–12 inches in circumference)
- Popsicle stick
- Masking tape
- Light bulb (150 to 250 watts) and bulb socket without a shade

INSTRUCTIONS

1. Push one end of the Popsicle stick into the Styrofoam ball. The Styrofoam ball represents the moon.

2. Tape the other end of the Popsicle stick to one end of the meter stick so that the Popsicle stick is perpendicular to the meter stick.

3. After turning off the overhead lights and making the room as dark as possible, the instructor will turn on the light bulb and hold it above his or her head. The light bulb represents the sun.

4. Stand up and hold the end of the meter stick with the Styrofoam ball up in the air with the other end poised on the tip of your nose. The angle of the meter stick should be about 45°. You represent the earth. (See Figure 5.1.) The 45° angle simulates a person's line of sight when looking at the moon.

5. Make sure you can turn around without bumping into someone else's meter stick. Keep your eyes focused on the Styrofoam ball. Slowly rotate and watch what happens.

6. Notice where the sun is in relation to your position and in relation to the moon for each phase of the moon.

7. Think about the data you collected from your actual observations of the moon and your questions.

8. Write down an explanation of moon phases using knowledge gained from direct observations and this activity.

9. Compare the explanation you wrote at the beginning of Classroom Activity 5.7 with your new explanation.

DISCUSSION QUESTIONS

- What did you learn from the actual moon phase observation?
- What did the simulation activity confirm about your actual moon phase observations?
- Why is it difficult to understand moon phase changes from pictures or illustrations?
- What point of view do pictures present? What is your point of view during the simulation activity?
- What specific concepts should children understand before they can understand changes in moon phases?
- In general, at what age should children learn about moon phase formation?
- Should children be given opportunities to learn about moon phases at different grade levels? Explain.
- What does this say about revisiting the same concepts at different grade levels?
- If a child says they already studied this in an earlier grade, how would you respond?
- What are the implications of learning about moon phases formation from pictures, diagrams, and illustrations?

FIGURE 5.1

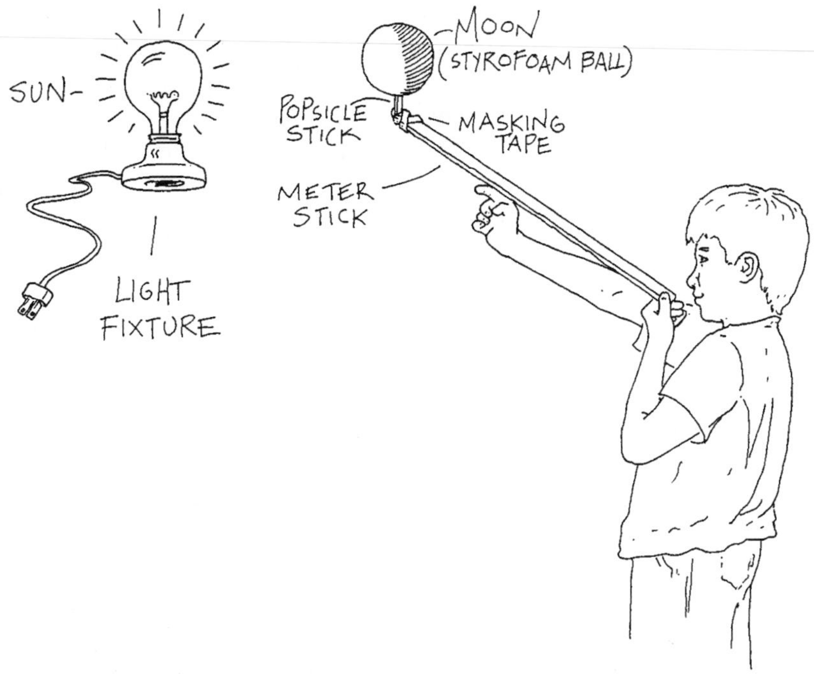

The following are examples of other long-term observation activities.

1. Plant seeds and keep track of the growth of plants.
2. Observe changes in butterfly chrysalises from caterpillars to adult butterflies.
3. Raise mealworms to watch the changes in beetles' life cycle.
4. Observe changes in terraria and aquaria with different ecosystems.
5. Observe changes in weather conditions.
6. Observe changes in the color of leaves in the autumn.
7. Start a mold culture and observe changes over a given length of time.

These long-term observation activities can be done at various grade levels. Primary children, however, may lose interest faster than older children and may not be able to make mental connections from one change to the next.

What mathematical operations and computations could be made with these activities? Discuss with your peers and instructor the appropriate use of mathematics with these activities.

Summary

All science and mathematics activities require children to be engaged through observations. Their prior knowledge, experience, and personal backgrounds will influence what they observe and learn (see Chapter 3). Children, especially primary children, learn best by using all their senses. However, many areas of scientific knowledge were developed through limited use of the senses. Inferences about these areas of scientific knowledge are represented by two- and three-dimensional models. Traditional science teaching often requires children to memorize models without experiencing how those models were developed. On the other hand, substituting processes for memorization does not guarantee that children will achieve the same level of understanding as scientists. The teacher must select activities, with the realization that what is learned from a given activity may be limited.

Observations are just as important to effective teaching as they are to accurate scientific and mathematical investigations. Teachers who collect data about how children learn will increase their knowledge about good teaching practices. Direct observations can be made about children's behavior and their reactions to activities and questions. It has been customary to base teaching practices on inferences and opinions with little reference to observable data. But it is difficult to know what children are thinking. Their minds are like black boxes and we can only surmise by collecting indirect data. Once knowledge bases are created, inferences from indirect observations become more accurate. For example, collecting observable data of children's behavior during hands-on science and mathematics activities can provide a knowledge base for making inferences about what children are learning from the activities. This is all part of assessment, which is continuous. This will be explained further in Chapter 13. Chapter 6 presents the other learning processes that are important to constructing mathematical and scientific knowledge.

> **Go back to the reflective questions at the beginning of the chapter and the answers you recorded in your journal.**
>
> **Add to or modify your answers based on what you learned from this chapter.**

APPENDIX A   *Mystery Box Template*

Select cardboard boxes with lids that have dimensions in the following range: 7 to 8 inches by 5 to 6 inches by ½ inch.

Directions for Making Mystery Boxes

The template in Figure 5.2 is based on using cardboard boxes with lids and Pick Up Stix™. Wooden dowels of the same length and diameter could be used instead of Pick Up Stix™. Close and seal the boxes. Insert one Pick Up Stix™ through the length of the box and two through the width of the box. Hang objects on the Pick Up Stix™ at various locations. The Pick Up Stix™ restrict the motion of the objects. Place one end of a rubber band around one of the protruding ends of a stick and stretch it underneath the box to the other end of the stick. Do this for all three sticks. If the rubber bands are tight enough, they will hold the sticks in place so that they do not slip out of the holes in the box.

Shoe boxes, gift boxes, and other boxes can be used to make the mystery boxes. If all the boxes are the same size and are the same inside, participants can be asked if they think the boxes are all the same inside based on the data collected by individual members of the class.

FIGURE 5.2

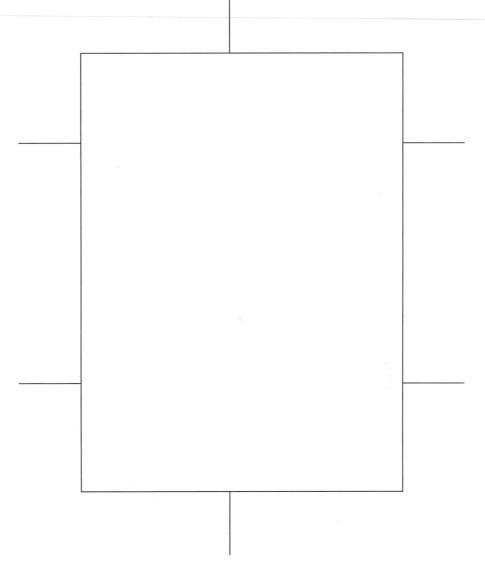

Instead of using Pick Up Stix™, objects can be placed in a box and allowed to roll around. Baffles can be added to direct the motion of the objects. Make baffles by cutting pieces of tagboard or index folders and glue them to the bottom of the box. Figure 5.3 shows how baffles can be placed in the boxes.

FIGURE 5.3

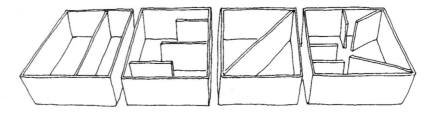

APPENDIX B   *Fossilized Prints*

FIGURE 5.4

Abruscato, J., and Hassard, J. (1976). *Loving and beyond.* Santa Monica, CA: Goodyear. Copyright © 1976 J. Abruscato and J. Hassard. Used by permission.

APPENDIX C   *Cupcake Geology*

You will need one package of white cake mix. Following the directions on the box, make the white cake batter. Divide the batter equally into four to five bowls. Add a different food coloring to each bowl of batter. These colors represent the different layers. Be creative and make colors such as brown to represent soil. One layer can be plain white.

Use aluminum foil cupcake holders to prevent looking at the layers from the side. Place approximately one teaspoon of each color of batter in each cupcake holder. Try to arrange the layers the same way in all the cupcake holders.

As the cupcakes bake, colored layers are formed (see Figure 5.5), but heat will affect the depth of each layer.

Bake at the temperature suggested on the box. Remove the cupcakes and let cool. When cool, cover each cupcake with frosting so that the layers are concealed.

FIGURE 5.5

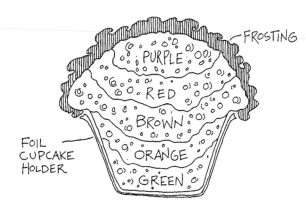

Bibliography

Bronowski, J. (1981). *The common sense of science.* Cambridge, MA: Harvard University Press.

Campbell, N. (1953). *What is science?* New York: Dover Publications.

Ford, G., and Monod, S. (1966). *Charles Dickens, Hard Times: An authoritative text: Background, source, and contemporary reaction and criticism.* New York: W. W. Norton.

Gleick, J. (1987). *Chaos: Making a new science.* New York: Penguin.

Hirst, P. (1974). *Knowledge and the curriculum: A collection of philosophical papers.* Boston, MA: Routledge and K. Paul.

Medawar, P. (1984). *The limits of science.* New York: Harper and Row.

National Council of Teachers of Mathematics. (1989). *Curriculum and evaluation standards for school mathematics.* Alexandria, VA: Author.

National Research Council. (1996). *National science education standards.* Washington, DC: National Academy Press.

Pearce, J. (1971). *The crack in the cosmic egg: Challenging constructs of mind and reality.* New York: Washington Square Press.

Pirsig, R. (1974). *Zen and the art of motorcycle maintenance.* New York: Bantam Books.

Thier, H., and Knott, R. (1993). *SCIS 3 teacher's guide level 4: Relative position and motion.* Hudson, NH: Delta Education.

Wheetley, M. (1994). *Leadership and the new science.* San Francisco, CA: Berrett-Koehler.

CHAPTER 6 | The Other Learning Processes

The child is curious. He wants to make sense out of things, find out how things work, gain competence and control over himself and his environment, do what he can see other people doing. He is open, receptive, and perceptive. He does not shut himself off from the strange, confused, complicated world around him. He observes it closely and sharply, tries to take it all in. He is experimental. He does not merely observe the world around him, but tastes it, touches it, hefts it, bends it, breaks it. To find out how reality works, he works on it. He is bold.

J. Holt, *How Children Learn*

JOURNEY PREPARATION

Reflective Questions

- Other than questioning and observing, what processes are used to learn science and mathematics content?

- What do the processes say about the nature of science and mathematics?

- What is the role of the processes in inquiry?

- What is the relationship of learning processes to developing knowledge of mathematics and science content?

- What learning processes are common to learning both mathematics and science knowledge?

- What are the relationships between "play" and learning?

- What is the role of processes in assessing children's learning?

- What are the implications of emphasizing learning processes over content for multicultural classrooms?

- What are the implications of the learning processes in terms of teaching mathematics and science?

Introduction

Children are active learners. Their activity is essential to constructing knowledge. These statements will be examined throughout this chapter. They are worth repeating throughout your journey with learning and teaching mathematics and science because they are so important to real learning. Active children use exploration and all of their senses to make the unfamiliar world familiar. Meaningful exploration involves the interaction of the senses with objects. Science is exploration to construct knowledge about the world. Exploring and interacting using the senses and using observation was addressed in Chapter 5. Chapter 4 gave an in-depth look at the act of questioning, which is essential to motivating exploration and construction of knowledge. Both observing and questioning are essential processes for teaching and learning mathematics and science.

The goal of this chapter is to examine other aspects of exploration or play in constructing organized knowledge through learning processes. Mathematics is a tool or language that helps to construct meaning out of exploration and to give structure and organization to the knowledge that emerges from the exploration. Some of the elements of the NCTM Standards 9 and 11 will be explored

TOUR GUIDE

National Council of Teachers of Mathematics (1989): Standard 9: Algebra

In grades 5–8, students should understand the concepts of variables, expressions, and equations; represent situations and number patterns with tables, graphs, verbal rules, and equations and explore the interrelationships of these representations; analyze tables and graphs to identify properties and relationships; develop confidence in solving linear equations using concrete, informal, and formal methods; investigate inequalities and nonlinear equations; informally apply algebraic methods to solve a variety of real-world and mathematical problems. (p. 102)

Standard 10: Statistics

In grades 5–8, the mathematics curriculum should include exploration of statistics in real-world situations so that students can
—systematically collect, organize, and describe data. (p. 105)

Standard 11: Statistics and Probability

In grades K–4, the mathematics curriculum should include experiences with data analysis and probability so that students can
—collect, organize, and describe data; construct, read, and interpret displays of data; formulate and solve real problems that involve collecting and analyzing data. (p. 54)

Standard 11: Probability (5–8)

In grades 5–8, the mathematics curriculum should model situations by devising and carrying out experiments or simulations to determine probabilities; model situations by constructing a sample space to determine probabilities; appreciate the power of using a probability model by comparing experimental results with mathematical expectations; make predictions that are based on experimental or theoretical probabilities; develop an appreciation for the pervasive use of probability in the real world. (p.109) in this chapter, including variables, tables, graphs, analyzing data and graphs, and developing expressions and equations to represent data patterns. We will also discuss making predictions and using probabilities.

Definition of Processes

The word *processes* is often used to describe action learning. The NCTM (1989) describes mathematics as " . . . 'doing' that, rather than 'knowing that'" (p. 7). Thus, processes are a series of actions with objects using the senses (sight, hearing, touch, taste, and smell) to extract relationships about the objects. Tobin and Tippins (1993) describe the processes as thinking processes, "such as using the senses to experience; representing knowledge through language, diagrams, mathematics, and other symbolic modes; clarification; elaborations; comparisons; justification; generation of alternatives; and selection of viable solutions to problems" (p. 9).

Processes are the connectors between physical interactions and mental operations. Relationships are such things as comparison of attributes or placement of objects in space in relationship to each other. Thus, processes are used in the development of logic and reasoning.

TOUR GUIDE

> ### National Research Council (1996)
>
> In the vision presented by the Standards, inquiry is a step beyond "science as a process," in which students learn skills, such as observation, inference, and experimentation. The new vision includes the "process of science" and requires that students combine processes and scientific knowledge as they use scientific reasoning and critical thinking to develop their understanding of science. (p. 105)

In other words, there are reasons for using processes. Processes are important in the development of knowledge. The processes are not specifically identified in the science standards, but are listed in Table 6.1 because they can be used as indicators of learning, that is, to assess learning. For example, if children are making accurate predictions, they must have some understanding of data. The processes in Table 6.1 are common to both science and mathematics. These processes are observable behaviors: Children can express these processes both verbally and physically. The "x" in the table indicates the grade level at which children can appropriately use the processes. Each of the processes will be explained later in this chapter.

Classroom Activities 6.1 and 6.2, "Objects That Swing" and "Whirling Paper," will give you a chance to engage in processes that lead to investigating variables in cause and effect situations. The data you collect can also be expressed in tables and represented in graphs. Verbal rules and equations can be developed to explore the relationships represented in the tables and graphs.

TABLE 6.1

Processes

Fundamental	Grade Levels		
	K–3	4–6	7–8
Observing	x	x	x
Questioning	x	x	x
Classifying	x	x	x
Ordering	x	x	x
Communicating	x	x	x
Using Numbers	x	x	x
Measuring	x	x	x
Predicting	x	x	x
Combined			
Inferring		x	x
Relating Time and Space			x
Interpreting Data		x	x
Designing Investigations		x	x
Controlling Variables		x	x
Defining Operationally			x
Formulating Models		x	x
Hypothesizing		x	x

Classroom Activity 6.1

Objects That Swing

GOALS

- To control variables
- To explore variables that affect the rate of swing of pendulums

GRADE LEVELS

- Middle to upper

MATERIALS

- Several types of string of various thicknesses
- Metal washers of various sizes
- Paper clips
- Wooden support (1–2 m long; 4 cm wide; 0.5–1 cm thick)
- Masking tape
- Stopwatch
- Meter stick

FIGURE 6.1

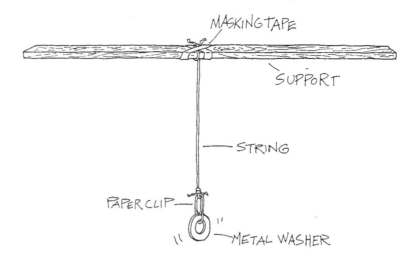

INSTRUCTIONS

Refer to Figure 6.1 as you read these directions to construct the support for the swinging object. The wooden board should be sturdy enough to support heavy swinging objects. Use masking tape to secure the ends of the wooden board (support) between two sturdy objects. The two sturdy objects can be two tables, desks, or chairs. Make as much room as possible between the sturdy objects because the swinging objects must have room to swing without hitting anything. Select a length of string and record its length in centimeters. Unbend a paper clip to form an "S" shape and tie one end of the string to the paper clip. Tape the other end of the string to the center of the wooden support. Record the string's length in centimeters. Hang a selected washer on the bent paper clip.

INVESTIGATIVE QUESTION

Which of the following variables affects the rate of swing: string diameter, length, and type; weight of object; release height?

INVESTIGATIVE PLAN

Identify other variables that might affect the rate of swing and devise a plan to investigate each variable. Address the following questions as you develop a plan:

■ What do you do about the other variables when you investigate one variable at a time?

■ What is considered a swing?

■ How will the rate of swing be measured?

MEASUREMENT SUGGESTIONS

■ Measure the length of the string in centimeters.

■ Designate a particular washer size as the unit of weight. For example, two washers of the same size weigh twice as much as one washer.

■ One swing is equal to a release and a return to the release point. Refer to Figure 6.2.

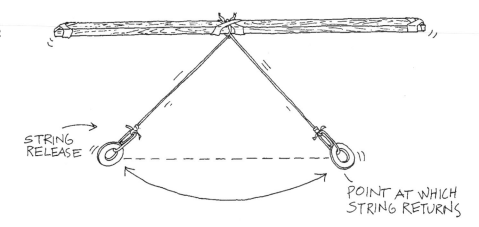

FIGURE 6.2

■ The rate of swing can be the number of swings per minute. To simplify, count the number of swings for 10 or 15 seconds and multiply to get the number per minute.

REST STOP 6.1

Validity and Reliability

The purpose of gathering data is to construct knowledge that is logical (*valid*) and credible (*reliable*) to predict future events. In other words, valid data can be confirmed by replicating the procedures and obtaining the same results. If the data are valid they can be used to predict future events.

What are some techniques for ensuring the accuracy or validity of the data? Discuss them with your classmates and instructor before reading further.

For example, assume that the width of a string is tested to determine if it affects the rate of swing of a pendulum. First, we would want to keep all other variables constant for each trial, such as the length of string, type of string, weight, and release angle. We would choose a range of different widths of strings, from very thin to very thick. However, we want to make sure that the number of swings per width of string is accurate, so we would try it several times. More than likely there will be differences due to human error. The number of trials can be averaged to compensate for human error. By using these procedures, we can assume that the data will have some validity and can be used to make predictions.

Go back to your own plans and incorporate these actions to ensure accuracy. Set up the apparatus and collect the data. Record the data on charts such as the one in Figure 6.3a. Graph the data for each variable using the graph form displayed in Figure 6.3b. Use centimeter graph paper and graph your results for each variable.

DISCUSSION QUESTIONS

Use your tables and graphs to answer these questions.

■ Which variables affect the rate of swing?

■ Which variables do not?

For each variable, choose quantities that were not recorded on the graphs to make predictions for rates of swing. For example, if 50 washers are used, what will be the rate of swing? What will be the rate of swing for 10 meters of string? Choose quantities that are between the first and last points on your graph as well as beyond the

FIGURE 6.3

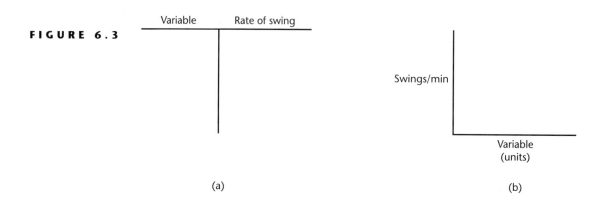

(a)   (b)

points on the graph. The act of predicting events with a given set of data is called *interpolation*. The act of predicting events beyond the known data set is called *extrapolation*. Testing these predictions will also provide information about the reliability of the data.

Develop a verbal rule for each variable to make predictions about the rate of swing of a pendulum. Express these verbal rules in the form of symbolic relationships. Develop an explanation about why and how the rate of swing is affected by the different variables.

SUGGESTIONS

- Make a five-foot pendulum. Attach the string to the ceiling and hold the end of the pendulum at the tip of your nose. Let go of the pendulum. Assuming that you are standing up straight and have not moved, what is the probability that the pendulum will hit you in the nose on its return swing?

- What happens to the rate of swing if you use rubber bands instead of string?

- What happens if you use a spring instead of string?

- What happens if you put water in a small plastic bottle, close the bottle, and use it as a weight on the end of the string? What happens if you vary the amount of water in the bottle?

- Create patterns on large sheets of butcher paper using colored sand dripping from a swinging cone-shaped cup. Make a hole in the bottom of the cup to allow the sand to drip onto the butcher paper. Does the size of the hole or the type of sand affect the pattern?

- Create patterns using other kinds of devices. For example, tie a colored marker to a string and let it swing to gently brush the butcher paper.

- Can you make two objects swing at the same rate if you use different weights?

- What will swinging objects do if you hang several on a swing? (See Figure 6.4.)

- Create water timers or metronome timers using such materials as clay, straws, and Styrofoam cups.

- How do swinging objects relate to everyday life?

- How is time regulated on a grandfather clock?

- Develop mathematical equations that express the relationships between the variables.

FIGURE 6.4

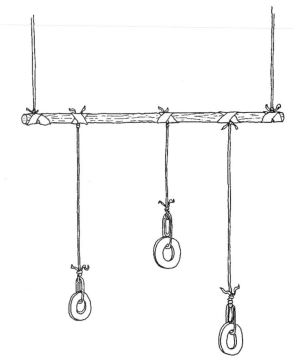

Discussion Questions

Think about this activity as a learner would. During a small group discussion, try to answer the following questions.

- What processes were used during the activity? Refer to Table 6.1.

- For which grade levels would this activity be appropriate? Why? Discuss this with your instructor.

- What science concepts will children learn from this activity?

Classroom Activity 6.2

Whirling Paper

GOALS

- To control variables
- To explore the effects of variables on the spin of the blades

GRADE LEVELS

- Middle to upper

MATERIALS

- $8^{1}/_{2}'' \times 11''$ paper
- Aluminum foil
- Construction paper
- Tag board or index cards
- Scissors
- Paper clips

FIGURE 6.5

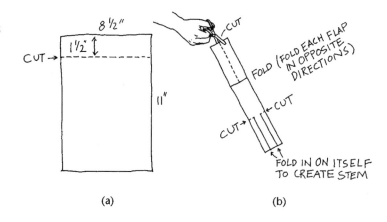

(a)   (b)

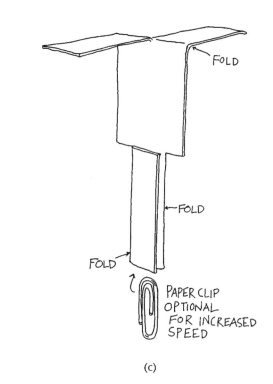

(c)

DIRECTIONS

This activity is often called "Whirlybirds" in science resource books.

Figure 6.5a: Fold the $8\frac{1}{2}$" × 11" paper into thirds. Cut with scissors or tear along the folds to make three strips. (Give two strips to two other classmates.)

Figure 6.5b: Fold one strip into thirds. Cut into the ends of one of the folds, approximately $\frac{1}{8}$" on both sides. Fold along the cuts.

Figure 6.5c: Cut or tear from the center of the other end of the fold.

Directions Summary

Fold the bottom third to make a stem. Cut the top down the center to the top third fold. Fold the two flaps in opposite directions along the top third fold line to create blades. Hold the object in one hand with the blades at the top. Raise your hand as high as possible and release the whirlybird. Watch it drop to the floor.

FIGURE 6.6

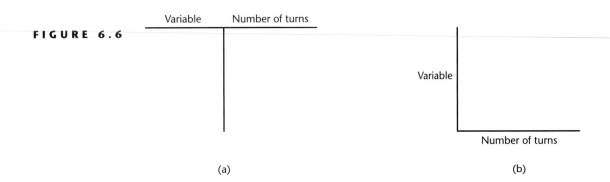

(a) (b)

INVESTIGATIVE QUESTIONS

Which of the following variables affects the number of turns the blades make as the whirling paper falls: weight (change weight by adding paper clips to stem), size of blades (width, length, or both), length and width of stem, type of material? (Change materials by using aluminum foil, construction paper, tag board, or other kinds of paper.)

Design an investigation to explore each of the variables.

- What other variables must be controlled to ensure accuracy of the data?
- How will you count the number of turns?

Use the chart in Figure 6.6 to record your data. Plot your data on graph paper.

Be sure the data in your charts and graphs are valid and reliable. Check the validity and reliability of the data by making predictions and testing for accuracy.

During a small group discussion, develop an explanation about why the whirling paper spins. Develop verbal rules to explain the effect of the variables on the whirling paper.

Discussion Questions

- List the things you were doing or the actions you took during both Classroom Activity investigations.
- From your experiences with these investigations, create a definition for each action you listed.
- Create an overall definition for action learning as it relates to mathematics and science. *Processes* is another word for action learning.
- Create mathematical equations to express the relationships between the variables.
- Based on past experience, are there different types of action learning for mathematics and science?
- Classroom Activities 6.1 and 6.2 include many types of action learning. Are some more appropriate for children at particular ages? Which ones do you think primary children can do? Which ones can all ages do?

REST STOP 6.2

Compare the "Objects That Swing" and "Whirling Paper" activities to the "Inference Boxes," "Digestive System Model," "Cupcake Geology," and "Fossilized Prints" activities. All of these activities require creating inferences because the senses do not reveal all of the cause and effect relationships. We cannot "see" the friction of the air slowing down a pendulum or acting on the blades of the whirling paper. The interaction of variables cannot be directly "seen." To understand the role of friction in Classroom Activities 6.1 and 6.2 requires using data to abstract ideas mentally. Thus, in general, these two activities are more appropriate for the upper grades than for primary grades.

Take a few minutes to think about the feelings you experienced during Classroom Activities 6.1 and 6.2. Discuss the following questions in a small group.

Discussion Questions

- How did you feel about having to follow specific directions?

- Did feelings from past experiences surface? What were they? What were the experiences?

- Were there times during these two activities when you wanted to explore without being obligated to follow directions?

- Did you feel restricted?

- Did you want to do your own investigating first before following the directions?

- Did the directions give you a sense of security in completing the activities successfully?

According to Rogers (1969):

When he chooses his own directions, helps to discover his own learning resources, formulates his own problems, decides his own course of action, lives with the consequences of each of these choices, then significant learning is maximized. There is evidence from industry as well as from the field of education that such participative learning is far more effective than passive learning. (p. 162)

The quotation from Holt (1967) at the beginning of this chapter is very similar. *What are the implications of these two quotations in terms of action learning?* Think about "Objects That Swing" and "Whirling Paper." *Do the two passages apply to these two activities?*

Think back to the "Cornstarch Mixtures" activity in Chapter 5. *What were your feelings during this activity?* You were given few directions and allowed to choose your own path of exploration. But these two activities were structured to ensure that you collected meaningful data. The cornstarch activity was less structured because more than likely you would get meaningful data regardless of what you did during the activity. You were allowed to "mess about" to understand that learning can take place during minimally structured activities. Another word for "messing about" is play. *What images are conjured in your mind when you think about children playing? What is the relationship between play and learning?* Scientists are playful and tend to "mess about." Refer to Rest Stop 5.2 in Chapter 5. Why do children, scientists, or anyone for that matter, play? Again, Holt (1967) gives us insight about play and learning:

> If the experience before us is completely new and strange; if there is much new material to be observed, material that doesn't seem to fall into any recognizable pattern or order; if we cannot tell what are the variables that influence the situation, much less isolate them, we will be unwise to try to think like a detective, or a scientist in a laboratory. (p. 145)

Discussion Questions

- Did you feel playful during the cornstarch activity?

- Were you learning anything during the cornstarch activity? If so, what was it?

- Play is part of learning. How might this knowledge be used for assessment purposes when children begin new investigations?

- What are some other implications for teaching and learning mathematics and science?

When experiences are strange and new, or puzzling, there is conflict between perceptions and reality. Often, this conflict may be resolved through innovative actions or play. If science and mathematics activities are chosen wisely to motivate children to learn, the activities will undoubtedly be about new and strange things, causing children to play. The act of doing in relation to learning is developmental. Doing begins with free exploration because of lack of knowledge about a phenomenon. Play makes the unfamiliar familiar. Once there is familiarity with the variables of a phenomenon, more precise data can be collected through a controlled experience. Thus, organized learning occurs. Now mathematics becomes important. Mathematics is the language that expresses relationships in shorthand. Symbols can express many words. Also at this stage, doing becomes organized or methodical. Preciseness leads to data or facts that can be accepted as reflecting reality. This reality can be accepted by others who explore the same phenomenon. The structure allows others to collect data in the same way to verify the findings and corroborate the reality. Thus play is natural to learning. Learn to distinguish between activity that is playful and inquisitive and activity that disrupts the learning environment.

Discussion Questions

- Would you structure the "Objects That Swing" and "Whirling Paper" activities to allow for play? What would you do to allow for play?

- For any given science or mathematics activity, how would you know whether or not to allow children to play?

- If the act of doing is developmental, what does this say about exploring in depth and creating a spiral curriculum? For example, "Objects That Swing" could be revisited each year by children.

- Suppose you were doing the cornstarch activity and a parent, another teacher, or the principal came into the room and said that the children were just playing. How would you respond? What would you say to defend the fact that play in the classroom is appropriate?

- What kinds of play are not related to learning? What would you do to prevent nonlearning play?

Fundamental Processes

Table 6.1 divides the processes into those that are fundamental and those that are combined. For the sake of discussion, these processes are separated. However, in reality they are integrated. In both "Objects That Swing" and "Whirling Paper" are found many if not all of the fundamental and combined processes. Go back to Chapter 5 and analyze the processes in that chapter's Classroom Activities.

The fundamental processes are important to the learner during the "play" phase of learning. The act of observing and questioning entices the learner to engage in exploration. That exploration continues with counting, classifying, and ordering. As the experience become more familiar, a learner can communicate observations and actions as well as begin to understand cause and effect relationships to make predictions and to quantify data through using numbers and measuring. Play is essential to young children's ability to use these processes. The processes with an "x" in the K–3 column develop through play.

The fundamental processes are more "physical" action than "mental" action, although mental operations are occurring. These processes are used continuously, no matter the age of the child. Following is a description of the fundamental processes.

Observing

The process of observing was extensively explored in the previous chapter. However, it is worth repeating: *Observing is fundamental to the use of other mathematical and science processes. Observations are made by children of all ages.*

Questioning

This process was explored extensively in Chapter 4. *Questioning is an active expression of curiosity.*

Classifying

This process will be discussed in detail in Chapter 8 in terms of a mental operation as well. Classifying involves the ability to group objects according to similarities and differences. However, classification is more than just grouping. It involves understanding relationships among objects. Understanding relationships between groups is necessary for mathematical operations.

Classification is an important mental operation. Scientists use classification to organize data about the natural world. Plants and animals are organized in classification hierarchies. The periodic chart of the elements is an organized system to show relationships between elements. Classification is useful for predicting and identifying objects that have not yet been identified by scientists. However, more importantly, everyone uses classification. For example, grocery and shoe stores place items in related groups. The postal system's zip code is a classification system. Understanding different levels of classification is a process that occurs over several years in elementary school.

Ordering

Just like classifying, ordering is a way to organize objects using relationships. Understanding ordering is important in understanding ordinal numbers; that is, knowing that 3 is greater than 2. Ordering also takes many experiences and many years to be understood. Ordering is explored in depth in Chapter 8.

Communicating

Communicating was addressed in Chapter 3 in terms of the problems of communication in a multicultural classroom and also to demonstrate that mathematics cuts across cultures and languages. Gallard (1993) says:

> It is the direct experiences of students and their everyday language that should be used to provide experiences that lead to conceptual understanding of science phenomena. The language of science is thus connected through everyday language and to the student's direct experiences. This involves creating and maintaining science classrooms that are rich in opportunities for students to use their everyday language as they attempt to make sense of the world. (p. 179)

Mathematics can be a vehicle for communication with people of other cultures and languages. The NCTM discusses mathematics and communications in Standard 2.

The communication of ideas, whether symbolically or qualitatively, involves expressing knowledge about relationships derived from experiences. Scientists and mathematicians communicate to others in their professions not only to share their knowledge but also to recognize the knowledge as valid information. The most common way for children to express mathematical and scientific ideas is through written or verbal words. However, children can learn to express relationships through graphic forms.

Communicating Through Graphs

Graphs are visual representations of data to illustrate different levels of relationships. Simple graphs such as pictographs and histograms (rectangular boxes used to illustrate the frequency of objects) make comparisons between discrete variables. Discrete variables are those that are quantifiably related to each other along a continuum of ordered numbers. Line graphs illustrate relationships along an ordered continuum. Circle graphs illustrate percentages or ratios of related parts to a whole. Pictographs and histograms do not require the level of abstract thinking that is necessary for making line graphs or circle graphs. Graphing will be described in terms of developmental levels. Primary-grade children can learn to make pictographs.

Level I: Actual Objects

Children can use real three-dimensional objects or symbolic objects to represent relationships.

TOUR GUIDE

National Council of Teachers of Mathematics (1989)
Standard 2: Mathematics and Communication

In grades K–4, students can relate physical materials, pictures, and diagrams to mathematical ideas; reflect on and clarify their thinking about mathematical ideas and situations; relate their everyday language to mathematical language and symbols; realize that representing, discussing, reading, writing, and listening to mathematics are a vital part of learning and using mathematics. (p. 26)

In grades 5–8, students can model situations using oral, written, concrete, pictorial, graphical, and algebraic methods; reflect on and clarify their own thinking about mathematical ideas and situations; develop common understanding of mathematical ideas, including the role of definitions; use the skills of reading, listening, and viewing to interpret and evaluate mathematical ideas; discuss mathematical ideas and make conjectures and convincing arguments; appreciate the value of mathematical notation and its role in the development of mathematical ideas. (p. 78)

Standard 13: Patterns and Relationships

In grades K–4, students can recognize, describe, extend, and create a wide variety of patterns; represent and describe mathematical relationships; explore the use of variables and open sentences to express relationships. (p. 60)

Standard 4: Mathematical Connections

In grades 5–8, students see mathematics as an integrated whole; explore problems and describe results using graphical, numerical, physical, algebraic, and verbal mathematical models or representations; use a mathematical idea to further their understanding of other mathematical ideas; apply mathematical thinking and modeling to solve problems that arise in other disciplines, such as art, music, psychology, science, and business; value the role of mathematics in our culture and society. (p. 84)

Standard 8: Patterns and Functions

In grades 5–8, students describe, extend, analyze, and create a wide variety of patterns; describe and represent relationships with tables, graphs, and rules; analyze functional relationships to explain how a change in one quantity results in a change in another; use patterns and functions to represent and solve problems. (p. 98)

Activity Example

Put a handful of M&Ms on top of a desk and ask children to arrange them in columns according to color. Have children write down the number of M&Ms in each column so they can "see" the number of each color in relationship to the others. All kinds of objects such as buttons, seeds, animal crackers, and even the children themselves can be placed in columns according to a single attribute. For example, children could line up in rows according to eye color.

FIGURE 6.7

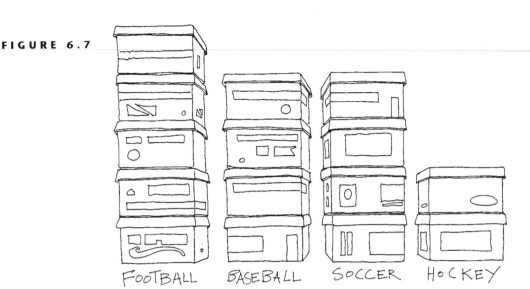

FOOTBALL BASEBALL SOCCER HOCKEY

Level II: Pictures or Drawings to Represent Real Objects

Activity Example

Rather than using the actual pieces of candy, cut out pictures of M&Ms from magazines and have children place the pictures in columns. Other objects that can be used to represent the M&Ms include colored circles drawn by the children or colored stickers.

Level III: Symbolic Representation Using Other Objects

Children can represent objects by using other, unrelated objects, which can be used to represent many ideas. If large objects are used, the representations can be made in front of the entire class. For example, shoe boxes (Baratta-Lorton, 1977) can be used. (See Figure 6.7.) Children have their own shoe boxes labeled with their names and attached photographs. These shoe boxes can be stacked according to a particular attribute. For example, the boxes in Figure 6.7 are arranged according to the children's favorite sports. Or the boxes can be stacked according to birthday months. Children can see the "histogram" and the number of children who have birthdays in each month.

Unifix cubes, Legos, plastic or wooden centimeter cubes, or other stacking objects can be used instead of shoe boxes. In that case children can work at their own desks to create columns representing a set of data.

Level IV: Pictorial Representation Using Coordinate Systems

Level IV use of graphing involves developing horizontal and vertical axes to show the relationship between two variables. The vertical axis represents a quantitative value such as actual number or percentage. The horizontal line represents qualitative attributes such as color, shape, or texture. A rectangular bar represents the relationship between the quantitative and qualitative variables.

FIGURE 6.8

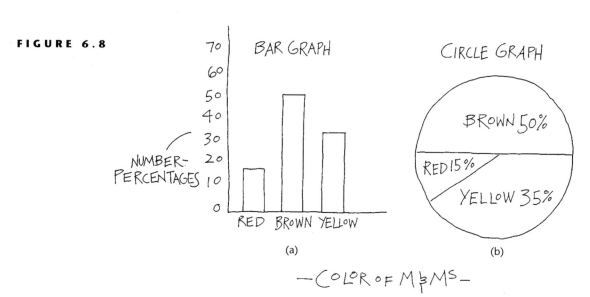

Bar graphs (Figure 6.8a) are symbolic of relationships between discrete variables. Circle graphs (Figure 6.8b) represent ratios of the parts to the whole.

Have children can gather data and represent it in graph form to answer the following questions:

- Which letter is the most common in alphabet cereal?

- What is the most common shoe size among children in a given classroom?

- What are different heights of children in the classroom?

- What are the children's favorite TV shows, movie stars, baseball players, football players, books, sports?

- How many birthdays are represented for each month?

- What kinds of pets do the children have?

- What is a favorite candy?

- How many seeds are found in the following: apples, oranges, green peppers, pumpkins, pears, peaches, bananas, tomatoes?

- What is a favorite cereal?

- What is a favorite soft drink?

- How much water will different types of paper towels absorb?

- Which paper towel weighs the most when it is wet?

- What is the relationship between the brightness of a bulb and the number of batteries used to light the bulb?

- What is the relationship between the size of drops of water when they hit different kinds of surfaces such as paper, waxed paper, glass, plastic wrap, aluminum foil, and Styrofoam?

- Does the type of material insulating an ice cube affect how long it takes to melt?

FIGURE 6.9

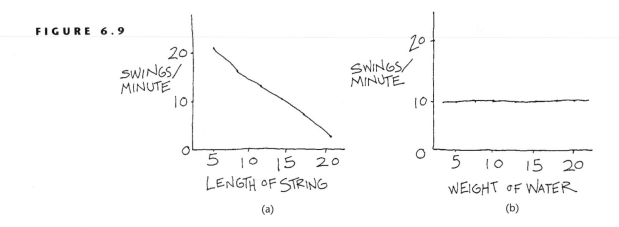

(a) (b)

Group Discussion Activity

Which type of graphing is the most appropriate for representing each of the questions above?

Level V: Illustrating Cause and Effect Relationships

The rate of swing of a pendulum is affected by the length of the string (Figure 6.9a). The rate of swing is not affected by the weight of the pendulum (Figure 6.9b).

REST STOP 6.3

The first paragraph of the discussion of Level V is a general illustration of how the graphs of Figure 6.9 might be interpreted with the given data. These statements do not explain what happens as the length of string reaches zero or what happens to the number of swings if the string is taken to extreme lengths. Obviously, there is a much more sophisticated explanation of the relationship than what is represented in the graphs. If you want to pursue that explanation, consult a physics instructor or text.

Linear graphs are set up with units on each axis. Segments of equal length along the axis have the same value and are cumulative, moving from zero or the intersection toward the end of the line. Units are typically in feet, yards, or meters; pounds or grams; liters or cups.

The answers to the following questions can be graphed to illustrate cause and effect relationships.

- How does the angle of an inclined plane affect the distance a toy car travels?
- How does the height from which a ball is dropped affect how high the ball will bounce?
- Is there a relationship between the height of an object and its shadow?
- What is the relationship between the number of turns of the crank of a windup toy and the distance it will travel?
- What is the relationship between how much a rubber band stretches and the amount of weight attached to it?

Children begin to understand graphing by making three-dimensional representations of data with the actual objects. They progress to using symbols to represent the objects. At the beginning levels, children make visual comparisons between variables of the same kind, but not necessarily those that depend on each other. Thus, children in primary and intermediate levels can explore graphing discrete variables using actual objects and pictures. In order for children to represent cause and effect relationships on graphs, they must "see" relationships between two variables and be able to translate those relationships to a visual representation in the form of a line. To create the vertices of the graph, children must understand the units of a particular measurement system.

Using Numbers

Using numbers is an active process of symbolically representing the relationship of individual objects to other similar objects. The members of a group or the groups themselves can be counted and compared. Using numbers is also developmental and is an outcome of understanding basic classification systems.

Measuring

Measuring is the action of describing attributes of objects and their placement by quantifying data. Attributes such as height, length, width, weight, volume, and surface area can be described accurately using scalar units. Objects can be located in different dimensions by using measurements. The location of a dot on a sheet of paper can be determined accurately by using two dimensions. The exact location of a chair in a room can be determined by using three dimensions.

Children learn the act of measuring first by creating their own units of measurement. This is essential to understanding and using standard units. Thus, measurement as a concept is developmental. Whether children use non-standard or standard units, requiring them to be precise will help them understand how measurement scales are developed.

Children need a variety of measuring experiences with standard units. Measurement as it relates to science and mathematics will be explored in Chapter 10.

Predicting

Predicting is a way of testing knowledge by using what is known to determine whether a future event will occur. Predicting is a reality check between the known and unknown, stated in terms of actions or behaviors rather than being based on data gathered from prior experiences. Predictions can be made according to patterns in the data. In science, predicting is a way to validate data and determine its usefulness in future situations.

Sometimes there is an element of guessing involved in predicting. In other words, predictions can be based on opinions supported by little or no evidence. These predictions may not be accurate, but making them gives us a feeling of security about an uncertain future.

Estimating is closely related to predicting and is useful in mathematics. Whereas predicting is related to cause and effect events, estimating is related to quantifying objects or events. Estimating is often useful when accuracy and precision are not needed. Estimation gives parameters for collecting precise data. Sometimes we do not need to be precise in measuring or defining the quantity of something. Children can estimate the number of pennies or gum balls in a jar, or the number of the leaves on a tree or bricks in a building.

TOUR GUIDE

National Council of Teachers of Mathematics (1989)
Standard 5: Estimation

In grades K–4, the curriculum should include estimation so students can
—explore estimation strategies, recognize when an estimate is appropriate; determine the reasonableness of results; apply estimation in working with quantities, measurement, computation, and problem solving. (p.

Probability is also related to predicting in the sense that the likelihood of an event occurring is quantified in terms of a ratio of the future event to past events. Young children can explore probability by flipping coins or bottle caps, rolling dice, or dropping other objects to see which way they land. After a series of trials, they can predict what is likely to happen for the next trial. Children can explore the probability of winning a lottery by picking numbers from a container. You can most likely think of some other activities that teach children about probability.

Combined Processes

The combined processes depend on the fundamental processes as well as other combined processes in terms of mental operations. The fundamental processes are embedded within the combined processes. In other words, observing, classifying, using numbers, and the other fundamental processes are used when making inferences, interpreting data, or the other combined processes. The use of the combined processes implies a higher level of thinking than for the fundamental processes. This higher level of thinking develops through experience and the use of the fundamental processes. Fourth-grade children who have had experience with the fundamental processes can begin to use the combined processes effectively.

Inferring

Inferences are interpretations of data or conclusions based on limited use of the senses. The accuracy of interpretations of data increases in terms of how much can be directly observed and measured. Inferences made with limited observations must be tested and retested through replication. No data are purely objective because the person observing is influenced by past experiences and their own knowledge base. Young children's knowledge base is tied to reality, which limits the possibilities of interpreting data.

Relating Time and Space

Relating time and space involves understanding events that occur in relation to time and motion, interpreted in terms of measurements. Pendulums involve the relationships between time and space. Moon phases involve relationships of the motions and distances over time of the earth, moon, and sun. The concepts of acceleration and speed are comparisons of several objects' motions in relation to one another. These ideas are highly abstract and difficult for elementary children to understand. However, appropriate activities that involve time and space relationships are addressed in Chapter 11.

Interpreting Data

Interpreting data requires the ability to analyze and see patterns and relationships among the facts collected through observations. The patterns and relationships may be based on observable attributes and quantitative measurements. Geometry involves both detecting patterns and measuring those patterns. Geometry will be further discussed in Chapter 9.

Designing Investigations

Designing investigations begins after the initial exploratory phase of learning. Designing investigations requires many steps, beginning with a central question that can be answered in quantitative terms. The type of question asked determines the design of the investigation. The central question leads to other questions. What sense or observational instruments will be used to collect data? What will influence the outcome of the investigation? How will variables be controlled? Once the data are collected, what is to be done with them? How will they be organized to look for patterns and relationships? How valid are the patterns and relationships? If the experiment is repeated, will the experimenter obtain similar results?

Designing an experiment involves choosing a series of steps that must be thought through prior to the investigation. The so-called "scientific method" is experimental design. However, there is no one "scientific method" to follow to answer a question or solve a problem. Children learn ways to collect data through experience. Using a series of questions such as those given here can help children construct their own investigation designs.

Controlling Variables

Variables can be thought of as attributes of objects that interact to create changes. To control variables requires one to become aware of all the possibilities that can affect the results of an investigation. Controlling variables means keeping conditions constant while manipulating one variable to see whether it has an effect on the outcome of an investigation. Children may learn to control variables by beginning with investigations that have only one variable. Variables that involve living things are difficult to control because of the unpredictability of behaviors. Certain variables may not surface until after the investigation is over. The investigation may have to be repeated to account for the variables unless the investigator determines that they have little effect on the outcome.

Defining Operationally

An operational definition involves describing an event in terms of relationships based on actions and ideas abstracted from the actions rather than reducing the relationships to symbols and formulas. For example, a formula is: Area is length times width ($A = L \times W$). An operational definition might be: Area is the surface covered within specific boundaries.

Formulating Models

Formulating models involves creating visual representations of ideas abstracted from data. They are visual representations of inferences. Models are needed to explain events and phenomena that are too small or too large to observe without the aid of technology. The visual representation may be in the form of symbols, diagrams, or three-dimensional objects that simulate the real thing. Products and ideas are often created from models. The process of formulating models was addressed in Chapter 5.

Hypothesizing

A hypothesis may be described as an assumption based on prior knowledge, which is insufficient to provide more than a tentative explanation. For example: *The length of a pendulum's string makes a difference because the pendulum gains momentum the farther and higher it travels. Gravitational pull prevents the pendulum from reaching the same height each time and it begins losing momentum until it eventually stops.* This tentative explanation is tested through logic by using a designed investigation, which was discussed in a previous section.

Predicting is foretelling a future event. Teachers commonly say that young children can hypothesize, but in reality children are making predictions. Remember, hypothesizing involves using logic. Probability is used to determine the likelihood of the hypothesis being true in quantitative terms.

The mathematics and science classroom activities found in the remaining chapters of this book will engage the reader in the learning processes that were described in this section.

Skills or Processes?

Just as the terms *hypothesizing* and *predicting* are often used interchangeably, *processes* and *skills* are often used the same way. *Skills* are specific sets of procedures, steps, or other types of actions that are methodical and that one can improve with practice. There are mathematical skills such as following the steps to add, subtract, multiply, or divide through a repetition of operations. A person can memorize and follow steps without understanding the logic behind the steps.

Many skills are common to both mathematics and science. These manipulative skills are found in the process of measuring. Children have to know how to use and read rulers, weighing scales, thermometers, graduated cylinders, and timing devices. Studying life sciences requires knowing laboratory techniques or skills. Children must know how to properly operate a microscope or prepare a microscope slide. Dissection requires using tools in specific ways. Telescopes and seismographs require specific skills. Many problem-solving investigations follow appropriate lab skills in order to ensure the control of variables. Creativity is limited, not only because of the controls but also for safety reasons. Lab skills are best learned through direct instruction and modeling to ensure proper use of equipment. In contrast to these skills, processes are mental operations that are enhanced by creativity.

One may wonder about making a distinction between skills and processes. In some cases, there seems to be no clear difference. For example, graphing can be considered a skill because a figure or some type of illustration is created to represent data. Graphing also involves processes that require certain levels of understanding. Line graphs have coordinate axes (horizontal and vertical). The lines of a graph have place values marked with equal spacing. The values are expressed in units of measurement. Thus, the assumption is often made that certain actions can be memorized and learned through practice. But certain actions learned by using processes are conducted more effectively through logic and understanding rather than memorization and practice. Graphing and measurement are two examples.

The following NCTM standards are related to the processes and skills discussed in this section. Certain elements of these standards will be discussed in other chapters as well. Notice that these standards involve real-world experiences and problem solving. Anytime this happens, the processes are being used. The standards also speak to estimating, creating models, and developing meaning from operations. These are all based on actions as described in the processes.

The Learning Processes and Science Disciplines

Schools typically teach life, physical, and earth sciences. The basic knowledge of these disciplines can be learned through the fundamental processes of *observing, classifying,* and *ordering.* These processes help the learner understand differences and similarities among plants, animals, rocks, minerals, and such physical properties as sound, heat, and magnetism. Differences and similarities are determined through watching, touching, listening, smelling, and sometimes even tasting. Differences can be *measured* and *predicted* as accuracy in collecting and *interpreting* data collection increases. The similarities and differences are expressed in different ways through *communicating* and *questioning* actions on objects.

The physical sciences provide the most direct hands-on experiences in using the senses. Children's senses receive immediate feedback through the manipulation of objects and observation of cause and effect relationships. Through manipulation, children's actions and knowledge become integrated. Concepts learned from manipulations such as interactions with magnets and paper clips, mirrors and light, or batteries and bulbs are clearly observable. The cause and effect relationships occur immediately. The immediate reactions hold children's attention. In most basic physical science investigations by elementary school children, variables can be identified and controlled. All the basic processes as well as the complex processes can be used in learning physical science concepts. Many of the basic physical science concepts are also fundamental to the life sciences and earth sciences. For example, the concepts of temperature and heat are important in understanding air patterns and the flow of magma. The chemical process of separating color pigments (chromatography) helps one understand the color content of leaves. Thus, physical science activities are necessary in elementary school curricula because they provide the most direct, active learning and provide the foundation for understanding other science areas. However, some areas of the physical sciences are difficult to learn through the learning processes. These will be discussed in forthcoming chapters.

Many basic life science concepts can be learned through hands-on activities that involve observing, classifying, and ordering living organisms according to their physical structures, methods of locomotion, or behaviors. Learning about living organisms is done through watching. Touching has to

TOUR GUIDE

National Council of Teachers of Mathematics (1989)
Standard 6: Number Sense and Numeration

In grades K–4, students can construct number meanings through real-world experiences and the use of physical materials; understand our numeration system by relating, counting, grouping, and place value concepts; develop number sense; interpret the multiple uses of numbers encountered in the real world. (p. 38)

Standard 7: Concepts of Whole Number Operations

In grades K–4, students can develop meaning for the operations by modeling and discussing a rich variety of problem situations; relate the mathematical language and symbolism of operations to problem situations and informal language; recognize that a wide variety of problem structures can be represented by a single operation; develop operations sense. (p. 41)

Standard 8: Whole Number Computation

In grades K–4, students can model, explain, and develop reasonable proficiency with basic facts and algorithms; use a variety of mental computations and estimation techniques; use calculators in appropriate computational situations; select and use computation techniques appropriate to specific problems and determine whether the results are reasonable. (p. 44)

Standard 5: Numbers and Number Relationships

In grades 5–8, students can understand, represent, and use numbers in a variety of equivalent forms (integer, fraction, decimal, percent, exponential, and scientific notation) in real-world and mathematical situations; develop number sense for whole numbers, fractions, decimals, integers, and rational numbers; understand and apply ratios, proportions, and percents in a wide variety of situations; investigate relationships among fractions, decimals, and percents; represent numerical relationships in one- and two-dimensional graphs. (p. 87)

Standard 6: Number System and Number Theory

In grades 5–8, students can understand and appreciate the need for numbers beyond the whole numbers; develop and use order relations for whole numbers, fractions, decimals, integers, and rational numbers; extend their understanding of whole numbers, fractions, decimals, integers, and rational numbers; extend their understanding of whole number operations to fractions, decimals, integers, and rational numbers; understand how basic arithmetic operations are related to one another; develop and apply number theory concepts (e.g., primes, factors, and multiples) in real-world and mathematical problem situations. (p. 91)

Standard 7: Computation and Estimation

In grades 5–8, students can compute with whole numbers, fractions, decimals, integers, and rational numbers; develop, analyze, and explain procedures for computation and techniques for estimation; develop, analyze, and explain methods for solving proportions; select and use an appropriate method for computing from among mental arithmetic, paper and pencil, calculator, and computer methods; use computation, estimation, and proportions to solve problems; use estimation to check the reasonableness of results. (p. 94) be limited because it interferes with natural behaviors. Creating controlled experiments often involves handling living organisms. Too much handling, probing, or other kinds of manipulations can harm animals and even destroy them. Children's curiosity may override their sense of respect for living organisms and they may treat them as if they were objects. Thus, having live animals in the classroom raises moral issues about their treatment and care. Many groups are against using animals in laboratory investigations. The National Science Teachers Association developed guidelines for the proper treatment and care of animals in classrooms; these guidelines can be found on their Web page. However, children can learn to respect living organisms and to handle them in nurturing ways. Animals must be treated with care and respect. Cause and effect types of investigations with living things must be carefully thought through and children must understand the rules for handling them.

The results of cause and effect investigations with living organisms sometimes are not clearly observable. Changes may occur over a long time span and children may lose interest. There are no instantaneous results. Living organisms' behaviors are complex, making it difficult to control variables or even determine which variable is causing the change. However, the study of living organisms is important for several reasons. Children will become sensitive to the natural environment and with the proper guidance can learn to respect life. They can learn how human beings are similar to other animals. Living organisms can be studied by taking nature walks, growing plants in the classroom, taking care of animals, maintaining terrariums and aquariums—in other words, being as unobtrusive as possible with living organisms so that what is learned represents their natural behaviors.

Earth science includes the study of weather, astronomy, and the components and characteristics of the earth. Earth science ideas depend on physical science concepts. Other than classifying minerals, rocks, and soils, understanding earth science concepts also means observing rather than directly manipulating objects because events occur on a large scale and over a long time. Data collected through watching is used to detect patterns and to make predictions; to create models about weather, volcanoes, earthquakes, the internal motion of the earth, the motion of stars and planets. Knowledge about earth science is learned by trying to understand cause and effect relationships by replicating conditions through simulations and models. Earth science ideas are understood through the complex processes. Time-space relations are important to understanding geological and fossil formations.

Children can learn many physical science concepts through the basic processes. Physical science concepts such as light, gravity, force, and sound, learned through hands-on science activities, are useful in understanding biological and earth science concepts. Children can classify and measure rocks, leaves, insects, soils, and seeds. But understanding big ideas such as genetics, plate tectonics, evolution, and weather patterns requires the ability to use complex processes such as modeling, hypothesizing, defining operationally, and relating time and space. Explanations of magnetism, sound waves, light waves, electricity, atoms, and molecules are also based on models and interpreting data. Young children must explore science ideas through basic processes before they can understand complicated science ideas through complex processes.

As Holt (1967) says, children are bold. They learn through acting with their environment. The learning processes are essential to the extrapolation of ideas from objects in the environment. Novel experiences are explored through play. Familiar experiences are explored in depth by controlling variables and quantifying data. The way children learn is similar to the way mathematicians and scientists learn. What is constructed when children are engaged in the learning processes? A theory of intellectual development is presented in Chapter 7 that explains the elements of constructing knowledge.

> **Go back to the reflective questions at the beginning of the chapter and the answers you recorded in your journal.**
>
> **Add to or modify your answers based on what you learned from this chapter.**

Bibliography

Baratta-Lorton, R. (1977). *Mathematics: A way of thinking.* Menlo Park, CA: Addison-Wesley.

Gallard, A. J. (1993). Learning science in multicultural environments. In K. Tobin (Ed.), *The practice of constructivism in science education.* Hillsdale, NJ: Lawrence Erlbaum Associates.

Holt, J. (1967). *How children learn.* New York: Dell.

National Council of Teachers of Mathematics (1989). *Curriculum and evaluation standards for school mathematics.* Reston, VA: Author.

National Research Council (1996). *National science education standards.* Washington, DC: National Academy Press.

Rogers, C. (1969). *Freedom to learn.* Columbus, OH: Charles Merrill.

Tobin, K., and Tippins, D. (1993). Constructivism as a referent for teaching and learning. In K. Tobin (Ed.), *The practice of constructivism in science education.* Hillsdale, NJ: Lawrence Erlbaum Associates.

CHAPTER 7

How Children Learn Mathematics and Science

The more we help children to have wonderful ideas and to feel good about themselves having them, the more likely it is that they will some day happen upon wonderful ideas that no one else has happened upon before.

E. Duckworth, *The Having of Wonderful Ideas and Other Essays on Teaching and Learning*

JOURNEY PREPARATION

Reflective Questions

■ How do we determine what content to teach at various grade levels?

■ Will all children doing the same hands-on activities at the same time learn exactly the same thing?

■ Under what conditions do facts become the most meaningful to the learner?

■ Explain concepts and their role in the development of intelligence.

■ Discuss the significance of learning from primary sources as opposed to secondary sources.

■ What are the key elements of Piaget's theory of intellectual development?

■ What is your definition of intelligence?

■ What are the implications of Piaget's theory for teaching and learning mathematics and science?

Whose Facts Do You Believe?

As a preservice elementary teacher, you are probably wondering what science and mathematics content should be taught and when. Like other preservice teachers, you may have said,

> I want to know the science and mathematics content so that I know what children are supposed to learn from activities. I can't do the activities unless I know the content. Just give me the facts! That is all I need to know!

This chapter discusses what science and mathematics should be taught in elementary school classrooms. In general, the concerns about what to teach in mathematics do not seem to be as serious as concerns about science teaching. Mathematics "content" or facts are fairly constant and do not change as rapidly as does science content. Exactly what are science facts? Where do they come from? Let's put scientific facts in the proper perspective by doing the following activity.

Classroom Activity 7.1   **The Search for the Truth**

INSTRUCTIONS

1. Obtain a science-based article that is at least two pages long on a topic such as genetics, evolution, astronomy, or ecology. *Time* and *Newsweek* are weekly magazines that frequently have science articles. *Science and Children,* a publication of the National Science Teachers Association, frequently has articles on selected science content. Find an article in *Science and Children* (for example, Capron, Brook, and Rieben, 1996) or in another journal. Give everyone in the class a copy of the same article.

2. Form groups of four to five people. Have each person in a group choose a portion of the article to read and search for three opinions, facts, and concepts. Remember, opinions are based on beliefs and perceptions. Facts are based on experiences, and concepts are mental abstractions from facts.

3. Read your section and select three opinions, facts, and concepts. Share your choices during a group discussion.

4. Have each group choose one fact, one concept, and one opinion from the selection.

5. Appoint someone in the group to present the three selections to the rest of the class. They can be presented orally or written on butcher paper or a chalkboard.

6. As a class, discuss whether each sample is truly representative of the category in which it was placed.

DISCUSSION QUESTIONS

- Why are opinions easy to identify and agree upon?
- Why are scientific facts difficult to agree upon?
- Why are scientific concepts difficult to identify?
- What does this say about the scientific facts presented in newspapers, magazines, and textbooks?
- How can we be sure of the validity of facts presented in newspapers, magazines, and textbooks?
- Whose facts are the most believable? (A person's own set? Those in magazines or books?)
- What are the implications for teaching and learning science?
- What are the implications for using textbooks as the only source for learning science?

Primary sources are learners themselves. Secondary sources are other learners, adults, reading materials, and other media sources. The most believable facts are those collected first-hand through active and mental engagement using the senses. These facts will have meaning because they are knowledge hard won. Facts from secondary sources such as books and magazines can be accepted, but may not be remembered. Facts learned from secondary sources have to be mentally "wrestled" from our own knowledge base and experiences. The learner may even have to go through new investigations to confirm secondary sources.

Facts presented in books, magazines, newspapers, and other media are often assumed to be true without question because of our faith in those who report them. However, if we understand that facts are subject to question, we can choose to accept them in good faith, or to question them and gather data to confirm or deny them in our own mind. This is how science operates. There are countless examples of new discoveries made by those who questioned the status quo. This is true of teaching as well. Change happens in teaching when the status quo is challenged through questions and data collection.

Scientific facts do not stay the same because scientists as individuals bring their own experiences and biases to their investigations. Driver, Guesne, and Tiberghien (1985) say:

> Individuals internalize their experience in a way which is at least partially their own; they construct their own meanings. These personal "ideas" influence the manner in which information is acquired. This personal manner of approaching phenomena is also found in the way in which scientific knowledge is generated. Most philosophers of science accept that hypotheses or theories do not represent so-called "objective" data but that they are constructions or products of the human imagination. (pp. 2–3)

This is important to remember when thinking about the implications for teaching science and mathematics. Traditionally science is viewed as objective data or data free of human constraints. In reality, data are subject to individual views of the world and interpreted through individual mental filters. Heredity, experience, and prior knowledge all act as filters.

Children are denied the rich experience of developing their own knowledge when they are required to learn facts from secondary sources and to accept them without question. By questioning and finding answers through investigating, learners may discover ideas that very few others think about. That is the way science works. If every scientist passively accepted the works of others, very few discoveries would be made.

In teaching there is a tendency to accept the work of others without questioning. For example, there is a belief among educators that all children will learn exactly the same science content from an activity and teachers can guide them to learn the same content. Is this an unrealistic expectation? Are there data to support this belief? Doesn't this belief deny that children are unique? And what does it mean to children when they are told to ignore their own sets of data?

Accepting one's own set of facts develops self-confidence in the ability to learn and to trust one's own observations. Recognizing that learners do have different sets of facts creates vitality and spontaneity and affirms the individuality of each learner.

Classroom Activity 7.2 **Fact Gathering**

INSTRUCTIONS

1. As a group, choose one of the following questions to answer:
   - What causes electricity?
   - What causes magnetism?
   - What is visible light?

2. Write down your own answer to the question chosen by the group. Compare your answers.

3. Have each person in the group find three textbooks o___ give an answer to the question. Coordinate your efforts so ___ different resources.

4. If you have the opportunity, include a physics professor's answer as o___ three. Have only one person in the group seek out a physics professor's ans___

DISCUSSION QUESTIONS

- Were you able to give an answer before you went to other sources? Why or why not?

- How does your answer compare with answers found by others in the group?

- Did all sources give the exact same answer? Why or why not?

- Would you choose one of these answers over the others as a point of information for teaching a unit on the topic?

- After reading and discussing the answers provided by the different resources, write an answer to the question chosen by the group. What difficulties do you encounter?

- Do you think all scientists have the exact same answer when asked to explain a scientific concept?

- Scientist A, who is an expert in the field, reads the explanation of a given concept by Scientist B, who is also an expert in the same field. What might be the reaction of Scientist A to Scientist B's explanation?

- What are the implications of giving children facts rather than allowing them to learn through their own experiences?

Field Experience Activity 7.1

What Is the Rationale?

INSTRUCTIONS

Interview elementary classroom teachers who regularly teach mathematics and science to find out how they choose the topics they teach. Predict what they will say. The following are some responses you may hear.

- I choose these topics because they are in the book.

- I choose these topics because I like them.

- Other teachers like these topics.

- Research says these topics are appropriate.

- Considering research studies and my own research, I choose topics that are relevant to this age group.

DISCUSSION QUESTION

Which of the statements above reflects a decision based on opinions? Facts? Concepts?

Research Base for Curriculum Decisions

Facts are important and children will learn facts if they are taught properly. How do children learn and remember facts? More importantly, what is the role of intelligence in learning facts? Research has shown that the development of intelligence is necessary for children to learn facts. However, what is taught is often based on other rationales rather than the development of intelligence.

s mentioned before, science and mathematics units and activities are chosen based on opinions rather than research: "I teach $A = L \times W$ .use that is the way it is presented in the book." "I teach about food chains ause I like the activity." "I teach about magnets because it is fun." These inions say nothing about whether children are learning from the experience r whether children's intelligence is developing. However, there is a research base that can help determine which activities are appropriate for learning mathematics and science for the development of intelligence. Part of that research base is familiar to you because of your own learning experiences. Learning occurs through hands-on and relevant experiences. When you are actively engaged with your senses and your mind, you will remember those experiences. You also know that learning takes time and is an individualized experience. Your pace does not necessarily match the pace of other learners. One person may understand something in high school and another person may not understand it until college. Piaget (1974b) says, "Conceptualization lags behind action—clear proof that the latter is autonomous" (p. 214). In other words, understanding does not necessarily occur at the same time as the actions responsible for the learning.

Piaget formulated a theory to explain the development of intelligence and how facts are learned. His theory, as you already know, says that the development of intelligence and real learning occurs through concrete experiences. Piaget and his colleagues developed one-to-one interview procedures to probe children's thinking about particular concepts. In the majority of the books written by Piaget, he gives examples of the interviews. Despite the fact that most of Piaget's work was done during the first half of the twentieth century, these interviews can be replicated to find out what today's children think. Thus, his theory has credibility because his results can be verified.

Piaget's theory of intellectual development is the basis for the constructivist view of learning. He says that intelligence " . . . constitutes the state of equilibrium towards which tend all the successive adaptations of a sensorimotor and cognitive nature, as well as all assimilatory and accommodatory interactions between the organism and the environment" (1966, p. 11). This definition will be explained in further detail in the following paragraphs. Basically, this view says that the learner constructs knowledge.

A common belief holds that Piaget only studied his own three children to develop his theory. But Piaget began studying children before his own were born and his theory was developed over time. By 1967 he had already spent nearly fifty years observing and interviewing children of all ages. The observations and interviews provided enormous sets of empirical data for the foundation of his theory (Ginsburg and Opper, 1969). Piaget produced over 30 full-length books and more than a hundred articles. He continued researching and publishing well into his eighties, a span of more than 60 years. Phillips (1995) states that Piaget studied over 2,000 children during this time span.

Gardner's (1993) theory of multiple intelligence is also popular among educators. He defines intelligence in terms of problem solving or creating products. The theory of multiple intelligence is based on several sources of information: (1) development of different kinds of skills in normal children; (2) the way these skills break down under conditions of brain damage; (3) special populations of learning disabled children, autistic children, and prodigies; (4) cognition in diverse animal species; and (5) correlations among psychological tests. Gardner says:

Alas, the kind of material with which I was working didn't exist in a form that is susceptible to computation, and so we had to perform a more subjective factor analysis. In truth, we simply studied the results as best we could, and tried to organize them in a way that made sense to us, and hopefully to critical readers as well. (p. 8)

Thus, the multiple intelligence categories are a way to organize data about children who exhibit special abilities in different areas of learning. However, these categories do not explain the construction of intelligence in relation to special abilities.

Major Elements of Piaget's Theory of Intelligence

Through a series of stages children construct intelligence, just as they learn to walk. Even though Piaget gives ages for these different stages of development, he did not imply that children all go through these stages at the same time. These ages are the time at which the stages are most likely to develop. As you read the descriptions of each stage, think in terms of concepts developing through a series of stages.

Sensorimotor Stage (Infancy)

Infants learn to use actions to explore objects in their environment, and respond to environmental stimuli by actions of random movement. Actions become organized through repeated responses to the same stimuli. Organized patterns of behavior are called *schemes*. Through repetition, infants learn to control their actions in order to satisfy specific needs such as thumb sucking.

Piaget (Ginsburg and Opper, 1969) describes *egocentrism* as one's own viewpoint, which is more important than actual data or the viewpoints of others. Infants believe that when an object is out of sight, the object no longer exists. This is an egocentric view of the world. Through experience, children learn objects have permanence even though they themselves are not present. They learn that an object's existence does not depend on their own existence. This is part of the *decentering* process, an ongoing process in the formation of intelligence. Perceptions give way to logic. Ideas are formed from ideas. Egocentrism decreases as a child progresses from perceptions to the development of abstract ideas. Intelligence becomes multidimensional and includes the viewpoints of others. Thus, the decentering process begins at birth and continues throughout life as ideas and concepts take form and change with new information. Hands-on experiences are essential for the decentering process so children become less egocentric about their view of the world.

Preoperational Stage (Approximately 2 Years Old)

At this stage, concepts are dominated by perceptions. Knowledge is based on opinions and beliefs rather than facts. In other words, thoughts are influenced by what is perceived to be true rather than by ideas held constant. What the child perceives is considered reality. For example, think back to being two or three years old, watching the moon from a moving car and thinking that the moon was moving with the car, or thinking that railroad tracks actually did meet somewhere "way down the line." These are egocentric points of view. After you observed the moon over many years, you understood that the moon does not move. Walking along railroad tracks for miles and miles will convince a person that the tracks do not meet.

For a child who has not internalized "ten," the concept may change according to the size of objects. For example, ten cents may be perceived as a smaller amount than a five-cent coin because a dime is smaller than a nickel. Ten poker chips may seem to be larger than twenty pennies because the chips are bigger. The world of a preoperational stage child may seem chaotic and confusing. Adults who provide stable environments and support children's exploration of the world through hands-on activities are helping them gain constancy in their lives.

Children learn to express their experiences and to cope with perceived changes through expressing mental images in play, imitation, drawings, and language. These are symbolic expressions of their experiences. They imitate the actions of adults, other children, and even animals through role-playing. Language develops through these experiences. Piaget's (1974a) data support the notion that language develops from experience rather than the other way around. Language gives children tools to express their experiences. Duckworth (1987) says: "In sum, his early insight was that language often is a misleading indicator of the level of a child's understanding; a second insight was that there is a good deal of logic in children's actions that is not revealed by their verbal formation" (p. 16). Counting to ten, adding numbers, and using adult words can be done by imitation of adults and without understanding the concepts behind the words.

The interactions of young children with objects are described as play or free exploration. Children become immersed in their actions on objects. These actions are spontaneous and diversified. Children encounter many novel experiences that they want to examine thoroughly and seem to abandon any coherent plan of investigation. Through action on objects, children begin to see that there is order and stability in the world independent of their own perceptions.

Concrete Mental Operations Stage (Approximately 7 Years Old)

Concrete refers to understanding objects as real three-dimensional objects, not pictures, drawings, diagrams, and symbols that represent three-dimensional objects. A mental operation is the action on objects and the abstraction of those actions to create internalized ideas. During this stage, the learner begins to develop relationships about objects through actions and the senses. The acts of touching and manipulating objects and watching what happens are essential to developing logical relationships. Children gather facts about objects, such as their attributes or their spatial relationships with other objects. Generally at this age, children learn that no matter what they do to the object the idea remains constant. The idea of "ten" remains the same regardless of the configuration or the size of the objects. This is knowledge hard won.

Piaget refers to the internalization of ideas as *conservation*. Children know that the moon does not really move with the car they are riding in even though it looks that way.

The development of mental images and ideas is tied to reality or children's experiences with the environment. Facts gathered from experiences are abstracted to create *mental structures* that consist of related ideas or concepts. The core mental structures remain constant (internalized) regardless of perceptual data. A good analogy for understanding mental structures is an object constructed with Tinkertoys. The rods are the facts and the spools are the concepts. As the rods and spools are connected, a structure is formed. Once the structure is in place, additional facts (rods) can be added to expand the structure. To add more rods, more spools are needed. For example, roses and daisies are part of the class of flowers and are included within the concept of flower. The concept of flower is a spool. The colors, shapes, and other characteristics of roses and daisies are the rods. Class inclusion is the first level within the classification structures that are all formed from action upon objects. All of the classification structures form a group indicating relationships between the individual mental structures.

According to Inhelder and Piaget (1964), there are four classification structures and four ordering and seriation structures that form a group of classification and relations. Classification and relations structures are important to the formation of logic and reasoning. These structures, explained in detail in Chapter 8, are:

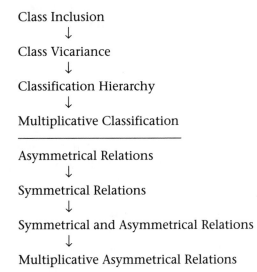

Class Inclusion
↓
Class Vicariance
↓
Classification Hierarchy
↓
Multiplicative Classification

Asymmetrical Relations
↓
Symmetrical Relations
↓
Symmetrical and Asymmetrical Relations
↓
Multiplicative Asymmetrical Relations

In addition to the *logical* groupings there are *infralogical* groupings. These groupings are based on the relationship of objects to one another and their spatial placements. (Chapter 9 is devoted to detailed explanations about spatial relations.) Infralogical groupings consist of spatial structures and time structures. Within the infralogical groupings, there are eight topological structures, eight projective structures, and eight Euclidean structures. Topological structures refer to the placement of objects on surfaces and their relationships to each other. Topological concepts include ideas such as beside, below, behind, to the right or left. Projective relationships refer to what can be seen of an object from different points of view. Objects can hide objects. Objects look different on one side than the other. Objects look different in relation to horizontal or vertical reference points. Shadows of objects take on different shapes and sizes in relation to the actual object. Euclidean structures deal with relationships of objects and the exact location of their position in three-dimensional space.

The number groups of additive whole numbers and multiplicative numbers develop from spatial relations and classification structures. Measurement groups of one and two dimensions assist in the location of objects with great precision. (Chapter 9 discusses measurement.) Phillips (1995) provides a detailed chart that shows the interrelationships among the various sets of structures: logical groupings of classification and relations as well as the infralogical groupings of topology, projective space, and Euclidean space.

Formal Operational Stage (Approximately 12 Years Old)

Formal operations involve mental operations on ideas rather than objects. Ideas are abstracted from ideas. Concepts are formed from concepts. Abstractions are made from abstractions. A child at the formal operational level is able to do the following when experimenting: properly design experiments, observe results accurately, and draw logical conclusions from the observations. Two basic formal operational structures are the combinatorial system and the INRC groups: identity (I), negation (N), reciprocity (R), and correlativity (C). Other structures include 16 binary operations, proportionality, probability, multiplicative compensations, correlation, multiple frames of reference, mechanical equilibration, and some conservation problems. The 16 binary operations are involved in the realm of hypothetical thinking. The experimenter imagines all of the possible determinants of the results (Ginsburg and Opper, 1969).

Influential Factors and Intelligence

Four factors affect intellectual development (Ginsburg and Opper, 1969): experience, physical maturity, social interactions, and equilibration. Exploring and manipulating objects to identify attributes (facts) are part of the definition of *experience*. The facts are attributes gleaned from the objects that the learner assimilates. Experience also involves abstracting specific ideas from the exploration. These are called *logico-mathematical* relationships. For example, the size of an object is an attribute of the object; the exact size is a relationship the learner derives by making comparisons to other objects, including comparison of height, diameter, placement, size, and number of objects in a given place. The relationships can be precise and quantified.

Children can have experiences with objects without forming relationships. But children do not arrive at school as empty vessels ready to be filled with facts, as described by Charles Dickens in *Hard Times*. Children have been experiencing the world since birth and bring knowledge to school that may or may not be based on perceptions or logic. Driver, Guesne, and Tiberghien (1985) have noted that children approach science and mathematics with preexisting ideas gained through experiences.

Physical maturation refers to the development of the brain. Children may not be ready to learn particular concepts because their brain may be lacking certain connections or synapses to process information. For example, five-year-olds are not capable of understanding the relationship between mass and volume.

Intellectual development is also influenced by interactions with other people. *Social interactions* are just as important to the decentering process as objects. Chapter 3 discussed the importance of social interactions to learning mathematics and science. Vygotsky's theory emphasizes social interactions as the most important factors in children's psychological development (Davydov, 1995). Children learn that there are other views of the world as well as differences in cultures. The interactions of primary children are egocentric. Observe kindergarten children and watch how they interact with each other. They want to express ideas and to be heard but do not necessarily hear what others say to them. As they interact with both objects and others, they gain similar experiences and can relate those experiences to each other by making comparisons of similarities and differences. Thus, cooperative groups are beneficial in terms of allowing children to mentally act upon the ideas of others, as was explained in Chapter 3. Piaget (1966) defines cooperation as the coordination of different viewpoints. Cooperation is mentally acting upon the ideas of others. Since cooperation is primarily a verbal experience, it is not a primary source of information. It requires abstracting ideas from the ideas of others, which may or may not be at the concrete or formal level. For example, a child who has not explored making tetrahedrons may encounter difficulty engaging in a conversation about geometrical theorems and proofs.

The concept of *equilibration* is the most important of the four factors affecting learning. Equilibration is the process of internalizing the abstractions formed from action on objects or ideas. When learning occurs ideas are assimilated and accommodated to existing mental structures. Piaget says that assimilation and accommodation occur together. *Assimilation* is the process of information becoming part of existing mental structures. *Accommodation* is the process of adapting the mental structure to the information that has been internalized. In a far-ranging discussion of educational concepts Piaget (Bringuier, 1980) said:

> Take, for example, an infant who's just discovered he can grasp what he sees; well, from then on, everything he sees is assimilated to the schemes of prehension, that is, it becomes an object to grasp as well as an object to look at or an object to suck on. But if it's a large object, for which he needs both hands, or if it's a very small object and he has to tighten the fingers of only one hand to grasp it, he will modify the scheme of prehension. (p. 43)

Again, using the Tinkertoy analogy, assimilation is adding new spokes and rods to the existing structure. Accommodation is the process of adapting and modifying the structure so that the new rods and spools can be added. Equilibration is never reached because human beings are continuously assimilating their environment and adapting the information. Piaget calls changes in understanding *transformations,* which he says are slow or occur over time. They are slow because sometimes new ideas are rejected. A person may not be ready for them because accepting the ideas may require a major overhaul in thinking. Thus, learning is *self-regulated.* Just as a person learns to regulate food intake, a person also regulates information acquired from experiences. Research data gathered by Driver, Guesne, and Tiberghien (1985) support this idea of self-regulated learning. Driver says: "It is often noticed that even after being taught, students have not modified their ideas in spite of attempts by a teacher to challenge them by offering counter-evidence" (p. 3).

Driver goes on to say that children have stable ideas until some factor changes them. For example, a child's physical brain may not be capable of equilibrating an idea or the experience does not lend itself to modifying the idea.

Piaget's theory of intellectual development is summarized in Figure 7.1.

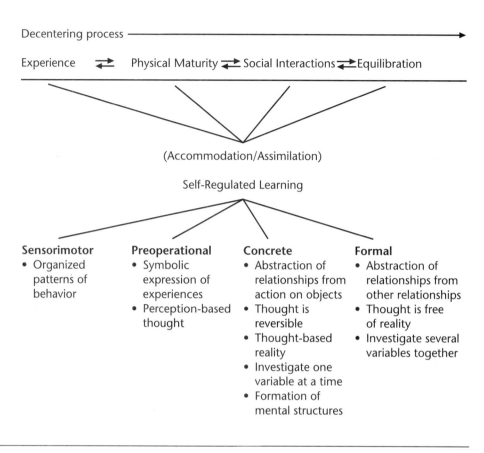

FIGURE 7.1
Summary of Piaget's Theory of Intellectual Development

Decentering process ⟶

Experience ⇄ Physical Maturity ⇄ Social Interactions ⇄ Equilibration

(Accommodation/Assimilation)

Self-Regulated Learning

Sensorimotor
- Organized patterns of behavior

Preoperational
- Symbolic expression of experiences
- Perception-based thought

Concrete
- Abstraction of relationships from action on objects
- Thought is reversible
- Thought-based reality
- Investigate one variable at a time
- Formation of mental structures

Formal
- Abstraction of relationships from other relationships
- Thought is free of reality
- Investigate several variables together

Classroom Activity 7.3

Group Discussion of Implications for Teaching

DISCUSSION QUESTIONS

▪ What are the implications of Piaget's theory for teaching mathematics and science?

▪ What types of teaching behaviors would be exhibited by a teacher who applies Piaget's theory?

▪ What would the physical learning environment of this teacher look like?

Children's Ideas about Selected Concepts

Piaget wrote extensively about children's development of understanding of the following concepts: movement and speed (1970); mirrors and reflections, weight and balance (1974b); concept of life, origin of the sun and moon, meteorology, origin of water, trees, mountains, and the earth (1979). Piaget also wrote about children's understanding of time (1969), classification and ordering (Inhelder and Piaget, 1964), and spatial relations (1967). A discussion of children's understanding of classification and ordering as well as spatial relations is presented in the following chapters.

Table 7.1 is drawn from research literature that discusses what elementary school children think about certain scientific concepts: energy, force, electricity, heat and temperature, light, earth science, and plants and animals. Wandersee, Mintzes, and Novak (1994), Osborne (1985), and Driver, Guesne, and Tiberghien (1985) have also presented data about the concepts listed in Table 7.1. The definitions in the table were drawn from Hazen and Trefil (1990), the American Association for the Advancement of Science (1989),

TABLE 7.1

What Do Scientists and Children Say?

Concept	Scientists say:	Children say:
Energy	■ The ability to perform useful work ■ Cannot be created or destroyed ■ Conversion from one type to another results in dispersion of energy from concentrated to less concentrated	■ Associated with living things, especially humans ■ Associated with images of movement and activity
Force	■ The thing that compels objects to change their state of motion ■ Objects continue in state of rest, or uniform motion in a straight line, unless compelled to change that state by forces impressed on them ■ For every action force there is an equal and opposite reaction force ■ Force equals mass times acceleration ■ Friction exists whether an object is moving or not ■ A force acts on a body causing changes in motion; forces can be acting in directions opposite to that of motion	■ When a force is applied to an object, it produces motion in the direction of the force ■ Under the influence of a constant force, objects move with constant velocity ■ The velocity of an object is proportional to the magnitude of the applied force ■ In the absence of force, objects are either at rest or, if moving, are slowing down ■ Force is inside an object ■ Friction is only associated with motion
Electricity	■ A circuit is a continuous path through material in which electrical charges can flow	■ Current leaves a battery and travels through one wire to a light bulb, which serves as a kind of electricity sink ■ Electricity leaves a battery from both terminals and travels toward a light bulb, where it is used up ■ Current flows in one direction through a circuit and becomes gradually weaker as it encounters successive components of a light bulb

**TABLE 7.1
(CONTINUED)
What Do Scientists and
Children Say?**

Concept	Scientists say:	Children say:
Electricity (continued)		■ Current flows in one direction and is distributed to and consumed equally by all components of the circuit; all bulbs achieve the same brightness ■ Current flows in one direction but follows laws of conservation of energy
Heat and Temperature	■ Heating and cooling cause change in motion of atoms ■ Atoms and molecules are perpetually in motion ■ The more vigorously molecules move, the greater the heat energy ■ Gas molecules are in constant motion ■ Empty space is found between particles ■ Temperature is a relative term to compare the motion of molecules in different objects ■ When the motion of molecules is the same in two bodies, the temperature is the same	■ Heat makes things rise ■ Heat and cold are material substances that are transferred from one object to another ■ Heat accumulates in some areas and flows to other areas ■ Large ice cubes take longer to melt than small ones because they are colder ■ Wax melts when heated because it is soft ■ Matter is continuous rather than particulate ■ There are no empty spaces between molecules
Light	■ A distinct entity located in space between its source and the effects it produces ■ Consists of electromagnetic waves that travel in all directions from the source ■ Travels in a straight line until it is absorbed or reflected by objects ■ Some electromagnetic waves are visible to the eye ■ Visible light is reflected from surfaces and detected by the eye	■ Brightens or illuminates objects ■ The eye reaches out and grabs images ■ The distance light travels depends on how far away the source is ■ Travels farther in the dark ■ Is in the sun, a light bulb, etc. ■ Is in a mirror

	Concept	Scientists say:	Children say:
TABLE 7.1 (CONTINUED) What Do Scientists and Children Say?	Earth Science	■ Earth's gravity decreases as the distance increases from the surface of the earth	■ Earth is flat ■ Earth is round but limited in space by a ceiling ■ Things fall down ■ Earth is round and bounded by limitless space; things fall down but not toward the center of the earth ■ Earth is round and bounded by limitless space; things fall toward the center of the earth ■ Gravity is associated with air ■ Gravity increases as the distance above the earth's surface increases; it is zero beyond the earth's atmosphere
	Plants and Animals	■ Plants synthesize their own food intracellularly ■ Animals consume energy-rich foods ■ Animals can move spontaneously and in rapid response to stimuli ■ Plants have cellulose cells	■ Animals are alive, have legs, move, have hair or fur, live outside or in the woods ■ Plants are alive and must eat ■ Plants are found in gardens ■ The heart is in the shape of a valentine; it cleans, filters, or manufactures the blood ■ Separate systems of tubes carry air to the heart and other body structures ■ Plants obtain food from the soil

Webster's (1987), and the National Research Council (1996). Some of the scientists' definitions have been simplified and some of the children's might raise eyebrows among scientists, but they reflect children's thinking. Remember that true understanding comes from primary sources of knowledge (hands-on experiences).

Discussion Activity 7.1   **Analyzing Children's Ideas**

Discuss Table 7.1 in terms of the definitions and what elementary school children think. Read what Foster (1996) found out about children's understanding of moon phases. What concepts do children need to understand moon phase formation?

DISCUSSION QUESTIONS

■ Think back to your childhood. What explanations did you have for the concepts in Table 7.1?

■ If you do not remember having any explanations, do you know why?

■ What are your current explanations for the concepts in Table 7.1? Are they different from what you understood as a child?

■ What cognitive levels (preoperational, concrete, or formal) must children have reached in order to understand the concepts in Table 7.1?

■ Why do children have alternative conceptions?

■ What are the implications of the data in Table 7.1 for teaching and learning science?

Field Experience Activity 7.2

Asking Children Questions

Visit an elementary school classroom and ask the teacher if you can interview individual children to find out what they understand about certain scientific concepts. Record their answers and bring them to class for discussion. Use the questions listed below or your own.

■ What is a plant?

■ What is an animal?

■ What is heat?

■ When a flashlight is turned on, why does the bulb light?

■ What is light?

■ What is gravity?

■ What causes moon phases?

The first answer children give may not reveal what they are thinking. Additional probing questions may have to be asked to get a better understanding of their thinking. Refer to Chapter 4 for suggestions about the types of questions to ask to reveal children's understanding.

Discussion Activity 7.2

Discussion of Standards and Piaget

Discuss the mathematics standard in the following Tour Guide in terms of the content of this chapter.

DISCUSSION QUESTIONS

■ How does this standard relate to Piaget's theory of intellectual development?

■ Are there mathematical concepts that children have difficulty understanding? What are they? Why would they be difficult?

■ As a child, what did you consider to be difficult mathematics concepts?

■ What are the implications for learning and teaching mathematics?

TOUR GUIDE

> *National Council of Teachers of Mathematics (1989)*
> *Standard 3: Mathematics as Reasoning*
>
> Children draw logical conclusions about mathematics using models, known facts, properties, and relationships to explain their thinking; justify their answers and solutions to processes; use patterns and relationships to analyze mathematical situations; and believe that mathematics makes sense. (K–4) (p. 29)
>
> Children recognize and apply deductive and inductive reasoning; understand and apply reasoning processes with special attention to spatial reasoning and reasoning with proportions and graphs; make and evaluate mathematical conjectures and arguments; validate their own thinking; appreciate the pervasive use and power of reasoning as a part of mathematics. (5–8) (p. 81)

Threads of Continuity

The beauty of Piaget's theory is that it has continuity and is holistic. Two main threads run throughout the theory. One thread is that learning occurs along a continuum. The construction of knowledge begins at birth and continues for a lifetime. At one end of the continuum, objects help to structure the world through play and exploration; at the other end, ideas help to structure the world. The senses of touch, taste, smell, hearing, and sight are the tools used to create mental frameworks that provide structures that continuously process information from the environment.

Infants begin processing information by learning how to coordinate actions to explore a foreign environment. As the child grows and the environment increases in familiarity, there is a need to communicate all of the processed information in the brain. Thus, the child expresses interpretations of the world through language, drawings, imagery, and writing. With a foundation in place, the child begins to form mental structures from objects in the environment. Finally, mental structures continue to form without acting upon objects. There is a continuum from the coordination of actions with objects to the coordination of ideas.

However, this continuum is not a smooth path with the learner progressing from one point to the next. The progression varies from concept to concept. A concept cannot be learned through formal operations before it is understood through concrete operations. This is also true in learning to walk. Infants learn to roll, then crawl on their stomachs, crawl on their knees and hands, learn to stand, and finally to walk. New concepts may only be understood perceptually. It is not until facts are gathered that concepts are supported by logic. Children who do not understand "number" as a concept cannot understand addition and subtraction. Children can memorize numbers and memorize how to add and subtract, but memorized knowledge is likely to crumble when put to the test because the knowledge is not internalized. That is one of the reasons why children who rely solely upon memorization are likely to do poorly on standardized tests. To construct knowledge means that the knowledge is internalized, forming a strong and stable foundation for future problem-solving situations.

A second common thread is that learning is uniquely individual and self-regulated. Heredity, social interactions, interests, and motivation are part of the self-regulation process, making the construction of knowledge highly variable. Infants who grow up in a nurturing, learning environment are provided with many objects. They decide whether to play with a particular toy. Parents know that not all toys will interest children. These parents are not likely to say to a child: "I want you to learn how to count with this toy." They accept the idea that children learn to count from a variety of toys when they are ready. However, school children are in an environment with restrictive choices for learning. All children in a class are expected to learn the same concepts, decided by the teacher, at the same time, and with the same materials.

Implications for Teaching and Learning Elementary School Science and Mathematics

1. Elementary school children's intellectual development is supported by the manipulation of concrete materials.
2. Children who have memorized content are more likely to have ideas based on perceptions than children who have learned facts through the manipulation of objects.
3. Each child must have his or her own sets of materials.
4. A variety of materials and experiences must be provided for children to learn any given concept.
5. Since learning occurs at different rates, the focus must be on the needs and interests of the individual learner.
6. Physical maturation, relevant experiences, social interactions, and equilibration influence learners' needs and interests.
7. Learning is facilitated through questioning and presenting discrepant events that create disequilibration about ideas.
8. Children must be allowed options for working by themselves or in groups.
9. Children may need concrete experiences for a given concept before they can benefit from working in a group.
10. Children must be allowed to take risks and explore their own ideas.
11. Learning is self-regulated and tolerance must be shown to children who are at different levels of understanding, rather than expecting all children to be at the same level.
12. Understanding mathematics and science concepts must begin with concrete objects rather than manipulating symbols.
13. Children will have varying interpretations of concepts even though they may work with the same object.

Piaget's theory of cognitive development is open to debate. However, his theory is based on facts collected through scientific research. These facts can be replicated through the same methods he used. The theory has stood up over time. It gives educators a base for making curricular decisions for teaching mathematics and science. It also explains the development of mental structures, which are used to assimilate and accommodate information acquired through hands-on experiences. These mental structures are the foundation for the development of logic. Chapter 8 examines these mental structures in detail.

> **Go back to the reflective questions at the beginning of the chapter and the answers you recorded in your journal.**
>
> **Add to or modify your answers based on what you learned from this chapter.**

Bibliography

American Association for the Advancement of Science. (1989). *Science for all Americans.* Washington, DC: Author.

Bringuier, J. (1980). *Conversations with Jean Piaget.* Chicago: The University of Chicago Press.

Capron, S., Brook, R., and Rieben, E. (1996). The high plains: Land of extremes. *Science and Children, 34*(1), 41–46.

Davydov, V. (1995). The influence of L. S. Vygotsky on education theory, research, and practice. (S. T. Kerr, Transl.). *Educational Researcher, 12,* 12–21.

Driver, R., Guesne, E., and Tiberghien, A. (1985). *Children's ideas in science.* Philadelphia: Open University Press.

Duckworth, E. (1987). *The having of wonderful ideas and other essays on teaching and learning.* New York: Teachers College Press.

Foster, G. (1996). Seeing the moon. *Science and Children, 34*(3), 30–33.

Gardner, H. (1993). *Multiple intelligences: The theory in practice.* New York: Basic Books.

Ginsburg, H., and Opper, S. (1969). *Piaget's theory of intellectual development: An introduction.* Englewood Cliffs, NJ: Prentice Hall.

Hazen, R., and Trefil, J. (1990). *Science matters.* New York: Doubleday.

Inhelder, B., and Piaget, J. (1964). *The early growth of logic in the child.* New York: W.W. Norton.

Inhelder, B., and Piaget, J. (1958). *The growth of logical thinking.* New York: Basic Books.

National Council of Teachers of Mathematics. (1989). *Curriculum and evaluation standards for mathematics.* Reston, VA: Author.

National Research Council. (1996). *National science education standards.* Washington, DC: National Academy Press.

Osborne, R. (1985). Children's own concepts. In W. Harlan (Ed.), *Primary science.* Oxford, England: Heinemann Educational.

Phillips, D. (1995). *Sciencing: Towards logical thinking.* Dubuque, IA: Kendall/Hunt.

Piaget, J. (1970). *The child's conception of movement and speed.* London: Routledge and Kegan Paul.

Piaget, J. (1979). *The child's conception of the world.* Totowa, NJ: Littlefield, Adams.

Piaget, J. (1974a). *The language and thought of the child.* New York: New American Library.

Piaget, J. (1974b). *Success and understanding.* London: Routledge and Kegan Paul.

Piaget, J. (1966). *The psychology of intelligence.* Totowa, NJ: Littlefield, Adams.

Piaget, J. (1969). *The child's conception of time.* New York: Basic Books.

Piaget, J., and Inhelder, B. (1967). *The child's conception of space.* New York: Norton Library.

Wandersee, J., Mintzes, J., and Novak, J. (1994). Research on alternative conceptions in science. In D. Gabel (Ed.), *Handbook of research on science teaching and learning.* New York: Macmillan.

Webster's ninth new collegiate dictionary. (1987). Springfield, MA: Merriam-Webster.

PART 3

The Constructed Framework

When children engage with learning processes they construct mental structures necessary for understanding scientific and mathematical ideas. Classification and ordering, the mental structures needed for organization of data, are discussed in Chapter 8. Spatial relations that are mentally constructed through hands-on activities are necessary to understand elements of geometry as well as many areas of biology (covered in Chapter 9), chemistry, and physics. Understanding measurement as a concept arises from experiences with spatial relations (Chapter 10). The theme of measurement is continued in Chapter 11, which presents activities that deal with forces and other physical science concepts. Chapter 12 also focuses on measurement, using appropriate biology and earth science activities.

CHAPTER 8 | Classes and Relations

We are so accustomed to the separation of knowledge from doing and making that we fail to recognize how it controls our conceptions of mind, of consciousness and of reflective inquiry.

J. Dewey, *The Quest for Certainty*

Reflective Questions

- According to Piaget, what are the mental operations that are important in the development of intelligence?

- How do the science and mathematics standards relate to these mental operations?

- What kinds of science and mathematics activities support the development of these mental operations?

- What are the characteristics of classification and ordering structures?

- What science and mathematics concepts are constructed through classification and ordering frameworks?

- How do mathematics symbols fit in the development of mathematical concepts and hands-on activities?

- Why are classification and ordering considered both processes and mental operations?

Introduction

In Chapter 6, classification and ordering were mentioned as basic processes used in learning. When children manipulate objects to form different kinds of groupings, they are actively engaged in the process. But when they are mentally acting upon the groups, children are developing classification and relations as mental operations. In this chapter, classification and relations will be examined in terms of the construction of the mental operations that are essential to understand basic mathematical and science concepts. Chapter 6 was about the processes or tools for learning; this chapter is about what is constructed when the tools are used.

The mental operations involve understanding relationships between objects according to differences between inherent characteristics and mathematical attributes. Phillips and Phillips (1996) provide an explanation that describes the differences between classification and relations. They explain that *classification* involves understanding parts to the whole in terms of undoing an action, for example, putting oranges with apples to make one group and then separating them into two separate groups. *Relationships* involve understanding parts to the whole in terms of where an object belongs according to a "*direction* of difference" (Phillips and Phillips, 1996). The number 5 is smaller than the number 9. The snake is longer than the worm. Jack is the brother of Sue. In each of these examples, a reverse statement can be made about the relationships but the relationships cannot be undone (Phillips and Phillips, 1996). In other words, the worm cannot become longer than the snake, nor can Sue become the brother of Jack, or 9 be smaller than 5.

Classification is an action and relations are verbal expressions of ordered relationships. Besides playing a role in the development of logic by creating mental structures, classes and relations are also processes since the mental operations are formed from the actions of the learner. The development of these structures is critical to organizing and understanding mathematical and scientific concepts. Their importance is reflected in the national science and mathematical standards.

TOUR GUIDE

> ### National Council of Teachers of Mathematics (1989)
> ### Standard 6: Number Sense and Numeration
>
> In grades K–4, the mathematics curriculum should include whole number concepts and skills so that students can construct number meanings through real-world experiences and the use of physical materials; understand our numeration system by relating, counting, grouping, and place value concepts; develop number sense; interpret the multiple uses of numbers encountered in the real world. (p. 38)
>
> ### National Research Council (1996)
> ### Content Standard B: Physical Science
>
> As a result of the activities all students should develop an understanding of properties of objects and materials.
> Physical science in grades K–4
> —Through observation, manipulation and classification of common objects, children reflect on the similarities and differences of objects. (p. 123)
> —In grades 5–8, students observe and measure characteristic properties to distinguish and separate one substance from another. (p. 149)

This chapter is about developing an operational sense through classification and relations that are relevant to addition, subtraction, multiplication, and division. Humans have given the world structure and organization through classification systems. By organizing objects, predictions can be made about them. For example, we can predict that oranges will be found with grapefruits and tangerines in the grocery store. We can also predict that there might be some unknown fruit that has the same characteristics as oranges and grapefruits. The periodic table was developed for such purposes. The periodic table is organized around the properties of chemical elements such as their physical attributes and characteristics of their atoms. The organization of the elements provided scientists a way to predict and find new and missing ones. Numbers have an order according to their place values and sizes. The terms fractions, ratios, and decimals describe relationships between parts to the whole.

Discussion Question

- What are the implications of the following statement for teaching and learning mathematics and science? "Classification is the doing and undoing of actions; relations are expressions of ordered differences."

Classification

Preclassification

Children progress through four preclassification stages before they begin classifying objects by attribute relationships (Inhelder and Piaget, 1964). These preclassification stages are:

1. Objects are placed in random order.

2. Objects are placed side by side in rows (trains). The child may be making patterns from attributes, e.g., shape, color, or size. For example, there may be rows of triangles, followed by rows of squares, and then rows of circles. These triangles, squares, and circles within each row or train may be different sizes and colors. The main characteristic of this stage is a continuous row of objects. The patterns of objects are side by side in a spatial arrangement.

3. Objects are placed to create symbolic representations of other objects. Children name the representations, such as "house," "dog," "moon," "sun," or "car." Remember from Chapter 7 that the preoperational stage is characterized by symbolic representation (graphic).

4. Objects are placed according to the same observable characteristic (groups). For example, the child makes groups according to color only. One group is red, another group is yellow, and another is blue. All red objects are piled in a group by themselves. Each color is in its own pile. They are distinct groups based on an attribute of the objects.

Phillips and Phillips (1996) describe a task interview to assess whether a child is working at the preclassification levels. The investigator interviews one child at a time using 37 paper shapes that consist of right and isosceles triangles, rectangles, squares, circles, semicircles, and half-rings in two different sizes and four different colors (see Figure 8.1).

The interview begins with the following question: "Here I have a set of objects. Can you put the objects together that go together?"

If the child creates piles of objects according to a single attribute, the following question can be asked: "Is there any other way that you can put the objects together that go together?"

Figure 8.2 shows examples from interviews conducted with kindergarten children.

Classroom Activity 8.1

Assessment of Examples in Figure 8.2

GOAL

- To identify the preclassification level for each example in Figure 8.2

DISCUSSION QUESTION

- At which level is a child likely to group the objects another way?

FIGURE 8.1

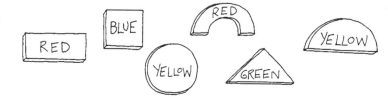

The author interviewed 60 kindergarten children and found that their responses varied, with no significant differences in the percentages of particular classification categories. Not only did children display the four major categories but also combinations of these categories. Intermediate levels between the four distinct levels might be (1) random order and trains, (2) trains and graphic representation, or (3) graphic representation and groups.

Field Activity 8.1

Interview Kindergarten Children

INSTRUCTIONS

Use the task interview in Phillips and Phillips (1996) to interview kindergarten children. Or give children sets of buttons or seeds and observe how they place the objects. Your set should include at least thirty to forty objects with a variety of different attributes. Interview three to four children and identify the levels that the children exhibit. Ask them if there is any other way they can group the objects.

Ask the following questions so that everyone is doing the interview the same way:

"Here I have some objects." (Show the objects to the child.) "Can you put the objects together that go together?" (Give the entire set of objects to the child.)

Allow enough time for the child to arrange the objects. After the child has completed the arrangement ask: "Is there any other way you can put together the objects that go together?"

Make drawings of the child's arrangements and bring them to class for discussion.

Classroom Activity 8.2

Observable Attributes

GOAL

- To collect observable characteristics for the purpose of classifying

MATERIALS

- One set of Creature Cards (Alberti, Davitt, Ferguson, and Oakey, 1974) per person

The creatures in the first row on the cards have the same characteristic(s). The creatures in the second row do not have that same characteristic(s). The third row consists of creatures with the characteristics of those of the first and second rows.

INSTRUCTIONS

Work in small groups. Discuss the attributes and decide which creatures in the third row have the same attributes as the creatures in row 1. It will take about fifteen minutes.

FIGURE 8.2

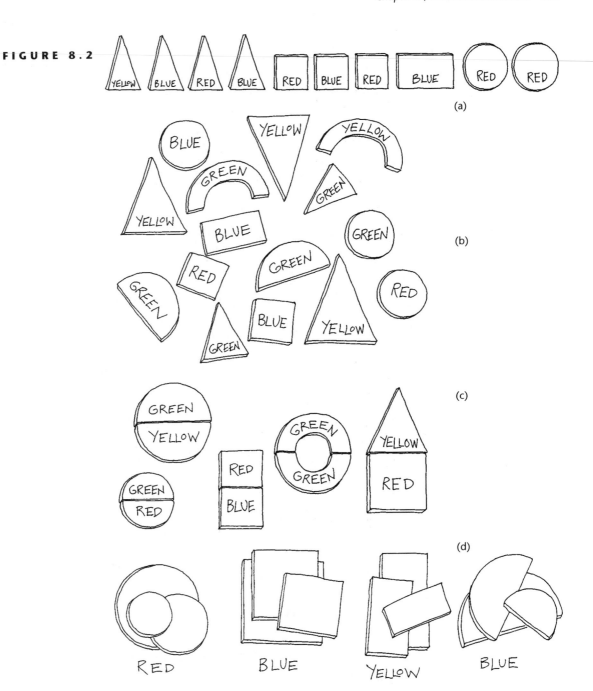

(a)

(b)

(c)

(d)

DISCUSSION QUESTIONS

■ What kinds of characteristics did you use to determine whether or not a creature belonged to the named group?

■ What do all of the characteristics on the cards have in common?

■ Why are these cards more effective for focusing on observable characteristics than using pictures of such things as animals, fruits, flowers, or vegetables?

FIGURE 8.3

Class Inclusion

Classification that describes the relationship between groups based on groups within groups is called *class inclusion* (Inhelder and Piaget, 1964). Both groups are related because they are part of the same set. The development of class inclusion as a mental structure is important in understanding addition and subtraction. For example, three red apples plus two green apples makes five apples. Or the reverse is true; take away two green apples and you have three red apples left of the apple group. Figure 8.3 illustrates class inclusion of apples. This is the first level of true classification (Inhelder and Piaget, 1964). Remember, classification involves creating, through actions, relationships between objects according to characteristics or attributes. Class inclusion is a concrete mental operation because relationships are based on images of real objects. The object does not have to be present; mental images from prior experiences can be used. Children who understand concepts at the concrete level base their thoughts on reality. Children who are at the preclassification level do not mentally "see" relationships between groups of objects.

Classroom Activity 8.3

Class Inclusion

GOAL

■ To understand class inclusion by using objects

MATERIALS

■ One set of plastic creatures per person

Creatures can be purchased from toy stores or teachers' equipment stores. The creatures should not be familiar farm or wild animals, insects, or dinosaurs. Find plastic creatures that represent fictitious beings from another planet or an unknown land. Each set should contain 15 different creatures that differ in color, shape, texture, or some other observable characteristic.

INSTRUCTIONS

1. Examine and identify the observable attributes of the objects.
2. List the characteristics you used to make the groups.
3. How many different groups can you make with your objects?
4. Make two groups using some of the objects. Name each group. Let's say that you name one group the humibugs and the other goup the fluffyduffs.

DISCUSSION QUESTIONS

■ Are there more humibugs or creatures? Why?
■ Are there more fluffyduffs or creatures? Why?

FIGURE 8.4

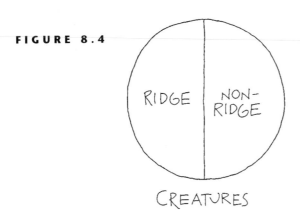

FIGURE 8.5

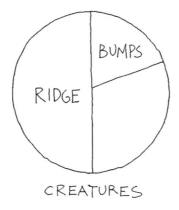

- If all of the humibugs are taken away, are there any creatures left? Why?
- If all of the creatures are taken away, are there any fluffyduffs left? Why?

Class Vicariance

Suppose we have some plastic creatures arranged in rows. Assume that the first row contains creatures with ridges, and the second row contains creatures without ridges. The group with no ridges is the counterpart to the group with ridges in relation to the overall group of creatures. Figure 8.4 illustrates that the ridge and nonridge groups together complete the entire group of creatures. It is like the phrase from the song: "You can't have one without the other!"

This relationship is called *class vicariance.* But what if the second row were called bumps rather than nonridges? What would the figure look like? See Figure 8.5.

Ridges and bumps limit the set of creatures because we know they have other characteristics as well. There may be creatures with spines or other protrusions similar to bumps. Which name, bumps or nonridges, would accommodate spines or other protrusions? The "non" category defines the remainder of the group by including *all* possible characteristics of the entire group of creatures. The "non" category gives the group completeness. Thus, mathematically, parts to the whole that express ratios, proportions, percentages, and fractions are expressing those groups that are part of a larger group.

Classroom Activity 8.4	**Class Vicariance**

GOAL

- To understand class vicariance by creating your own set of Creature Cards

GRADE LEVELS

- Middle to upper

INSTRUCTIONS

1. Make a row of five plastic creatures that have an observable characteristic in common. Give the row a name.

2. Make a second row of five plastic creatures that do not have the characteristic found in the first row.

3. Create a third row with creatures that have characteristics of the first row as well as characteristics of the second row.

4. Ask another classmate to identify objects in the third row that have the same characteristics as the objects in the first row.

5. Take turns doing this.

Classification Hierarchy

A *classification hierarchy* consists of relationships that are both horizontal and vertical. Groups, subgroups, and groups within subgroups are all related. A classification hierarchy of dogs, for example, shows relationships between different breeds. Shelties and sheepdogs are subgroups of collies; standard poodles and miniature poodles are subdivisions of poodles. See Figure 8.6a.

The same thing can be done with numbers by making a factor tree (Figure 8.6b). At each level the two factors are identified. The 2s and the 3 are prime numbers. Thus 2 times 2 is 4; 4 times 2 is 8; 8 times 3 is 24. This clearly indicates the relationship between 24, its factors, and its prime numbers. Thus, a classification hierarchy can be made with or without the "non" category.

Classroom Activity 8.5	**Binary Classification Hierarchy**

GOAL

- To create a binary classification system, based on dividing into two groups at each level and using the "non" category as one of the groups

GRADE LEVELS

- Middle to upper

MATERIALS

- 14 plastic creatures, different in size, shape, color, or texture

FIGURE 8.6

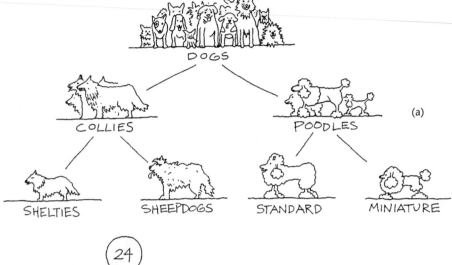

(a)

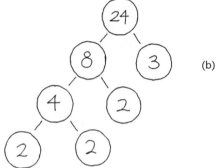

(b)

FIGURE 8.7

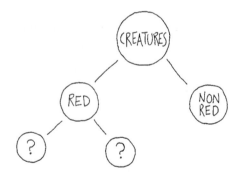

INSTRUCTIONS

1. Create a hierarchy by dividing the creatures into two groups until each creature ends up in its own category. Figure 8.7 is an example that illustrates how the binary system will begin to take shape as you classify the creatures.

2. Continue the hierarchy until you have used all 14 of the creatures. Each creature should end up in its own category.

3. Create a name for your entire group of creatures.

DISCUSSION QUESTIONS

■ How many levels will you have altogether if you place all 14 creatures in their own category?

Once you have completed your hierarchy, take a fifteenth creature and see where it fits in your hierarchy.

- Did you have to make major changes to make it fit?
- If the binary system were not used, would that have created problems in placing the object? Explain.

Exchange your hierarchy and creatures with a classmate. Use each other's creatures and binary chart and place the creatures in the correct categories. After both of you have completed the task, explain to each other why you placed the objects in particular categories.

- Did you both make the exact same hierarchy? Why or why not?
- What are the implications for the development of scientific classification systems?
- When working with a partner's hierarchy, was there any difficulty placing the objects in the correct places? Explain.
- What makes it easy or difficult to place the objects in the correct places?

Think about your experiences learning classification systems.

- If you studied biology, how did you learn about the classification of animals and plants?
- If you studied chemistry, did you have to memorize the periodic table of elements or were you allowed to reflect on and reason out the development of the chart?
- What are the implications for children learning classification?
- What numerical symbol is used in mathematics for the "non" category?
- How are binary numerical systems used?
- What does Classroom Activity 8.5 say about memorizing terms and concepts?

The hierarchy that you developed is a good illustration of the relationship between facts and concepts. The entire chart represents the concept "creature." The facts are the attributes or observable data (shape, color, size, etc.) used to create the different levels. The lines and levels represent the different relationships between the objects. Not only does each sublevel represent attributes of the creatures, they also represent subconcepts of "creature." The concept "creature" is made up of many attributes.

Attributes give definition to concepts. Children learn language by identifying attributes and naming them. Language develops by observing objects and their attributes. Remember, science is an organized body of knowledge. Your classification system of creatures is an organized body of knowledge. Mathematics is used to quantify the relationships within the hierarchy. The hierarchy presents a visual representation of mentally structured knowledge. Knowledge is constructed and structured by creating relationships between facts and concepts. Assimilation and accommodation are the processes of adding new data to existing structures (adding the extra creature) and modifying the mental structure to accommodate the new data.

Again, think about the importance of the "non" category. Did you use the "non" category in your hierarchy? Why or why not? What are the advantages

FIGURE 8.8

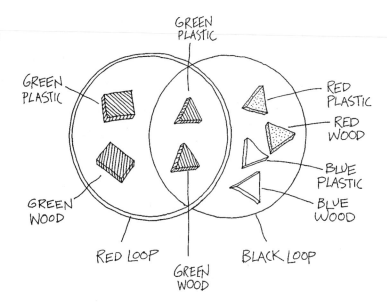

of using the "non" category? A binary system based on the "non" category is called a *dichotomy*. A group can be divided into two subgroups by naming one of the groups by a characteristic and naming the other group the opposite or "non" category. For example, a group is divided by the characteristic of color into the red group and the nonred group. A plant has green leaves or non-green leaves to distinguish photosynthesizing plants from fungi. Numbers are either positive or negative, prime or nonprime, even or uneven. One category complements the other.

The "non" category is important in solving problems because the range of solutions is almost unlimited. For example, an algorithm is a finite set of steps to solve a problem. However, if we think about nonalgorithms, we open up a whole range of possibilities. Thus, classification hierarchies are important in everyday living. But remember that putting people into groups and nongroups has created barriers and conflicts. When working with children of different racial, ethnic, cultural, and religious backgrounds, focus on individuals and their unique characteristics. Promote harmony among people rather than viewing humans as having only group characteristics.

Multiplicative Classification

A higher level of classification beyond hierarchies is multiplicative classification. At this level, classification involves understanding specific characteristics shared by more than one group (Phillips and Phillips, 1996). These shared characteristics can be between one set of attributes to several attributes or between several attributes to several attributes. For example, objects can be squares that are green and either plastic or wood. Another group can be red, blue triangles that are plastic or wood. What is the relationship between these two sets of objects? Study Figure 8.8.

The intersection illustrates what the objects have in common. Figure 8.8 is also called a *Venn diagram,* which is used to illustrate multiplicative relationships. A child who understands Venn diagrams understands class inclusions and hierarchies. Variables that affect the outcomes of experiments can be thought of as attributes.

FIGURE 8.9

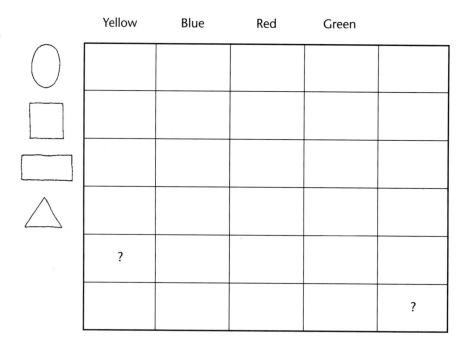

Two or more criteria are considered at the same time, which is illustrated in the matrix in Figure 8.9. The attribute in the columns is color and the attribute in the rows is shape. Objects can be identified according to shape and color. The object that goes in the first cell is a yellow oval. A child can take the objects and put them in the correct place in the matrix.

Discussion Questions

■ What objects would go in the boxes with question marks?

■ How are matrices useful to scientists and mathematicians?

Let's use a 2×2 matrix, Figure 8.10, as an example.* The colors yellow and red can be represented as symbols (C = color, R = red, and Y = yellow). Their relationship would look like the following: $C = Y + R$. The same can be done for the attribute of shape. *Sh* will represent shape, O will represent oval, and S will represent square. Their relationship can be stated as follows: $Sh = O + S$. Putting the two relationships together will create the following expression: $C \times Sh = (Y + R) \times (O + S)$. Since $\times$ means times, $C \times Sh$ represents multiple relationships that consist of yellow plus red that intersect with oval plus square. What we have is yellow oval plus red oval plus yellow square plus red square, which can be expressed as $C \times Sh = YO + RO + YS + RS$.

Matrices are useful in understanding algebra. In algebra, letters represent numbers. Here the terms of one equation are multiplied by the terms of another equation. The result is yellow ovals (YO) plus red ovals (RO) plus yellow squares (YS) plus red squares (RS). Each one represents an intersection of two attributes.

*This discussion is adapted from Phillips and Phillips (1996).

FIGURE 8.10

	Yellow	Red
○	yellow oval	red oval
☐	yellow square	red square

TOUR GUIDE

> ### National Council of Teachers of Mathematics (1989) Standard 9: Algebra
>
> In grades 5–8, the mathematics curriculum should include explorations of algebraic concepts and processes so that students can—
> understand the concepts of variable, expression, and equation; represent situations and number patterns with tables, graphs, verbal rules, and equations and explore the interrelationships of these representations; develop confidence in solving linear equations using concrete, informal, and formal methods; investigate inequalities and nonlinear equations informally; apply algebraic methods to solve a variety of real-world and mathematical problems. (p. 102)

Relations: Seriation and Ordering

There are two main differences between seriation and classification. The first is that a relation can be perceived while a class as such cannot, and the second is that a serial configuration constitutes a "good form" perceptually. (Inhelder and Piaget, 1964, p. 247)

Ordinal relations involve placing objects according to differences that increase or decrease. For example, dowel rods are placed in order according to their length. (See Figure 8.11.) This order can be in either direction.

A child can take a group of randomly placed different-sized rods and perceptually place the sticks in order because a perceptual design is created. However, when asked to insert other rods of different lengths, the child may not be able to complete the task. This is because he or she sees the original set as a whole and has difficulty breaking it apart while maintaining the "good form" (Inhelder and Piaget, 1964). Let's use a set of numbers: 3, 11, 2, 20, 15, 16, 10. These can be ordered as 2 > 3 > 10 > 11 > 15 > 16 > 20 or they could be ordered in the reverse. A child who is asked to place 5 and 13 in the correct order within this group of numbers may look at each number in the arrangement as being independent of the others. Another child may place 5 and 13 correctly because he or she can mentally picture their placement by thinking about the whole arrangement.

Ordinal relations can be gradations of differences for a single characteristic, such as sound, height, diameter, color, length, or weight. Understanding

FIGURE 8.11

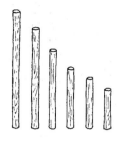

FIGURE 8.12

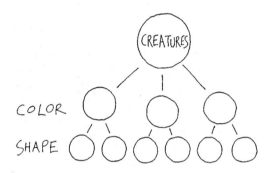

ordinal relations is important in understanding basic ideas of mathematics. A child can memorize the numbers from 1 to 100 but if the child is asked if 35 is bigger than 55, he or she may not understand the difference conceptually.

The first level of relations is *asymmetrical* because the relation is ordered according to direction. The next level of relations is *symmetrical*. Phillips and Phillips (1996) illustrate the symmetry by using family relations. Ted is the brother of Sam and Sam is the brother of Ted. This relationship is expressed in both directions simultaneously. Each relationship is equal and not directional. A mathematical example is the following: The teacher asks Susie to give every student in the room a ruler. There are 22 children in the class but Susie picks up only 21 rulers. Why did Susie only pick up 21 rather than 22 rulers?

The next level of ordering is a combination of *symmetrical and asymmetrical relations* found in a classification hierarchy. Each level of the hierarchy uses the same criterion: color, shape, or some other characteristic. For example, "creature" is the group of objects. The first division may be by color and the second division may be by shape. Each division has the same number of groups. "Color" may have three groups and "shape" two groups because each group on the first level may be divided into colors. Those groups may be further divided by shape. Each group at a particular level is divided by the same number. For example, the first level may have three groups and those three groups are divided into two groups at the next level. Figure 8.12 illustrates this point. The symmetry is at each level (horizontal). Asymmetry is created by following a line of attributes vertically (Phillips and Phillips, 1996).

The final level of relations is the *multiplication of two or more series of asymmetrical relations* (Inhelder and Piaget, 1964). A set of dowels can be ordered by two attributes: length and diameter. Figure 8.13 illustrates the relationships between the dowels. The rows show increases in length and the columns show increases in diameter. The order of objects is determined by adhering to two criteria at the same time.

You might remember seeing a matrix hanging in your chemistry class: the periodic table of chemical elements. The elements are ordered according to the

FIGURE 8.13

Diameter (mm)	Length (cm)					
	5	8	10	15	20	22
1						
4						
6						
8						
10						
15						
20						

number of electrons each has, which creates rows of elements with similar properties. For example, the column of helium, neon, argon, krypton, xenon, and radon have two electrons in their outer shells. They are all gases. This ordering of known objects was conceived by Mendeleyev in 1869. As new elements were discovered, their characteristics aided scientists in placing them on the periodic table. Blank spaces within rows were soon filled. As the search for new elements continues, scientists have an available framework for their placement. Asymmetrical matrices are valuable for organizing data and making predictions from the data.

■ How does the matrix relate to mathematics? Find mathematical matrices that are useful for making computations.

Table 8.1 summarizes the stages of classification and relations.

Summary

Classification and relations are not only processes but also mental structures important to the development of logic. Logic involves understanding the relationships of groups or classes and ordering or seriation. Children develop these relationships by using their senses to interact with objects and their characteristics. Classification and relations involve more than just grouping things according to various observable characteristics. The relationships among the objects can have various levels and multiple attributes.

Traditional ways of learning classifications in biology require children to memorize the characteristics of plants and animals from pictures, photographs, illustrations, and videos. But requiring children to memorize existing classification schemes is a lesson in futility. They are being asked to memorize someone else's data, which is a secondary source of information. Photographs, pictures, diagrams, illustrations, and videos do not adequately represent the actual objects. Visual representations limit objects' characteristics because they may be neither in proportion nor multidimensional. Children must explore objects from all angles and observe all of the characteristics with all their senses, not just sight. Language and especially the under-

TOUR GUIDE

> ### National Council of Teachers of Mathematics (1989)
> ### Standard 3: Mathematics and Reasoning
>
> In grades K–4, the study of mathematics should emphasize reasoning so that students can—
>
> draw logical conclusions about mathematics; use models, known facts, properties, and relationships to explain their thinking; justify their answers and solution processes; use patterns and relationships to analyze mathematical situations; believe that mathematics makes sense. (p. 29)
>
> In grades 5–8, reasoning shall permeate the mathematics curriculum so that students can—
>
> recognize and apply deductive and inductive reasoning; understand and apply reasoning processes, with special attention to spatial reasoning and reasoning with proportions and graphs; validate their own thinking; appreciate the pervasive use and possession of reasoning as a part of mathematics. (p. 81)
>
> ### Standard 4: Mathematical Connections
>
> In grades K–4, the study of mathematics should include opportunities to make connections so that students—
>
> link conceptual and procedural knowledge; relate various representations of concepts or procedures to one another; recognize relationships among different topics in mathematics; use mathematics in other curriculum areas; use mathematics in their daily lives. (p. 32)

standing of mathematical and scientific terminology develops from the exploration of objects using all the senses.

For example, I remember learning that an elephant is a mammal, but my only source of information was the writing and photographs found in books. This had little meaning until I was able to stand next to an elephant and feel its skin. I saw and touched the hairs on its body, which are characteristic of mammals. Most colored photographs do not show fine details. It is the touching and seeing at the same time that is convincing. The word *mammal* took on a new meaning for me.

There are multiple characteristics used to place an animal in the mammal category. Children who are asked to memorize these characteristics only through pictures are deprived of experiencing reality through the senses. Their own classification structures are not developed, but they must memorize the characteristics anyway. In that case children who have difficulty memorizing are considered poor learners.

It is important for children to be actively engaged in classification as a process to construct mental operations, which can then be used to solve everyday problems. Understanding classification and relations is important in many mathematical operations. By grouping, regrouping, and counting objects in groups, children learn to add and subtract. Younger children learn that symbolic representations of numbers (written or verbal) always represent the same quantity, no matter the arrangement. They also learn that numbers have particular values, which are larger or smaller in relation to other numbers. Comparing objects and their sizes leads to understanding characteristics of

TABLE 8.1
Summary of Class and Relation Mental Operations

PRECLASSIFICATION		
*Stages**	*Descriptions*	*Concepts*
Random	Individual objects are scattered	None
Rows	Objects are placed side by side (usually horizontally) whether the same or different	None
Graphic	Objects are placed together to create shapes of other objects	None
Groups	Objects are placed in piles having one attribute in common	None
CLASSIFICATION		
*Stages**	*Descriptions*	*Concepts*
Class Inclusion	Relationships between groups, based on groups within groups	Addition and subtraction
Class Vicariance	Parts to the whole, groups that are part of a larger group	Ratios, proportions, percentages, and fractions
Classification Hierarchy	Horizontal and vertical relationships	Biological classification systems
Multiplicative Classification	Specific characteristics shared by more than one group	Venn diagrams Matrices Algebra
RELATIONS		
*Stages**	*Descriptions*	*Concepts*
Asymmetrical	Gradation of differences for a single category; objects create a whole with "good form"; directional	Placing numbers in order
Symmetrical relations	Relationships expressed in both directions at the same time	Family relationships
Symmetrical and asymmetrical relations	Part of classification hierarchies; each level uses the same criterion	Biological classifications
Multiplicative asymmetrical relations	Objects ordered according to more than one attribute	Periodic table of chemical elements

*Stages are listed in developmental order for preclassification, classification, and ordering.

numbers such as decimals, ratios, and fractions. By expressing these relationships orally, children learn place values and can then express them in written symbolic form.

When children create matrices, Venn diagrams, and hierarchies with objects, they are learning about multiplication and division. Understanding mathematical relationships begins with arranging and rearranging objects and expressing these relationships. Eventually children can replace the objects with symbols. These symbols can be words as well as numbers.

The development of classification and relations is critical because these operations provide a structure for understanding scientific and mathematical relationships. Classification and ordering allow children to construct ideas, explore the world, and explain it.

TOUR GUIDE

> *National Council of Teachers of Mathematics (1989)*
> *Standard 6: Number Sense and Numeration*
>
> In grades K–4, the mathematics curriculum should include whole number concepts and skills so that students can—
>   construct number meanings through real-world experiences and the use of physical materials; understand our numeration system by relating, counting, grouping, and place value concepts; develop number sense; interpret the multiple use of numbers encountered in the real world. (p. 38)
>
> *National Research Council (1996)*
> *Content Standard B: Properties of objects and materials (K–4)*
>
> Objects have many observable properties, including size, weight, shape, color, temperature, and the ability to react with other substances. (p. 127)

Classroom Activities

Primary (K–4) Classrooms

In general, children in the primary grades are on a developmental continuum. Activities must be designed to take into account this range of individual differences. Studying the attributes of objects assists children through a logical and sequential approach to mathematics. First, they learn about the attributes of objects by grouping according to those attributes. As they work with objects and make various groupings, they can be encouraged to orally express the mathematical relationships. These verbal expressions represent fundamental story problems and they can create real or fictitious stories by using the objects. For example, Jack buys 10 black beans and 5 brown beans. How many beans does he have altogether? Besides helping with language development, verbal expressions help children conceptualize and relate ideas with their actions.

Next, expressions can be represented through symbolism. However, it is important to keep the objects with the verbal representations. For example, a child working with a set of beans counts 10 beans in the set. The words "ten beans" can be printed on paper and placed with the beans. Eventually the symbol "10" can be substituted and placed by the beans. Finally, children can work with symbols only. By this time they should understand the concept of numbers and other mathematical relationships such as addition and subtraction. As children group and regroup their beans they can learn multiple mathematical operations. These processes can be represented as words and eventually as symbols. (See Baratta-Lorton, 1979.) Table 8.2 summarizes how a teacher might help children learning mathematics concepts progress from concrete objects to symbols. The teacher's questions are only suggestions and do not imply an ordered series of steps. The questions depend on individual children and what they understand.

Primary classrooms should have a variety of sets of objects that children can classify or order using the observable attributes of the objects. Sets should have at least 50 objects with a variety of attributes such as length, color, diameter, texture, and shape. With a variety of sets, children can choose according to their interests and ability levels. Sets can be stored in containers such as gallon plastic milk containers with the tops cut off, washtubs, coffee cans, plastic storage containers, or resealable plastic bags. Label the containers so that children can associate the word with the objects. Clear containers are ideal so that children can see the objects that are inside. Have the containers readily accessible so that children can retrieve them and return them where they were found. Encourage children to empty the contents in their work area so that they can see each individual piece. Define each child's work area and encourage him or her to stay within those boundaries. Boundaries can be imaginary or real by using hula hoops, jump ropes, spaces between desks and tables, or carpeted areas. Children should work on the floor so that pieces do not fall off desks and tables. Remember, children need to have real objects, not pictures, drawings, or diagrams of objects. For example, pictures of fruit are inappropriate for classifying. Children need to see the actual sizes, colors, and shapes and how they feel to the touch.

If the following types of classification and ordering sets are available to you, examine them in terms of the number and kinds of attributes children can use to create a variety of groups.

Examples of Sight and Touch Sets

Seeds and Nuts

Use vegetable and fruit seeds such as beans, watermelon seeds, corn kernels, sunflower seeds, pumpkin seeds, squash seeds, and peas. The seeds should not be so small that their characteristics cannot be observed or that children will have difficulty handling them. Nuts such as walnuts, peanuts, hickory nuts, almonds, and pecans are abundant during holiday seasons.

Make mixtures of seeds or nuts and place them in Ziploc bags. These can be used for classification and ordering. Other sets of seeds of the same kind can be placed in baby food and canning jars (pints and quarts). These seed containers can be used for addition and subtraction, multiplication and division, and estimation. After estimating how many seeds are in a jar, children can go through the process of finding out exactly how many seeds the jar actually contains. Provide containers of various sizes so that they can create sets and multiply them instead of counting each individual seed.

Seeds can be purchased at grocery, hardware, and gardening stores. Ethnic grocery stores will have a variety of seeds from other countries. Children can find out about the countries where the seeds are produced.

Child's Actions	Concepts	Teacher's Questions
Explores object attributes	Discriminates attributes	Are there other ways to put the object together? Why did you put these here?
Creates individual groups	Number	What other ways can you make groups? Why did you put these in this group? How many objects are in this group? Here is the word for "five." Place it with the five group. Write out the number words and place them by the appropriate piles. Here is the symbol for "5." Place it with the appropriate group. Write out the number symbols and place them by the appropriate groups.
Moves objects from group to group	Addition and subtraction	Can you keep the same number of objects in your group? If you put these two groups together, how many do you have? If you take these away, how many are left in the group? Explain what you are doing when you make new groups. Make a story about what you are doing and tell me about it. I can write down what you are doing or you can do it. The phrase "2 beans plus 2 beans equals 4" is written on the card. Show me how you would represent the phrase with the beans. I have written the symbols 2 + 2 = 4. Can you show that to me with your beans?
Creates multiple groups and groups within groups Creates hierarchies and matrices with the objects	Multiplication and division	Make a drawing to show how the different piles are related to each other. Place the objects in a row according to size. Make a row that goes down using another attribute. Put the appropriate objects in the rows. (The same series of questions as for addition and subtraction can be used to have children express their actions orally and then with symbols.)

Feathers

Purchase different sizes, textures, and colors of feathers at craft stores.

Nuts and Bolts

Purchase different sizes of nuts and bolts at hardware stores.

Nails

Find different sizes and types of nails at hardware stores.

Wooden Dowels

Use dowels of various lengths and diameters. The ends can be painted different colors to add another observable characteristic.

Buttons

Choose buttons that have different colors, textures, diameters, shapes, and number of holes.

Yarn

Yarn is available in various diameters, lengths, colors, and textures.

Drinking Straws

Create sets by using various lengths, diameters, colors, and patterns of straws.

Dry Pasta

Select various shapes, colors, and sizes of pasta. Plain pasta can be dyed with food coloring or spray painted.

Geometric Shapes

Create sets by cutting construction paper shapes such as triangles, squares, rectangles, circles, rings, half-rings, and semicircles in different colors and sizes. Cut shapes from sponges, Styrofoam, or foam rubber, or use commercially made plastic sets.

Sand and Gravel

Pet stores that carry aquarium supplies will have different colors of sand and gravel. Use sieves in various dimensions for sifting sand. Sieves can be made from window screen.

Fabric

Glue pieces of fabric on tongue depressors so children can order and match patterns or textures.

Paint Chips

Paint chip samples are found in hardware and paint stores. Cut them into individual pieces. Children can order and group them according to different colors and different shades.

Colored Water

Use red, blue, green, and yellow food coloring to create colored water samples. Store the samples in pint-sized plastic freezer containers. Give children small samples of each of the four colors in small vials. Give them droppers to transfer drops into other small containers. Children can create different colors from the four colors. Older primary children can write down the number of drops used to create a certain color. They can make different shades, or try to match their clothing, paint chips, or colored markers.

Leaves

Collect leaves in the fall. Order and group the leaves according to different shades of yellow, brown, red, and green.

Rattles

Use small empty plastic or cardboard containers with lids, such as from frozen orange juice, potato chips, and soft margarine. Plastic Easter egg containers can also be used. Fill the containers with different amounts of rice, buttons, or metal washers to create different sounds. Children can place the containers in order (loudest to softest or high to low pitch).

Scrapers

Glue different grades of sandpaper onto large craft sticks, tongue depressors, or wooden shims (thin tapered pieces of wood, which can be purchased at hardware or lumber stores). Children can create different sounds by rubbing the sticks together.

Bottle Blowing

Fill plastic bottles such as soda pop containers with various amounts of water. Children can make sounds by blowing across the open top of the bottle and varying the sound according to the amount of water in each bottle.

Bottle Tapping

Fill glass containers with various amounts of water. Children can make sounds by tapping on the side of the bottle with a pencil.

Smelling Jars

Place different spices and herbs in separate containers, such as baby food jars. Cover the opening of the jars with thin cloth to allow the scent to escape. Also cover the sides of the jars so that children cannot identify the scent by seeing the actual herb or spice. Place drops of liquids such as peppermint extract and vanilla on cotton balls. Children can describe the smells. Collect scented plant leaves, stems, or flowers. Dry them and place them in separate jars like the herb and spice jars.

DISCUSSSION QUESTIONS

The following are examples of questions you can ask to accompany the above activities.

"More and Less" Questions

- Are there more two-hole buttons or four-hole buttons?
- If you take away the four-hole buttons, are there any buttons left?
- Are there more seeds or beans?

Grouping Questions

- Is there another way to group the objects?
- How many objects are in each group?

- How many objects will you have if you put these two groups together?
- How did you make your groups?
- How many different groups can you make?
- Can you make two groups using all of the objects?
- If two objects are taken away from this group, how many objects will be left?
- Is there a way to know how many objects you have without counting every individual object?

Ordering Questions

- Which rod is the longest? Which one is the shortest?
- Can you make stair steps using these wooden dowels?
- Can you arrange the buttons from the smallest to the largest?
- Where would this button go in your line of buttons?
- Can you arrange the feathers from the shortest to the longest?

The classification sets above are examples. You can think of many other objects to make classification and ordering sets. Since classification is developmental, children in the primary grades must have opportunities grouping objects in different ways, not only by their characteristics but also in a variety of sets. When allowed to make groups, they have the opportunity to understand the relationships between groups within groups using single attributes. This provides a foundation for understanding classification and ordering using more than one attribute and creating hierarchies of relationships.

Middle/Upper Grade Classrooms (5–8)

Keep in mind that some of the classification sets recommended for the primary level may also be appropriate for children in grades 5–8. In general, if children have had classification experiences in the primary grades, they can classify objects using more than one attribute and can develop multilevel and symmetrical hierarchies, matrices, and Venn diagrams.

Objects within the sets must have multiple characteristics. Allow children to create their own classification systems and then compare them to those commonly accepted by scientists. Magnifying lenses as well as microscopes are often useful in identifying characteristics. Use binocular microscopes for objects that are opaque.

Rocks and Minerals

Children can collect their own rocks or purchase commercially prepared sets. Purchase commercial sets of minerals to use for classifying. Rocks are more difficult to classify than minerals because rocks vary in their mineral content and may be too smooth on the outside for their composition to be identified.

Children will have to break rocks open to see their mineral contents. Challenge them to determine the percentage of each mineral in a rock.

Children can use metal nails or glass to see which rocks can be scratched.

Dilute hydrochloric acid can be used to identify rocks that contain limestone. However, require children to wear goggles and have water readily accessible to dilute and clean up spilled acid. Children need a very small amount of acid. Place only one drop on the rock.

Children can weigh rocks and use water displacement to compare their densities. The density is found by dropping a rock into a container that allows the displaced water to be collected and its volume measured. The weight of the rock is then divided by the volume of water to get the density. For example, if the weight of a rock is 50 grams and it displaced 25 grams of water, it has a density of 2.

Have reference books available so children can look up the names of rocks and their characteristics.

Shells

Teacher or children can collect shells from oceans, lakes, and even woods. Snail shells can be found around lakes and in forests. Hundreds of varieties of sea shells can be collected from beaches around the world. Choose only empty shells that are commonly found in these areas. Shells are the dwellings of snails and other animals. They vary from coiled (univalve) to enclosed containers formed from two symmetrical halves (bivalve). Univalves have coils going in different directions, horizontally or vertically. Bivalves can be flat, rounded, and have ridges. Shells have many different colors from solid to speckled patterns. Classification and relations matrices can be created using shells.

Insects

Insects can be classified according to body shapes, wings, and coloring. Children can also measure the lengths of their bodies and wings. Talk to a high school biology teacher or university biologist about the best ways to care for live insects and to make insect collections. Children can create hierarchies that involve both symmetrical and asymmetrical relations.

Leaves

There are multiple ways to classify leaves. Edges, veins, shapes, and having a single leaf on a stem or many small leaves on one stem are attributes for classifying leaves. Leaves can also be measured. Tree leaves are the best to use. Challenge children to create matrices using the color of the leaves and some other characteristic.

Flowers

Flowers can be difficult to classify because flower parts are not always distinct. Some plants have fused flower parts or many tiny flowers are compacted together. Some of the parts are very small and require the use of magnifying lenses and binocular microscopes.

Flowers are classified according to the multiples of their parts. For example, some flowers have parts that are even or divisible by 2. Other flowers have uneven parts such as multiples of 3 or 5. Petals, stamens, and pistils are divided into parts of 3, 4, 5, and even 6. Find books that illustrate the structure of flowers and show different representations of flowers with different numbers of parts. If a child creates piles of objects according to a single attribute, you can ask, "Is there any other way that you can put the objects together that go together?"

Twigs

Twigs can be classified according to the color of the bark, the texture of bark and stems, or the placement of buds and branches on the stem. Measurements can be made of the distance between buds and the diameters of branches. This is a great activity during the winter when many trees have no leaves.

Venn Diagrams

Make Venn diagrams by using different colored loops from shoelaces, colored craft cord, clothesline, and hula hoops. Make loops that are one to two feet in diameter.

FIGURE 8.14

Volume from smallest to largest container

Beans from smallest to largest	5 mm	10 mm	20 mm
black	number of beans?	?	?
lima	?	?	?
navy	?	?	?
great navy	?	?	?

Place objects such as beans or buttons in one of the loops, add loops one at a time, and place similar objects in the additional loops. Decide what objects will go in the overlapping areas of the loops.

Matrices

Matrices can be created by using large sheets of tagboard (two feet by three feet) that are divided into columns and rows. Children can fill in the matrix using two attributes at a time (e.g., shape and color). Place the actual objects on the matrix template. Beside the objects already mentioned (leaves and shells), other sets of objects can be used. Look at Figure 8.14. Does the matrix represent classification or ordering? Describe the mental process needed to complete the matrix. Look at a pile of beans and predict the number of beans for each cell.

Gears and Pulleys

Find old mechanical toys, clocks, and other worn-out mechanical devices that contain gears and pulleys. Create hierarchies, matrices, or Venn diagrams using the gears and pulleys. Compare the size of the gears and pulleys to ratios between the number of turns, number of gears, and size of gears.

The following activities are complex because they include not only classification and ordering but also many of the learning processes. You should do these activities yourself before doing them with children.

Fingerprint Classification

GOAL

■ To develop a classification hierarchy using a set of fingerprints

GRADE LEVELS

■ Upper

MATERIALS

■ Washable ink pad

- Index cards cut into 4 cm squares
- Magnifying lenses

INSTRUCTIONS

Each child will make a set of prints for every other child in the classroom. For example, if there are 20 children in the class, each child would make 19 prints. For consistency of data, all participants should choose the same finger or thumb on either the right or left hand.

1. The children press thumb or finger on the washable ink pad and then press and roll it on a 4 × 4 cm piece of index card or some other heavy-duty white paper. The print should show the lines and shape of the thumb or finger.

2. Children may have to practice making prints so that lines and shapes are clearly observable. An alternative is to press the thumb or finger onto graphite and roll it on the index card pieces.

3. Children put their initials in the top upper right corner of the printed index card. This helps to identify the source of the print and to indicate the top of the print.

4. Children turn in their sets, which are then redistributed to the class. However, a select number can be used if the class is large. The remaining prints can be used in the activity extension. For example, in a class of 20 children, choose 10 prints to create classification systems. The remaining 10 prints can be used in the activity extension.

Figure 8.15 shows basic fingerprint patterns. Fingerprints can be any combination of these patterns. The patterns can lie to the right or left of the center of the print. The lines of the prints can vary by widths between lines. The number of lines in a whorl, arch, or tent can be counted. The heights of the whorls and arches can be measured.

Challenge students to answer the following question: "Can fingerprints be used to identify individuals?" Children can answer this question after they have made their classification hierarchy.

Children need to use inherent characteristics of the prints. They may require help to distinguish the inherent characteristics. For example, the color of the ink is not inherent to the individual print.

Stress that children should quantify as many characteristics as possible.

Have children draw their hierarchy indicating the characteristics used at each level. Each fingerprint should end up in its own individual categories. Children can list their prints with a description to determine whether or not each print is unique and different.

This activity requires more than understanding class inclusion. It requires children to see relationships between fingerprints at different levels. They are looking at the data from general attributes to specific attributes of individual prints. All prints have characteristics in common, but each print has characteristics or combinations of characteristics that make it unique in comparison to other prints.

ACTIVITY EXTENSIONS

Instruct children to exchange their system with another person. Challenge children to identify a set of prints using the classification system. Ask them to suggest how the systems could be improved.

Suggest that children create a binary hierarchy, which involves using the "non" category at each level.

FIGURE 8.15

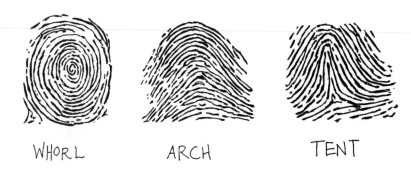

WHORL   ARCH   TENT

Use the additional prints to see where they would fit into the classification systems the children created.

DISCUSSION QUESTIONS

- Does the classification system have to be changed in order to add the additional prints?
- What has to be done to make the additional prints fit the system?
- Are the additional prints different from all the prints that are part of the system?
- Find out how fingerprints are used to identify people. What categories are used?
- How are fingerprints used in identifying crime suspects?
- How is DNA mapping used to identify people?

Mystery Powders

GOALS

- To organize and classify data to identify individual powders when they are mixed together
- To use chemical reactions to identify attributes inherent in the powders

GRADE LEVELS

- Upper

MATERIALS

- Four white powders (boric acid, baking soda, sugar, and cornstarch)
- Magnifying lenses to look at the shapes of individual pieces of the powders
- Plastic spatulas such as coffee stirrers to measure small amounts
- Four liquids (phenolphthalein mixture, iodine solution, vinegar, and water)
- Coin packets for the powders
- Dark medicine bottles with droppers for the liquids
- Aluminum foil to create small vessels to heat the powders
- Wooden clothespins with a spring as forceps for holding the aluminum foil
- Alcohol burners for heating
- Safety glasses for children to wear when using alcohol burners
- Small plastic vials are needed for mixing the powders with the liquids

CAUTION

- Make sure children wear safety glasses and keep their hair tied back when using the alcohol burners.

- Do not let children heat phenolphthalein mixtures since it contains alcohol.

INSTRUCTIONS

1. The objective of this investigation is to find characteristics of the powders that will provide positive identification when the powders are mixed together. Each powder has its own "fingerprint." Its characteristics are created when the powder is mixed with the liquids, heated, or placed directly in a flame. In most cases, these characteristics will always be seen whether the powders are separate or in a mixture. Thus, visual identification is not enough because the powders could change in appearance, such as becoming crystals. Children need to conduct tests on the known powders to identify their characteristics before they begin to identify powders in unknown mixtures.

2. Number the four white powders and always refer to them by their number rather than by their name. Identify the liquids by a letter rather than by name. If students know the powders and liquids by name, they may lose interest and not pursue identifying their characteristics.

3. Prepare packets of different combinations of the powders for each student. The packets could contain only one powder or all four.

4. Have students organize the data that will be useful in identifying powders in the mixtures. For example, "If some of the mixture does not dissolve in water, add solution B and observe what happens." Some powders will not exhibit a particular characteristic when it is in a mixture. Students can check out this possibility by creating mixtures using known powders to see if they get the same results.

5. Make sure children use tiny amounts of powders and liquids: for liquids, drops from droppers, and for powders, the amount that can fit on a plastic spatula.

6. Keep all utensils and containers clean. Never pour liquids back into their original containers. Take small liquid samples from their containers and place them in vials to mix with the powders. Clean containers before using them again.

7. Children learn to organize their data by creating matrices from the attributes of the powders that are helpful for identification purposes. They learn to collect valid data by quantifying the data and replicating experiences. The following are additional tests that can be used to distinguish powders.

Heat Test

Use a 5 cm × 5 cm piece of aluminum foil to create a vessel for holding water. Place one spatula of powder in the vessel. Add several drops of water. Mix the powder and water. Use a spring clothespin to hold the aluminum foil vessel over an alcohol flame burner. **Caution:** Do not look at the mixture while it is above the flame. Some of the mixture may "pop out" and hit the face or hair could get into the flame. Look at the mixture only after removing it from the flame.

Flame Test

Unbend a metal paper clip. Dip one end into water and then into the powder. The powder should stick to the wet paper clip. Holding the paper clip with a spring clothespin, place the paper clip with powder in the flame and observe the changes.

Characteristics of the Powders When Subjected to Tests

- Baking soda turns pink in phenolphthalein solution.
- Starch turns purple when iodine is added.
- Mixing baking soda and vinegar produces bubbles.
- Starch heated in water thickens and develops into an opaque, thick white liquid.
- Baking soda will not burn in a flame.
- Boric acid placed directly in a flame turns the flame green.
- When heated, sugar melts, turns brown, and gives off a distinctive odor familiar to anyone who has roasted marshmallows. The same thing occurs when placed directly in a flame.

The activities given here for upper grades involve complex mental operations of classification and ordering. They help children understand classification and relations structures as well as how to apply them to scientific investigation. The experiences of organizing data and sorting multiple variables can lead to understanding combinatorial logic, which is a formal operation.

Classroom Activity 8.6

Analysis of Hands-On Activities

GOAL

- To analyze hands-on activities to determine the level of classification children are using

INSTRUCTIONS

1. Search resource books, commercial science and mathematics curriculum materials, and/or the World Wide Web for activities that specifically involve classification and ordering.

2. Find five activities. Analyze them by answering the following questions:
   - Do children use real objects rather than pictures or models?
   - How many attributes are available to create groups?
   - Do the activities allow children to enter at their own level of understanding?
   - What developmental levels of classification are involved in the activities?
   - What do you suggest is the appropriate grade level for these activities?

3. Look at five other activities that are not specifically designed to teach classification.
   - Do they require children to use classification and ordering? Explain.
   - Do you think all hands-on science and mathematics activities require children to use classification and ordering to some degree?

This chapter explained the mental structures of classification and relations, which are important in the development of logic. These mental structures are also important in the internalization of information gathered through hands-on activities. The activities presented in this chapter will facilitate the development of classification and relations as mental structures. Chapter 9 explains the characteristics of spatial relations, which are important in the understanding of mathematical and scientific concepts.

Go back to the reflective questions at the beginning of the chapter and the answers you recorded in your journal.

Add to or modify your answers based on what you learned from this chapter.

Bibliography

Alberti, D., Davitt, R., Ferguson, T., and Oakey, S. (1974). Attribute games and problems: Classification and relationships among classes. New York: McGraw-Hill.

Baratta-Lorton, M. (1979). *Work jobs II: Number activities for early childhood.* Menlo Park, CA: Addison-Wesley.

Dewey, J. (1929). *The quest for certainty.* New York: Minton, Balch.

Inhelder, B., and Piaget, J. (1964). *The early growth of logic in the child.* New York: W. W. Norton.

National Council of Teachers of Mathematics. (1989). *Curriculum and evaluation standards for school mathematics.* Reston, VA: Author.

National Research Council. (1996). *National science education standards.* Washington, DC: National Academy Press.

Phillips, D. G., and Phillips, D. R. (1996). *Structures of thinking: Concrete operations,* 2d ed. Dubuque, IA: Kendall/Hunt.

CHAPTER 9

Geometry and Spatial Relations

This is children's strong tendency to interpret reality only according to the way it is perceived from their own perspective (their egocentric frame of reference).

J. Nussbaum, "The Earth as a Cosmic Body"

Reflective Questions

- Why are spatial relations important to understanding mathematical and scientific ideas?

- What mathematical ideas are constructed through spatial relations?

- What scientific ideas are constructed through spatial relations?

- Explain the different stages of development of spatial relations.

- What kinds of hands-on activities are appropriate for developing spatial relations?

As a young child, I believed that the moon traveled alongside a moving car. I thought that long, flat stretches of highways ended in a "point." What similar perceptions do you remember from your childhood? Even adults' perceptions about natural phenomena can contradict reality. People once believed that the world was flat and that it was the center of the universe. Perceptually, objects appear to change in size and position. The sun appears to move around the earth and appears to be flat because the ocean seems to end at the horizon. Adults can correct their perceptions once they have the appropriate experience and knowledge. For young children it is not that simple; their knowledge base is limited. Young children view the world through their perceptions more than through knowledge. This can make a child's world confusing. A baby thinks that its parents, who are not in sight, have disappeared. When the sun sets, it no longer exists. Learning about spatial relations through objects creates constant mental models regardless of the individual's perspective. Understanding objects' relative positions to each other is important in understanding many scientific and mathematical concepts.

The Mental Development of Spatial Relations

This chapter explores the mental development of spatial relationships according to the psychological research conducted by Piaget and his colleagues (Piaget and Inhelder, 1967). Anyone skeptical about Piaget's explanations of spatial relations development must replicate his interviews to understand the validity of the data that support his theory.

The spatial relations constructed through coordinated actions on objects become mental representations. These mental representations are internalized, forming structures used to manipulate data necessary to understanding spatial or geometrical relationships. This means quantifying the relationship of objects. For example, a child may look at a pile of beans and think there are fewer beans than when they were spread all over the floor. By placing the beans in different arrangements, the child learns that the actual number of beans is not influenced by the way they are arranged. To give another example, railroad tracks may appear to meet in the distance. However, a child who walks alongside the tracks learns that the two tracks will not meet regardless of his or her perceptions. Thus, manipulating the spatial relationships of objects helps bridge the gap between perceptions and reality.

Piaget presents his research findings by discussing topological space, projective space, and finally Euclidean space. The definitions of these structures are psychologically based. Piaget emphasizes that topological space and projective space may develop independently of each other. However, both are necessary for the development of Euclidean concepts.

Topological Space

Topology refers to the placement of objects in space within boundaries or enclosures (Gleick, 1987):

> Topology studies the properties that remain unchanged when shapes are deformed by twisting or squeezing. Whether a shape is square or round, large or small, is irrelevant in topology, because stretching can change those properties. Topologists ask whether a shape is connected, whether it has holes, whether it is knotted. . . . topology is geometry on rubber sheets. (p. 46)

In the development of spatial relations, topological relationships are first, despite the fact that topology develops independently of projective spatial relations: "Topological relationships are first in order of appearance because they are inherent to the simplest possible ordering or organization of the actions from which shape is abstracted" (Piaget and Inhelder, 1967, p. 67).

The development of topology begins in the infant years, "since topological relationships express the simplest possible coordination of the dissociated elements of the basic motor rhythms" (Piaget and Inhelder, 1967, p. 68).

The relationships between objects are not taken into consideration. More than one object may be seen as one whole object. Relationships are inherent within the object. For example, a young child draws a picture of the mother's face but cannot place the eyes in the correct position in the circle. Each eye is drawn independently, as are the nose, mouth, and ears. An infant who sees a face from different angles may think that parts of the face appear longer or rounder. It is as if the face shape stretches or shrinks. Thus as the view changes, perceptually the object has changed.

Topology is observing objects and recognizing that individual objects have shape. However, a group of objects may also be considered as a unit with distinctive patterns.

Topology consists of relationships of proximity, separation, order, surrounding, and continuity. *Proximity* is the nearness of objects; *separation* is knowing the distinction between objects rather than blurring or blending them. *Order* is the succession of spatial events. For example, a baby learns that with the opening of the bedroom door a person appears with food. *Surrounding* is recognizing boundaries such as that the nose is enclosed by the face or that a picture is enclosed within a frame. *Continuity* is understanding the relationships between boundaries and objects within those boundaries, the parts to the whole and the whole to the parts. For example, the child understands that a line is made up of a series of points and a row of points can create a continuous line. Topology has to do with the relationships between various parts of objects or patterns created by the objects.

Projective Space

The railroad track view is an example of projection. Looking at the tracks in the horizon is a perspective that appears distorted. Projective space involves understanding relationships of objects from different points of view other than that of the viewer. The simplest form of projection is placing objects in a straight line (Piaget and Inhelder, 1967). Children's abilities to place objects in a straight line were assessed by asking them to arrange toy telephone poles in a straight line. The poles had to be placed between two points separated by a distance of two to three feet. The two points were marked by toy houses. A lake figure was placed between the two points, as an obstacle to placing them in a straight row without using them as a line of sight. The only way to line them up correctly was to view them straight on rather than from the top.

Piaget and Inhelder (1967) also assessed children's understanding of straight lines from perspectives other than their own. The child sits in front of the interviewer. First, the child is asked to draw an object, such as a needle, as it would appear from his or her own viewpoint. The needle is held perpendicular to the horizon. The child is asked to draw the needle in the same position but from a viewpoint at a right angle to his or her own. Then the object is rotated to a 45° angle toward the spot that is at a right angle to the child's viewpoint. Finally, the interviewer rotates the needle so that it is parallel to the horizon and pointing to the right-angle view. The child is asked to draw what the needle would look like for each point of view. It is important for the child to focus on the apparent shape rather than the actual shape and not to be led astray by an inability to draw (Piaget and Inhelder, 1967). Figure 9.1 illustrates the rotation of the needle and how it would look at different angles. As the perspective changes the needle appears shorter until it is parallel to the horizon, at which point only the end can be seen.

Children's understanding of projection was also assessed by having them predict the shape of an object's shadow. The shadow of a cone was projected onto a screen at different angles to a light source. In both assessments, children have to divorce themselves from their own viewpoint in order to understand the shadows from different viewpoints. Thinking about one's own viewpoint is a change in position; thinking about another viewpoint is a change in depth. In other words, it is the mental process of becoming completely aware of one's own viewpoint and coordinating it with the viewpoint of others. Imagery of other viewpoints occurs in the mind that goes beyond imagery of the viewpoint from one's own experience.

Children's understanding of different perspectives of a group of objects was also researched by Piaget and Inhelder (1967). An example of a group of objects is a cone, cylinder, pyramid, and cube. Piaget used a three-dimensional model of a cluster of mountains. The interviewer asks the child to describe the

FIGURE 9.1
Subject viewers' perspective of straw as it is tilted toward them in six stages.

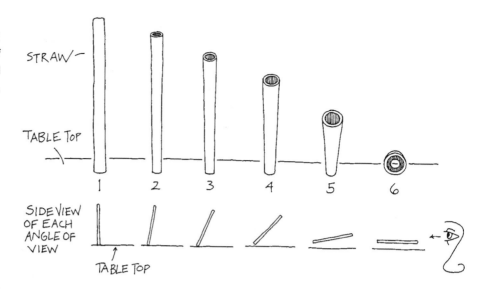

objects as they would look from different points of view without directly viewing them. A child has to consider the reversal of left and right and what parts of each object would be shown in the different perspectives or changing viewpoints. In other words, the child is required to coordinate the different perspectives from all points of view. The child links a number of objects into a single whole by reasoning "through a coordination or 'multiplication' of relationships" (Piaget and Inhelder, 1967, p. 240).

Euclidean Space

The transition from projections to Euclidean space depends on understanding and conserving several relationships: "Coordination of objectives relative to each other and to a system of reference points arranged along different dimensions leads to Euclidean space" (Piaget and Inhelder, 1967, p. 247).

The idea of angles develops concurrently with that of parallel lines. The knowledge of parallel lines and angles leads to the understanding of rectangles and triangles. This knowledge leads to the development of similarity and proportionality; i.e., triangles can be different sizes but have the same angles and sides. Once these concepts are in place a system of reference is constructed. For example, the child knows the water level in an enclosed container is always parallel to the horizon no matter which way the jar is turned. Next comes the development of a coordinate system that determines the exact location of objects in space, from one dimension, to two dimensions, and finally three dimensions. "Euclidean space is based upon the construction of systems of reference and coordinates" (Piaget and Inhelder, 1967, p. 375). Understanding a coordinate system depends on understanding distance and length, perimeter, area, and volume.

"Coordinates, . . . which express the structure of Euclidean space, link together objects considered as such, in their objective positions and displacements, and at relative distances" (Piaget and Inhelder, 1967, p. 418). All relationships, such as the distance of objects from other objects and their appearance from different viewpoints relative to their positions, are taken into consideration at the same time. The mental imagery is holistic in terms of objects and their relationships in space. For example, a large wooden block, a

TABLE 9.1
Summary of Spatial Relations

Topology	
Description	*Concepts*
■ Boundaries on a surface ■ Properties remain unchanged when shapes are deformed (rubber sheet geometry) ■ Relationships inherent in objects	■ Knot tying ■ Shapes (circles, squares, triangles) ■ Position of objects (near, far, behind, below, above, next to)

Projections and Perspectives	
Description	*Concepts*
■ Relationships of objects and between objects from different points of views	■ Lining things up ■ Shadows ■ Coordinating left and right, front and back

Euclidean	
Description	*Concepts*
■ System of references or coordinates to locate objects in space ■ Leads to understanding measurement and time	■ Geometry, calculus, fractions, ratios, distance, parallel lines, angles, frames of references, similarities and proportions, depth, perimeter, area, volume ■ Genetics (DNA, genes, etc.) ■ Chemistry (atoms, molecules, bonding, etc.) ■ Earth science (planetary systems, rocks, minerals, earth layers)

*Topology and projective spatial relations may develop at the same time but before Euclidean relations.

basketball, and a megaphone are all sitting on a desk in close proximity. We can think about their relative position and distance to the floor, ceiling, and walls. We can also visualize what they look like from different angles, even if the basketball hides part of the view of the megaphone when viewed from behind or the wooden block is completely hidden from view by the basketball. Table 9.1 summarizes the three main groups of spatial relations we have discussed.

Key Points about Spatial Relations

Spatial relations development is crucial to the development of logical thinking and intelligence. These concepts exist in parallel to the structures of classification and ordering, which are logico-mathematical relationships: ". . . Their function is to produce the concept of the object as such, in contrast to collection of objections (logico-mathematical)" (Piaget and Inhelder, 1967, p. 450).

The development of spatial relations begins when the child distinguishes one object from another and recognizes objects with definitive shapes. Objects have boundaries and individual characteristics that make up shapes. The child may see a group of objects as one discrete object. At the same time as the child studies objects, he or she forms mental images and internalizes what an object may look like from another viewpoint. Using these operations, the child can coordinate different viewpoints of multiple objects into a whole system in a given space.

> A spatial field is a single schemata embracing all of the elements of which it is composed and uniting them in one monolithic bloc, whereas a logical class is a collection of discontinuous elements linked by their resemblance, regardless of spatio-temporal location. (Piaget and Inhelder, 1967, p. 454)

With these structures in place the child can locate objects in space with accuracy. This accuracy leads to the development of measurement and of quantifying exact locations in relationship to others. A line can be identified as having a specific length by comparing it to another object. Understanding area and volume depends on the ability to coordinate more than one dimension and their exact relations to one another. Thus, measurement is a mental structure derived from Euclidean spatial relations.

Understanding spatial relations is developmental through the action on objects. Spatial concepts are internalized actions that become organized into mental operations called structures. Topological, projective, and Euclidean spatial relations are mental structures built through mental operations.

> These internalized actions are linked together in the form of a mental structure of space as a continuous system. Thus, between perception and imagination there lies a whole series of increasingly systematized actions, internalized in the form of images. (Piaget and Inhelder, 1967, p. 272)

This system consists of images that conserve mathematical concepts such as distance, parallel lines, angles, frames of references, similarities, proportionality, depth, perimeter, area, and volume. Spatial relations are important to understanding fractions and ratios. Many scientific concepts such as the structure of atoms and molecules, DNA and genes, plate tectonics, and the solar system are images created by using systems of coordinate spatial relations. Understanding geometry, calculus, and coordinate systems depends on the development of spatial structures.

Having children memorize the structures of atoms and molecules is a waste of time. Ideas about atoms, their structure, and their components were developed by scientists using sense data to create images of what they think atoms and molecules look like. Many scientists have proposed theories of what molecules and atoms look like. Our current ideas about their structure are based on years and years of research. Hazen and Trefil (1991) explain that the Greek philosopher Democritus proposed the idea of atoms in the fifth century B.C. and describes his argument in the following manner: "Imagine that you have a very sharp knife and a piece of cheese. Cut a piece off the cheese, then cut that piece, then cut the resulting piece smaller and smaller, and so on and on" (p. 55). However, Democritus' idea probably did not originate from cutting up a piece of cheese but from other kinds of experiences! To understand the concept behind the idea of atoms, a child has to visualize relationships of objects that are broken down to many sublevels that cannot be seen with the naked eye.

Many educators expect children to understand atoms by memorizing one-dimensional symbolic representations of three-dimensional models that were created in the minds of scientists. Scientists have created sophisticated technologies to "see" atoms and molecules to verify the theories based on mental images. The same can be said for theories of magnetism, electricity, genetics, radiation, light waves, and energy. These concepts were once based on mental images derived from inferences. Memorizing concepts such as these provide little understanding about them.

Yes, we can take scientific knowledge and transmit this content to children. This content, which was arrived at through processes by using the senses, was transmitted by scientists into scholarly publications and then into textbooks. Teachers explain this knowledge to children. By the time it reaches children, the information is reduced to simplified ideas (content) of which they have no ownership (relevancy). This point was discussed in Chapter 7. The important process of deriving the information is missing. It is through the processes that knowledge becomes internalized and relevant. You can spend hours upon hours reading explanations of scientific and mathematical concepts. However, if you do not internalize the concepts through experiences, your learning will dissipate.

Activities That Focus on Spatial Relations

All activities that engage children in manipulating objects involve spatial relations. However, certain activities focus mainly on spatial relations and also support the development of logico-mathematical concepts. Thus, activities have a dual role in the development of intelligence. The activities in this section will support the development of spatial relations and are congruent with the NCTM standards. The activities contain sample questions and suggestions for extensions of the activities. You will identify many more suggestions as you work through the activities on your own and with children. Each activity is open-ended. The topology activities will probably be the most meaningful to primary children because they are descriptive and exploratory. Some of the projection and Euclidean activities will also be appropriate if children are allowed to explore the patterns and attributes of the objects. Activities that require children to construct line graphs and tables will be more relevant to children in upper grades. However, activities can be adapted for different age levels by adding questions and challenges related to quantifying and organizing results. Questions should challenge children to think about other alternatives. Questions can also be used to assess what children understand.

Topology Activities

Topological spatial relations develop at a relatively young age. Activities to support the development of topology are appropriate for preschool to kindergarten classes. The following hands-on activities require children to explore concepts such as *besides, next to, on top of, below, near,* and *far.* Any activities that involve exploring patterns are also beneficial. Children can draw and color patterns they have created. Whenever children make patterns, have them communicate their patterns orally as well as through drawings.

National Council of Teachers of Mathematics (1989)
Standard 9: Geometry and Spatial Sense (K–4)

In grades K–4, the mathematics curriculum should include two- and three-dimensional geometry so that students can describe, model, draw, and classify shapes; investigate and predict the results of combining, subdividing, and changing shapes; relate geometric ideas to number and measurement ideas; recognize and appreciate geometry in their world. (p. 48)

Standard 12: Geometry (5–8)

Identify, describe, compare, and classify geometric figures; visualize and represent geometric figures with special attention to developing spatial sense; explore transformations of geometric figures; represent and solve problems using geometric models; understand and apply geometric properties and relationships; develop an appreciation of geometry as a means of describing the physical world. (p. 112)

Standard 13: Patterns and Relationships (K–4)

Recognize, describe, extend, and create a wide variety of patterns; represent and describe mathematical relationships; explore the use of variable and open sentences to express relationships. (p. 60)

Bead Stringing

GOALS

- To learn topological concepts such as *next to*
- To create patterns that repeat and reverse

GRADE LEVELS

- Primary grades

MATERIALS

- Multicolored beads in different shapes (oval, circular, cubic, rectangular) and different materials (plastic, wood)
- Long shoestrings or craft cords

INSTRUCTIONS

Give each child a set of beads and strings. Have children place the beads on the strings and see whether they make patterns or just place them randomly. The following questions can be asked after determining children's level of understanding.

QUESTIONS

- Can you make the same pattern on another shoestring?
- Can you repeat the pattern that you have completed so far?
- How many different patterns can you make using these beads?
- Count the number of red (blue, green, yellow) beads you have on the string.
- Can you do the pattern backwards?

Hanging Clothes on a Clothesline

GOALS

- To explore topological concepts such as *next to* and *beside*
- To make patterns

GRADE LEVELS

- Primary grades

MATERIALS

- Doll clothes
- Colored tissue paper
- Ribbons in different textures, patterns, and colors
- Miniature clothespins
- Craft cord

INSTRUCTIONS

Hang doll clothes or other objects on the clothesline to create patterns.

QUESTIONS

- How would you arrange the clothes on the line?
- Can you hang the clothes that all have the same color?
- Can you hang the clothes that all have a different color?
- Can you hang all the dresses next to each other?
- Can you hang a dress and then a pair of pants and repeat the pattern?

Patterns with Cubes, Blocks, and Beads

GOALS

- To create patterns
- To describe the location of objects in relation to each other

GRADE LEVELS

- Primary grades

MATERIALS

- Plastic cubes that can be linked together, such as Unifix Cubes
- Multicolored pop beads, such as Snap Beads
- Sets of colored wooden or plastic blocks

INSTRUCTIONS

Have children link the cubes or beads together, or arrange the blocks together. Prepare some patterns ahead of time and challenge children to reproduce the same patterns.

QUESTIONS

- Can you match the pattern I have made with these Unifix cubes?
- Can you put three of each color together to make a long row of cubes?
- Can you alternate red and blue colors five times?
- Make a pattern and have someone else match your pattern.
- How many times does your pattern repeat itself?
- How many different colors did you use?
- Can you alternate colored beads?
- Can you put two beads of each color together to make a necklace?
- Can you make a string of beads using only two different colors?

Matching Ribbons*

GOAL

- To explore patterning by matching patterns

GRADE LEVELS

- Primary grades

MATERIALS

- Tongue depressors or large craft sticks
- Assorted ribbons in different colors and patterns

INSTRUCTIONS

1. Cut pieces of ribbon that are half the length of a tongue depressor.
2. Glue a piece of ribbon to one half of a tongue depressor. Glue another strip of ribbon to the other half of the tongue depressor.
3. Make at least 10 pairs of tongue depressors with the same ribbon pattern for each child.
4. Make several sets so that more than one child can work with them. Children can exchange sets.
5. Give a child a mixed set of 10 pairs. Say: "Can you find the ones that go together?"
6. Allow child to match pairs on their own.

Toy Villages

GOALS

- To describe the position of objects in relation to each other
- To encourage children to use terminology such as *in front of, behind, beside, next to*

GRADE LEVELS

- Primary grades

---

*Adapted from L. B. Gilbert, *I Can Do It! I Can Do It! 135 Successful Independent Learning Activities*. Mt. Rainier, MD: Gryphon House, 1984.

FIGURE 9.2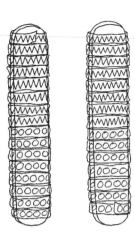

MATERIALS

■ Miniature plastic toy people, animals, houses, trees, and fences

INSTRUCTIONS

Create villages from circles of cloth, jump ropes, or thick cord. Children place the toy animals, people, and houses within the villages. The size of the village will be proportional to the number of objects the children use and how close they place the objects. The rope or cloth gives boundaries to the village. Ask questions that will encourage children to use phrases like *in front of, behind, next to,* and *on top of.* The children can talk about their placement of objects.

QUESTIONS

■ Where is the boy's dog?

■ Where will I find the two houses?

■ What is closest to this house, the boy or the dog?

Sifting Sand

GOALS

■ To sort objects according to size

■ To order by making spatial comparisons

GRADE LEVELS

■ Primary grades

MATERIALS

■ Aquarium sand in various sizes, each size a different color

■ Sifters made from different sizes of screen or commercially made sifters*

INSTRUCTIONS

Have children use the sifters to sort the different sands. They must determine the order of sifters to use to successfully sort the sand. You might begin by saying: "See what you can find out about the sand."

*Sifters can be ordered from Delta Education; see address at end of chapter.

FIGURE 9.3

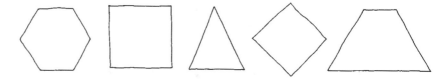

QUESTIONS

- How would you keep the smallest sand from falling through the sifter?
- To sift a different-sized sand in each sifter, which sifter would you use first? Second? Third?
- Can you take this mixture of sand and sort the particles according to their size?

Pattern Blocks

GOALS

- To create symmetrical patterns using different geometrical shapes
- To describe these patterns using topological terminology

GRADE LEVELS

- Primary grades

MATERIALS

- Pattern Blocks

INSTRUCTIONS

Pattern Blocks consist of different geometric shapes and colors. The shapes are squares, triangles, hexagons, diamond-shaped parallelograms, and trapezoids. Children can create patterns using the blocks. (See Figure 9.3.) Say to the children: "Here is a tub of blocks of different colors and shapes. See what you can find out about these blocks."

QUESTIONS

- What kinds of patterns can you make?
- Can you make the blocks fit together to cover this piece of paper?
- How many different kinds of blocks do you have in your pattern?
- How many yellow (blue? green? red?) blocks do you have in your pattern?

Tessellating (Patterning or Tiling)

GOAL

- To create patterns using pieces of the same shape and size

GRADE LEVELS

- Primary to upper grades

MATERIALS

- Pattern Blocks
- Wooden or plastic colored tiles
- Plastic stencils

FIGURE 9.4

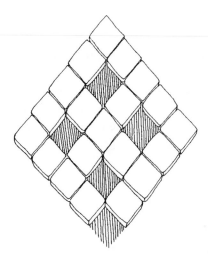

BACKGROUND INFORMATION

Tessellating is the act of making a mosaic, covering an area without gaps or overlaps using the same or congruent shapes. According to Webster's, the word *tessellation* originates from the Latin word *tessella* or *tessera,* meaning little square stones or tiles. The people of ancient Rome decorated their buildings, floors, and streets with tiles, and other cultures of the Middle East and Spain used tiles as part of buildings. Tessellation includes creating patterns with polygons as well as shapes with curves. The drawings and paintings by the Dutch artist M. C. Escher are tessellations because the figures fill space in a repetitive pattern. His paintings were originally influenced by his interest in Moorish art (Ranucci and Teeters, 1977). Seeing the patterns in numbers and data is essential in mathematics.

INSTRUCTIONS

Either give children objects with which to make patterns or let them select their own. Patterns can also be given to them to duplicate on another sheet of paper. In Figure 9.4, a diamond shape was used to make the pattern. The shadowed pieces represent blanks where no pieces were traced. Say to the children: "Using one shape, make a pattern that is repetitive and covers an area without any gaps or overlapping."

SUGGESTIONS

- Draw a pattern by flipping the object from one side to the other.
- Draw a pattern by turning the object 45° or 90° to the right or to the left.
- Draw a pattern by rotating the object so that one side touches the line drawn for the other side.
- Take an object and count the number of turns, rotations, or flips to make patterns while covering an entire sheet of paper.
- Make some rules for making patterns. For example, using a square, make two 45° turns to the right, one flip to the left, and five rotations. Repeat this pattern until the paper is covered.
- Investigate Turtle Geometry and LOGO to make patterns on the computer (Papert, 1980).

Perspectives and Projection Activities

Working with shadows, mirrors, and rubber stamps gives children opportunities to develop perspectives and projections. Building with multishaped blocks provides experience in seeing objects from multiple perspectives and mentally coordinating these perspectives. Piaget has pointed out that the development of topological spatial relations and projective spatial relations can occur at the same time. Thus objects such as Pattern Blocks and Geoblocks can help in developing both of these mental structures.

Making Shadows

GOAL

- To compare the shapes of objects and their shadows

GRADE LEVELS

- Primary to upper grades

MATERIALS

- Clear adhesive tape
- Straws, dowels, or craft sticks
- Meter stick
- White sheets of paper
- Bare light bulb (60–70 watts, depending on the darkness of the room) in a porcelain-base socket
- Paper tagboard objects (5 to 7 cm in size) in geometrical shapes such as squares, circles, triangles, ovals, rings, and half rings

INSTRUCTIONS

1. Use clear adhesive tape to attach paper objects to straws, dowels, or craft sticks.
2. Make a screen by taping together white sheets of paper and hanging them on a flat surface.
3. Place one end of the meter stick next to the light bulb and the other end touching the screen. (See Figure 9.5.) Tape the meter stick to the surface to prevent it from moving.
4. Hold the paper objects vertically and move them between the light source and the screen so that they project shadows on the screen. The size of the shadows will depend on the distance of the objects from the wall.
5. Measure and record the distance from the light bulb to the object and the shadow to the object. Measure and record the size of the object. Predict and record the size of the shadow, then measure and record the actual size of the shadow.
6. Suggest points at which to hold the objects and then allow children to choose their own. Table 9.2 shows suggested object shapes and one suggested set of distances.

QUESTIONS AND SUGGESTIONS

- Predict shadow sizes for distances of more than 1 meter.
- What patterns do you find in the data you recorded about the relationships between distances and size of shadows?

FIGURE 9.5

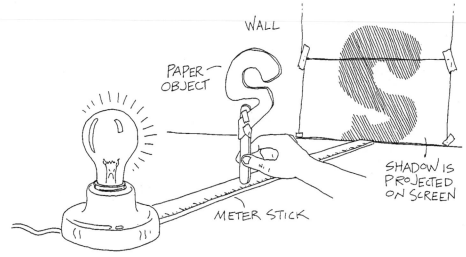

TABLE 9.2

**Chart for Recording
Measurements of Shadow and
Object Relationships**

Object Shapes	Shadow to Object (cm)	Light Bulb to Object (cm)	Actual Object Size (cm)	Predicted Shadow Size (cm)	Actual Shadow Size (cm)
▭	50 cm	50 cm			
▭	75 cm	25 cm			
⬭	30 cm	70 cm			
⊖	70 cm	30 cm			
⬭					
△					
◺					

- Make bigger or smaller shapes than the ones used to collect the initial set of data. Predict the size of the shadows in relation to the distances.

- Graph the data.

- Can you make an algebraic expression that symbolizes the relationships between the variables?

- Make shadow hand puppets.

- Cut shadow puppets from paper.

- Research shadow puppets from other cultures. Make shadow puppets like those from other cultures and create plays.

Solid and Transparent Objects

GOALS

- To compare the shape of objects with the shape of their shadows
- To compare the shadows of transparent objects to those of translucent objects

GRADE LEVELS

- Primary to middle grades

MATERIALS

- Objects in different geometric shapes, made of opaque plastic, wood, or paper, and clear plastic
- Overhead projector or the apparatus used in the "Making Shadows" activity

INSTRUCTIONS

Have children place objects on the overhead projector to observe the shapes projected onto a screen or wall. Encourage children to predict the shape before placing the object on the overhead projector. Objects can be rotated in different positions.

QUESTIONS

- How many different shadow shapes can be made with each object?
- What objects give the same shadow shape as the actual objects, no matter their orientation?
- What objects give only one different-shaped shadow?
- Can you get shadows within shadows?
- Compare shadows of the transparent objects to the opaque objects

---

Season Shadow Simulations

GOAL

- To simulate the changing seasons by studying shadow lengths using an artificial light

GRADE LEVELS

- Middle to upper grades

MATERIALS

- Flashlight
- Pencil, drinking straw, or wooden dowel
- Modeling clay

INSTRUCTIONS

1. Anchor the pencil in a tiny piece of clay so that it is perpendicular to a surface.

2. Move a lit flashlight over the top of the pencil, starting at one side of the surface and going to the other side. (See Figure 9.6.) This simulates the sun directly overhead moving from east to west.

3. Repeat this step, except start at an angle of 15° away from the top of the pencil. (See Figure 9.7.)

4. Repeat this step again, moving 30° away from the pencil.

FIGURE 9.6

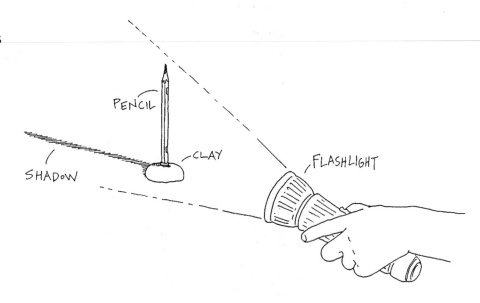

FIGURE 9.7

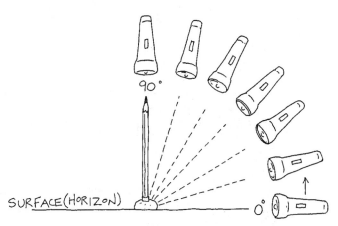

5   Move 45° away from the pencil until the flashlight is perpendicular to the pencil on one side.

6.   Now move the flashlight approximately 10° away from the top of the pencil at different angles.

7.   Measure the length of the shadows and record the data in Table 9.3.

8.   Do the same thing except as you move the flashlight from horizon to horizon, move it 45° away from the top of the pencil. Record the data in Table 9.4.

Figure 9.7 illustrates how the flashlight is placed at a different angle to the pencil. The flashlight moves in the same direction as when it moved over the top of the pencil.

Remember, this is only a simulation. The sun does not move like the flashlight. It is the earth's angle to the sun that creates the seasons and different lengths of shadow. You may want to try moving the tilt of the pencil to different angles and keeping the flashlight in a constant position as you move it from one horizon to the next.

Moving the flashlight over the top of the object (Figure 9.8a) simulates the sun moving across the sky in the summer over the northern hemisphere or the sun moving over the tropics. Shadows will be short. Moving the flashlight at a 45°

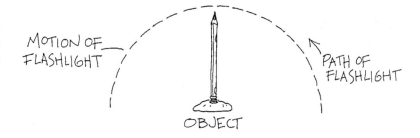

FIGURE 9.8a
Flashlight Motion:
Directly over Object

TABLE 9.3
Length of Shadow
for Every 15°

Angle of Flashlight from Horizon to Object (degrees)	Length of Shadow (mm)
15°	
30°	
45°	
60°	
75°	
90°	

angle away from the object (Figure 9.8b) simulates the winter months. Shadows are long.

SUGGESTIONS

- Make a graph illustrating the length of shadows with the movement of the sun. Place two lines on the graph that represent the two angles: 90° and 45° above the horizon.

- Move the flashlight at other angles across the horizon and measure shadows at every 15°. Add this new information to the graph.

- Label each line on the graph with the name of the season they represent.

- Find out the angle of the earth to the sun. Use a ball or some other sphere to simulate the earth and move the ball around a flashlight or a freestanding lit bulb. Keep the angle constant as the object moves around the light source.

Sun and Shadows

GOAL

- To study positions, shapes, and lengths of shadows caused by the sun

GRADE LEVELS

- Primary to upper grades

MATERIALS

- Meter sticks or wooden dowels of similar length

- Pieces of chalk

FIGURE 9.8b
Flashlight Moves from
Horizon to Horizon: 45° Angle
Away from Object

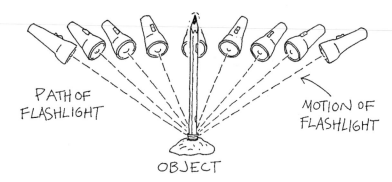

PATH OF FLASHLIGHT

MOTION OF FLASHLIGHT

OBJECT

TABLE 9.4
Length of Shadow
for Every 15°

Angle of Flashlight 45° Away from Object	Length of Shadow (mm)
15°	
30°	
45°	
60°	
75°	
90°	

INSTRUCTIONS

Challenge children to find ways to make shadows while standing in the sunlight.

SUGGESTIONS

- Use your body to make the biggest shadow possible.
- Use your body to make the smallest shadow possible.
- Play shadow tag.
- Look around and find the longest shadow on the playground (a tree, flagpole, swings). Measure the shadow.
- Find the shortest shadow on the playground (blade of grass, insect). Measure the shadow.
- Have someone draw your shadow with a piece of chalk. If you stand in the exact same spot, where will your shadow be in 15 minutes? How long will it be? Predict what will happen to your shadow after 15 minutes, 30 minutes, and 1 hour. Stand in your shadow for each of the suggested time intervals. What happens each time? Predict the length and shape of the shadow in a different season of the year.
- Hold a meter stick or some other object of similar length perpendicular to the ground. Trace its shadow. Predict the length of the shadow after 15 minutes; 30 minutes.

FIGURE 9.9

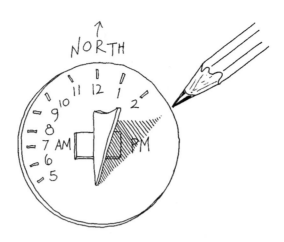

Making a Sundial

GOAL

■ To create timing devices using sunlight and shadows

GRADE LEVELS

■ Middle to upper grades

MATERIALS

■ Plastic lids from 5 pound coffee cans

■ Pencil or wooden dowel of the same length

■ Felt-tip markers with permanent ink

INSTRUCTIONS

1. Punch a hole the size of a pencil in the center of a coffee can lid. Place a pencil upright in the center of the lid.

2. Place the coffee can lid in a sunny spot. Push the end of the pencil into the ground to hold the lid in place.

3. Using a felt-tip marker, outline the shadow on the lid and label the line with the appropriate time to the nearest 15 minutes.

4. Leave the coffee can lid in the same position and location. Return in one hour. Draw the shadow and label the time.

5. Continue doing this for several hours until you see a pattern. Using the pattern, draw the lines to represent the rest of the 24 hours of the day.

6. The completed sundial consists of a coffee can lid with lines drawn for each hour and a pencil in the center of the lid to cast a shadow. (See Figure 9.9.) Leave the completed sundial outside and check it periodically to see if the shadow matches the appropriate time.

QUESTIONS

■ If you wanted to use your sundial to know the time, what would you have to do to adjust for the changing seasons?

■ How accurate can you make your sundial? To the nearest half-hour? Quarter-hour? Minute?

FIGURE 9.10

Printing

GOALS

- To explore spatial relations through printing letters
- To explore the correct position of stamps to print letters correctly

GRADE LEVELS

- Primary grades

MATERIALS

- Individual rubber alphabet stamps glued onto corks
- Ink pad
- Paper
- Hand mirror

INSTRUCTIONS

Give the set of letters, the ink pad, and the paper to the children. Say: "See what you can find out about these letters by stamping them on paper." (See Figure 9.10.)

QUESTIONS

- In what position should you hold the stamp to make a letter correctly?
- What letters can be made by using other letters?
- What kinds of pictures can you make using the letters?
- Can you write a message using a mirror? Hold the mirror so that one of its edges is standing upright on the surface of the paper.

SUGGESTIONS

Take objects such as potatoes, green peppers, apples, sponges, pieces of clay, and bars of soap. Make cross sections and print with the objects, or cut designs into the surface of a cross section and make prints.

Mirrors and Reflections

GOALS

- To create patterns using mirrors and objects
- To create symmetrical patterns using mirror images

GRADE LEVELS

- Primary grades

MATERIALS

- Plastic mirrors
- Pattern Blocks
- Colorful pictures from magazines

INSTRUCTIONS

Children are working with the concept of symmetry when looking at patterns using mirrors. Instruct children to hold a mirror upright to an object or picture and look in the mirror to see what kind of image is created.

SUGGESTIONS

- Ask children to predict what an image will look like when a mirror is placed perpendicularly to a colorful picture or Pattern Blocks.
- Have children draw the pattern they see in the mirror on a piece of paper behind the mirror.
- Have children draw colorful "stained glass" images, place a mirror on one of the edges, and look at the images that are created. Ask them if they can make other "stained glass" images from the ones that appear in the mirror.
- Use two or more mirrors and look at the patterns that are created.

Projective and Euclidean Activities

Euclidean structures are abstracted from experiences with topology, perspectives, and projections. "Euclidean structures are concerned with absolute relationships within and among objects" (Phillips, 1994, p. 294). Distances, dimensions, shapes, parallels, angles, and proportions are all constant in Euclidean space; point of view is of no consequence. Through the exploration of objects these concepts become constant in the children's minds. Space is now conceived as a "container" composed of sites or positions, which remain fixed in a continuum of possible sites.

Geometrical Cross Sections

GOAL

- To predict and examine cross sections made through a variety of objects

GRADE LEVELS

- Middle to upper grades

MATERIALS

- Modeling clay
- Cheese knife
- Fruits such as apples, pears, lemons, oranges, kiwi, and other exotic fruit
- Vegetables such as green peppers and cucumbers
- Tempera paints and paper

INSTRUCTIONS

Have children make slices of objects and look at the shape of the surface created by the slice.

TABLE 9.5

Side Views of Three-Dimensional Objects	Side Views Angle sliced:			Top Views Angle sliced:		
	0°	45°	90°	0°	45°	90°
□ (square)	▭	△	?	☐	▯	?
▭ (rectangle)						
○ (circle)						
△ (triangle)						
⬭ (oval)						
?						

SUGGESTIONS

- Make a variety of shapes (5 to 12 cm in size) with modeling clay: cubes, pyramids, cylinders, rectangular tetrahedrons, cones, spheres, and ovals. Create different shapes such as tetrahedrons and spheres by cutting at different angles through the clay shapes.

- What do the cross sections look like? Make a chart such as that shown in Table 9.5.

- If you cut through a sphere at different angles, what shape is formed by the cross sections?

- If you cut a pyramid at different angles, what shape is formed by the cross sections?

- Cut the fruits and vegetables at different angles. What shapes are formed? Describe the shapes in words. Look at the seed patterns too.

- Use the different sections to make prints with tempera paints.

Creating Geometric Models

GOAL

- To create geometric shapes from paper

GRADE LEVELS

- Upper grades

MATERIALS

- Solid geometrical figures: ovals, spheres, cubes, cones, rectangular tetrahedrons, and pyramids

- Centimeter graph paper

- Scissors

- Clear cellophane tape
- Oranges

INSTRUCTIONS

Have children draw on graph paper what the shapes of the solid objects would look like if their sides were flattened. Then they can cut out these drawings, fold them, and tape the sides to recreate the original shape of the objects.

SUGGESTIONS

- Observe these solid geometrical shapes and imagine what shape they would be if you could unfold them and lay the sides flat on a surface. Draw these shapes on graph paper. Cut out the shapes and then see if you can reconstruct the solid geometrical shapes.

- If you could peel an orange and keep the entire peel in one piece, what would its shape look like? Peel an orange in one piece. Draw the shape before peeling. After peeling the orange, check to see if the shape is the same as the one you drew. Draw this shape on graph paper. Cut out the shape and reconstruct a sphere.

Geoblocks

GOALS

- To create shapes using other shapes
- To balance objects by building
- To explore fractions, ratios, and parts to the whole

GRADE LEVELS

- Primary to upper grades

INSTRUCTIONS

A set of Geoblocks consists of hundreds of blocks in a variety of shapes and sizes. Children can make big blocks from the small blocks or construct towers. They can make objects with the triangles and rectangles. Instruct children to find out what they can about the Geoblocks.

SUGGESTIONS

- Make a tower using only the rectangles and then make a tower the same height using cubes. How many cubes did it take to make the tower the same height? What is the ratio of cubes to rectangles?
- Use a variety of Geoblocks to make the tallest tower possible.
- Make a model city, town, or neighborhood.

Tangrams

GOAL

- To explore the relationship of area to shape

GRADE LEVELS

- Middle to upper grades

FIGURE 9.11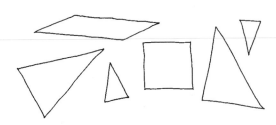

BACKGROUND INFORMATION

Tangram sets consist of seven puzzle pieces: triangles, squares, and a parallelogram. (See Figure 9.11.) The set also includes geometric figure outlines in which these puzzle pieces will fit. Children learn that there are a variety of ways to fit these pieces in the puzzle. The areas of the pieces do not change but their shapes change. Children learn that area can be constant regardless of shape.

There are three sets of puzzles that increase in difficulty. Instructions are given at the beginning of each set about which puzzle pieces to use. Children should begin with the first set. If they skip a set, they may become frustrated and want to stop.

Children can make their own puzzle shapes using the puzzle pieces. Super Tangrams are also available. They contain more pieces and different shapes from the original Tangram set.

INSTRUCTIONS

Have children begin with the first set of Tangrams and continue through sets 2 and 3.

QUESTIONS

- Can you create your own Tangram patterns?
- Can you complete the pattern without putting the pieces into the pattern?
- How many new patterns can you make?
- Give someone else the patterns you created and see if they can fit the pieces of puzzle into them.

Pattern Blocks

GOALS

- To understand concepts of parts to the whole and fractions
- To explore area using different-shaped objects

GRADE LEVELS

- Primary to upper grades

MATERIALS

- One set of Pattern Blocks

INSTRUCTIONS

Say to children: "See what you can find out about these colored blocks." (See Figure 9.12.)

QUESTIONS

- Can you cover your desk or this piece of paper with the blocks by piecing them together?

FIGURE 9.12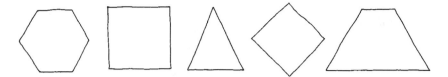

- What can you build with the Pattern Blocks?
- How high can you build with the Pattern Blocks?
- Can you make images of objects using Pattern Blocks?
- What pieces can be used to construct other pieces in the set?
- How many different patterns can you make with the Pattern Blocks?

Cuisenaire Rods

GOALS

- To explore part to whole relationships
- To place objects in order
- To balance objects by building
- To explore addition and subtraction

GRADE LEVELS

- Primary to upper grades

INSTRUCTIONS

Say to children: "See what you can find out about these colored rods."

QUESTIONS

- What can you build with these rods?
- How high can you go?
- Can you build two towers using different sets of rods?
- Can you spell your name with the rods?
- How many of one color rods does it take to equal the length of another color rod?
- Can you tell the rods by feel? Place rods in a paper bag and determine the colors by feeling them.
- How many rods of one color equal one rod of another color?
- How many rods of two different colors equal one rod of another color?

Mirrors and Angles

GOALS

- To explore the angle of reflection
- To measure the angle of reflection using more than one mirror

GRADE LEVELS

- Middle to upper grades

FIGURE 9.13

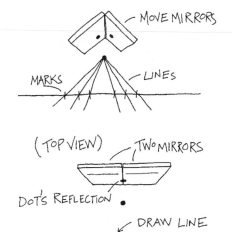

TABLE 9.6

Images	Angle
one	180°
two	?
three	?

MATERIALS

- Two mirrors
- $8\frac{1}{2}'' \times 11''$ sheets of paper

INSTRUCTIONS

1. Draw a line on a sheet of paper.

2. Position the mirrors behind the line so that the entire line can be seen in the two mirrors when they are parallel to the line.

3. Draw a dot on the paper behind the line at the point where the two mirrors touch each other so that the dot appears as one image. (See Figure 9.13.)

4. Complete Table 9.6 by moving the two mirrors toward each other and marking the spot on the paper where two images of the dot are seen.

5. Continue moving the mirrors, marking the position of the mirrors on the line each time the number of dots increases.

6. Draw lines from the dot to the markings and estimate the angle for each position. Use a protractor.

QUESTIONS

- What is the greatest number of images that can be seen in the two mirrors?
- How are the two mirrors positioned to display the greatest number of images?
- How much do the angles change as the mirrors are moved together?
- Use three mirrors to form an equilateral triangle. Place a dot in the center of the three mirrors. How many images are formed? Kaleidoscopes are based on three reflective surfaces that form the shape of a triangle.

FIGURE 9.14

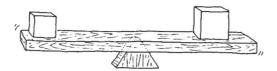

Seesaw Balance

GOALS

- To explore balancing using a fulcrum
- To explore horizontal relationships
- To explore the weight and position of objects on a balance beam

GRADE LEVELS

- Primary to upper grades

MATERIALS

- Wooden beam (35 cm × 4 cm × 5–7 mm)
- Wooden fulcrum,* rounded on top, covered by sandpaper, 6 cm × 4 cm × 2.5 cm
- Wooden or plastic blocks of various sizes, or washers of various sizes
- Other objects to balance on the beam

INSTRUCTIONS

Give the children a beam, a fulcrum, and a set of objects that are all the same size and weight. (See Figure 9.14.)

SUGGESTIONS

- Balance the beam on the fulcrum so that it is parallel to the horizon.
- Place same-sized blocks on one side and then on the other side to keep the beam balanced.
- Use different-sized blocks on either side and keep the beam balanced.
- Balance larger objects with smaller objects.
- Place the beam off balance. Put blocks on both sides to make it balanced again.
- Can you balance one beam on top of another? How many beams can you balance on each other?
- How high can you stack blocks on each side of the balance beam without them falling?

T-Balance

GOALS

- To explore the relationship of position and weight of objects on a T-balance
- To explore the ratio of number of objects on each side of the balance

GRADE LEVELS

- Middle to upper grades

---

*Fulcrums can be ordered from Delta Education; see address at end of chapter.

FIGURE 9.15

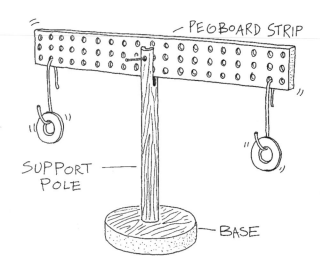

MATERIALS

- Pegboard strip
- Upright support with base
- Paper clips
- Metal washers

INSTRUCTIONS

1. Secure the pegboard to the upright support with a straightened paper clip. Insert the straightened paper clip through the appropriate holes so that when it is attached to the upright support it is balanced. (See Figure 9.15.) If the pegboard does not balance, add a small piece of clay at the appropriate spot on the pegboard or attach another paper clip to achieve balance.

2. Unbend other paper clips to hang washers at different points on the pegboard. Children should begin with the same size washers before using different sizes.

QUESTIONS

- If you place a washer in hole #2 on the left, where would you place the same size washer on the right side?

- Can you keep adding washers on one side and maintain the balance by adding washers on the other side?

- If you use a small washer on the left side, where do you have to place a bigger washer on the right side to keep the pegboard balanced?

- If you place three small washers in hole #3 on the left, how many large washers have to be added to the right side to keep the pegboard balanced?

- Remove the pegboard beam and reattach it so that it is no longer balanced. Use the same size washers and place them in the appropriate spots to make the beam balanced.

Hanging Balance

GOALS

- To explore the relationship of balancing objects on each side of a hanging balance

- To compare the weight and position of objects

FIGURE 9.16

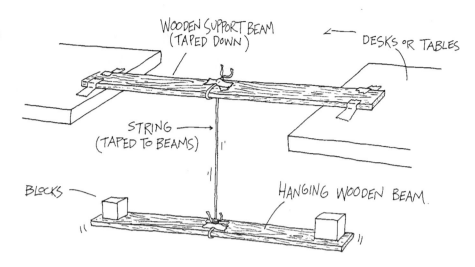

GRADE LEVELS

■ Middle to upper grades

MATERIALS

■ Wooden support beam (1.5 m long)

■ Hanging beam (1 m long)

■ Masking tape

■ String

■ Wooden and plastic blocks in assorted sizes

INSTRUCTIONS

Show children how to set up the apparatus. (See Figure 9.16.) They must balance the hanging beam. Challenge the children to place blocks on the beam without letting them fall off. Have children begin with the same size blocks.

QUESTIONS

■ How many blocks of the same size can you place on both sides of the beam without them falling off?

■ Use two different-sized blocks on each side of the beam. Can you keep the beam balanced?

■ How many blocks of two different sizes can you place on each side and keep the beam balanced?

■ Can you keep the beam balanced by using a variety of blocks?

■ Place the beam off balance. Can you add blocks to the beam to make it balanced again?

Mobiles

GOAL

■ To explore balancing objects by creating mobiles using different kinds of objects

GRADE LEVELS

■ Middle to upper grades

FIGURE 9.17

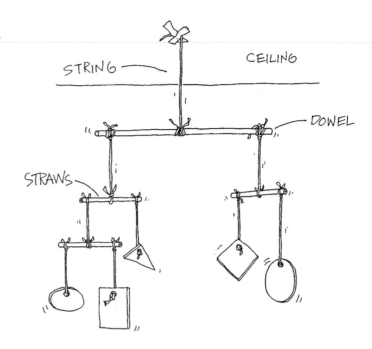

MATERIALS

- Wooden dowels (0.5 cm in diameter and 25 cm long)
- Straws
- String
- Scissors
- Paper clips
- An assortment of objects to build the mobile, such as construction paper, nuts and bolts, nails, spoons, feathers, radio parts, clocks and mechanical appliances, leaves, berries, pine cones, twigs

INSTRUCTIONS

Attach one end of the string to the wooden dowel and the other end to a ceiling, door frame, or some other support that allows the dowel to hang freely without hitting anything. Children must work with the mobile as it is hanging. Balance the dowel on the string. Add another layer to the first dowel. Continue to balance and layer until the mobile is complete. (See Figure 9.17.) Add other layers using straws, string, and miscellaneous objects. Keep each layer balanced.

QUESTIONS

- How many layers can you make and retain an overall balance?
- Can you make a mobile starting with each support level off balance and balancing them by adding objects?
- Can you predict where to place an object so that the support stays balanced?
- Create "theme" mobiles: snowflakes, gears, trash, nails, paper shapes, holiday themes.

FIGURE 9.18

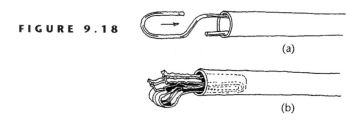

(a)

(b)

Straw Towers

GOAL

■ To explore balancing by building structures

GRADE LEVELS

■ Middle to upper grades

MATERIALS

■ Drinking straws

■ Paper clips

INSTRUCTIONS

Unbend a paper clip so that it forms an "S" shape. Insert one end into one straw and the other end into another straw. (See Figure 9.18a.) Insert another "S" shaped paper clip into the opposite end of one of the connected straws. Attach another straw to the paper clip connector and bend it in a different direction. You now have three straws attached to each other. The paper clips can be bent to put the straws in different positions. You have created a joint. Other straws can be added to this joint in the same manner.

Using clay to make joints does not work because the clay softens and weakens the structure. Twist ties can be used instead of paper clips but are not as strong (Figure 9.18b). Fold a twist tie back on itself. Fold the two ends back on themselves. Insert the folded side into one straw and the folded two ends into another straw. The twist tie has to be thick enough on both ends to fit snugly into both straws. This will give the joints strength.

A straw tower must be balanced to keep it from falling. Thus, the kind of structure children create and how it is balanced will determine how high they can go before it falls. Children can explore which foundational shape produces a strong framework upon which a tall tower can be built.

Show children how to connect the straws with the bent paper clips. Tell them they can be creative and create their own designs for making towers by connecting the straws with the bent paper clips. Children should construct their towers on their own. The questions that follow can also be used to help children think about how to construct a tower. The idea here is to challenge children to think about ways to build a tower that will not fall over. Of course, older children will likely be more successful than young children. The more experiences children have with this activity, the more they will understand how to build a tower. This is why the activity is appropriate for all grade levels.

Note: A tower does not necessarily have to be anchored if it has a wide base and a strong frame. It will stand without falling over. Some children will understand this and others will not. Children who do not understand this idea can use tiny pieces of clay to anchor the straws of the base to a solid surface such as the

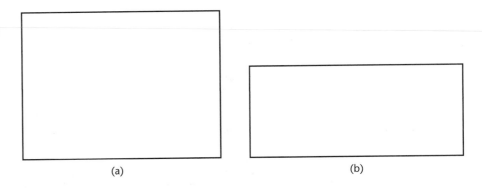

FIGURE 9.19

(a)   (b)

floor, a table, or a desk. However, please note that clay can be messy and children have a tendency to use too much clay for anchoring their towers. Monitor children closely so that they do not leave excess pieces of clay on furniture or the floor. As an alternative, children can anchor their towers to sturdy pieces of cardboard.

QUESTIONS

- How high can you build a tower without it falling over?
- Who can build the highest tower?
- Who can build a tower to look like a real building?
- What is the best shape for building the tallest tower?

Area and Perimeter

GOALS

- To explore the relationship between area and perimeter
- To understand the formulas for area and perimeter

GRADE LEVELS

- Upper grades

MATERIALS

- Straight pins
- Centimeter graph paper
- Sewing thread
- n Styrofoam or cardboard tiles (30 cm × 30 cm)

INSTRUCTIONS—PART 1

Have children answer the following questions on a sheet of paper.

1. What does $A = L \times W$ mean?

2. Assume that Figure 9.19a and Figure 9.19b were made with the same length of string. An ant walks around the string making one complete trip. Does the ant walk the same, more, or less around Figure 9.19a as compared to Figure 9.19b? Explain your choice.

3. Pretend that there is grass inside both figures. Does Figure 9.19a have the same, less, or more grass to be mowed as compared to Figure 9.19b? Explain your choice.

FIGURE 9.20

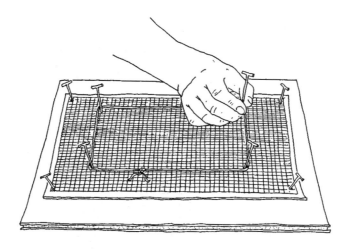

INSTRUCTIONS—PART 2

Cut a piece of thread 50 cm long and tie the two ends together. Place an 8½″ × 11″ piece of centimeter graph paper on a tile. Pin down the paper in each of the four corners. Create a square using the piece of thread and pin it to the tile. (See Figure 9.20.) Using the lines on the graph paper, determine the distance around the string. Determine the amount of surface within the string. Remove the pins and place them in different positions to create new shapes.

Continue making different shapes and finding the distances around the string and the surface within the string. Make a variety of shapes, both rectangles and triangles.

Create a chart of your data as in Table 9.7. Look for patterns in the data. Once you have established a pattern, predict what will happen with other shapes. Collect data to confirm or deny your prediction. Go back to the formula $A = L \times W$ and explain it using the data you collected. Explain it in terms of the squares, rectangles, triangles, trapezoids, parallelograms, and even circles that you made with your string.

QUESTIONS

- Does the perimeter change for each shape?

- What shape contains the most area?

- What shape contains the least area?

- Use your data to write down the formulas to find the following: perimeter of rectangles and triangles; perimeter of circles (circumference); area of rectangles; area of triangles; area of circles. Express these written explanations in algebraic form.

Determining the Origin of Pi

GOAL

- To derive pi using objects

GRADE LEVELS

- Upper grades

TABLE 9.7
Relationships of Shapes to Distance and Surfaces

Shapes	Distance Around	Surface Within
▭	?	?
▢	?	?
?	?	?

TABLE 9.8

Cylinder	Circumference	Diameter	Ratio: Circumference/Diameter
Cylinder #1	?	?	?
Cylinder #2	?	?	?
Cylinder #3	?	?	?

MATERIALS

■ A variety of small cylinders approximately 2–5 cm in diameter and 4–10 cm in length

INSTRUCTIONS

First, explain what the following formula means: Pi (π) = 3.14+.

Use the following procedures and collect data to find answers to this question. Determine the circumference of each cylinder by rolling graph paper around each one. Determine the diameter of each cylinder using graph paper as well. Determine the ratio of the circumference of each cylinder to its diameter. Once you have established a pattern, try to explain the results of your data. Record the data in Table 9.8.

SUGGESTIONS

■ Use your data to explain the rationale for the following formulas:

Circumference of a circle: $C = \pi D$

Area of a circle: $A = \pi r^2$

Area of a cylinder: $A = 2\pi r(r + h)$

Relationships between Volume and Surface Area of Cubes

GOAL

■ To compare the surface area of three-dimensional objects when the volume is constant

GRADE LEVELS

■ Upper grades

TABLE 9.9

Shape	Outside Surface	Inside Volume
▢	?	?
▭	?	?
⌐▭	?	?

MATERIALS

- 36 wooden blocks of the same size (2 × 2 cm)

INSTRUCTIONS

Create different shapes with the blocks to explore the relationship between volume and surface area. Record your data in Table 9.9.

Count the number of exposed block surfaces for each shape in the table. Remember this includes the surfaces that you see on all sides of the shape including those in contact with the table or desk. Write the results of the total amount of block surface for each shape in the "Outside Surface" column. Each block surface is one unit of area. Determine the volume for each shape made with the blocks. The volume is the space occupied by the shape the blocks create. One block represents one volume unit. Write the results for the total amount of volume for each shape in the "Inside Volume" column.

QUESTIONS

- What shape has the most surface area?
- What shape has the least surface area?
- What is the relationship between surface area and volume in cubes?

The next page shows a stack of blocks. The stack is 3 blocks high, 3 blocks wide, and 3 blocks deep.

Figure 9.21a is a side view of the stack of blocks. One row of blocks is moved and placed on top of another row to create Figure 9.21b, also a side view.

QUESTIONS

- Assume that all of the exposed sides of the blocks are windows. Are there more, less, or the same amount of windows to clean in Figure 9.21a compared to Figure 9.21b? Explain your choice.
- Assume that the blocks are hollow and a bird can fly around inside. Does the bird have the same, less, or more amount of room to fly around in Figure 9.21a as compared to Figure 9.21b?
- Collect data to support your answers by using the blocks to make different figures.

FIGURE 9.21

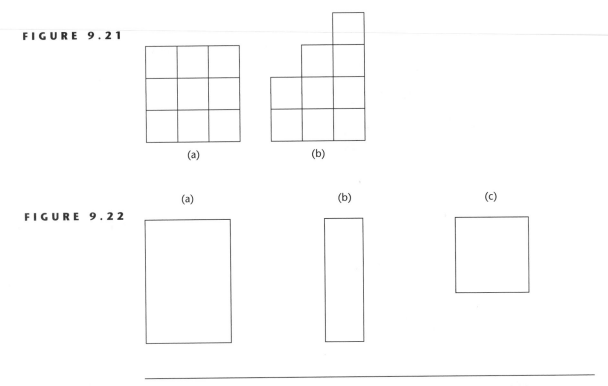

FIGURE 9.22

Determining Relationships between Surface Area and Volume of Polyhedrons

GOAL

■ To compare volume when surface area is constant

GRADE LEVELS

■ Upper grades

BEFORE BEGINNING THE ACTIVITY

Two polyhedrons (Figures 9.22b and 9.22c) were made from the same amount of paper (Figure 9.22a). Figures b and c are three-dimensional and are hollow.

■ If they were to be painted, does it take the same, less, or more amount of paint to paint Figure b compared to Figure c? Explain your choice.

■ Will Figure b hold the same, less, or more sand than Figure c? Explain your choice.

INSTRUCTIONS

Use graph paper to make the figures. Keeping the amount of paper constant, construct various polyhedrons. Fill the polyhedrons with sand, rice, beans, or wooden centimeter cubes. Compare the amounts that each holds. Complete Table 9.10.

QUESTIONS

■ Which figure holds the least amount of material?

■ Which figure holds the most amount of material?

■ What is the relationship between surface area and volume for polyhedrons?

TABLE 9.10

Shape	Surface Number of Centimeters Square	Inside Amount of Material
	?	?
	?	?

TABLE 9.11

Type and Shape	Number of Centimeter Squares Covering the Surface	Number of Objects to Fill the Inside
Shoe box	?	?

Covering Geometric Shapes

GOAL

- To explore the relationship between outside area and inside volume of three-dimensional objects

GRADE LEVELS

- Upper grades

MATERIALS

- Assorted boxes: cereal boxes, shoe boxes, and other cardboard packages
- Centimeter graph paper
- Objects to fill the boxes, such as beans, rice, centimeter cubes

INSTRUCTIONS

Find the surface area of the containers by using centimeter graph paper. Find the inside volume of the containers by filling them with objects. Develop a chart like Table 9.11.

SUGGESTIONS

- Compare the amount of material each box holds.
- Which boxes have the same amount of surface area?
- Which boxes hold the same amount of material but have different surface areas?
- Fill plastic polyhedrons with water. How much water does it take to fill each one? Determine the amount in milliliters.
- Fill the plastic polyhedrons with wooden centimeter cubes. How does the number of cubes compare to the amount of water?

Activities about Patterns in Nature

Geometrical shapes can be found in nature. Crystals are identified by shape. Leaves and flowers have definite geometrical shapes. Scientists classify plants according to the veins in the leaves and whether they are parallel lines. Flowers can have odd or even numbers of parts. Even bubbles can be studied in terms of their geometric shape. Scientists study the shape of bubbles to understand the relationship between structure and form.

Making Crystals

GOAL

■ To create crystals and identify their geometric shapes

GRADE LEVELS

■ Upper grades

MATERIALS

■ Table salt, Epsom salt, boric acid, sugar

■ String, buttons, washers, paper clips

■ Hot plate

■ Plastic and glass containers

■ Mineral and crystal sets

■ Magnifying lenses and/or binocular microscopes

BACKGROUND INFORMATION

Crystals can be created by heating water to boiling and then adding a substance, such as those listed above, to make the solution supersaturated. In other words, the substance is added until no more will dissolve. The substance will begin to precipitate to the bottom. When the water is very hot, it can hold more of the substance than when it is cool. As the water cools, the substance condenses into a solid form. If the substance cools slowly without being disturbed, large crystals form. Some crystals form on the bottom or side of the container; others form on a surface such as a string. Crystals will also form on a suspended string weighted with a paper clip or heavy button.

INSTRUCTIONS

1. Heat a small amount (5–10 ml) of water to boiling in a Pyrex container on a hot plate. Pyrex will not break when heated and cooled rapidly.

2. Add sugar, Epsom salt, boric acid, or table salt. Add the substance slowly while stirring. Stirring will make the substance dissolve quickly.

3. Continue adding and stirring until some of the substance no longer dissolves. Carefully pour the substance into glass or plastic containers. Set the containers where the solutions will not be disturbed.

4. A piece of string may be added to the solution to act as a surface on which the crystals can attach. A button, paper clip, washer, or other heavy object can be tied to the end of the string to add weight and prevent the string from floating. However, metal washers and paper clips may rust, which may disturb the growth of the crystals. Some types of crystals form very quickly; other crystals take several days to form.

5. Repeat the steps for each type of substance.

Have children examine the shapes of the crystals and identify them. Commercial crystal-making sets are also available.

Minerals are made of crystals. Find a mineral set and identify the geometric shape of its crystals.

CAUTION

Wear safety goggles around the boiling water. Use hot pads to remove the boiling water solution from the burner. Pans may be used instead of Pyrex containers. Pour the solution into glass jars but make sure the glass will not crack because of the sudden change in temperature. Canning jars work well.

SUGGESTIONS

- Maintain records of how long it takes crystals to form.
- Measure and weigh the biggest crystals that form.
- Make drawings of the crystals.
- Examine crystals with magnifying lenses and binocular microscopes.

Making Bubbles

GOAL

- To explore bubble geometric shapes in relation to objects that create the bubbles

GRADE LEVELS

- Primary to upper grades

MATERIALS

- Dishwashing liquid, water, and glycerin
- A variety of objects such as strainers, other kitchen items, plastic six-pack rings, canning jar rings, hula hoops, window screening, other objects with holes
- Plastic swimming pool or plastic washtubs
- String and drinking straws

INSTRUCTIONS

To every gallon of water add one cup of dishwashing liquid soap and a tablespoon of glycerin. Stir. Let the mixture sit overnight.

Give children small amounts of the solution in washtubs. To make bubbles, submerge the bubble maker in the solution. This activity works best outside on a sunny, warm day!

Create the skeletons of polyhedrons from drinking straws by using paper clips as suggested in the "Straw Towers" activity or by inserting string through the straws and tying the joints together. Pipe cleaners may be inserted into the straws to hold the sides in place. To make a bubble maker, use approximately three feet of string. Thread two drinking straws onto the string and tie the two ends of the string together. Using two hands, hold the two straws to form a rectangle. Dip this into the bubble solution with the string loose. Bring the two straws close together and pull the string through the air. Large bubbles will form and float away.

QUESTIONS

- Is it possible to make a square bubble? Why or why not?
- What shapes of bubbles can you make?

TABLE 9.12

Materials	Description	Concepts
Mira	Translucent, red, "I" shape	Congruence, symmetry, flips, slides, rotations
Tangrams	7 piece puzzle with patterns with different levels of difficulty	Area, spatial relations, patterns
Geoblocks	335 solid hardwood blocks	Spatial relations, proportions, ratios of volume, building, balancing
Pattern Blocks	250 hexagons, trapezoids, diamonds, triangles, and squares	Spatial relations, patterns, symmetry, fractions
Geoboards	Plastic board with pins to make shapes with rubber bands	Shapes, angles, sets, number patterns
Pentominoes	12 pieces, each 5 inches square, but different rectangular shapes	Similarity, congruence, area, perimeter, tessellations
Cuisenaire rods	74 rods in 10 colors, each color a different length, basic length is 1 cm cubed	Ratios, proportions, fractions, units of measurement, place values, building, balancing
Unifix Cubes	Interlocking plastic cubes in 10 colors	Patterns, numbers, place value

- What is the largest bubble you can make?
- How many bubbles can you make at one time?
- Examine the shape of bubbles formed with the tetrahedron skeletons.

Sources of Materials

Certain geometry activities require purchasing commercial materials. Table 9.12 provides information about the materials and the concepts they teach.

The following companies are vendors of the materials listed in Table 9.12. Delta is the only company that sells Geoblocks.

1. Creative Publications
   5623 W. 115th St.
   Worth, IL 60482-9931

2. Cuisenaire Company of America, Inc.
   P.O. Box 5026
   White Plains, NY 10602-5026

3. Dale Seymour Publications
   P.O. Box 10888
   Palo Alto, CA 94303-0879

4. Delta Education
   P.O. Box 3000
   Nashua, NH 03061-3000

Summary

Exploring objects through multiple perspectives is vital to the development of scientific and mathematical knowledge. Abstractions from these experiences create mental images or structures that form the foundation of theories and formulas. Exploring objects and understanding them from multiple perspectives is also important in understanding the viewpoints of others. Understanding begins with the child's own viewpoint. "This is because thought can only replace action on the basis of the data which action itself provides" (Piaget and Inhelder, 1967, p. 454).

How can children be expected to understand the scientific ideas of others if they have not had the experience of formulating their own? This doesn't mean that children need to reinvent the wheel, but to emphasize the importance of object exploration in the development of ideas and intelligence. For too long the emphasis has been on the product rather than the process that produces the product. One study dealt with the development of the brain. A scientist said the brain actually "creates" itself through a child's experiences using the senses, a process called "sculpting." Brain cells are added and the brain is structured through experiences. Thus, physiological research data supports the importance of children learning through experiences. The brain actually takes shape and becomes structured through experiences.

The use of measurement was stressed many times in this chapter. Measurement as a concept develops from understanding numbers, ordering, and Euclidean spatial relationships. Measurement will be examined and explored in the following chapter.

> **Go back to the reflective questions at the beginning of the chapter and the answers you recorded in your journal.**
>
> **Add to or modify your answers based on what you learned from this chapter.**

Bibliography

Gilbert, L. B. (1984). *I can do it ! I can do it! 135 successful independent learning activities.* Mt. Rainier, MD: Gryphon House.

Gleick, J. (1987). *Chaos: Making a new science.* New York: Penguin.

Hazen, R. M., and Trefil, J. (1991). *Science matters: Achieving scientific literacy.* New York: Doubleday.

National Council of Teachers of Mathematics. (1989). *Curriculum and evaluation standards for school mathematics.* Reston, VA: Author.

Nussbaum, J. (1989). The earth as a cosmic body. In R. Driver, E. Guesne, and A. Tiberghien (Eds.), *Children's ideas in science*. Milton Keynes, England: Open University Press.

Papert, S. (1980). *Mindstorms*. New York: Basic Books.

Phillips, D. (1994). *Sciencing: Towards logical thinking* (2d ed.). Dubuque, IA: Kendall Hunt.

Piaget, J., and Inhelder, B. (1967). *The child's conception of space*. New York: W.W. Norton.

Ranucci, E., and Teeters, J. (1977). *Escher-type drawings*. Mountain View, CA: Creative Publications.

Webster's ninth new collegiate dictionary. (1987). Springfield, MA: Merriam-Webster.

| # Measure for Measure

All measuring implies at least three conditions: (1) a division cutting off from the main body, one part selected as the unit; (2) a change of location allowing the unit part to be transferred to the remains of the part of that same whole, or to those of a separate whole; (3) a transitional relationship permitting the conclusion that if A = B *and* B = C, *then* A = C.

J. Piaget, *The Child's Conception of Movement and Speed*

JOURNEY PREPARATION

Reflective Questions

- Why is measurement considered both a process and a developmental concept?

- What kinds of measurement activities are most appropriate for primary-age children?

- Why is measurement important to scientific inquiry?

- Why is it important for children to learn about time through hands-on experiences?

- Why is the concept of density difficult to understand?

Introduction

Measurement was identified as a learning process in Chapter 6. In other words, measurement is a behavior used to quantify attributes of objects. However, measurement is mentally constructed from the development of the Euclidean infralogical groupings (see Chapter 9). The understanding of measurement begins with acting on objects and defining those objects in mathematical and logical concepts. The concepts are defined as relationships of distances and perimeters, areas, and volumes to geometric shapes. In Chapter 9 mathematical formulas were presented for these concepts that are used in measuring objects. This chapter discusses mathematical relationships of measurement as well as other concepts that children need for understanding these relationships. Density requires understanding the relationship between volume and weight. Temperature is a measurement that defines heat in relative terms. Time is one of the units of measuring motion of objects. The forces associated with motion can also be quantified through linear measurements.

Scientific literacy includes knowing that measurements are vital to scientists. "Evidence for interaction and subsequent change and the formulation of scientific explanations are often clarified through quantitative distinctions—measurement. Mathematics is essential for accurately measuring change" (National Research Council, 1996). Measurement is essential to science because it allows scientists to replicate and verify, with accuracy, the discoveries of others. Again, measurement becomes a way to communicate in precise terms.

Measurement involves comparing one set of objects to another set of objects, defining the parameters of objects, and locating objects in specific terms: Object A is twice as long as Object B. Object A is the same length on all sides. The object can be found suspended halfway down the wall or halfway across the room. The understanding of measurement develops from Euclidean spatial structures that involve knowing objects in precise terms. Objects can be compared, defined, or located in space in terms of one, two, and three dimensions. The more dimensions used, the more the object is defined.

Children begin with their own views of these relationships, which are neither mathematical nor precise. Their views are different from standards, which were developed by someone else.

TOUR GUIDE

National Council of Teachers of Mathematics (1989): Standard 10: Measurement

In grades K–4, the mathematics curriculum should include measurement so that students can understand the attributes of length, capacity, weight, mass, area, volume, time, temperature, and angle; develop the process of measuring and concepts related to units of measurement; make and use estimates of measurement; make and use measurements in problem and everyday situations. (p. 51)

Standard 13: Measurement

In grades 5–8, the mathematics curriculum should include extensive concrete experiences using measurement so that students can extend their understanding of the process of measurement; estimate, make, and use measurement to describe and compare phenomena; select appropriate units and tools to measure to the degree of accuracy required in a particular situation; understand the structure and use of systems of measurement; extend their understanding of the concepts of perimeter, area, volume, angle measure, capacity, and weight and mass; . . . develop formulas and procedures for determining measures to solve problems. (p. 116)

National Research Council (1996): Content Standard B

As a result of activities, all students should develop understanding of

- Properties of objects and materials
- Position and motion of objects (pp. 123, 149)

Initially no tools need to be used, but children eventually learn that they can add to their descriptions by measuring objects—first with measuring devices they create and then by using conventional measuring instruments such as rulers, balances, and thermometers. (p. 126)

In grades 5–8, students observe and measure characteristic properties, such as boiling points, melting points, solubility, and simple chemical changes of pure substances and use those properties to distinguish and separate one substance from another. (p. 149)

The science standard, quoted above, states that children can create their own measuring devices. This is the starting point of working from their own point of view. If this premise is used for teaching measurement, children will develop an intuitive sense of it as a mental operation. They will understand that individual measuring systems are difficult to communicate to each other and that standards overcome those barriers. Traditionally, it was assumed that children can inherently adapt and understand standard units of measurement. For the most part, children were given rulers and explanations of the units and expected to use them as if understanding measurement is an instantaneous learning process. The notion that understanding measurement is developmental was ignored.

Measurement for Primary Children

Young children need opportunities to make mathematical comparisons between objects to understand height, distance, and perimeter. These comparisons can be made by using a variety of objects such as paper clips, string, their feet, hands, and fingers. Making general comparisons helps children learn about estimations. Filling containers with sand, rice, and water to compare how much they hold helps children to understand volume. Weight can be understood by playing on teeter-totters, lifting objects, or putting objects in pan balances. By describing measurements, children are using fractions, proportions, and ratios: Tower A is twice as high as Tower B. There is three times as much water in this container as in the other container. Quantifying the relationships leads to understanding the units used in measurement.

Primary children learn about measurement as a concept through exploratory activities and everyday experiences rather than structured worksheets and activities. In addition, they learn measurement through interactions with each other. Allow children to explain to each other how they measure objects because verbalizing helps them integrate concepts.

When children are learning measurement through exploration, use questions that encourage them to answer in quantifiable terms. Units of measurement can be emphasized by having children state the length of an object in paper clips or the height of an object in terms of the number of blocks. Measuring sticks can be made by replicating metersticks. Boards that are the thickness and width of metersticks or yardsticks can be purchased at building supply stores, and cut to the same length as a foot ruler, yardstick, meterstick, or some other length. Children can measure with them without any units marked on them and gradually add units as needed by marking them on the boards. For example, if children measure their desks using blank foot rulers and find that the desks are one and a half times the ruler's length, they can mark the halfway point on the ruler.

Questions to Facilitate Understanding of Measurement

- How much taller are you than your sister?
- How many paper clips does it take to measure the width of your desk?
- If this side is ten paper clips long, how long is the other side?
- How many paper clips long is the length of string?

- How much longer is your foot compared to Johnny's foot?
- Which is longer?
- How much higher is the door than the tallest person in the room?
- How much bigger around is this tree compared to the other tree?
- How much heavier is the cat compared to the dog?
- How much heavier is this book compared to the other book?
- How much hotter is it today than yesterday?
- Which day had the strongest wind?
- How much Kool-Aid does glass A contain compared to glass B?
- If you pour the water into the container, where is the water level?
- How much more water do you have to add to fill the glass?
- Can you find an accurate way to measure the length of this desk?
- Which is easier to use in measuring the desk, paper clips or pencils?

As children interact with objects' attributes, use comparison questions to help them focus on mathematical relationships.

Measurement for Upper-Grade Children

In general, older children can use formulas and measurement to quantify relationships between area, volume, weight, distance traveled, time, and temperature, and to understand major concepts such as density, heat, energy, and force.

Measurement Activities

Volume Measurement of Irregular Objects

GOAL

- To use water displacement as a technique for determining the volume of irregularly shaped objects

GRADE LEVELS

- Upper grades

BACKGROUND INFORMATION

The volume of regular-shaped objects such as polyhedrons can be determined by filling the objects with blocks, sand, or water. Their volume can also be determined by measuring their height, length, and width ($V = L \times H \times W$). This formula was addressed in the last chapter, which also mentioned that one milliliter (liquid volume) of water is equal to 1 cubic centimeter ($V = L \times H \times W$). Centimeter units of measurement are used for determining the length, width, and height of solid objects. The volume of irregular objects such as rocks or objects without definitive sides can be determined using the water displacement method. Every milliliter of water displaced is equal to the volume of the irregular object in cubic centimeters.

DISCUSSION QUESTIONS

When a rock is placed in a container of water, what happens to the water level? Why? Where does the water go when the rock is added to the water? How much water is pushed out of the way?

FIGURE 10.1

Discuss these questions with each other and your instructor before continuing. Water displacement is an abstract concept and children as well as adults may have difficulty understanding it. Why is an abstract idea so difficult to understand?

At what grade level would the study of water displacement be most appropriate? What kinds of mental structures are needed to understand the concept of water displacement?

Explain the concept of water displacement to each other.

MATERIALS

- A variety of small pieces of rocks
- Metal cubes
- A variety of graduated cylinders (10, 100, 1000 ml)
- Drinking cups
- Drinking straws
- Small amount of florist (oil-based) clay

INSTRUCTIONS

Water Displacement in a Graduated Cylinder

Put enough water in a graduated cylinder to cover an object. Record the water level, then gently place the object in the water so that no water splashes out. Record the new water level. The difference of the two readings is the volume of the object. Since one milliliter of water equals one centimeter cubed, the amount of milliliters can be converted to cubic centimeters.

Overflow of Displaced Water

This method involves catching and measuring the water that overflows when an object is placed in a container that is completely filled with water. The container has to be big enough so the object can rest on the bottom, and not so wide that the rise of the water level is too small to measure. Small objects can be measured in regular-size Styrofoam or plastic cups.

Make a hole in the cup approximately 2/3 from the bottom. The hole should be no bigger than the diameter of a drinking straw.

Cut a straw so that it is four centimeters long. Insert the straw into the hole at approximately a 45° angle to the side of the cup in a downward position. The end of the straw must be flush with the wall inside the cup. Use the clay to seal around the hole and straw so that no water leaks from the cup. Figure 10.1 shows the completed overflow cup.

Fill the cup with enough water so that water flows into the straw spout. If it begins dripping, you have enough water in the cup. Place a graduated cylinder below the spout to catch the water. When it stops dripping, discard that excess water.

Place an object in the cup. Any water that runs out of the cup when the object is placed in it represents the volume of the object. Measure this volume of water in the graduated cylinder.

QUESTIONS

- Compare the volume of a regular solid measured linearly to the volume found through the water displacement method. Are they the same?

- Will the volumes be different for various rocks and minerals that weigh the same?

- How can you measure the volume of an object that floats using the water displacement technique?

Density Activities

The water displacement technique is also used to find the density of objects. Do you remember the formula $D = m/v$ (D = density, m = mass, and v = volume)? What is mass? What is density?

The following three activities provide different experiences to help children understand density. Each activity results in "observable" data to help them formulate the concept of density. Work through the activities yourself to see if they give you a better understanding of density.

Children may not understand the concept of density after a single activity or experience. Before children can understand density they have to understand volume and mass. At what grade levels would exploring density be developmentally appropriate? Refer to previous chapters on concept development to find an answer. Is density directly observable through the senses? Explore these activities to help yourself understand density.

Rising Raisins

GOAL

- To explain density in terms of sinking and floating raisins

GRADE LEVELS

- Upper grades

MATERIALS

- 12 oz clear bottles of seltzer water
- Raisins, grapes, mothballs
- Newspaper
- Paper towels (to wipe up any spilled seltzer water)

INSTRUCTIONS

Cover the work area with newspaper. Carefully open a small bottle of seltzer water and place several raisins in the water. After a few minutes, notice what they do. Look closely at them to see if you can explain their actions. Write down an explanation for their motion. Go back to your explanation of density. Compare your explanation to the formula for density.

SUGGESTIONS

Try other objects such as grapes and mothballs to see if they react the same as the raisins. Try other liquids that contain carbon dioxide.

Sink 'n Float

GOAL

- To explain density in terms of the shape and volume of objects

GRADE LEVELS

- Upper grades

MATERIALS

- Oil-based clay (floral clay)
- Washtub half full of water
- Aluminum foil
- Straight pins
- Metal washers
- Paper clips
- Pennies and other objects such as metal and plastic washers, pieces of window screening, soda pop cans (unopened), fruit, pieces of wood, rocks
- Newspaper
- Paper towels

INSTRUCTIONS

Cover the surface area with newspaper. Start by taking a small amount of clay and making a boat. Make it float in a tub of water. Explore the concept of density by doing the activities and answering the questions in the following section.

QUESTIONS AND SUGGESTIONS

- How many objects will the clay hold before it sinks?
- Given the same weight of clay and the same type of objects, who can get their clay to hold the most number of objects?
- Compare objects by determining the ratio of the number of objects placed on the clay boat to the type of objects, for example, 10 metal washers and 20 plastic washers.
- Make a clay submarine.
- Make an aluminum foil boat. How many washers will it hold compared to the clay boat?
- Compare the weight of the clay boat to the aluminum foil boat. How many more objects does it take to sink the aluminum foil boat than the clay boat?
- How much aluminum foil does it take to equal the weight of the clay boat?
- Will the aluminum foil float if it has pinholes in it?
- Can you make a piece of aluminum foil sink without adding anything to it?
- Can you make an aluminum foil submarine?
- Will a piece of window screen float?

- What other objects will float?

- What other objects will sink?

- Can you get an object that floats to sink?

- Can you get an object that sinks to float?

- Place unopened soda pop cans in the water. Be sure to add enough water to cover them. What do you observe? Explain.

- Go back to your definition of density and see if it explains why certain things float or sink. Rewrite your definition if your data support a modification.

- What will be the density of objects that float or sink when compared to water?

- Will an orange sink or float? Peel an orange and predict whether it will sink or float.

- Which fruits sink or float? Can you predict which ones and why?

- Can you find wood that sinks?

- Can you find rocks that float?

Closed Systems

GOAL

- To explain density in terms of the change in volume of objects that sink and float

GRADE LEVELS

- Upper grades

MATERIALS

- One large test tube (diameter = 2.5 cm, length = 20 cm)

- One small test tube (diameter = 1 cm, length = 7.5 cm)

- One 9-inch round rubber balloon

- Rubber bands

- Plastic washtub

- Clear plastic 2-liter soda pop bottles with caps

- Other assorted plastic bottles in different shapes and sizes

INSTRUCTIONS

Fill the washtub half full of water. Place the large test tube in the tub and fill it with water. Place the small test tube in the tub and fill it with water.

Will the small test tube sink or float in the large test tube when it is completely filled with water? What will the small test tube do if it is inverted with no water inside? Will it sink or float?

Put your finger over the opening of the small test tube to prevent the water from escaping. Keeping your finger in place, invert the test tube and gently drop it into the water of the larger test tube. Find a way to make the bottom of the small test tube even with the water level in the large test tube when it is turned upside down. (See Figure 10.2.) How much water is needed in the small test tube?

Cut a round balloon in half by cutting around the balloon, not across it. Stretch one of the halves across the opening of the large test tube. Tie a rubber band around the stretched balloon and test tube. Figure 10.3 shows the completed system. (The national science standards define *system* as "an organized

FIGURE 10.2

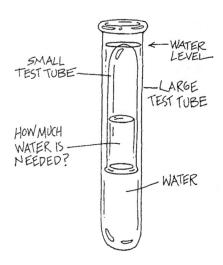

FIGURE 10.3

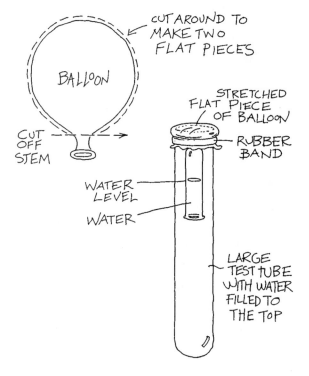

group of related objects or components that form a whole"; National Research Council, 1996, p. 116.) Once the balloon is secure, push down on it with your thumb and watch what happens to the small test tube. Release your thumb and watch what happens to the small test tube. Try this several times, watching what happens so that you can explain the motion of the small test tube.

Why does the small test tube move up and down? Explain this in terms of your definition of density. Where should the water level be in the small test tube to make the bottom of the small test tube level with the water in the large test tube?

A closed system can be made with a clear 2-liter bottle. Place the small test tube in the bottle, replace the cap and screw it down tightly. Squeeze the sides of the bottle. Watch what happens.

FIGURE 10.4

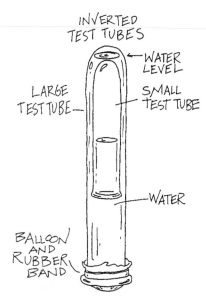

Using the formula D = m/v, *how can you determine whether an object will sink or float in water?*

The weight of water is 1 g/ 1 ml. Thus the density of water is 1. For all practical purposes, mass* and weight are the same. For example, if an object weighs 10 grams and has a volume of 20 milliliters, its density is one half.

Will the object sink or float? If the object weighs 50 grams and the volume is 10 milliliters, will the object sink or float? Why?

The density of objects can be determined by weighing the objects and finding their volumes. Unknown objects can be identified by their densities. Pure gold has a different density than fool's gold (pyrite). Minerals and rocks have different densities.

QUESTIONS AND SUGGESTIONS

■ The liquid, the container, and the small test tube are variables that will affect the small test tube's ability to sink. It is important to note the liquid level in the small test tube each time one of the variables is changed, because the changes are likely to affect the liquid level in the small test tube.

■ Does it matter how much water is inside the large test tube?

■ Can you make the small test tube stand suspended at the bottom of a large test tube when the bottom of the test tube is pointed upward? (See Figure 10.4.) The balloon is stretched across the opening of the large test tube. When you press on the balloon, the small test tube will sink toward the balloon.

■ Can you find a way to make the small test tube move either up or down?

■ What would happen if you used salt water to fill the large test tube? Oil? Vinegar? Rubbing alcohol?

■ What would happen if you used hot water?

■ What would happen if the small test tube contained a different liquid or a liquid at a different temperature than the large test tube?

---

*Mass is the material itself. The weight of the mass is created by the force of gravity. Thus, the mass can be defined in terms of weight on the earth. On the moon, the same mass would have a different weight because of the difference in gravitational pull.

- Using one 2-liter bottle, can you get several small test tubes to move at different speeds?

- Create a water game. For example, try making a small test tube move inside a medium-size test tube in a 2-liter plastic bottle.

- Use plastic pipettes to make divers. Purchase long-stemmed plastic pipettes and cut off all but about 1–2 cm of the stem. Put water inside the pipettes and add small hex nuts to the stems. The amount of water inside the pipettes plus the weight of the hex nuts will help them sink.

- Poke a hole with scissors or some other sharp object in the center of a circular piece of transparency just big enough to insert the stem of the pipette. The diameter of the circular pieces should be slightly larger than the bulb of the pipette. Make 5 to 6 notches into the circle and bend back the pieces to make blades. Make a hole in the center of the circle the size of the pipette stem. Place the circle on the pipette. When the pipette sinks, observe what happens. Explain.

- Can you make a test tube sink in a glass bottle?

- Rather than using round plastic bottles, try using plastic bottles with flat sides. What do you have to do to make a small test tube sink in these bottles?

Weather Measurement Activities

Children from primary to upper grades can measure different weather variables. They can measure wind speed and precipitation by using nonstandard comparisons. (*Note:* Nonstandard refers to creating a personal measurement system that has not been agreed upon by others. It is usually difficult to use by others because there is no preciseness in measurement scales. For example, children can "measure" the temperature of the room by ranking the temperature on a scale from very cold to very hot. The number 1 could be very cold and the number 10 could represent very hot. There are likely to be variations in how children interpret the temperature using this type of scale.) Upper grade children can create thermometers to measure indoor and outdoor temperatures. They can measure relative humidity and the dew point. However, changes in barometric pressure are normally slow with little fluctuation over long intervals. Barometric pressure instruments have to be very sensitive to changes in atmospheric pressures. This fact makes them difficult to assemble with any kind of accuracy.

Making a Thermometer

GOAL

- To use the concept of expansion and contraction of liquids to make thermometers

GRADE LEVELS

- Upper grades

BACKGROUND INFORMATION

Heat is produced by the motion of molecules. Since only the results of this motion can be detected and not the motion itself, heat is another abstract concept. Temperature is the measurement of this motion in relative terms. Several temperature scales have been developed: Fahrenheit, Celsius, and Kelvin. Thermometers are temperature-measuring tools. The most common thermometer consists of a long, thin tube connected to a receptacle containing a liquid that expands when heated and contracts when cooled. A scale can be made from the lowest point at which the liquid contracts to the highest point at which the liquid expands. Understanding the concept of a scale means "understanding that different characteristics, properties, or relationships within a system might change as its dimensions are increased or decreased" (National Research Council, 1996, p. 118). The temperatures at which water freezes and boils are two good benchmarks for making units of measurement. The Celsius thermometer is based on freezing at the 0° mark and boiling at the 100° mark.

However, water is impractical as a medium for a thermometer because of the limited range between boiling and freezing. Thermometers are usually made with alcohol or mercury, which are more sensitive to temperature changes and have lower freezing points than water. Mercury thermometers can be used to measure a wide range of temperatures. Alcohol freezes at a much lower temperature than water but will boil before water does.

What liquid is best for weather thermometers? What liquid is best for scientific measurements?

Mercury is very poisonous and extreme caution must be used if the thermometer breaks. Do not allow mercury to come in contact with the skin. It can be absorbed and cause damage to the brain and other vital organs.

Children can go to the library or use the Internet to learn more about the various types of thermometers and their uses.

How do thermostrips measure temperature?

Other thermometers, such as those used in thermostats, are made of metal strips that bend and contract with changes in heat. They are used to measure extremely high temperatures. Temperature probes can be connected to calculators and computers to automatically record temperatures. Instantaneous readings can be taken for a variety of microclimates.

MATERIALS

- Clear plastic straws or glass tubing
- Vaseline
- Colored water
- Cork or rubber stoppers
- Test tubes or some other receptacles for water
- Tongue depressors

SAFETY PRECAUTIONS

Put a tiny amount of Vaseline on the glass tubing. To insert the glass tubing into the stopper, twist and push at the same time. Pushing on the glass tube without twisting may cause it to break in your hand. Always wear safety goggles around flames and boiling water.

INSTRUCTIONS

Place glass tubing through a rubber stopper and insert it in a test tube containing water. The glass tubing has to be long enough so that when the water in the test tube is heated it will not rise out of the tubing. The less water in the test tube, the less it will rise.

FIGURE 10.5

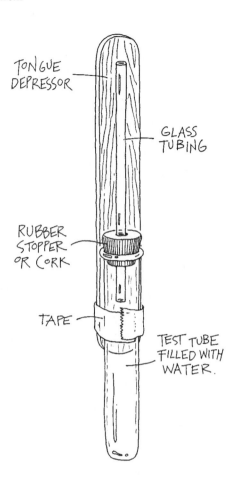

Fill the test tube with water so that the water level in the tubing rises above the rubber stopper. Attach a tongue depressor to the glass tubing with rubber bands (see Figure 10.5) and place the test tube in crushed ice. Allow the water in the test tube to become as cold as possible. When the water level stops dropping, mark that point on the tongue depressor as zero or freezing. Place the test tube in boiling water and allow the water to rise to the highest point possible. Mark this point as 100 or boiling. Then mark units of 10 between zero and 100.

For safety, classroom thermometers can be made instead from thin plastic tubing, plastic straws, and plastic or metal 35 mm film canisters. Drill a hole in the film canister lid to insert the straw. Put clay around the contact point between the straw and the lid to prevent the water from leaking. Since plastic is more of an insulator than glass, the water inside a plastic container will take longer to heat or cool than the water inside a glass container. Water will be more sensitive to temperature changes and will rise higher in tubing that has a small diameter.

Can you explain why?

The size of the container is also a factor in determining how fast the thermometer will respond to temperature changes. The volume of water in the container will affect the length of time it takes for the water to move up or down in the tube.

Water is used in this experiment since it is the safest. It is not poisonous and will not boil over and ignite like alcohol.

Additional Resources for Thermometers

Other small (3–4 cm long, 1 cm diameter) clear plastic containers can be used instead of test tubes, such as plastic flower holders, which are small, clear plastic vials with a stopper. The stopper has a flexible hole so that flowers with different-sized stems can be inserted. Hospitals and research laboratories may sell or donate small plastic vials. Science supply companies may also have them. Contact high school science teachers for additional suggestions.

QUESTIONS

■ According to the thermometer you made, what is the room temperature?

■ Find a commercial thermometer. How does its temperature reading compare to the temperature reading on your thermometer?

■ Place your thermometer in other locations to determine the temperature. Is the temperature the same or different?

■ How does the temperature vary when a thermometer is placed in the sun and then in the shade? Record your findings. Explain your results.

■ Does your thermometer's readings agree with those of your classmates?

■ Where do you think you will locate the coldest spot in the room? The warmest?

Measuring Precipitation

GOAL

■ To create devices that will collect moisture from rain and snow to measure the amount of precipitation

GRADE LEVELS

■ Upper grades

MATERIALS

■ Containers whose openings vary in diameter, such as cans, glass and plastic jars

■ Plastic funnels

INSTRUCTIONS

Rather than purchasing rain or snow gauges, allow children to explore making their own precipitation gauges. Remember that a container's opening is just as important as its size. Wide-mouthed containers collect more water, but because their diameters are large it is difficult to create a scale equal to inches; the volume of water spreads out over an area of little depth. Small-mouthed containers are more suitable to collecting inches of precipitation but the same problem arises if the container's diameter is large. Funnels help to catch rain in containers with small openings. Let children explore using different containers to see if they can find a way to measure precipitation.

QUESTIONS AND SUGGESTIONS

■ Place the "gauges" outside, away from buildings, shrubs, and trees. Use funnels in containers that have a small opening.

■ How do meteorologists measure precipitation?

■ Liquids are measured in volumes such as ounces, pints, and quarts or milliliters, deciliters, or liters, but meteorologists measure snow and rain in inches.

Why? Use the library as a resource or interview a meteorologist to find out how precipitation is measured and collected.

- What does it mean to measure precipitation in inches?

- Measure the amount of moisture collected in the containers and compare it to what is recorded in the daily newspaper.

- What shape of container seems to give the most accurate reading? Why?

- Measure, in milliliters, a given volume of snow. Bring it in the classroom and allow it to melt. Measure the volume again. What is the proportion of snow before and after melting? Collect snow on different occasions. Is the proportion the same?

Measuring the Wind

GOAL

- To develop instruments to measure wind motion and speed

GRADE LEVELS

- Upper grades

BACKGROUND INFORMATION

Wind is measured by an instrument called an anemometer. It consists of cone-shaped cups attached to dowels projecting from a center point.

QUESTIONS AND SUGGESTIONS

- Observe the American flag as it blows. Develop criteria that describe the strength of the wind. For example, no movement might have a value of zero. A very strong wind that extends the flag perpendicular to the pole might have a value of 10. Numbers between 1 and 10 can represent other positions of the flag when the wind is blowing.

- How many spins does a pinwheel make when the wind is very strong?

- How much do the angles of tree branches change when the wind is strong?

- How many times do leaves rustle in the wind during a given time?

- Make an anemometer using drinking cups. Capron, Brooks, and Rieben (1996) provide directions for making an anemometer.

- Make a wind sock. Many people have decorative wind socks in their yards.

- Make toys with parts that move when the wind blows (for example, pinwheels, sailboats, and windmills).

- Find out how sailors determine the speed of the wind.

Finding the Dew Point

GOAL

- To develop a technique for measuring the dew point

GRADE LEVELS

- Upper grades

BACKGROUND INFORMATION

The dew point is the temperature at which water vapor in the air condenses to a liquid on objects. Moisture in warm air will condense on a cold glass of water. After a warm, humid day, dew will form on the grass in the early morning when the temperature is usually at its lowest. The dew point is important in the formation of rain.

MATERIALS

- Glass, plastic, Styrofoam, and metal containers
- Water
- Thermometers

QUESTIONS AND SUGGESTIONS

- Place water and ice in various containers. Stir the water and ice and watch for the formation of water droplets on the outside of the containers. Record the temperature when the water droplets begin to form. This is the dew point. Compare the rate at which the dew point forms on the different containers. On which container does the dew form the fastest? Slowest? Can you explain why? Try this activity at various times throughout the year to compare the dew point at various temperatures.

- What kinds of drinking glasses are the best to use for cold drinks?

- Develop ways to prevent dew from forming on cold drink containers.

- Why does a ring of water form on surfaces where a cold drink has been placed? What can be done to prevent the ring from forming?

Relative Humidity

GOAL

- To develop a method for measuring relative humidity

GRADE LEVELS

- Upper grades

MATERIALS

- Thermometers
- Cotton gauze
- Water

INSTRUCTIONS

The amount of moisture or humidity in the air can fluctuate depending on the temperature of the air. Typically, warm air holds more water vapor than cold air. In the summer, warm days can feel very humid while winter days can feel very dry. Desert areas are extremely hot with very little moisture in the air during the summer, and other areas with abundant lakes feel very humid during the winter. Water can evaporate very quickly in a dry climate. As it does, it lowers the temperature of the surface from which it is evaporating. The temperature created by evaporation is compared to the actual air temperature to calculate the relative humidity.

Relative humidity is the ratio of the amount of water vapor in air to the greatest amount possible at the same temperature. You can determine the relative humidity by attaching cotton gauze (the kind used to bandage cuts and bruises) to the bulb of a thermometer, soaking the gauze in water, and rapidly moving the thermometer through the air to evaporate the water. The lowest temperature at which the evaporation occurs, compared to the actual air temperature, is used to calculate the relative humidity. There is a point at which the water-soaked gauze will no longer lower the temperature reading on the thermometer. For example, if the lowest temperature of the thermometer with the wet gauze reads 50° after the evaporation takes place and the air temperature is 70°, we divide 50 by 70 to get the relative humidity of approximately 71%. This percentage means that the air contains 71% water vapor.

QUESTIONS AND SUGGESTIONS

- If the evaporation temperature is 70 and the air temperature is 70, describe the amount of moisture in the air.

- If the evaporation temperature is 10 and the air temperature is 70, describe the amount of moisture in the air.

- Determine today's relative humidity by using the precedures described above. Compare your data with newspaper and TV weather information.

- "Dew point" is easier to understand than "relative humidity" because children can see the condensation of water on containers and measure the temperature at which condensation occurs. What mathematics and science concepts must children know to understand the concept of relative humidity?

- What makes it difficult to understand the concept of relative humidity? What are some ways to help children understand it?

The Measurement of Time

It goes without saying that the development of psychological time involves physical time, since the coordination of actions performed at different rates presupposes that some work has been done in the first place, and since all work is sooner or later incorporated into the external world. Hence personal memory is the memory of things and actions in the external world as much, if not more so than, the memory of things and actions in the inner world. (Piaget, 1969, p. 277)

Time in both cases is therefore the coordination of motions, and the direction of its flow can only be deduced from the causal chain, because causes necessarily precede their effects. Now if causality is the general system of operations enabling us to correlate physical events, it is clear that before we can establish the existence of a causal relationship by experiment, we must first be able to correlate our measurements and this involves appealing to our memory or to reconstruct characteristics of psychological time. This is precisely what we mean when we say that physical time implies psychological time, and vice versa. (Piaget, 1969, p. 278)

Understanding time as a measurement involves understanding time as a concept. Time does not exist without motion. Years, months, days, hours, minutes are units of measurement in relation to the motion of the earth. Young children who do not understand time as a standard or units for measuring time can relate to it by becoming conscious of their own actions over a given time period. For example, ask them, "Which took longer, building the sand castle or building the wooden block castle?"

As Piaget points out above, primary-age children will develop a sense of time connecting their memory of things and the actions associated with them. Use objects with regular motions to make comparisons. For example, sand timers, metronomes, heartbeats, dripping water, or analog clocks can be used to time events such as building with blocks, jumping rope, running, or jumping. Children have to see or hear time passing in relation to their own actions in order to understand it. For example, children can compare how long it takes to build a block tower by using a sand timer.

Primary-grade children do not learn time by moving pointers around a numbered paper plate. This type of activity requires children to make a mental jump from no reference point to understanding a standard unit of measurement foreign to their own viewpoint. Clocks and watches will have no meaning until the motion of the child and the motion of the hands of the clock are coordinated. Digital watches and clocks do not give a continuous visual sense of time passing compared to those that have moving hands. Children learn about time first by understanding seconds and minutes, which digital clocks and watches may not show in terms of motion and numbers. Keeping track of hours is a task that can be beyond the attention span of young children.

Upper-grade children who have a sense of seconds and minutes can explore time using the following activities.

Time Measurement Activities

Water Absorption Clocks

GOAL

- To compare the passing of time to the motion of water absorption

GRADE LEVELS

- Upper grades

BACKGROUND INFORMATION

Water can adhere to the molecules of other kinds of materials and move through the spaces between the molecules. The water is absorbed by the material. Depending on the type of paper towel, water will travel through the paper towel at a certain rate or distance for a given time period. Water and paper towel timers can be created using this knowledge.

MATERIALS

- Assortment of types and brands of paper towels
- Water
- Plastic containers for water
- Rubber bands
- Centimeter rulers

INSTRUCTIONS

Create a two-minute timer using a paper towel and water. The water must soak into the paper towel and reach a designated mark at the end of 2 minutes.

Cut strips of paper towel 3 cm × 30 cm. Place approximately 2 cm of water in a container. Hold two different strips of paper towel in the water and time how fast the water travels to the top of the paper towel.

FIGURE 10.6

QUESTIONS

- Does water travel at different rates through different brands or types of paper towels?

- Does the shape of the paper towel affect how fast water travels through it? Rolled? Flat? Twisted?

- Does the position (horizontal or vertical) of the paper towel affect how fast water travels?

Water Drip Clocks

GOAL

- To compare the passing of time to dripping water

GRADE LEVELS

- Upper grades

MATERIALS

- Bottle-top caps with spouts from dishwashing liquid or other liquid cleaner dispenser bottles
- Paper cone cups
- Lids from jars and liter bottles

INSTRUCTIONS

Develop a timer that lets water drip in 1-second intervals for 3 minutes. The hole has to be the right size to allow one drop of water to drip each second. (See Figure 10.6.)

QUESTIONS

- Can you make a water drip clock that makes a container fill up in 3 minutes?

- Can you make a water drip clock that makes objects move, such as a water wheel?

- Can you make a water drip clock that will fill up one container, overflow into another container, and create a waterfall?

FIGURE 10.7

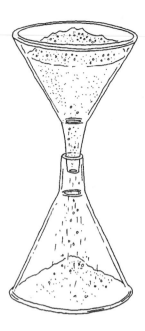

Sand Clocks

GOAL

■ To compare the passing of time to sand dropping through a funnel

GRADE LEVELS

■ Upper grades

MATERIALS

■ Sand in different sizes

■ Different sizes of plastic or metal funnels

■ Paper cone cups

■ Jar lids

INSTRUCTIONS

You can find sand at pet and aquarium stores, ocean and lake beaches, and science supply companies. With the help of Figure 10.7, create a 3-minute timer that lets sand completely run out of one container into another. The amount of sand and the size of the hole from which it descends are factors that affect the time.

QUESTIONS

■ Can you make a 5-minute timer and reverse the flow of sand, like an hourglass?

■ What size sand is the best for making a timer?

■ Can you make a swinging 3-minute timer from which sand runs out onto paper, making a pattern?

Candle Clocks

GOAL

■ To compare the passing of time to the change in length of a burning candle

FIGURE 10.8

EACH MARK
REPRESENTS
A TEN-MINUTE
INTERVAL

GRADE LEVELS

- Upper grades

MATERIALS

- Candles with different diameters
- Safety glasses

INSTRUCTIONS

Figure out ways to use a burning candle to make a 3-minute timer. (See Figure 10.8.)

SAFETY PRECAUTIONS

Don't let candles fall over. You can place a candle at the front of the room for observation. If children work with candles at their desks or tables, they must wear safety goggles. Make sure candles are anchored so that they will not tip. Candles can be anchored to metal lids or glass plates by setting them into some melted wax. Caution children not to lean over the flame and to keep their hair tied back.

QUESTIONS

- Is there some way to make the candle go out when it reaches the 3-minute mark?
- Can you predict how tall a candle will be after it burns for 5 minutes?
- Does the shape of a candle affect how fast it burns?
- Do paraffin candles burn quicker than beeswax candles?

Rolling Marble Timer

GOALS

- To compare the passing of time to an object rolling down an inclined plane
- To use the angle of reflection to determine the path of a marble

GRADE LEVELS

- Upper grades

MATERIALS

- Rectangular table, approximately 60 cm × 120 cm
- Marbles
- Heavy construction paper, tagboard, or manila folders
- Masking tape

FIGURE 10.9

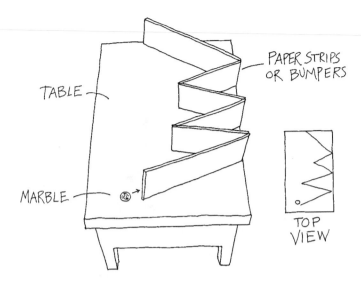

INSTRUCTIONS

The purpose of this activity is to get a marble to roll down a table in one minute. Raise one end of a table so that a marble will roll from one end to the other in 10 seconds. Then use strips of heavy paper to slow the speed of the marble. Anchor the paper to the table with masking tape. (See Figure 10.9.)

To slow down, the marble's direction must change so that it rolls against the pull of gravity. The pieces of construction paper are "bumpers" that change the direction of the marble. The bumpers must be placed at various angles to make the marble change direction. Thus, children have to consider the *angle of incidence* (the angle at which the marble hits the bumper) and the *angle of reflection* (the angle at which the marble bounces off the bumper) when planning the placement of the bumpers. The angle of incidence and the angle of reflection are equal to each other.

Pendulums

GOAL

- To measure time using pendulums

GRADE LEVELS

- Upper grades

BACKGROUND INFORMATION

Pendulums are important parts of clocks and metronomes. The pendulum in a clock moves gears, which in turn move the hands of the clock. A metronome is designed to move back and forth at different tempos.

MATERIALS

- String, springs, rubber bands, wooden dowels, clay, drinking straws, metal washers, plastic bottles, Styrofoam cups, paper clips, wooden blocks, beads

INSTRUCTIONS

Choose objects from the materials list to make a pendulum and a metronome.

FIGURE 10.10

SUGGESTIONS AND QUESTIONS

- Make a pendulum that swings back and forth in exactly one second.
- Create a pendulum that swings back and forth for exactly one minute.
- Create an object that rocks back and forth, up and down, or sideways for a given amount of time.
- Make a metronome that moves 10 times in 10 seconds.
- Can you make a metronome change its speed?
- What is the longest time you can make the metronome continue to swing?

Twister Alarm Clocks

GOAL

- To measure time using twisting objects

GRADE LEVELS

- Upper grades

MATERIALS

- String, wooden dowels, bottle caps, tin cans, nuts and bolts, cardboard tubes, drinking straws, tin cans

BACKGROUND INFORMATION

Twister alarm clocks are based on the idea of a pendulum, except that objects are hanging from two strings rather than one. (See Figure 10.10.)

SUGGESTIONS

- Hang objects such as wooden dowels, cardboard tubes, and straws using two pieces of string of equal length. Twist the strings around each other and release. How long does it take the strings to unravel?
- Make a twister alarm clock that will unravel in 3 minutes.
- Make a twister alarm clock that makes an alarming noise at the end of 3 minutes. The alarming noise can be made by a wooden dowel hitting tin cans as the strings unravel. Bottle caps, nuts and bolts can be used to make the alarm noise.

Melting Ice Cubes

GOAL

- To measure time using melting ice cubes

GRADE LEVELS

- Middle to upper grades

MATERIALS

- Plastic containers such as ice cube trays and other plastic containers in different sizes and shapes
- Balloons and other spherical objects that can be filled with water and frozen
- Pieces of cloth, Styrofoam, aluminum foil, newspaper, cardboard (these materials are used to develop investigations that explore the melting rate of ice)

INSTRUCTIONS

The shape of ice may affect how long it takes to melt. Children can fill different containers with water and freeze them to investigate the shape of ice and how long it takes to melt. The amount of water used should be the same for all shapes. Children can also explore ways to speed up or slow down the natural melting process. They can do this without using direct heat from flames or other heating devices that may not be safe in the classroom. Have them weigh the ice cubes they make to try to keep them uniform so they can make comparisons.

QUESTIONS

- Can you melt an ice cube in one minute?
- Experiment with melting an ice cube as quickly as possible.
- How long can you keep an ice cube from melting?
- Does the shape of ice affect how long it takes for it to melt?
- What shape takes the longest to melt?
- What shape takes the shortest time to melt?
- Can you make a 3-minute timer using ice?

Summary

Measurement is essential to scientific inquiry because it provides quantifiable data for replication and verification. Understanding measurement is also essential for everyday living. Challenge children to be exact whenever they collect data. Ask questions like, "How do you know for sure?" "What is the exact weight?" "Exactly how much smaller is it than the other object?" If children do not understand standard measurements they can be exact with whatever measuring device they choose. Encourage children to talk with each other about nonstandard units of measurement so that they develop a need for using standard units.

Understanding measurement is a developmental process. Assess what children understand and provide a variety of concrete experiences that will lead to their understanding of standard units of measure. This natural process of development may occur over years and needs to be articulated through the different grade levels.

Measurement is also important to understand relationships among forces. The next chapter provides discussions and activities that facilitate understanding physical forces as concepts and quantifying their relationship through measurements.

Go back to the reflective questions at the beginning of the chapter and the answers you recorded in your journal.

Add to or modify your answers based on what you learned from this chapter.

REST STOP 10.1

Metric System Units of Measurement

The metric system is based on units of 10. The prefix *centi* means 100 units smaller than 1. The prefix *milli* means 1000 units smaller than 1. The prefix *kilo* means 1000 units greater than 1.

The English system is not included here since we are familiar with it. Conversions are not included since they are difficult for children to understand. Children can make comparisons by measuring in both systems.

Abbreviation	Unit	Length
mm	millimeter	$\frac{1}{1000}$ meter (.001)
cm	centimeter	$\frac{1}{100}$ meter (.01)
dm	decimeter	$\frac{1}{10}$ meter (.1)
m	meter	1
dam	dekameter	10
hm	hectometer	100
km	kilometer	1000

Abbreviation	Unit	Area (based on linear measurements)
cm^2	square centimeter	$\frac{1}{1000}$ (.001)
km^2	square kilometer	1,000,000
ha	hectare	10,000

Abbreviation	Unit	Mass (weight)
mg	milligram	$\frac{1}{1000}$ (.001)
cg	centigram	$\frac{1}{100}$ (.01)
dg	decigram	$\frac{1}{10}$ (.1)
g	gram	1 (equal to 1 cubic centimeter of water)
dag	dekagram	10
hg	hectogram	100
kg	kilogram	1000

Abbreviation	Unit	Liquid Volume
ml	milliliter	$\frac{1}{1000}$ (.001)
cl	centiliter	$\frac{1}{100}$ (.01)
dl	deciliter	$\frac{1}{10}$ (.1)
l	liter	1
dal	dekaliter	10
hl	hectoliter	100
kl	kiloliter	1000

Abbreviation	Unit	Temperature
°C	degrees Celsius	(0° is freezing and 100° is boiling)

Bibliography

Capron, R., Brooks, R., and Rieben, E. (1996). The high plains: Land of extremes. *Science and Children, 34*(1), 41–48.

National Council of Teachers of Mathematics. (1989). *Curriculum and evaluation standards for school mathematics*. Reston, VA: Author.

National Research Council. (1996). *National science education standards*. Washington, DC: National Academy Press.

Piaget, J. (1969). *The child's conception of time*. New York: Basic Books.

Piaget, J. (1970). *The child's conception of movement and speed*. New York: Basic Books.

| # Measurement of Forces

Hence, whatever time is available in the curriculum for physics topics ought to be used first for considering the difficult and abstract concepts involved. Giving prime importance to mathematical statements relating to these concepts will only continue to hide the clear inconstancies between the beliefs of students and the tenets of physics.

R. Gunstone and M. Watts, "Force and Motion"

Reflective Questions

- Why are concepts such as force, electricity, light, and sound difficult to comprehend?

- What can children learn about these concepts through hands-on activities?

- How can mathematics be incorporated in these activities?

- What part of these concepts can be understood only through models, books, and other secondary sources?

- Why do scientists measure forces?

Introduction

Time and motion are used to measure forces. Actions and motion are caused by forces. Gravity is a force that causes pendulums to swing or marbles to roll down an incline. Energy is released whenever motion occurs over a distance. Energy is an abstract idea because it is mentally conceptualized from the relationships between forces and motion. We know that energy exists because products such as heat, light, and chemical changes result from the energy released from motion and forces.

The activities in this chapter focus on cause and effect relationships that result from the interactions of a variety of physical forces. This chapter is a continuation of Chapter 10 because measurement is important for comparing data. In Chapter 6, the pendulum and the whirly bird activities studied how gravity and friction affect motion and speed. In this chapter, motion and speed are further explored through inclined planes, gears and pulleys, elastic energy, and air pressure. Other activities explore characteristics of other types of forces such as magnetism, electromagnetism, light, and sound. Scientific explanations for these concepts are based on inferences since causes of these phenomena are found at the molecular, atomic, and subatomic levels. A brief explanation is given for the causes of these phenomena to provide the reader with some background information. However, it is advisable to read other resources for further comprehension. The most important thing to remember is that there is no substitute for experience. The activities provide opportunities to explore observable behaviors and characteristics of these concepts. This is more important than trying to understand scientific explanations that are based on behaviors and characteristics of molecules, atoms, and their components. The national science standards declare that these concepts of physical science should be understood by children in grades 5–8, and that primary children can learn about the motion and position of objects.

Since motion is created through cause and effect events, data about motion can be organized to determine patterns and functions. Statistics and probability are important concepts used in analyzing forces. The activities are appropriate for learning mathematical concepts that are described in the NCTM Standard 11 for grades K–4 and Standards 8 and 10 for grades 5–8. Some of the activities have sample data tables; tables will have to be created for other activities. Children can also create graphs for the data collected from these activities.

In some cases, data will be qualitative and must be quantified by creating standards for making comparisons. For example, rather than using sophisticated measuring instruments, changes in bulb brightness can be measured by using the brightness of a bulb. This brightness can be given a value of 1. If the brightness of another bulb increases, the brightness will have a value greater than 1; if it is dimmer than the designated bulb, less than 1. This, of course, is an example of a nonstandard measurement that illustrates how bulb brightness was historically determined by comparing it to that of a burning candle. The term "candle power" originated from this comparison. All variables should be constant, i.e., the same size of a battery or a light bulb. Using nonstandard measurements is fraught with errors, since a judgment is being made and variables such as the strength of a battery and the type of bulb will affect brightness. However, using nonstandard measurements can give an appreciation for the development of standards. Encourage children to quantify, organize, and graph the data that result from the activities in this chapter.

Activities to Measure Motion

. . . the fact is that the movement is an indivisible whole, and the path traversed is directly formed out of the series of positions successively occupied in the course of this movement, thus division into homogeneous units is impossible. (Piaget, 1970, p. 69)

The speed at which an object moves is called *velocity* and is measured in units of time. For example, water can drip one drop per second or two drops per second. The falling drops move a given distance for a given time. Thus the speed of the drops is expressed in distance covered in a given amount of time. A car traveling 70 miles in one hour is another example of velocity or rate of motion. Acceleration, on the other hand, is the change in speed for a given distance covered in a given amount of time. The car accelerates from 60 miles per hour to 70 miles per hour. The swing of a pendulum decelerates over a given amount of time until it eventually stops swinging.

Explore the following activities yourself before doing them with children.

National Council of Teachers of Mathematics (1989)
Standard 11: Statistics and Probability (K–4)

In grades K–4, the mathematics curriculum should include experiences with data analysis and probability so that students can collect, organize, and describe data; formulate and solve problems that involve collecting and analyzing data; explore concepts of change. (p. 54)

Standard 8: Patterns and Function

In grades 5–8, the mathematics curriculum should include explorations of patterns and functions so that students can describe, extend, analyze, and create a wide variety of patterns; describe and represent relationships with tables, graphs, and rules; analyze functional relationships to explain how a change in one quantity results in a change in another; use patterns and functions to represent and solve problems. (p. 98)

Standard 10: Statistics (5–8)

In grades 5–8, the mathematics curriculum should include exploration of statistics in real-world situations so that students can systematically collect, organize, and describe data; construct, read, and interpret data tables, charts, and graphs; make inferences and convincing arguments that are based on data analysis; evaluate arguments that are based on data analysis; develop an appreciation for statistical methods as powerful means for decision making. (p. 105)

National Research Council (1996)
Content Standard B: Physical Science (K–4)

All students should develop an understanding of position and motion of objects. (p. 123)

The position of an object can be described by locating it relative to another object or the background. An object's motion can be described by tracing and measuring its position over time. The position and motion of objects can be changed by pushing or pulling. Sound is produced by vibrating objects. (p. 127)

Light travels in a straight line until it strikes an object. Light can be reflected by a mirror, refracted by a lens, or absorbed by the object. Heat can be produced in many ways, such as burning, rubbing, or mixing one substance with another. Electricity in circuits can produce light. An electrical circuit requires a complete loop through which an electrical current can pass. Magnets attract and repel each other and certain kinds of other materials. (p. 123)

As a result of their activities in grades 5–8, all students should develop an understanding of motion and forces. (p. 149)

The motion of an object can be described by its position, direction of motion, and speed. That motion can be measured and represented on a graph. (p. 154)

Energy is a property of many substances and is associated with heat, light, electricity, mechanical motion, sound, nuclear, and the nature of chemical. Energy is transferred in many ways. (p. 155)

Inclined Planes

GOAL

■ To explore the relationships between the attributes of rolling objects, the height at which they are released, and surfaces

GRADE LEVELS

■ Upper grades

MATERIALS

■ Wooden board 40–50 cm wide, 1–2 m long

■ Metersticks

■ Masking tape

■ Stopwatches, clocks, or wristwatches with second hands

■ Marbles (glass, wooden, and metal) with different diameters

■ Balls (rubber, Styrofoam, plastic) with different diameters, both hollow and solid (tennis balls, baseballs, softballs, Ping-Pong balls, golf balls, Whiffle balls)

■ Soup cans (unopened)

■ Wind-up toys with wheels

■ Coffee cans filled with different materials: marbles, rocks, salt, or sand

BACKGROUND INFORMATION

In this activity children work with a variety of variables and measurements and have to organize the data for it to make sense. Children can explore the effects of the height of the inclined plane, the weight of a rolling object, whether the object is solid or hollow, the size of the rolling object, and the surface area on how far an object rolls. It is important that children explore one variable at a time and keep the others constant. Some third- or fourth-grade children may see the relationship between the height of the inclined plane and/or the weight of the object on how far the object rolls.

INSTRUCTIONS

Using the materials listed, construct a ramp like the one in Figure 11.1. Hold an object in place at the top of the ramp with a meterstick. Raise the meterstick straight up in the air to release the object. Use a stopwatch to time how far the object travels. Maintain time as a constant when measuring distance and distance as a constant when measuring time. Table 11.1 is an example of keeping the time constant.

Have children do several trials and then average the results of the trials. This will account for errors in the measurement of time or distance.

QUESTIONS AND SUGGESTIONS

■ What are the different variables that affect how far an object rolls down an inclined plane?

■ Try rolling coffee cans filled with different substances such as rocks, sand, marbles, or salt. What happens? How far will they go?

■ Does the fact that an object is hollow or solid affect how far it rolls?

■ How far will wind-up toys travel up an inclined plane? Change the number of turns of the spring as well as the angle of the incline.

FIGURE 11.1

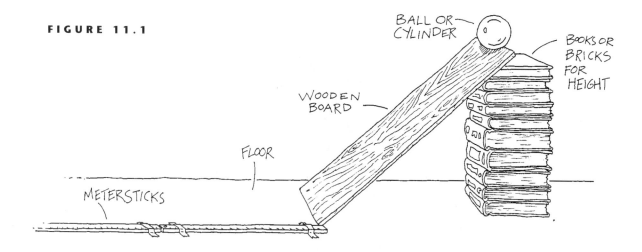

TABLE 11.1

Marble	Marble Weight (gm)	Distance Traveled (cm)	Time (sec)	Speed
A	1 g	20 cm	20 sec	1 cm/sec
B	2 g	40 cm	40 sec	2 cm/sec

- Which toy takes the fewest number of winds? Why?

- Which toy takes the most number of winds? Why?

- What happens to rolling objects if the inclined plane surface is covered with sandpaper, aluminum foil, Styrofoam, cloth, or waxed paper?

- Have soup can races. Does the consistency of the soup affect how far the cans roll? For example, will cans of mushroom soup roll farther than cans of chicken broth?

- Place liquids of different consistencies in clear bottles and roll them down the inclined plane. Watch what the liquids do inside the bottles as they roll. Use liquids such as water, oil, liquid soap.

- Cut out different-sized wheels from cardboard, and use dowels to make axles. Attach the wheels to a shoebox lid or some other object to make a cart. Does the size of the wheel affect how far the object travels?

- What happens if the front wheels are a different size than the back wheels?

- What happens if you put different-sized wheels on each side of the cart?

- What happens if you add weight to your cart? Does the weight change the speed at which the cart travels?

Flexible Tracks

GOAL

- To explore the motion of rolling objects on different types of curved tracks

GRADE LEVELS

- Primary to upper grades

FIGURE 11.2

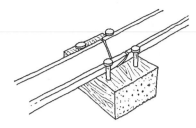

MATERIALS

- 8-foot sections of plastic corner wall molding
- Assorted balls, such as Ping-Pong balls, golf balls, plastic, and rubber
- Assorted types and sizes of marbles
- Bucket or wastebasket
- Headed nails
- Blocks of wood (10 cm square, made from 2 × 4 lumber)

BACKGROUND INFORMATION

Primary children can explore the relationship between the distance of the bucket and the angle of the track. Upper-grade children can explore the motion of rolling objects when the curvature of the track is changed. They can also add sections to make numerous curves and circular tracks.

INSTRUCTIONS

The plastic corner molding is used to finish paneled walls where they meet at corners. The molding is grooved, which creates a nice track. You can make an inclined plane track or bend the molding into a circular shape. Connect sections of molding with blocks of wood and nail guides. Don't pound the nails into the wood all the way. Keep them raised so that the track can be slipped underneath the nail heads and rest snugly on the wood. (See Figure 11.2.)

QUESTIONS AND SUGGESTIONS

- Hold individual strips of molding at different angles and roll an object down the molding to see if you can get the object into a bucket. (See Figure 11.3a.) How far away can you stand from the bucket and still make the rolling object go into the bucket? What happens if you change the angle of the molding?
- Can you use one strip of molding to roll a marble into another strip of molding held by someone else?
- Bend a strip of molding in a circle. Can you get a marble to go completely around the molding without falling? Is there a way to keep the marble moving around the circle? (See Figure 11.3b.)
- Set up a track using several sections of molding and wooden block joints to make a roller coaster with loops, twists, and turns. How far can you get a marble or ball to move along the track on its own?

FIGURE 11.3

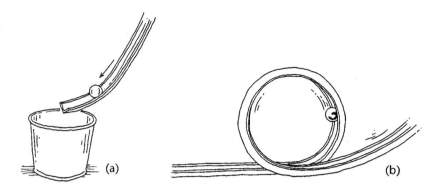

(a)　　　　　　　　　　　　(b)

TABLE 11.2

Type of Ball	Average Height #1	Average Height #2	Average Height #3	Average No. of Seconds	Average Speed
Tennis					
Rubber ball					
Golf					

Bouncing Balls

GOAL

■ To measure the relationship between the height from which an object is dropped and how high it bounces

GRADE LEVELS

■ Primary to upper grades

MATERIALS

■ Assorted sizes and types of balls such as tennis balls, golf balls, toy plastic, and rubber balls. The assortment should include different sizes, and hollow and solid balls.

■ Metersticks

■ Stopwatches

BACKGROUND INFORMATION

Primary children can explore one variable such as type of ball and how high it bounces. Upper-grade children can explore a variety of variables by collecting data through measurements.

INSTRUCTIONS

Drop balls from different heights. Record how high they bounce and the time it takes to reach the highest point of a bounce. Drop the balls from heights of 1 cm, 3 cm, and 5 cm. Other heights can be used as well. This will give validity to the resulting conclusions. Do three or more trials per height and record the averages in a table like Table 11.2.

FIGURE 11.4

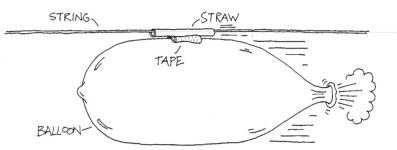

QUESTIONS

■ What is the relationship between how far the ball drops and the height of its return bounce?

■ Drop balls down a stairwell that is two stories or higher. Time them as they drop past the floors. Is there a change in speed as they pass the different levels?

■ What is the relationship between the size of the ball and how high it bounces?

■ What is the relationship between the contents of a ball and how high it bounces?

■ Can you get two different kinds of balls to bounce to the exact same height? How do you accomplish this?

■ What happens to the height of the bounce when you drop the balls on different surfaces?

■ Can you prevent a ball from bouncing when it is dropped from a certain height?

Racing Balloons

GOALS

■ To explore and measure the effects of air pressure on a moving object

GRADE LEVELS

■ Upper grades

MATERIALS

■ Various sizes and shapes of balloons

■ Kite string, thread, or fishing line

■ Drinking straws

■ Masking tape

BACKGROUND INFORMATION

This activity is suitable for older children since it requires manual dexterity and measuring.

INSTRUCTIONS

Cut a piece of string approximately 4 m long. Thread a straw onto the string. With masking tape, attach one end of the string to a wall. Pull on the other end to make the string taut. Blow up a balloon and hold the end closed to prevent the air from escaping. Fold a piece of masking tape with the sticky side on the outside. Attach the masking tape to the balloon and to the straw that is threaded on the string. Figure 11.4 indicates how the apparatus looks. Release the opening of the balloon and the balloon itself and watch what happens.

TABLE 11.3

Balloon Shape/Size	Distance Traveled	Time	Speed	Angle
10" round				
10" oblong				

FIGURE 11.5

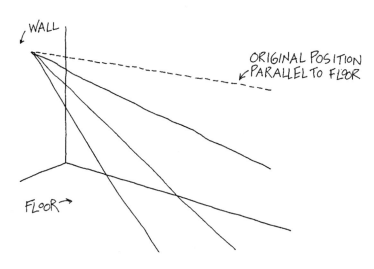

Measure how far the balloon travels along the string. You can also measure the time if the string is long enough.

Use Table 11.3 to determine the speed of the balloons. (For all practical purposes the weight of the two blown-up balloons [round and oblong] will be very similar.)

QUESTIONS

- How might you weigh a balloon that is full of air? Does the shape of the balloon determine how far it travels?

- Put the string at different angles and perpendicular to the floor. How far does the balloon go?

Figure 11.5 illustrates the different positions in which the string can be held when you release the balloon.

- What is the farthest you can get a balloon to travel?

- If you attach two balloons together, will they travel twice as far?

- What is the mathematical relationship between the angle of the string and how far the balloon travels?

Hovering Balloons

GOAL

- To apply the force of air pressure to make an object hover

GRADE LEVELS

- Upper grades

FIGURE 11.6

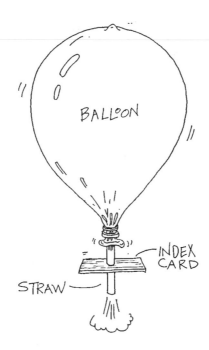

MATERIALS

- Assorted balloons
- Index cards, manila folders, or paper
- Drinking straws
- Rubber bands

BACKGROUND INFORMATION

This activity is suitable for older children because the manipulation of the variables requires patience.

INSTRUCTIONS

The weight of a balloon can be changed so that it will rise slowly as air is released. Its wild, unpredictable motion can also be stabilized by adding weight.

Take a small piece of index card (approximately 3 cm × 3 cm). Make a small hole in the center and insert a straw. The size of the balloon and the index card are variables that will affect the motion of the balloon. Place the other end of the straw in the neck of a balloon and secure with a rubber band. (See Figure 11.6.) Blow up the balloon. The straw and rubber band will add weight to the balloon. Release the balloon.

The card slows down the motion of the balloon. It acts as a stabilizer to prevent the balloon from spiraling haphazardly in the air. The card also adds weight to the volume of the balloon. The volume changes as the air in the balloon is released, but the weight remains the same. Thus, the density of the system changes. Gravitational pull eventually becomes stronger than the upward force caused by the escaping air.

QUESTIONS AND SUGGESTIONS

- Experiment with different types and sizes of cards to act as stabilizers and slow the ascent of the balloon.
- How high can you get a balloon to rise in the air?
- How long can you get a balloon to stay in the air?

- What shape of balloon is best if you want it to rise without a zigzagging motion?

- Is there any way to control the amount of air that escapes from the balloon?

- Experiment with a variety of stabilizers by changing materials, sizes, and weights. Which type of stabilizer keeps a balloon on a straight path? Which stabilizer helps a balloon to travel the highest? Which stabilizer helps keep the balloon in the air the longest?

Rubber Band Toys

GOAL

- To explore the force of elastic energy by using rubber bands

GRADE LEVELS

- Third to eighth grade

MATERIALS

- Hollow plastic eggs that are made in two sections (can be purchased at craft stores in the spring)

- Assorted rubber bands

- Paper clips

- Hollow plastic beads

- Straws, dowels, stirring sticks

- Electric drill

BACKGROUND INFORMATION

In this activity children investigate the number of twists of the rubber band and how far the egg travels. The straw acts as a guide and provides resistance as the egg moves. The bead acts as a bearing. It allows the rubber band to uncoil without rubbing against the straw. The thickness of the rubber band, the size of the object, and the straw guide are variables that will affect how far the object moves. Other objects that can be used are coffee cans, potato chip canisters, yogurt containers, or other plastic containers with lids. You must drill a hole in each end of the containers.

INSTRUCTIONS

Use an electric drill to make a hole (approximately 0.5 cm in diameter) in each end of the plastic egg. (A nail and a hammer can be used to make the holes but the plastic may crack when you pound on the nail.) Thread a rubber band through one of the holes and anchor it with a paper clip so that the rubber band cannot slip back into the egg. Thread the other end of the rubber band through the other half of the egg and close the two halves. Thread that end of the rubber band through a hollow plastic craft bead resting against the egg. Pull on the rubber band and insert a straw. The rubber band will hold the straw in place against the bead. (See Figure 11.7.) The straw has to be long enough to touch the floor when the egg is placed on the floor.

Turn the straw to wind up the rubber band. The paper clip on the other end must remain stationary so that the rubber band will remain twisted until released. If the paper clip moves, push part of it into the hole in the egg to prevent it from moving. When the rubber band is completely wound, set the egg on the floor with the long end of the straw touching the floor. Release it and watch the egg move.

FIGURE 11.7

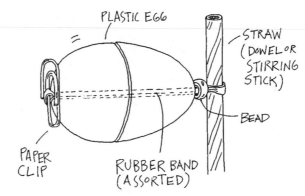

FIGURE 11.7

QUESTIONS

■ What is the relationship between the number of turns of the rubber band and how far the egg travels?

■ Does the egg travel in a straight line?

■ If not, how can you make it travel in a straight line?

■ How far can you make the toy travel?

■ How straight can you make the toy go?

Activities to Measure Mechanical Forces

Gears

GOAL

■ To explore motion in relation to the number and sizes of gears

GRADE LEVELS

■ Third to eighth grade

MATERIALS

■ Commercial sets of plastic gears

■ Gears from clocks (with second hands) and appliances

■ Gears cut from cardboard or plastic

BACKGROUND INFORMATION

Gears are made in different diameters. They are used as movable parts to transfer energy in different directions. Children can make arrangements of gears of different sizes and explore the ratio of the number of turns of a crank to the number of turns of a gear. They can use this knowledge to predict how far objects will move according to the number and size of the gears.

QUESTIONS

■ How many gears can you get to turn at the same time?

■ How many turns of the crank does it take to move the largest gear around once compared to the smallest gear?

■ Can you get gears to move in opposite directions?

■ Can you make a clock using a set of gears?

FIGURE 11.8

Pulleys

GOAL

- To use pulleys to explore the ratio of weight lifted to distance

GRADE LEVELS

- Middle to upper grades

MATERIALS

- String
- Pairs of bottle caps glued back to back
- Thread spools
- Miniature yo-yos
- Commercial pulleys
- Spring scales and/or rubber band scale

BACKGROUND INFORMATION

Pulleys help disperse weight so heavy objects can be lifted. This is easier with a pulley system than trying to lift the object directly. Very heavy objects are lifted with a series of pulleys and ropes called a block and tackle. Children can lift objects from the floor to the desk by using pulleys and comparing the amount of weight involved in the lifts.

Pulleys can also be used to control the motion of an object. For example, a toy car can be attached to a weight with a string. The string is threaded through a pulley with the weight hanging below it. (See Figure 11.8.) If the car is on an inclined plane, the weight can either slow the car's motion or stop it. The weights on the ends of the string are counterbalanced. The difference between the weights causes the car to move either forward or backward.

INSTRUCTIONS

The stretch of the rubber band can be measured on a ruler to compare the weights of objects. This apparatus does not give weight in grams or ounces; it only presents comparative weights. A rubber band attached to a wooden ruler can be used to measure the pull of gravity. (See Figure 11.9.) Thumb-tack a rubber band to the "zero" end of the ruler. Unbend a paper clip into an "S" shape. Hook one end of the paper clip over the other end of the rubber band. Hook the object on the other end of the "S" shaped paper clip. Attach an object to a rubber band scale and lift the object from the floor to the table. Measure the stretch of the rubber band.

FIGURE 11.9

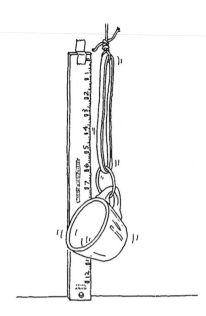

FIGURE 11.10

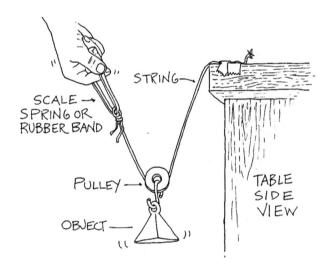

The spring coil is covered with a metal or plastic which is marked with a scale in grams. An arrow attached to the spring moves along the marked scale according to the amount of weight hanging from the hook.

Compare the weight of an object hanging from a scale (use either the rubber band scale or a commercially made spring scale) with and without a pulley. To make the comparison do the following:

- Attach one end of a piece of string to a desk top with tape.

- Run the string through a pulley and attach the object to the pulley (see Figure 11.10). If the pulley doesn't have a hook, make an "S" shaped hook from a paper clip.

- Attach the other end of the string to the bottom of the scale.

- Use your hand to move the scale and pulley system up and down.

- Record the weight of the object as you lift it. How much does the object weigh?

- Compare the reading to that obtained from lifting the object without the pulley.

SUGGESTIONS

- Create a system using one pulley to move objects that are at different heights from the floor.

- Create a system of two or more pulleys to move objects from the floor to the top of a desk.

- Create a pulley system as shown in Figure 11.8. Investigate the relationship between the weight of the car and the counterweight. Can you control the speed of the car? Can you control how far the car will go before stopping? Create a table and graph to represent the changes. Can you create an algebraic expression that illustrates the relationships? (Speed is distance traveled for a given amount of time.)

Activities to Measure Magnetic and Electrical Forces

Magnetism

GOALS

- To explore and measure the characteristics of magnetism

GRADE LEVELS

- Primary through eighth grade

MATERIALS

- Assorted magnets: bar and horseshoe-shaped steel, ceramic, and rubber magnets

- Iron filings

- Assorted magnetic and nonmagnetic materials: wood, pieces of zinc, copper strips, pennies and other coins, aluminum foil, nails, paper clips (bare and plastic coated), plastic pieces, pipe cleaners, paper, glass, magnetite (magnetic rock), Styrofoam

SCENIC VIEW 11.1

Children as well as adults are fascinated by magnets. They are used in many products: for example, in appliances such as can openers and in speakers in sound systems.

Iron magnets lose their magnetism after a time, especially if they are dropped or stored improperly. However, they are more permanent than steel magnets, which are often referred to as temporary magnets. Steel magnets, composed of iron and carbon, should be stored so that they are not touching each other. Steel magnets are difficult to remagnetize; consult a high school physics teacher for help. Ceramic magnets keep their magnetism much longer than iron or steel magnets. Ceramic magnets are powerful for their size, but they break into pieces when they are dropped. Ceramic magnets are found in electronic stores. They are made in a variety of shapes and some have holes so they can be stacked on pencils or dowels. Rubber magnets, which are sold in strips at craft stores, are used for refrigerator molding and for attaching objects to refrigerators. Their strength is limited. Items such as nails and paper clips can be magnetized by rubbing them across iron or steel magnets in one direction.

Basically, theories of magnetism say that iron molecules orient themselves in an orderly fashion to produce magnetic forces. Rather than moving randomly, the electrons (negative charge) seem to congregate or cluster together instead of being evenly dispersed around the nucleus or the protons (positive charge). This creates clusters of iron molecules that have the same characteristics of uneven charges as the individual atoms (Hazen and Trefil, 1992). The whole iron object is magnetic because of these clusters of molecules. Areas of negative charges line up next to areas of positive charges throughout the iron material. If a magnet is cut into pieces, each piece will have opposite poles of attraction. Two magnets placed next to each other are attracted to each other in the same way. The earth acts as a giant magnet because of the flow of molten iron ore at its center. The molten iron ore moves in an orderly direction, setting up these clusters of uneven charges.

Our understanding of magnets is based on inferences; children cannot directly observe the behavior of molecules. However, children can create explanations or theories about the causes of magnetism and then test their theories. Provide books and give them time to browse the Internet to find scientific explanations of the causes of magnetic force.

INSTRUCTIONS

Prepare bags that contain both magnetic and nonmagnetic materials. Have children sort the materials into magnetic and nonmagnetic piles and list the items in each pile. After completing the list, they can use magnets to check their predictions.

QUESTIONS AND SUGGESTIONS

- What objects in the classroom are magnetic? Make a list and check your predictions.

- Place a small amount of iron filings between two overhead transparencies and seal the edges with masking tape. Place a magnet under the transparencies. What shapes do the iron filings create? Does the iron filing arrangement change when you use a different shape of magnet? Can you tell which part of the magnet has the strongest magnetic force?

- Draw the head of a person on a sheet of paper and place it under the transparency sheets. Move the iron filings around with a magnet to make hair and other facial features.

- Which magnet picks up the most paper clips?

- Can you get a magnet to move an object when something such as paper, a book, or a piece of wood is placed between the magnet and the object?

- What is the thickest object you can place between a magnet and a paper clip and still allow the magnetic force to attract the paper clip?

- Can you magnetize an object such as a paper clip, nail, or pin and use it to pick up other objects?

- Can you make a magnet spin by using other magnets?

- Make a game using magnets.

- Find ways to move objects around (without touching them) using magnets.

- Will magnets attract objects placed in water?

- Place magnets on toy cars and have races.

- Using one magnet, can you make another magnet float in mid-air?

- Can you make a magnetic boat and make it move on water using another magnet?

FIGURE 11.11

- From how far away will a magnet attract an object?

- Read several books about theories of magnetism. Do scientists agree about what causes magnetism?

- What is the magnetic North Pole?

Electricity

GOALS

- To explore and measure the characteristics of electricity

GRADE LEVELS

- Middle to upper grades

MATERIALS

- Bare copper wire in various diameters. Bare copper wire is used in this activity so that children can see that it is the wire and not the coating that carries electricity. The coating acts as an insulator. The wire, not the coating, must touch the metal parts of the battery and the bulb. If the wire is covered, the coating must be stripped away so that the bare wire is exposed. Some wires appear bare, but have a thin coating of plastic. This coating has to be scraped or burned to expose the wire. Thin copper wire is likely to have this type of insulation.

- Miniature lamps in various sizes, the kind used for flashlights and Christmas tree strings. Use old strings of lights. The bases of the lights can be cut from the string (Figure 11.11). The lights have protruding wires which can be connected directly to wire and then to a battery. Use clear bulbs so children can see the wires inside the bulbs.

- A, C, and D dry cell batteries. Store dry cell batteries so that their ends are not touching each other, pieces of wire, or any other kind of metal. When they touch metal the electrons move through the ends of the batteries and weaken them. The electrons disperse very slowly into the air. The electrons are concentrated in the batteries and move to a less concentrated area over time. Therefore the ends should be covered with an insulator such as paper. Store batteries in plastic tubs or other containers. Layer the batteries standing up and place paper on top of them as an insulator. Flashlights not in use should be disassembled.

- Commercial battery and bulb holders. An alternative: Lay the batteries end to end (positive to negative) and roll them up in a sheet of notebook paper folded to fit the length of the batteries. Put a rubber band lengthwise around the paper and batteries. The rubber band holds the batteries in place and provides a place to attach wire on each end of the batteries. Wires can be taped to bulbs rather than using bulb holders. Batteries and bulb holders should not be used until children understand how the wires, batteries, and bulbs must be connected to make a bulb light. They are used for convenience when multiple batteries, wires, and bulbs are used.

SCENIC VIEW 11.2

Electricity and magnetism are related because both forces are caused by the clustering of electrons. However, electricity is caused by the movement of excess electrons from one position to another; magnetism is caused by electrons that remain around an atom. Electricity is created by excess electrons (negative charge) moving to areas with excess protons (positive charge). Electrical current is a continuous flow of electrons; static electricity is a sudden, short flow of electrons. In both cases, electrons move from an area of high concentration to an area of low concentration. The charge is neutralized when the number of electrons and protons are equal. Many metals allow the flow of electrons. They are called *conductors.* Materials that prevent the flow of electrons are called *insulators.*

Batteries contain chemicals that react and create a buildup of electrons. The electrons move from areas of high concentration to areas of low concentration, which will be into wires and bulbs if they are connected to the battery. Batteries are sealed tightly to prevent the moist chemicals from drying out. If there is wire, the electrons will move through the wire and anything else in the same path. *Resistance* is the term used to describe how well electrons can move through objects. Resistance is basically friction caused by the motion of electrons. If the electrons cannot move easily, the material is said to have resistance. When a metal has a great amount of resistance it may become so hot that light is created as well. Batteries and wires can feel warm to the touch because of this motion of electrons and their resistance. Resistance is also caused by the size of the wire. Large amounts of electrons have a difficult time flowing through very thin wire. Light bulbs are constructed using these principles. Wire inside a light bulb is extremely thin and made of a metal that resists the flow of electricity. *Wattage* is a unit to measure the brightness of a bulb. Originally, when bulbs were first made, their brightness was compared to the brightness of a burning candle.

The more resistance, the more power or *volts* it takes to make electricity run through an object. Metal wire or conductors have the least resistance to the flow of electrons as opposed to glass, plastic, wood, or insulators. Electricity seeks the path of least resistance. Thus, if two wires are touching each other, the electricity will flow through the contact point rather than through a bulb because the bulb increases the resistance. This is called a *short circuit.* An analogy that is often used to explain the flow of electricity is water running through pipes. Water runs easier through a large pipe than a small pipe.

Lightning is created by the resistance of the electrons moving through the air. The buildup of electrons is tremendous and they will move through objects (trees and houses) regardless of the amount of resistance.

Batteries are marked plus and minus to indicate the differences between the two ends. These markings do not necessarily indicate the location of electrons and protons or the flow of electrons. A battery is called a *cell* because it is one unit of power. Volts represent the power of the battery. Batteries such as AAA, AA, C, and D are called dry cells. The number of volts is indicated on the sides of these batteries. A D cell battery, for example, can provide 1.5 volts of electricity.

FIGURE 11.12

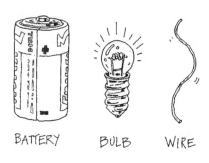

BATTERY   BULB   WIRE

INSTRUCTIONS

> We might start by instructing our pupils to set up a wide range of simple circuits and encourage them to describe their observations in terms of the supply of electrical energy to the lamps which form their principal elements. In this way we might begin to form a bond between the acceptable term "electrical energy" and the idea children already have of what is "used up" in a circuit, to light lamps, run motors, etc. (Shipstone, 1985, p. 48)

Begin by lighting a bulb using only one bare wire and battery. (See Figure 11.12.) Instruct children to draw different battery and bulb configurations, indicating how the bulbs and batteries are connected and where the wire touches the battery and bulb. State whether the bulb lights.

QUESTIONS AND SUGGESTIONS

- How many ways can you get the bulb to light?

- How many ways can you prevent the bulb from lighting?

- Once you have figured out the ways the bulb lights, trace the flow of electricity. Write a description of the path that the electricity follows. Write a general principle to explain what must be true in order for a bulb to light.

- Can you get two bulbs to light using one wire and one battery? How many bulbs can you light using one wire and one battery?

- What materials in the classroom will conduct electricity?

- Plan investigations to answer the following question: What affects the brightness of a bulb? Identify the variables that affect the brightness. How can you quantify brightness?

- Using the same size bulb, determine its brightness as you add more batteries and bulbs.

- Create a circuit using three bulbs and two batteries. Unscrew one of the bulbs. Did the other two bulbs stop lighting? A series circuit is created by having electricity flow through all of the bulbs, one after the other. Why do the other bulbs stop lighting?

- Using three bulbs and two batteries, can you create a circuit that allows you to remove one lit bulb without affecting the others? Create a circuit using five bulbs and four batteries so that if you remove more than one bulb the others will stay lit. This type of circuit is called parallel. Explain why. Try varying the number of bulbs and batteries. Remove more than one bulb while keeping the others lit.

- Compare the brightness of the bulbs in series and parallel circuits.

FIGURE 11.13

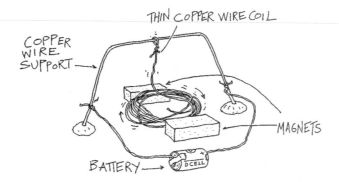

- In a series circuit, predict what the brightness will be (in quantifiable terms) as you add bulbs. Assume that the number of batteries and the size of the bulb remain the same.

- Take apart a bulb and look at the inside. Use a standard 40-watt light bulb. To break the glass, place the bulb in a paper bag and gently hit the glass with a heavy object. If you hit the bulb too hard, the wires may be destroyed. Draw a diagram of the inside of the light bulb. Light the bulb. What happens?

- Make your own bulb.

- Cover a work area with newspaper. Take apart a battery. Test the battery to see if it will still light a bulb at various stages of disassembly.

- Does the thickness of the wire affect the brightness of a bulb?

- Does the length of the wire affect the brightness of a bulb?

- Does the type of wire affect the brightness of a bulb?

- Create a circuit using five batteries. How bright is the bulb compared to a circuit using one battery? Take one of the batteries in the center of the row and reverse it. Will the bulb still light? Reverse the direction of another battery and test the bulb. Keep doing this until you have reversed all the batteries. Can you explain why the bulb lights or does not light?

- To make an electromagnet, use very thin copper wire and wind it around a nail so that it is completely covered. The wire does not have to be bare but the ends must be bare. Attach the two ends of copper wire to a battery and try to pick up paper clips with the nail. Add more batteries to increase the strength of the magnetism.

- Electrical motors are made by placing a coil of thin copper wire between two magnets (Figure 11.13). When this coil of thin copper wire is attached to a battery, it becomes magnetized because of the motion of the electrons around a circle, causing a directional force. If the coil is free to rotate and centered between regular magnets it will move in a circle. The coil rotates because of the attraction and repulsion of the different areas of the wire as they move past areas of the magnets.

- Batteries can be made using lemons, potatoes, and other fruits and vegetables that have a high acidic content. Push a penny and an iron nail into opposite ends of a lemon. Attach a piece of copper wire to the penny and another piece to the nail. Attach the other ends of the wire to a voltmeter. The voltmeter should register an electrical current. Each potato or lemon represents one cell, like a battery. Add more lemons to increase the voltage. If enough lemons are used, a very tiny bulb will light.

FIGURE 11.14

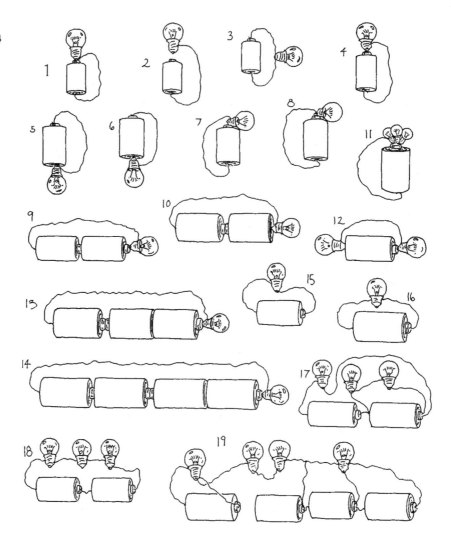

- Figure 11.14 shows drawings of different types of circuits. In which circuits will the bulbs light? Test these circuits to confirm your predictions.

- In circuits that have more than one bulb, will the brightness of the bulbs change?

Assessment of Mystery Circuits

GOAL

- To assess children's ability to "visualize" unseen circuits by using the properties of electricity that affect the brightness of bulbs

GRADE LEVELS

- Middle to upper grades

MATERIALS

- Shoebox lid

- Brads

- Copper wire

FIGURE 11.15

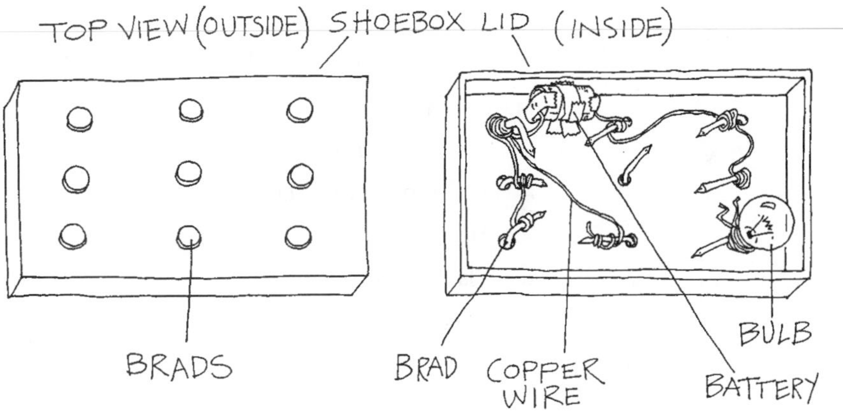

TOP VIEW (OUTSIDE)   SHOEBOX LID (INSIDE)

BRADS

BRAD   COPPER WIRE

BULB   BATTERY

- Bulbs
- Batteries

BACKGROUND INFORMATION

Mystery circuits can be used to assess what children understand about electricity. In order to identify the mystery circuits, they have to know how to light a bulb and what happens to the brightness of a bulb in a series circuit. They also have to know what happens to the brightness of a bulb when another battery is added to a series circuit. Children may have difficulty understanding how the unseen wires and bulbs inside the box are connected to those outside the box. They must use spatial reasoning.

INSTRUCTIONS

Stick two rows of three brads into the cover of a shoebox. (See Figure 11.15.) On the inside of the shoebox lid, bend the brads into place. Wrap the brads with wire and connect them to each other. A miniature lamp on the outside of the box will light when using the wired circuits on the inside of the lid, if the following is done: The base of the bulb touches brad "A" that has a wire running from it to another brad "B," inside the box lid. On the outside, one end of another separate wire must touch the side of the bulb and the other end of the wire must touch one end of a D cell battery. The other end of the D cell battery must touch brad "B" that is connected by wire on the inside to brad "A." Batteries and light bulbs can also be added to the circuits on the inside of the lid. Place the lid on the shoe box and seal with masking tape so that the wires, batteries, and bulbs cannot be seen. Challenge children to figure out the placement of the wires, bulbs, and batteries. Each box can have a different configuration of wires, bulbs, and batteries. Some boxes may contain only one wire connecting two brads, others may have wire connecting several brads. Bulbs and batteries can be added to boxes without being connected. Children will feel the weight but will not know whether the weight is a battery or something else. Children can diagram the mystery circuits.

Static Electricity

GOALS

- To observe and measure the behavior of objects that are charged with static electricity

GRADE LEVELS

- Middle to upper grades

MATERIALS

- Large round balloons
- Different kinds of cloth
- Hair combs
- Plastic wrap
- Styrofoam
- Puffed rice
- Thread
- Pepper
- Small pieces of newspaper or tissue paper
- Banana
- Meterstick

SCENIC VIEW 11.3

Static electricity is the buildup of electrons in one area. They "jump" to another area that has a lesser concentration of electrons. This creates a crackle and even a spark. Lightning is produced in this way. Electrical shocks are produced when you walk across a carpet because the excess electrons build up on your body from the friction. If you touch metal or an electrical appliance such as a television the electrons "jump" to that object, causing the "shock."

QUESTIONS AND SUGGESTIONS

- What kinds of materials produce the most static electricity when rubbed on a balloon?
- Blow up a balloon and rub it with different kinds of cloth. Use the same number of rubs. How many pieces of paper or puffed rice can you pick up with your balloon after rubbing it? Does one type of cloth produce better results than another?
- Instead of balloons try combs, plastic wrap, and Styrofoam. Keep the number of rubs constant. How many pieces of paper or puffed rice can you pick up?
- How far away can you keep a balloon or another charged object and still have it attract objects? Measure the distance.
- Tie two blown-up balloons to two ends of a 20 cm length of thread. Rub one balloon and bring it near the other one. What happens? Charge both balloons and bring them near each other. What happens? What do you have to do to make the two balloons repel each other?
- Tie a piece of puffed rice on a piece of 5 cm long thread and bring it near a charged balloon. What happens? What happens after the puffed rice touches the balloon?
- Bring a charged balloon near a small pile of pepper. What happens?
- Hang a banana using 20 cm of sewing thread. Make sure the banana is balanced and hanging freely. Once the banana stops turning, slowly bring a charged balloon near the banana. What happens? Can you make the banana move in a circle without touching it?

■ Suspend a meterstick with a piece of thread and do the same thing. What happens?

■ Turn on a water faucet and bring a charged balloon near the stream of water. What happens?

Activities to Measure Sound Forces

SCENIC VIEW 11.4

Molecules in the air move and vibrate to produce sound. Children can explore this force by constructing musical instruments. They can hear, see, and touch the vibrations emanating from the instruments. They will begin to understand what affects pitch and the range of sounds that are produced. Children can make string, wind, and percussion instruments.

Vibrating objects cause molecules to move in waves from their point of origin. The following activities allow children to experience sound through hearing, touching, and seeing vibrations. Children can attempt to measure how fast an object vibrates. They can order pitches according to how high and low they are. They can create musical notes by using the instruments that they make.

Straw Whistles

GOAL

■ To observe the properties of sound through simulated musical instruments that use reeds and/or the vibration of air across a set of holes

GRADE LEVELS

■ Primary to upper grades

MATERIALS

■ Plastic drinking straws

■ Balloons

■ Paper

■ Scissors

INSTRUCTIONS

Cut one end of a plastic drinking straw to form an upside-down "V" (see Figure 11.16). Flatten the upside-down "V" by pressing it with your teeth. This creates a "reed." Place the "reed" between your lips and blow. When the whistle works correctly, the "reed" will vibrate, making sounds. Your lips will feel the vibrations.

QUESTIONS AND SUGGESTIONS

■ What happens to the sound if you cut ¼ off the straw from the end? ½ off the straw? ¾ off the straw? How does the sound change? Why?

■ Place the straw perpendicular to your lower lip. Blow straight across the opening. The air has to travel across the opening rather than through the straw. You can also cut into a straw, leaving it attached on one side. Bend the top part 90° to the bottom part. Blow directly into the top part. The air should travel across the opening of the bottom part. (See Figure 11.17.)

FIGURE 11.16

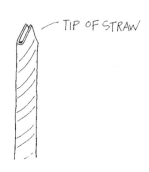

TIP OF STRAW

FIGURE 11.17

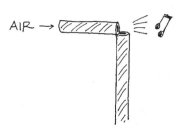

AIR →

FIGURE 11.18

FIGURE 11.19

BLOW ACROSS OPENING

- Take another straw and cut diamond-shaped notches along its length. Place your fingers over the notches and blow through the straw (Figure 11.18). What happens to the pitch as you cover and uncover the holes?

- What happens if you cover the bottom of the straw as you blow?

- Can you cut the straw or put holes in the straw to make the sound higher or lower than it was?

- What do you have to do to make the sound lower and lower?

- Insert a small straw into a large straw. Move the large straw back and forth over the small one as you blow across the opening of the small straw. (See Figure 11.19.)

- Can you take a series of straws and cut them at different lengths to change the pitch from highest to lowest?

- Make a chart of the lengths of the straw in relation to the change in sound. Use fractions to express the change in sound. For example, the sound from a 2-inch straw is 1/4 as high as the original sound.

- Can you make a set of panpipes varying in pitch by cutting the straws at appropriate lengths? How many straws are needed for the scale? What lengths would you need?

FIGURE 11.20

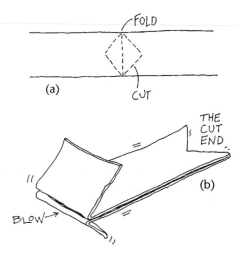

- Can you play tunes on your panpipes?
- What musical instruments are played by blowing over an opening?

Paper Reeds

GOAL

- To observe the properties of sound through simulated musical instruments that use reeds

GRADE LEVELS

- Primary to upper grades

MATERIALS

- Various types of paper
- Scissors

INSTRUCTIONS

Cut a piece of paper to 3 cm by 20 cm. Fold it in half and cut a notch in the fold (Figure 11.20a). Fold back the opposite ends approximately ½ inch. Press the folded ends to your lips and keep your mouth slightly open while blowing. The whole strip of paper will vibrate.

SUGGESTIONS

- Cut the strip of paper in different lengths to see how that affects the sound from the paper whistle. Can you predict the pitch as you change the lengths of paper?
- Try different types of paper to see what happens to the sounds.

Musical Bottles

GOALS

- To explore sound by blowing across the tops of narrow-mouthed bottles filled with water
- To explore the sound of bottles by hitting them with a soft mallet

GRADE LEVELS

■ Primary to upper grades

MATERIALS

■ Narrow-necked glass and plastic bottles of all sizes and shapes

■ Water

INSTRUCTIONS

Collect all kinds of narrow-necked bottles. Plastic soda pop bottles work well. Blow gently over the opening of the bottle by slightly pressing your lower lip on the rim of the bottle opening. Hold the opening of the bottle at a 90° angle to your lower lip. As an alternative, softly hit each bottle with a mallet.

QUESTIONS

■ Where do you feel the vibrations?

■ Where does the air go? How does this create sound?

■ Add water to the bottles and blow over the opening. Be sure to keep track of the amount of water and the water level in relation to the different sounds. Try hitting them with a mallet.

■ What happens to the sound as water is added? Can the sound be compared to the sound made by a whistle?

■ What other objects can you use instead of bottles to get a sound by blowing over the opening?

■ Add water to several 2-liter soda pop bottles. Vary the amount of water in each one. Blow across the openings to make sound. Adjust the water levels to get different pitches. Can you play a song?

Musical Percussion

GOAL

■ To observe the properties of sound through simulated musical instruments that require beating on a surface stretched across a hollow interior

GRADE LEVELS

■ Primary to upper grades

MATERIALS

■ Large balloons

■ Containers such as coffee cans, butter tubs, plastic bowls, small cardboard boxes, yogurt containers, oatmeal containers

INSTRUCTIONS

Stretch sheets of rubber or pieces of balloons across the opening of the containers and secure with rubber bands.

QUESTIONS AND SUGGESTIONS

■ Hit the stretched balloon with a pencil. What happens?

■ What do you have to do to make the sound higher or lower?

■ Place pieces of rice or puffed rice on the stretched balloon. What happens when you strike the stretched balloon?

- Collect assorted glass containers and fill them with different amounts of water. Gently hit their sides with a pencil. Watch what the water does when you strike the glass containers.

- What makes the sound?

- What happens to the sound when the water level is increased or decreased?

- Can you place the correct amount of water in each container to raise or lower the sound by half of what it was before?

Stringed Instruments

GOAL

- To observe the properties of sound through simulated musical instruments that require strumming stretched strings

GRADE LEVELS

- Primary to upper grades

MATERIALS

- Rubber bands, fishing line, string, and very thin wire

- Tacks, brads, adhesive tape

- Shoeboxes, butter tubs, pie tins, cigar boxes, plastic bowls, cardboard boxes, waxed paper cups

INSTRUCTIONS

Take a piece of string or wire, or rubber bands. Stretch it across the opening of a container. (Stretch the rubber bands around the object.) Anchor string and wires with tacks, brads, or strong adhesive tape. Pluck the strings and listen to the sounds.

QUESTIONS

- In your opinion, which of the following makes the best sound: strings, wires, or rubber bands?

- Which kinds of containers produce the best sound?

- Using the same container and strings, how can you change the sound?

- What musical instruments use strings?

- Poke a hole in the bottom of a waxed paper cup and thread approximately 20 cm of string through the hole. Anchor it with a wooden toothpick. Gently hold the bottom of the cup with one hand and pull the string through your fingers with the other hand. The wooden toothpick anchor will be inside the cup. The string will hang out of the bottom of the cup. What kind of sound do you get? Try wetting the string and pulling it through your fingers. What does that do to the sound? Try this using containers like yogurt cups, Styrofoam cups, aluminum cans. Try a variety of strings.

- Cut a 4-foot length of cord and put it through a hole punched in the corner of a cardboard box. Secure it by tying a pencil to it inside the box. Take a broom handle and tie the other end of the cord to it so that it is taut when placed on the box. Put the box on the floor with the broom handle on top of the box. (See Figure 11.21.) Pluck the string. What sounds do you hear? What instrument is similar to this one?

FIGURE 11.21

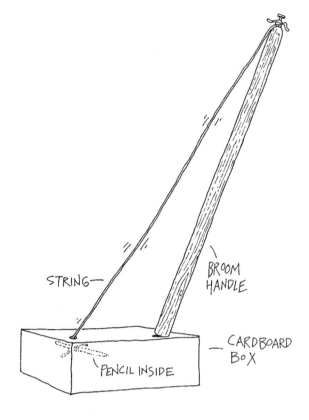

STRING—

BROOM HANDLE

PENCIL INSIDE

CARDBOARD BOX

Activities to Measure Color and Light

Often a teaching course will start by establishing the propagation of light in a straight line. To accomplish this, it will show pupils that they cannot see a candle's flame through a series of holes punched in a card unless the holes are aligned. Children cannot appreciate this demonstration; they cannot interpret the experiment in terms of the path of the light from the object to the eye, when they do not link the vision of the flame to a reception of light by the eye. (Guesne, 1985, p. 29)

SCENIC VIEW 11.5

Light is also a force because it travels and can move objects. Probably you have seen the small black and white paddle wheels enclosed in a glass globe. The paddle wheels spin very fast when placed in direct sunlight because heat energy is absorbed by the black sides of the paddles and reflected by the white sides. Solar energy is used to heat water and homes and can be converted to electrical power.

Light can be absorbed, transmitted, or scattered. Visible white light consists of all the colors of the rainbow: red, yellow, green, blue, indigo, and violet. These colors make up the spectrum. Any transparent medium that bends white light will create the spectrum, such as triangular glass prisms, beveled glass, and raindrops. Light consists of electron wave lengths. The variation in the distance between wave crests creates different colors. Different wave lengths bend sooner than others when they pass through a transparent medium. This causes the colors to separate.

Opaque objects scatter light as well as absorb it. When all the colors are absorbed, black is produced. Black is the absence of color. When all colors are reflected, white is produced. The colors we see are reflected back to the eye. Thus, green is reflected to the eye from a green surface which absorbs the other colors.

FIGURE 11.22

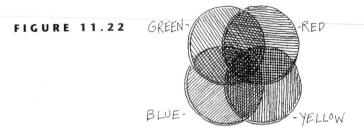

When liquid pigments such as green, yellow, and red are mixed together, a black color is produced because no particular color is reflected back to the eye. White is the absence of pigments and all light of the spectrum is reflected back to the eye. Different proportions of pigments create different shades of colors.

Colored Cellophane

GOAL

■ To explore colors created by colored transparencies

GRADE LEVELS

■ Primary grades

MATERIALS

■ Blue, green, red, and yellow pieces of cellophane

INSTRUCTIONS

Hold different-colored pieces of cellophane in front of your eyes and look toward a light source.

SUGGESTIONS

■ Figure 11.22 illustrates the overlapping of four colors of cellophane. What colors are produced at each intersection?

■ Look at colored objects through the colored cellophane. What colors do you see?

■ Go outside and scatter colored toothpicks in the grass. How many can you find when you cover your eyes with colored cellophane? How does this relate to how animals camouflage themselves?

■ Write a message on paper that can only be deciphered when certain colors of cellophane are placed over the message. (Use different-colored markers or pens.)

■ Create pictures or words that appear three-dimensional when colored cellophane is placed over your eyes.

Colored Water

GOAL

■ To create a variety of colors by combining drops of red, yellow, green, and blue colored water

GRADE LEVELS

■ Primary to upper grades

MATERIALS

You will need stock solutions of red, yellow, green, and blue water made from concentrated food coloring. They can be kept in closed quart-sized plastic freezer containers. Each child will need:

■ 3-ounce clear cups

■ 1-ounce clear party favor cups

■ Eyedroppers

■ Plastic or Styrofoam food trays

■ Paper towels

■ Newspapers

INSTRUCTIONS

Prepare separate containers of red, blue, yellow, and green colored water from food coloring. (Keep the bottles of concentrated food coloring away from the children. Giving children concentrated food color containers invites a messy experience with stained fingers and clothes.) Provide each child with a small amount of red, blue, yellow, and green water in four 3-ounce cups. Primary children can mix colors on Styrofoam plates or trays, or on white paper towels. Older children can mix colors in small plastic party favor cups. Put newspaper underneath the food trays. Children can use eye droppers to mix colors in the small party favor cups. Have plenty of paper towels available for spills.

Older children can record the number of drops of each color used to produce new colors. For example, this could be how purple is made: 2 red + 3 blue = 5 drops of purple. Children can create names for the new colors they create. For example, 3 yellow + 6 red + 1 green = 10 drops of "lush lavender." They can create equations such as: 3 yellow + 6 red + ? green = 10 drops of "lush lavender."

QUESTIONS AND SUGGESTIONS

■ How many shades of each of the four colors can you make?

■ Determine the ratio or percentages of drops of each color used to make a new color.

■ Can you make a color wheel?

■ Reproduce the colors that you see in clothing worn by children in the class.

■ Make colors that match paint strips obtained from hardware or paint stores.

■ Exchange color formulas with your classmates.

■ Create colors never seen before.

■ Create clear water by using the four colors.

■ Can you make white?

■ What is the lightest color you can make?

■ What is the darkest color you can make?

FIGURE 11.23

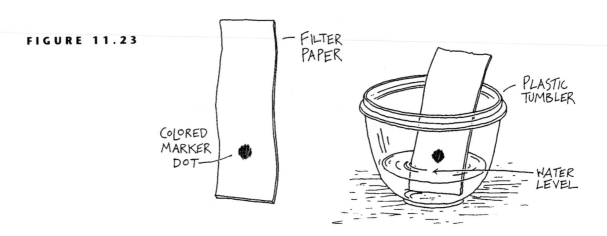

Chromatography

GOAL

■ To separate color pigments that are suspended in solutions

GRADE LEVELS

■ Upper grades

BACKGROUND INFORMATION

Chromatography is the separation of color. Pigments spread through a paper towel or coffee filter when the paper is soaked with colored water. Some pigments travel farther than others from the point of impact. Thus, pigments that are mixed together can be separated. Colored markers consist of combinations of pigments, which can be sorted by chromatography. (The colors of permanent colored markers will not separate in water; rubbing alcohol has to be used as the solvent.)

MATERIALS

■ Assorted water-soluble colored markers

■ Shallow cups or dishes

■ Water

■ Coffee filters or white paper towels

■ Centimeter rulers

INSTRUCTIONS

Cut a strip of coffee filter or white paper towel approximately 2 cm wide. With a marker, make a dot on the paper towel or coffee filter in the center of the strip near one of the ends. (See Figure 11.23.)

Place the strip in a cup with a tiny amount of water in the bottom. It is important not to let the dot come in contact with the water, or the color will bleed into the water without the separation occurring. If the dot is too high, it will take several minutes before the water reaches it. The dot must be placed just above the water line (Figure 11.23). The strip can rest on the side of the glass tumbler or be attached to a pencil laid across the top of the tumbler.

QUESTIONS AND SUGGESTIONS

- If black marker or pen is used, what colors are likely to appear on the strip?

- If you use a brown marker or pen, what colors are likely to appear on the strip?

- If a red marker is used, what colors are likely to appear on the strip?

- Find a way to identify different ballpoint pens using chromatography.

- Measure the height of each color as they separate. Do the same colors always reach the same height?

- Make a drawing or write your name on the filter paper and allow the water to absorb through it. What happens?

- The pigments in Kool-Aid packets and M&Ms can also be separated. Make a concentrated solution of Kool-Aid or dissolve the M&Ms in water. Place a strip in the water dye. Remember, the solution has to be concentrated for the color to show up on the strip.

- Pigments of leaves and fruits can also be separated using either water or alcohol as the solvent. You will have to experiment to see what works best. Some fruits, leaves, or blossoms are not water soluble. Crush the fruit to make a concentrated solution.

- What other material could be used for chromatography?

Light Tubs

GOAL

- To explore the characteristics of white light

GRADE LEVELS

- Upper grades

MATERIALS

- Large round cardboard ice cream tub

- Porcelain-base lamp fixture with cord and plug

- Nuts and bolts

- A 150–200 watt light bulb with a vertical filament (A light bulb with a vertical filament will give a sharper light than one with a horizontal filament. These bulbs may have to be purchased at electrical supply stores.)

- Pieces of colored cellophane

- Prisms

- Mirrors

- Black paper, white butcher paper, masking tape

- Assorted convex and concave lenses

- Assorted tubes to hold water and other liquids

INSTRUCTIONS

To make the light tubs (prepare these in advance):

1. Obtain a round 5-gallon ice cream bucket.

FIGURE 11.24

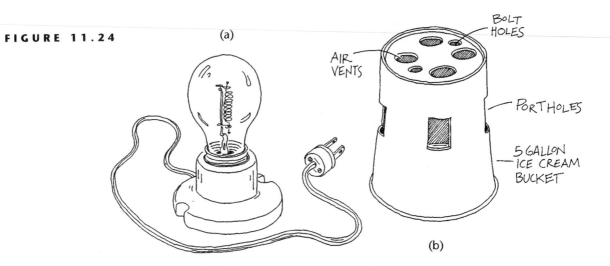

(a)

(b)

2. Cut four round holes (approximately 5 cm in diameter) in the bottom of the bucket. (See Figure 11.24b.) The four round holes allow heat to escape from the light bulb.

3. Attach approximately 6 m of electrical cord to the porcelain lamp base. (Figure 11.24a)

4. Make a small hole in the bottom of the ice cream tub and thread the electrical cord through the hole.

5. Make two additional small holes in the bottom of the tub and insert two bolts.

6. Run the two bolts through the holes on the side of the porcelain lamp base and secure them by tightly screwing down the nuts.

7. Attach an electrical plug to the end of the electrical cord.

8. Cut four portholes (approximately 9 cm × 6 cm) around the ice cream tub (Figure 11.24b). Each porthole serves as a workstation. Four children can work at one light box.

9. Screw in the light bulb with the vertical filament and turn the tub upside down.

10. Cut out four pieces of black paper to cover the portholes.

11. Cut a long slit into the black paper with a razor blade.

12. With masking tape, cover the portholes with the black paper.

13. Cover the table with white butcher paper secured with masking tape.

14. Secure the light tub to the butcher paper with masking tape.

15. Plug the electrical cord into an electrical outlet.

16. There should be a very narrow, straight ray of light emanating from the slits cut into the black paper. You should see these rays of light on the butcher paper. If the light beam is too diffused, seal the slit and make a narrower one in the paper.

QUESTIONS AND SUGGESTIONS

■ What colors do you see when you hold different combinations of cellophane over the narrow ray of light?

■ Prisms are triangular pieces of glass or plastic that can vary according to length and angle. Stand a prism on one of its ends and place it on the light ray. Rotate the prism slowly until the spectrum appears.

FIGURE 11.25

- Use a pencil and outline the spectrum. Label the colors and determine the angles of each color. Try using several prisms and bending the light in different directions.

- Using several prisms, make the spectrum revert to white light.

- Cover the spectrum with different pieces of colored cellophane. What happens to the colors?

- Can you tell by the order of the colors in the spectrum and the angles they form, which ones have the shortest wave length and which have the longest wave length?

- What causes red sunsets?

- Move a lens along the ray of light. The light ray should pass through the lens.

- Using the lenses, project an image of an object onto a white sheet of paper held vertically to the table top. To do this, place a small object between the lens and the paper. (See Figure 11.25.) Move the lens, the object, or the sheet of paper until you get a clear image. Measure the height of the actual object, the image, the distance from the lens to the object, and the distance from the object to the screen. Do this for each lens. What patterns do you see?

- Note the position of the image on the screen.

- Water in small plastic vials will also act as lenses. Try them as well.

- Bend the ray of light using mirrors. Can you bend the light so that it goes around the tub?

- What happens to the light intensity as more mirrors are added? Why does this happen?

- Try combinations of colored cellophane, prisms, mirrors, and lenses to see what you can discover about light.

Kaleidoscopes

GOAL

- To create kaleidoscopes using the ideas of refraction and reflection

GRADE LEVELS

- Middle to upper grades

FIGURE 11.26

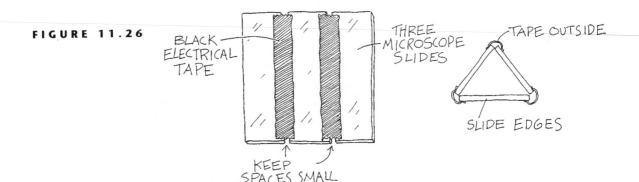

MATERIALS

- Microscope slides
- Black electrical tape
- Clear plastic party favor cups with lids
- Sequins and colorful plastic beads

INSTRUCTIONS

Place three microscope slides side by side, almost touching each other. (See Figure 11.26.) Attach the three slides with lengthwise strips of black electric tape. Fold the three slides to make a triangle, keeping the taped sides outside. If the slides are too close, they will not bend to make a triangle and if they are too far apart, they will move around in the tape. Insert the triangle into a toilet paper roll. If you do not have a toilet paper roll, cover the surfaces of the slides with black tape. Make sure all the glass is covered. You have made a kaleidoscope.

SUGGESTIONS

- Look at objects while slowly rotating the triangle. What do you see? How does the kaleidoscope work?
- Put some sequins and beads into a clear plastic party favor cup and cover it with a lid. Place the bottom of the party favor cup in the toilet paper roll and slowly rotate it. What do you see? You can also make designs on the party favor cup with markers.
- Think of other ways to make a kaleidoscope. For example, you can cut out a circle from an overhead transparency and spin it in front of the kaleidoscope.
- Put oil and sequins in a long closed tube. Shake the tube and place it perpendicular to the end of a kaleidoscope. Look through the kaleidoscope and watch the sequins fall through the oil as they pass by the kaleidoscope.
- Put a mirror at the end of the kaleidoscope. What do you see?

Summary

In this chapter, science concepts that involve forces were studied through hands-on activities. Forces occur whenever there is motion. Heat, light, and electromagnetism are also the result of forces. *Force* is an abstract idea that is difficult to understand at a concrete level.

It is Newton's laws that form the basis of school physics. The formula $F = ma$ is the one that pupils are most frequently asked to work with. Seldom, however, are the subtleties that lie behind it made clear. The law requires a recognition of forces exerted on one body by another. Only by clearly distinguishing the individual forces acting on a body can one hope to make sense of the laws at all. An understanding of $F = ma$ is made all the more difficult because it often contrasts with pupils' intuitive conceptions of motion. (Gunstone and Watts, 1985, p. 91)

Force is equal to mass times acceleration ($F = ma$). Mass is measured by weight and acceleration or the quickness of motion, and can be measured by changes in distance over time. Both mass and acceleration can be detected by the senses. However, their intersection to form the concept of force is abstracted mentally rather than through observable data. Thus, formulas such as $F = ma$ are difficult for children to understand if they have no knowledge of the components of the formula.

Thus, activities in this chapter focused on the attributes of forces that can be detected through the senses. Experiencing these attributes and quantifying them mathematically through a variety of hands-on activities will support the understanding of abstract concepts such as force.

The theme of measurement will continue in the next chapter, whose activities will help children learn some of the other major concepts in earth and life sciences. Keep in mind that whenever data are quantified in one way or another, mathematics is being used.

> **Go back to the reflective questions at the beginning of the chapter and the answers you recorded in your journal.**
>
> **Add to or modify your answers based on what you learned from this chapter.**

Bibliography

Guesne, E. (1985). Light. In R. Driver, E. Guesne, and A. Tiberghien (Eds.), *Children's ideas in science* (pp. 10–32). Philadelphia: Open University Press.

Gunstone, R., and Watts, M. (1985). Force and motion. In R. Driver, E. Guesne, and A. Tiberghien (Eds.), *Children's ideas in science* (pp. 85–104). Philadelphia: Open University Press.

Hazen, R., and Trefil, J. (1992). *Science matters: Achieving scientific literacy.* New York: Doubleday.

National Council of Teachers of Mathematics. (1989). *Curriculum and evaluation standards for school mathematics.* Reston, VA: Author.

National Research Council. (1996). *National science education standards.* Washington, DC: National Academy Press.

Piaget, J. (1970). *The child's conception of movement and speed.* New York: Basic Books.

Shipstone, D. (1985). Electricity in simple circuits. In R. Driver, E. Guesne, and A. Tiberghien (Eds.), *Children's ideas in science* (pp. 33–51). Philadelphia: Open University Press.

| # Liquids, Earth, and Life

And they are not self-evident: mass, energy, mind, the nervous system, the ecology of host and enzyme: these were not obvious to Aquinas and ready to be shuffled into laws by the first gifted mathematician. On the contrary, just as laws unite the facts, so the concepts of science unite its laws into an orderly world which hangs on those bold knots of the network.

J. Bronowski, *The Common Sense of Science*

JOURNEY PREPARATION

Reflective Questions

- What are appropriate activities that allow children to construct meaning about the earth and its life?

- What do you know about water and liquids?

- What are some basic earth science concepts that you understand?

- What life science activities are appropriate for elementary school children?

- How can mathematics be integrated with physical, earth, and life sciences?

Introduction

Chapters 10 and 11 emphasized measurement of forces. This chapter focuses on biology and earth science activities within a framework of problem solving. Activities related to water and other liquids begin the chapter. Science Content Standard B (see below) addresses the properties of liquids.

The life science and earth science activities in this chapter were selected based on children's ability to learn from direct observation. Thus, the life science activities include observing behaviors and structures of plants and animals that were not addressed in previous chapters. However, some simulation activities are included because they are the next best thing to direct experiences. Mathematical standards are included here to remind readers that science activities give children opportunities to use mathematics to solve problems quantitatively. The theme of measuring motion, time, and forces continues in this chapter.

Activities That Explore Liquids

The behaviors of water and other liquids are influenced by molecular forces and gravity. Because of the configuration of water molecules, a slight electrical charge is produced. Water molecules cling to each other and to other materials. This attraction between water and other materials is called *adhesion*. *Absorption* occurs when water or other liquids penetrate each other or other kinds of materials. Because of water's ability to penetrate many different

National Council of Teachers of Mathematics (1989)
Standard 1: Mathematics as Problem Solving

In grades K–4, the study of mathematics should emphasize problem solving so that students can—

use problem-solving approaches to investigate and understand mathematical content; formulate problems from everyday and mathematical situations; develop and apply strategies to solve a wide variety of problems; verify and interpret results with respect to the original problem; acquire confidence in using mathematics meaningfully. (p. 23)

In grades 5–8, the mathematics curriculum should include numerous and varied experiences with problem solving as a method of inquiry and application so that students can

—use problem-solving approaches to investigate and understand mathematical content; formulate problems from situations within and outside mathematics; develop and apply a variety of strategies to solve problems, with emphasis on multistep and nonroutine problems; verify and interpret results with respect to the original problem-solving situation; generalize solutions and strategies to new problem situations; acquire confidence in using mathematics meaningfully. (p. 75)

National Research Council (1996)
Content Standard B

As a result of their activities in grades K–4, all students should develop an understanding of properties of objects and materials. (p. 123)

Materials can exist in different states—solid, liquid, and gas. Some common materials such as water can be changed from one state to another by heating and cooling. (p. 127)

As a result of their activities in grades 5–8, all students should develop an understanding of properties and changes of properties in matter. (p. 149)

A substance has characteristic properties, such as density, a boiling point, and solubility, all of which are independent of the amount of the sample. A mixture of substances often can be separated into the original substances using one or more of the characteristic properties. (p. 154)

liquids and materials, it is called the universal solvent. Water is also used as a standard for comparing the density of other liquids. Water has a density of 1 g/ml. The density of everything else is less than or greater than water. The uneven attraction between water molecules causes surface tension because the molecules at the surface are being pulled down by those below the surface. This action results in a very thin film forming on undisturbed water. Certain insects can walk on the surface of water because of this film. Soap breaks down the bonds between water molecules and breaks the surface tension.

The water activities in this chapter provide opportunities to explore the physical characteristics of the surface tension of water and other liquids. Knowing how liquids interact with each other is useful for making salad dressing, cleaning clothes, and removing oil spills from oceans. And, of course, water is essential to the growth and survival of living things.

Liquid Drops

GOAL

■ To explore the properties of liquids by dropping them on different types of surfaces

GRADE LEVELS

■ Primary to upper grades

MATERIALS

■ Pipettes, straws, or eyedroppers

■ Small cups (paper, Styrofoam, coated and uncoated)

■ Materials such as aluminum foil, waxed paper, Styrofoam, glass, plastic, wood, construction paper, plastic wrap, newspaper, paper towels

■ Metersticks

■ Pennies

■ Glass slides

■ Liquids such as vinegar, vegetable oil, rubbing alcohol (91%), dishwashing liquid soap, water

■ Paper clips, toothpicks, tubing

INSTRUCTIONS

Children can begin with an eyedropper, water, and a penny to see how many drops they can pile onto the penny. A straw can be used like an eyedropper by placing it in water and holding a finger over the other end. The water will go into the straw and remain there until the finger is removed. After working with water, other liquids can be used to see how many drops can be piled onto pennies. After working with pennies and drops, children can explore drops landing on different surfaces from different heights.

QUESTIONS AND SUGGESTIONS

■ How many drops of water can you place on a penny before the water spills over the edge?

■ How many drops of other liquids can you get on a penny?

■ What happens to drops of water when they hit different surfaces (such as aluminum foil, waxed paper, plastic wrap, Styrofoam, glass, construction paper, paper towel, newspaper)?

■ What happens to drops of water when they hit different surfaces from different heights?

■ Drop other liquids from different heights. Look for patterns in the shapes of drops in relation to the liquid and to the surface.

■ Measure the diameter of the drops after they hit the various surfaces.

■ Drop water on different kinds of paper towel. Which ones allow the water to spread the fastest? Which ones allow the water to spread the farthest? Measure the area over which the water spreads.

■ What are the relationships between the height from which the liquids are dropped and the size of the drops?

- Can you pull around a drop of water? Which surfaces work the best to pull a drop of water around?

- Can you pull around other liquids?

- Have drop races: Cover an inclined plane with different kinds of materials. How far will different liquids run down the inclined plane? How fast does each liquid run down the inclined plane?

- Can you place a drop of water within another drop of water? Can a drop of one liquid be placed within a drop of another? How many drops of water can you get in another drop of water? How many drops of one liquid can you get into another liquid?

- What is the biggest drop you can make using water? What is the biggest drop you can make with another liquid?

- What is the smallest drop you can make using water? What is the smallest drop you can make with another liquid?

- Fill small cups to the brim with water. Continue adding water to each cup drop by drop. How many drops can you add to each cup before the water spills over the edge? Describe what the water looks like before it spills over the edge.

- Fill a clean cup with water to the brim. Float a paper clip on top of the water. Then put a tiny amount of liquid soap on the end of a toothpick. Touch the water at the edge of the cup with the soap. What happens to the paper clip?

- Repeat the experiment, using clean water, but put pepper on top of the water and touch the sides of the cup with a tiny drop of soap. What happens?

- Can you explain how soap cleans clothes?

- Using tubing, can you get water to run uphill from one container to another?

- Using tubing, can you get water to flow from one jar to another and another? How many jars can you add?

- Can you get water to flow through several containers and back to the original container?

Mixing Liquids

GOAL

- To explore the densities of liquids

GRADE LEVELS

- Middle to upper grades

MATERIALS

- Pipettes, eyedroppers, or straws

- Small cylindrical containers approximately one ounce in size

- Vinegar, vegetable oil, liquid dishwashing soap, molasses, syrup, rubbing alcohol (91%), salt water, lemon juice, glycerin, other liquids

- Food coloring

- Aluminum foil

- Small plastic beads

FIGURE 12.1

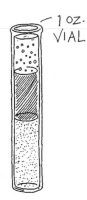

BACKGROUND INFORMATION

Liquids have different densities and can be layered on top of each other according to their densities. Water has a density of 1 and any liquid that floats on water will have a density of less than 1. Any liquid with a density of greater than 1 will sink. To find the density of a liquid, divide volume by mass: for example, 10 milliliters of a liquid that weighs 5 grams has a density of 0.5 g/ml.

Lava lamps are made using liquids that have different densities and will not dissolve in each other. Oils do not readily dissolve in water. Thus, when oil spills occur, the oil floats on top of the water.

QUESTIONS

- Using pipettes, carefully place drops of different liquids into a vial. Can you make layers of liquids? (See Figure 12.1.)

- Can you predict which liquids should go in first to make layers?

- How many layers can you make?

- What happens if you shake up the layers?

- What happens if you use hot water rather than cold water to make the layers?

- Can you reverse the order of the liquid layers?

- Can you place objects in each layer? Put a piece of aluminum foil in one layer and a small plastic bead in another layer.

- Can you make a liquid stay inside a layer of another liquid?

- Can you trap a liquid underneath another liquid?

- If you use the same amount of liquid for each layer, are the heights of each layer the same?

Activities That Explore Living Systems

For the time being, it need only be said that the extension of the notion of "life" seems to indicate the presence in the child's universe of a continuum of free forces endowed with activity and purpose. Between magical causality, according to which all things revolve around the self and the dynamism of material forces the notion of life forms an intermediary link. Born of the idea that all things are directed towards an end and that this end supposes a free activity as the means of attaining it, the notion of life gradually becomes reduced to the idea of force or of being the cause of spontaneous movement. (Piaget, 1979, p. 206)

Forces and motion can also be studied through the behavior of living organisms. Children can investigate the effects of light on plant growth. They can stand carnations or celery stalks in colored water and observe the water rising in the stems by capillary action; in other words, the effect of surface tension and adhesion on water molecules. Children can observe animals such as earthworms, mealworms, and sow bugs. The following hands-on activities involve observations of plant and animal behavior. Since plant behavior occurs over long periods of time, plants can be observed throughout the year in conjunction with other classroom activities.

Other concepts that are related to living organisms are difficult to learn through direct observations. Photosynthesis is a chemical process occuring at the molecular level. Examining plant and animal cells may be difficult for children because they have to learn how to use a microscope and to know the difference between microscopic inert objects and parts of living cells. Making diagrams of the photosynthesis process and creating models of cells are more like art exercises than learning about biological functions.

However, focusing on plant and animal behaviors and structures offers an excellent opportunity to use many mathematical operations. Children can use concepts of measurement and time to record changes, and they can work with estimation, percentages, ratios, fractions, and decimals. (See Chapter 6 for details of mathematical standards 5 and 7.)

TOUR GUIDE

National Research Council (1996) Content Standard C

As a result of activities in grades K–4, all students should develop an understanding of

- the characteristics of organisms
- life cycles of organisms
- organisms and environments (p. 127)

As a result of activities in grades 5–8, all students should develop an understanding of

- structure and function in living systems
- regulation and behavior
- populations and ecosystems
- diversity and adaptation of organisms (p. 155)

Seed Germination

GOALS

- To compare (by means of ratios) the size of seeds before and after soaking them in water
- To compare the ratios of the number of seeds that germinate to those that do not

GRADE LEVELS

- Middle to upper grades

MATERIALS

- Beans: lima, kidney, black, navy, pinto
- Pint or quart containers
- Water
- Weighing scales
- Plaster of Paris
- Small paper cups

QUESTIONS AND SUGGESTIONS

- Measure the dimensions of lima beans. What is the average size of the beans? Weigh the lima beans. What is the average weight of a lima bean?

- Fill a quart jar half full with lima beans and add enough water to cover the beans. How much water did it take to cover the beans? Record the number of beans, the level of the beans, and the level of the water.

- Check the beans the next day. What happened to the water? How much water is left?

- Measure the size of the beans. How much bigger are they now? How much more do they weigh than the previous day?

- What would happen if you filled the jar completely full of lima beans, covered them with water, and tightly screwed a lid onto the jar?

- Try other beans. Compare the change in size and the amount of water absorbed for each type of bean.

- Make a mixture of plaster of Paris and water. Fill small paper cups about half full with the mixture. Push several beans down into the liquid mixture. Predict what will happen to the beans after setting for several days in the solid plaster of Paris.

- Obtain a seed sprouting kit; usually an amber-colored quart jar with a jar ring that has a screen cover. The kits contain seeds that can be sprouted as salad greens. Use these seeds and seeds of beans, peas, radishes, lettuce, and corn. Place them in the jar, wet them thoroughly, and drain off the excess water. Place the jar in a cool place such as a refrigerator. The seeds must be rinsed daily as they sprout to prevent mold growth. The seeds will begin to sprout within a day.

- Which seeds begin to sprout or germinate roots and leaves first? Which seeds germinate last? Make a graph to illustrate germination times of seeds.

- Pour out the germinating seeds and examine them with a hand lens. Which seeds are germinating? How many of each type of seed are germinating?

- Which seeds have two halves? What does the seed look like inside when the two halves are separated?

- Observe the growth of the roots and leaves. Which start growing first?

- How much do the roots grow each day?

- What type of seed has the longest or shortest root at the end of a designated time period?

FIGURE 12.2

- What type of seed has the biggest or smallest leaves or stems at the end of a designated time period?

- Do all seeds have the same kind of root formation?

- How long does it take for the leaves to begin to form?

- How long does it take for the leaves to turn green?

- Examine the seeds daily until the shape of the leaves and roots can be distinguished. Classify the sprouts according to the root types and leaf shapes. After studying the sprouting seeds, put them on a salad and enjoy!

- Find out what other seeds can be sprouted in water. For example, avocado seeds can be sprouted in water. Suspend the seed by inserting four toothpicks and resting the toothpicks on the rim of a glass. Pour in enough water to cover the bottom of the avocado.

Observing Root, Stem, and Leaf Growth

GOAL

- To measure changes in root, stem, and leaf growth

GRADE LEVELS

- Middle to upper grades

MATERIALS

- Bean seeds
- Quart-size freezer bags
- Paper towels
- Water

INSTRUCTIONS

1. Put flat layers of moist paper towels in a quart-size freezer bag.
2. Place soaked bean seeds between the paper towel layers and around the edges of the bag.
3. Staple the bag and paper towel together to hold the seeds in place. (See Figure 12.2.)
4. Observe the seeds after a few days. Continue to observe them on a regular basis while the first few roots and leaves develop.

QUESTIONS

- Which way do the roots grow?
- Which way do the leaves grow?
- What happens to the growth of the roots and stems if you change the bag's position daily?
- How long will the sprouts continue to grow in the bag?
- Do all roots, stems, and leaves grow at the same rate?
- Do all roots, stems, and leaves grow to be the same size?

Note: Some seeds will become moldy since they cannot be rinsed. To reduce the amount of mold, rinse the seeds in water containing a small amount of chlorine bleach.

Seed Germination in Soil

GOAL

- To determine which seeds will germinate in soil

GRADE LEVELS

- Middle to upper grades

MATERIALS

- Plant pots such as plastic pots, fiber pots, paper cups, clay pots, tin cans
- Trays
- Garden soil
- A variety of seeds such as grass, radishes, beans, and peas; seeds from tomatoes and green peppers; fruit seeds such as apple, pear, grapefruit, lemon, lime, kiwi, watermelon, cantaloupe; seeds from outdoors such as nuts and seeds from trees, weeds, and garden flowers

INSTRUCTIONS

The pots should have good drainage. Fill pots with soil. Place pots on trays to catch excess water. Plant seeds in the soil. Depending on their size, several seeds can be planted in a single pot. Maintain records of the number of seeds in each pot. Keep the soil moist, but the seeds should not sit in water. Place the pots in a sunny window or under grow lights. Late winter and spring are good times to grow seeds because of the increasing hours of daylight.

QUESTIONS AND SUGGESTIONS

- Estimate how many seeds will actually germinate.
- Keep a record of the number of seeds that germinate in each pot and for each type of seed.
- What is the percentage of seeds that sprout?
- What is the ratio of seeds that sprout per pot?
- How many days does it take for the seeds to germinate?
- On a regular basis measure the height of the plants as they grow.
- Which type of seed germinates first?

- In midwinter dig up some soil from outside and place it in a pot. Keep it moist. Do plants begin to grow? How long does it take? How many plants begin to grow? How many kinds of plants begin to grow?

- Place some pots in a cabinet or a closet. What happens to the growth of these plants compared to those that are in a sunny spot? Can you explain the growth behavior of the plants that are located in the dark?

- If you cover plants with different colors of cellophane, will it affect the way they grow?

- Prepare graphs to compare the growth rate of plants under different conditions.

- Cover a leaf with black paper. Check the leaf on a regular basis. What happens?

Germination of Roots from Leaves and Stems

GOAL

- To determine what kinds of plants can be grown from stem and leaf cuttings

GRADE LEVELS

- Middle to upper grades

BACKGROUND INFORMATION

Some plants will produce roots from leaves or stems. For example, forsythia and pussy willow stems will produce roots. Geraniums, violets, and ivy are examples of houseplants that can be started from leaves placed in water. Late January or early February, depending on the climate, is a good time to make cuttings from outdoor shrubs and bring them into the classroom.

SUGGESTIONS

- Cut stems from houseplants and outdoor plants. Which ones develop leaves and flowers as they develop roots? Once the roots have developed, place the plant in a pot containing soil.

- Violets and philodendrons will produce roots if you place the stem of the leaf in water. Find out what other plants can produce roots this way.

- Grow potato plants by placing a piece of the potato tuber (section of a potato that contains an eye spot) in water. Keep the eye spot above the water level. Stems will grow from the eye spot. Weigh the potato tuber before beginning. Weigh the tuber periodically while the roots, stems, and leaves form and grow. Does the weight change? Why? Keep the piece moist while the potato grows.

- Cut the tops of carrots, beets, and radishes and place them in dishes of water. Do leaves begin to sprout? How long does it take for the leaves to sprout? Record the growth of roots on a daily basis. Is the growth rate the same every day?

Studying Plants and Animals

The best way to study plant and animal communities is to walk around the playground, the neighborhood, and other natural habitats. (Chapter 3 also contains suggestions for studying plant and animal communities.) Children can count the number and type of plants and animals they see. A plot of land can be roped off and children can investigate the area to see how many plants and animals they can find. During the winter children can take walks in the snow to find animal tracks. They can make bird feeders to attract birds and watch their behavior. Microhabitats can be created in the classroom by setting up herbariums, aquariums, and terrariums.

The balance of the type of plants and animals in a community must also be considered. The study of their interrelationship with their environment is called *ecology*. Children may observe examples of the *food chain*, the order in which members of an ecological community use each other as food. However, children may have difficulty understanding these concepts because these relationships cannot always be directly observed. The balance of nature, or the ecological makeup of a natural community, sometimes must be implied by events that happen in response to overpopulation, destruction of habitat, or changes in weather conditions.

Observing Plant and Animal Microcommunities

GOALS

- To observe changes in living organisms
- To observe the interactions between living organisms

GRADE LEVELS

- Primary through upper grades

BACKGROUND INFORMATION

Plant and animal communities can be observed by creating herbariums, terrariums, and aquariums. These microcommunities must have the right balance of living organisms and environmental factors such as light, air, moisture, and temperature. Children can study the ecology of these microcommunities. Children in upper grades can help make the environments and maintain records of the changes and interactions that occur in the microcommunities.

Making an Herbarium

Different kinds of plant environments can be created in large, clear plastic gallon jars that have a wide opening. Clear plastic two-liter bottles can also be used. Cut the top off the bottles. Put sand in the bottom for a desert community; garden soil for a tropical or temperate plant community. Place small pieces of charcoal in the soil to absorb the acidic conditions created by the water, soil, and decaying organisms. Add enough water to make the soil moist; for the desert community, sprinkle water on the soil without soaking it. Tropical and desert plants can be purchased at nurseries and garden stores. Plants of temperate regions can be found in the neighborhood. Loosely cover the opening of the bottle with plastic wrap to prevent moisture from escaping and to allow air to circulate.

Which community needs to have water added from time to time? What type of plants will grow in each community?

Making a Terrarium

Use five- to ten-gallon aquariums. Set up a particular plant community and add animals; for example, crickets, salamanders, and toads can be added to a temperate region community, land snails and frogs to a tropical rain forest community, and small snakes, horned toads, and kangaroo rats to a desert community. Many of these animals can be purchased at pet stores. Make sure the animals and insects have the right kind of food. Observe their behavior.

Making an Aquarium

The easiest fish to take care of are goldfish, which can tolerate water temperature fluctuations. If the water lacks oxygen they will come to the surface for air. Water plants, tadpoles, and water snails can be added with the goldfish.

Tropical fish need aerated, filtered water with a constant temperature. The easiest tropical fish to raise are guppies. Other tropical fish are more susceptible to disease when the temperature fluctuates. Some tropical fish are aggressive and will eat other fish.

QUESTIONS AND SUGGESTIONS

- Watch for condensation of moisture on the sides of a terrarium. Does it occur on a regular basis?
- Count the number of animals and plants in your microcommunity.
- Record the behavior of animals. Can you tell if they are breathing? How do they eat their food?
- Which ones fly? Which ones crawl? How many legs do the animals have?
- Record the number of animals that become food for other animals or die because of other reasons.
- Observe plant growth. Do some plants take over the habitat? What is the dominant species?
- What is the percentage of each type of plant in the habitat? Which species is rare?
- What is the tallest plant? What is the shortest plant?
- What is the largest animal? What is the smallest animal?
- Do some plants have more leaves than others? What is the ratio of leaves on one plant compared to another in the different environments? Is there a correlation between the environment and the number of leaves the plants have?
- What different shapes of leaves do you see? Which shape is the most predominant?
- Which plants have flowers? Which have the most flowers? Express in percentages the number of flowers each plant has to the total number of flowers found on all of the flowering plants.
- How many different colors do the flowers have? Is there a dominant color?

Creating Plants

GOAL

- To explore the relationships between the structure of plants and their environments

GRADE LEVELS

- Upper grades

MATERIALS

- Floral tape and wire

- Liquid plastic
- Colored tissue wrapping paper
- Pipe cleaners

INSTRUCTIONS

The floral wire or pipe cleaners can be bent and easily shaped to resemble plant parts. The shaped wire can be dipped in green liquid plastic to create leaves. Or use colored tissue wrapping paper to make leaves.

SUGGESTIONS

- Make a plant that lives in cold, dry conditions.
- Make a plant that lives in water.
- Make a plant that lives in a swamp.
- Make a plant that lives in dark conditions.
- Make a plant that lives in very hot, dry conditions.
- Make a plant that lives in very hot, wet conditions.
- Make a plant that lives in very cold, wet conditions.

Exploring Fibonacci Numbers

GOAL

- To look for the Fibonacci sequence of numbers in nature

GRADE LEVELS

- Upper grades

MATERIALS

- Pine cones
- Sunflower blossom that has gone to seed
- Flowers that are similar to sunflowers
- Twigs, stems, or branches of flowering plants, bushes, and trees

BACKGROUND INFORMATION

Leonardo of Pisa, also known as Fibonacci, was an Italian mathematician who discovered a sequence of numbers that occur in nature. The sequence is the sum of the previous two numbers. The sequence of numbers is 1, 1, 2, 3, 5, 8, 13 . . .

INSTRUCTIONS

Observe the arrangement of seeds, petals, and leaves on plants and flowers. Do you see the Fibonacci sequence in the number of seeds, petals, or leaves? Are Fibonacci numbers represented in nature in other ways?

Observing Butterflies

GOAL

- To observe butterfly larvae, pupae, and adults

GRADE LEVELS

- Primary to upper grades

MATERIALS

- Milk cartons (quart size)
- Clothes hanger
- Cheesecloth, fiber mesh, screening, or netting
- Broom handle or dowels
- Thread, tape
- Jar lid, cotton balls, sponges

BACKGROUND INFORMATION

Some insects undergo a four-stage metamorphosis or change of development. Each stage serves a specific purpose. Butterflies, moths, beetles, and bees are examples of insects that develop through four stages. The egg stage is the beginning of the insect's development. The larva, or caterpillar or wormlike stage, is the time when the insect eats and experiences the most growth. Next, the pupa stage is the time when the larva changes to the adult form. The pupa becomes encased within a protective covering; the larva of a moth creates a cocoon, the larva of a butterfly creates a chrysalis. A cocoon consists of coarse fibers; a chrysalis is usually smooth and hard. The pupa of a beetle does not form a cocoon or a chrysalis, but has a vague resemblance to the body of an adult beetle. Inside the cocoon or chrysalis the wormlike shape changes to that of an insect with six legs, wings, antenna, and some form of mouth parts. Growth is complete and the cycle is ready to renew itself because the main function of the adult stage is to reproduce. The adult needs minimal nourishment and its life span is short.

Butterfly pupae can be purchased from science supply companies. Children can watch the pupae develop into adult butterflies. To see the larva stage, children can catch butterflies during the summer months and keep them in terrariums in the classroom. Children can keep track of the number of days it takes for the butterfly to emerge from the chrysalis. They can watch the butterflies emerge and see how long it takes for their wings to dry and they are able to fly.

INSTRUCTIONS

To make an insect-catching net, bend a clothes hanger into a circular shape. Sew the mesh or netting around the clothes hanger. Untwist the ends of the clothes hanger and tape them to the end of a pole. To make a viewing container, cut openings or "windows" on the four sides of a milk carton. Tape nylon mesh or screen across the openings. The butterfly or other insects can be observed through these windows. Find a tree twig to lean inside the carton. The twig will be a place for the butterfly to rest. Put a small jar lid full of water inside the carton. Butterflies need moisture. Try other things that hold water such as cotton balls and small pieces of sponge.

Butterflies can be collected during the late summer or early fall while the weather is still warm. Handle them carefully so that their wings are not damaged. Release them after several days of observation. Watch for chrysalises and cocoons attached to plants. Leave them attached to the leaves or branches and gently place the whole branch in the carton. They can be observed throughout the school year. Finally, watch for butterfly and moth larvae. They can also be placed in the viewing container but will need food. When collecting them, notice what plants and parts of plants they eat. Put these plants inside the viewing container.

The viewing container can be used to observe other insects such as beetles, grasshoppers, and crickets. Make sure to give these insects the proper food.

QUESTIONS

- How do butterflies and moths hold their wings while resting?
- What do larva of butterflies and moths eat? How much do they eat? How much of their time do they spend eating?
- Can you determine how insects breathe? Watch them.
- How long does it take for a butterfly or moth to emerge from a cocoon or chrysalis?
- How long does it take the larva of a butterfly or moth to make a cocoon or chrysalis?
- How do butterflies and moths drink water?

Observing Mealworms

GOAL

- To observe the behavior of mealworms in response to different environmental conditions

GRADE LEVELS

- Middle to upper grades

MATERIALS

- Trays
- Colored cellophane
- Hand lenses
- Ice
- Black construction paper
- Pieces of apple and lettuce
- Water

INSTRUCTIONS

The mealworm is the larva stage of a beetle. Mealworms can be purchased at pet stores. They will grow in flour, cornmeal, or bran flour. Keep the mealworms in a closed container with tiny air holes. Add pieces of apple or lettuce for moisture and food. The mealworm eventually changes to the pupa stage and then to the adult beetle. (The eggs are too tiny to observe.) The complete life cycle of a mealworm is approximately two weeks.

Find out how mealworms react to environmental stimuli such as heat, light, and moisture.

SUGGESTIONS

- "Adopt" a mealworm. Find some way to identify it and watch it go through the pupa stage to the adult stage.
- Look closely at mealworms. Do all mealworms look the same? Can you draw them?
- Are all mealworms the same length? What is the average length of several mealworms?
- How much does a mealworm weigh? What is the average weight of several mealworms?

- How do they move?

- Can you find the mouth? Watch them eat.

- Place mealworms on trays. Cover one half with black paper. Expose the other half to a bright light. What do they do?

- Do mealworms prefer one color over another? Experiment by covering the tray with two different colors of cellophane. Repeat each experiment several times before drawing conclusions.

- Do all mealworms react the same way to environmental conditions? How can you be as sure as possible?

- What does a mealworm do if one half is hot and the other half is cold? To find out, put a mealworm on a tray with one half of the tray above a light bulb that provides heat and the other half above ice.

Observing Sow Bugs

GOAL

- To observe the behavior of sow bugs in response to different environmental conditions

GRADE LEVELS

- Middle to upper grades

MATERIALS

Use the same materials listed for the mealworm activity.

BACKGROUND INFORMATION

Children often call sow bugs roly-polys because they roll up into a ball when touched. They are also called wood lice or pill bugs. Sow bugs are not insects; they belong to a group called isopods. Crustaceans are other isopods, which makes sow bugs related to crayfish and lobsters.

Sow bugs live in moist soil under rocks and logs. They can easily be found in yards and gardens. Sow bugs can be kept alive in containers with moist soil and pieces of lettuce.

INSTRUCTIONS

Find out how sow bugs react to light, heat, and moisture. Try the same experiments as in the mealworm activity.

SUGGESTIONS

- Describe the bodies of sow bugs. How many legs do they have?

- What do sow bugs do when they are touched?

- Explain how they move. Can you get them to move through a maze? How fast do they move?

- What patterns do they make when they move? Do they move in circles? Do they move in a straight line?

Observing Earthworms

GOAL

- To observe the behavior of earthworms in response to different environmental conditions

GRADE LEVELS

- Middle to upper grades

MATERIALS

Use the same materials listed for the mealworm activity.

INSTRUCTIONS

Earthworms can be found in the soil in backyards or purchased at bait shops. Keep earthworms in containers with moist soil and pieces of lettuce, apples, and coffee grounds. The containers need air holes. Try the same experiments as in the mealworm activity.

QUESTIONS AND SUGGESTIONS

- Examine earthworms with magnifying lenses. What can you observe about their body structure? How do they move?

- Touch an earthworm and feel the differences between body parts. How many body segments are there?

- Do earthworms have mouth parts? Can you tell where the mouth is?

- Can earthworms see? Do they have eyes?

- Place earthworms in a jar of moist soil to which an inch or so of sand has been added. Earthworms will surface at some point and leave castings (soil and organic matter that has gone through their digestive system). They look like small, black piles of soil. Cover the jar with black paper. Uncover the jar after several days. What do you see?

- Place earthworms in a large container of moist soil and add pieces of vegetables, newspaper, coffee grounds, and other organic material. Observe what happens to the organic material after several days.

- Place an earthworm on the glass of a flashlight and turn on the light. Watch what the earthworm does. Can you see parts moving inside the earthworm? What do you think the moving parts are?

Finding Animals in the Soil

GOAL

- To find and describe living animals in the soil

GRADE LEVELS

- Primary through upper grades

MATERIALS

- Hand lenses

- Probes: pencils or pens

- Trays

- Newspaper

INSTRUCTIONS

Dig up soil at various times of the year. Obtain approximately a pint of soil. Cover the work surface with newspaper and place the soil on a tray on top of the newspaper. Use a pencil or pen as a probe to carefully search for animals in the soil. Use a magnifying lens to aid in the search.

QUESTIONS

■ How many living insects can you find? Are there other types of animals as well?

■ How many different kinds of animals can you find? Are there more than one of each type?

■ What is the percentage of each type of the total animal population?

■ If you were to take another sample of soil from another spot, what do you predict you would find? What is the probability of finding one particular animal?

■ In the winter take a soil sample from different layers (surface, five inches, and 10 inches deep). Allow the soil to warm to room temperature. Which layers contain life? Why?

Making a Spider Web

GOAL

■ To observe the patterns of spider webs

GRADE LEVELS

■ Primary through upper grades

MATERIALS

■ Dead tree branches or stems from other sturdy plants

■ Kite string or sewing thread

INSTRUCTIONS

Spiders are not classified as insects since they have eight legs. Spiders can spin intricate webs to catch prey for food. Look for spider webs in nature. Take a picture or draw a picture of the webs and go back to the classroom to build a spider web. Using the string, try to duplicate the web on a forked branch.

Capture spiders and place them in containers with twigs. Watch to see if the spiders will spin webs.

Create a spider web support: two wooden dowels or twigs connected by a horizontal twig. The two upright twigs should be anchored by floral clay in a water tray. Place a spider on the support apparatus. The water tray prevents the spider from escaping.

QUESTIONS

■ Can you predict the type of web a spider will spin?

■ Look at the shapes in a spider web. What shapes do you see? How many different shapes are there?

■ What is the distance between threads in a web?

Observing Leaf Veins

GOAL

- To compare the patterns and shapes made by leaf veins

GRADE LEVELS

- Primary through upper grades

MATERIALS

- Fallen leaves
- Hand lenses

BACKGROUND INFORMATION

Slugs will eat leaves. Slugs, which look like snails without shells, are part of the diverse life of the forest. They can be seen crawling on the damp forest floor or even on grass wet from dew or rain. They eat the soft part of a leaf and leave the veins.

INSTRUCTIONS

Look for leaves that have been eaten by slugs or put slugs in a terrarium with leaves for them to eat. Observe the veins of leaves the slugs eat and the behaviors of the slugs.

SUGGESTIONS

- Describe the structure of the leaf veins.
- Make rubbings of leaves before and after slugs have eaten them.
- Trace the veins from the largest to the smallest.
- What patterns do you see in the veins?

Making Bird Nests

GOAL

- To compare the structures of bird nests

GRADE LEVELS

- Upper grades

MATERIALS

- Twigs
- String
- Paper
- Dead grass

INSTRUCTIONS

Observe bird nests in a natural setting. Build a bird nest like one that you saw.

QUESTIONS AND SUGGESTIONS

- In the spring, locate a bird that is building a nest. Find out how long it takes for the bird to complete the task. What objects are used to build the nest? How are the objects placed to create the nest?
- How does the bird nest you build compare to the one you tried to copy?

Reconstructing Animal Skeletons from Owl Pellets

GOALS

- To examine animal skeletons
- To discover which animals are in a food chain

GRADE LEVELS

- Upper grades

MATERIALS

- Owl pellets
- Tweezers
- Hand lenses

INSTRUCTIONS

Owl pellets can be obtained from science supply companies. Owls eat rodents such as moles and field mice. What the owl cannot digest is regurgitated in the form of a ball, which consists of bones and fur. Skeletons of the animals the owl ate can be reconstructed from the pellets. Owl pellets are disinfected and wrapped in aluminum foil before being sold. Children can use tweezers to pull the pellets apart.

QUESTIONS AND SUGGESTIONS

- Weigh the owl pellet before and after extracting the bones. What percentage of the owl pellet is bone?
- Reconstruct the skeletons found in the owl pellets. Which pieces are missing? How many different pieces are missing? What could account for this?
- How many animal skeletons are in one owl pellet?
- Find a book that shows pictures of the skeletons of small rodents. Can you identify the animals found in the owl pellets?
- Glue the skeletons to black construction paper for display. Draw in the missing pieces.

Reconstructing Bird Skeletons

GOAL

- To examine the skeleton and bones of a bird

GRADE LEVELS

- Middle to upper grades

MATERIALS

- Chicken bones
- Cornish hen bones
- Turkey bones

INSTRUCTIONS

Save the bones from chicken, Cornish hen, and turkey carcasses. Boil the meat off the bones. Dip them in a chlorine bleach solution to kill any bacteria and clean them.

Place a complete skeleton in a bag and give it to children to see if they can fit the different bones together.

SUGGESTIONS

- Make bags with mixtures of bones from turkeys, chickens, and Cornish hens. Have children match the bones to the appropriate bird.
- Compare the weights and sizes of chicken, turkey, and Cornish hen bones.
- Look at the inside of mammal and bird bones. Are they different? Are some bones more hollow than others? (Mammal bones can be obtained from butchers in grocery stores as well as owl pellets.)
- Measure the lengths and diameters of the bones. Compare the bones of the different species.

Creating a Model Human Skeleton

GOAL

- To make a model of the human skeleton

GRADE LEVELS

- Upper grades

MATERIALS

- Paper towel rolls
- Toilet paper rolls
- Plaster of Paris
- Dowels
- Clothes hangers

INSTRUCTIONS

Children can work in groups to build a life-size skeleton that represents a member of the group. They can measure the length and diameter of the model's bones and reproduce them using a variety of the materials that are listed above.

QUESTIONS AND SUGGESTIONS

- Build the skeleton without using reference books.
- Which bones are easy to identify? Which bones are the most difficult?
- How many bones can you reconstruct without the use of references?
- Use a reference to complete the skeleton.

Growing Mold

GOAL

- To determine the best growing conditions for mold

GRADE LEVELS

- Upper grades

MATERIALS

- Organic material for growing mold

- Containers for the organic material
- Tweezers
- Magnifying lenses
- Binocular microscopes (optional)
- Books with illustrations of mold structures

BACKGROUND INFORMATION

Anyone who has stored food for a long time knows that certain foods become moldy. Mold is a nongreen plant that lives on other organisms. Besides food, mold can be found growing in the soil, on plants, and even on clothing. Mold spores are found in the air and on objects.

Mold organisms are important to the decaying process of living matter because mold creates enzymes that break down organic matter. Mold plants grow in colonies. They are characterized by their colors and the shapes of the colonies. Spores, which are part of the reproductive cycle, form last and often give the mold a different color. To see an individual plant, separate a very tiny amount of mold from the colony and observe it using magnifying lenses or binocular microscopes.

Some molds create allergies in some people; other molds are important in fighting diseases and infection. Penicillin is a derivative of a mold.

INSTRUCTIONS

Test what happens when organic matter such as bread, fruit, or cheese comes in contact with the floor, a door handle, or another surface. Touch the food source to the surface and then place it in a container. Decide where the container should be kept and whether it should be covered. Make observations. Set up experimental conditions to find out what kind of environment is the best for growing mold.

QUESTIONS

- Who can grow the most mold? How can this be quantified?
- How many different types of mold can you grow?
- How many different colors are there?
- How many different shapes do the mold colonies create?
- What does an individual mold plant look like?
- Do mold plants from different colonies look the same?
- How long does it take to grow mold colonies?
- What is the size of the largest colony?
- What is the size of the smallest colony?
- Do mold colonies grow on other mold colonies?
- What environmental conditions are conducive to growing mold?

Activities That Explore Earth Science

With regard to teaching the Earth concept, educators have the illusion that providing some proofs of the spherical shape of the Earth will convince pupils about the Earth's shape and, as a by-product, will change their understanding of the "nature" of cosmic space. Such proofs when given without considering pupils' preconceptions and without confronting them explicitly, often do not serve this purpose. They do not have the intended effect of causing pupils to

TOUR GUIDE

> ## National Research Council (1996)
> ## Content Standard D
>
> As a result of their activities in grades K–4, all students should develop an understanding of
>
> - properties of earth materials
> - objects in the sky
> - changes in earth and sky (p. 130)
>
> As a result of their activities in grades 5–8, all students should develop an understanding of
>
> - structure of the earth's systems
> - earth in the solar system (p. 158)

modify their belief about the Earth's shape and, needless to say, they do not influence pupils' notions of cosmic space. The notion of cosmic space requires direct and explicit didactic treatment. (Nussbaum, 1989, p. 190)

Earth science involves the study of the earth's composition, its layers and the activity within the layers, oceans, and weather systems. The study of astronomy is often included. Much of what is known about the earth and the rest of the universe is based on inferences. Thus, as Nussbaum (1989) points out, much of earth science has to be taught through didactic methods. It is difficult to collect data through direct observations because changes occur on a grand scale and over very long periods of time. The formations of most earth science concepts were developed by using sophisticated technology. Theories of plate tectonics, for example, were developed in part by collecting samples from hundreds of feet below the earth and the ocean in different parts of the world. Seismographic data collected over many years was also used to develop an explanation for the movement of earth plates. The same is true for astronomy. Thus, making papier-mâché planets does not lead to understanding anything about them. This is merely an art exercise. Usually the planets are not made to scale and their surfaces are not reproduced accurately either.

These science concepts have been incorporated into curriculums with little consideration as to whether children are developmentally ready to understand them. The plate tectonics theory was first introduced into the science curriculum at the high school level. Students collected actual data about earthquakes and volcanic activity. They studied maps of the continents and read about the composition of land masses to understand how they may have fit together at one time. However, now the study of plate tectonics can be found in the first grade. Children cut out continent shapes and glue them together, or make them out of clay and push them over each other to simulate what happens when continents collide. Thus a theory developed through a complex process of collecting data and drawing inferences has been reduced to a demonstration of showing objects moving over each other. This representation has no meaning to primary children, since the concepts are so far removed from their own experiences and they are not developmentally capable of understanding them. Remember, plate tectonics is a theory that is not based on direct observations. It is an explanation that most scientists accept based on the data they have.

The following activities are basically simulations with observable data. (For the cupcake geology activity see Chapter 5.)

Scale Models of Planets

GOALS

- To simulate the distances and diameters of the planets of the solar system
- To create scale models based on a ratio of the actual distances and diameters of the planets to one another

GRADE LEVELS

- Upper grades

MATERIALS

- String
- Construction paper
- Popsicle sticks

INSTRUCTIONS

Representing the distances and sizes of planets mathematically can be very helpful for students in understanding the tremendous differences in measurements in outer space. Have children find out the actual distances, in kilometers, between the sun and the planets of the solar system. Create ratios of kilometers to meters. Cut lengths of string, in meters, that represent the distances between the planets and the sun. Find out the actual diameters or circumferences of the planets. Use the metric scale to make circular cutouts of each planet, represented in centimeters. Write the names of the planets on the circular cutouts. Glue them to popsicle sticks. Attach one end of the string to the planet cutout.

Take children outside to a large area. One student represents the sun and holds the unattached end of all the strings. Other students hold the planet cutouts and walk away from the sun until the string lengths are fully extended. The planet holders slowly walk in a circle around the sun to see how far each planet has to travel to make one complete orbit. Children whose planets are closer to the sun will complete the circle before the child holding the earth. Children with planets that are at a greater distance from the sun will take longer to complete their orbits. Children can count the number of earth circles for each planet to know the number of years it takes for other planets to complete their orbits around the sun.

Plaster of Paris Volcanoes

GOAL

- To create a model of lava flow

GRADE LEVELS

- Upper grades

MATERIALS

- Plaster of Paris

FIGURE 12.3

- Crayons
- String
- Hot plate
- Paper cups
- Metal container for boiling water
- Safety goggles

BACKGROUND INFORMATION

To simulate volcanic activity, crayons submerged in plaster of Paris are placed in boiling water. As the water boils, the heat penetrates the mold and melts the crayon. Pressure builds, forcing the melted crayon to travel up the string to the outside. The water has to boil long enough for the crayon to melt inside the plaster of Paris. This simulates underground volcanic action as well as the movement of molten rock. Before doing this activity, children can read about the various types of volcanoes and identify the types that are shown in the simulation.

SAFETY PRECAUTIONS

Children must wear safety goggles as they make observations around the boiling water. Make sure the boiling water is not too close to the edge of a table and that no one trips over an electrical cord. Children can make observations in small groups.

INSTRUCTIONS

Take a piece of string approximately 6 centimeters long and rub it with a piece of wax to coat it. Tie a piece of crayon to one end of the string. Prepare a mixture of plaster of Paris. Cover the bottom of a paper cup with the plaster of Paris mixture. Place the crayon in this mixture and add more plaster of Paris until the cup is between one-half to two-thirds full. The end of the string should protrude from the plaster. (See Figure 12.3.) Let the cup set overnight so that the plaster of Paris dries. On the following day, strip away the paper cup. Place the plaster of Paris mold in water in a metal pan. The pan should be deep enough so that the water covers about two-thirds of the mold. Place the pan on a hot plate and bring the water to a boil.

SUGGESTIONS

- Note where the molten crayon emerges from the plaster of Paris.
- Explain why it comes out from several different places.
- Compare what books say about volcanic activity with what happens in this simulation.

Classifying Soil Particles

GOAL

- To compare the sizes and shapes of particles found in soil

GRADE LEVELS

- Primary through upper grades

MATERIALS

- Samples of soil from the schoolyard, forest, beach, backyard, desert
- Hand lenses
- Rubber tubing
- Variety of plastic jars and tubs
- Large shallow pans
- Funnels
- Commercial soils: sand, gravel, clay, black soil

BACKGROUND INFORMATION

Soil varies in composition from pure clay to soil that contains mainly organic materials. Organic soils are usually dark in color, containing decomposed leaves, stems, and animal remains with various amounts of clay, silt, and sand. Clay soils consist of microscopic particles that compact when dry and swell when wet. Ranging from browns to reds, clay soils originate from the weathering of shale rock. In between pure clay soil and soil rich in organic materials are the sandy soils. They may range from fine to coarse sand. Sandy soils can originate from the weathering of sandstone and other rocks such as granite. Silty soils contain various amounts of clay and fine particles of sand. Depending on the composition of soil, its water retention varies. This activity studies the effects of water on various types of soil.

SUGGESTIONS AND QUESTIONS

- Examine each of the different soils. Sort the particles in a variety of ways.
- What do the soils have in common?
- What is the proportion of each type of particle found in the soil samples?
- Place small piles of different kinds of soil in a pan. Drop water onto the soils. What happens?
- Place soil in a pan and pour water on it. Watch what the soil and water do. Repeat this for each type of soil studied. Which type of soil does the water run through the fastest?
- Place soil in a funnel and run water through it. Watch the behavior of the soil. Try different types of soils.
- Place different types of soil in jars of water and shake. Observe what happens after you stop shaking the bottle. Place a mixture of all the soils in a jar, add water, replace the lid, and shake. Can you identify the different soils after shaking?

Summary

This chapter completes the part of this book with activities for learning mathematics and science. The activities in this part are based on science concepts but require the use of mathematical operations to quantify data. Reputable science cannot exist without mathematics. Measurement is a way to compare the changes that occur in both living and nonliving things.

Background information was given for some science concepts in this and preceding chapters, because this information cannot be obtained from direct observations and hands-on activities. However, there is a danger in presenting this information. First, it may be construed as something that needs to be transmitted to children. Second, scientists could argue about the authenticity of the information, that it is too simple or too general, or that it is not comprehensive enough. Scientists often disagree among themselves about the explanations of particular concepts. This background information should inspire you to delve further into the concepts and find out what other scientists have to say about them, not just to transmit information to children whether or not they are interested and want to know, which will undermine the construction process of learning.

The last two parts of this book examine the learning processes and how children learn during hands-on, inquiry, science and mathematics problem-solving activities. Chapter 13 presents ideas for assessing children's use of the learning processes and suggestions for assessing teaching behaviors during hands-on inquiry activities.

> **Go back to the reflective questions at the beginning of the chapter and the answers you recorded in your journal.**
> **Add to or modify your answers based on what you learned from this chapter.**

Bibliography

Bronowski, J. (1978). *The common sense of science.* Cambridge, MA: Harvard University Press.

National Council of Teachers of Mathematics. (1989). *Curriculum and evaluation standards for school mathematics.* Reston, VA: Author.

National Research Council. (1996). *National science education standards.* Washington, DC: National Academy Press.

Nussbaum, J. (1989). The earth as a cosmic body. In R. Driver, E. Guesne, and A. Tiberghien (Eds.), *Children's ideas in science.* Philadelphia: Open University Press.

Piaget, J. (1979). *The child's conception of the world.* Totowa, NJ: Littlefield, Adams.

PART 4 Building Inspection

Part 4 emphasizes assessment of teaching and learning mathematics and science rather than evaluation. Evaluation is judgmental. Assessment is based on collecting evidence to describe what one does as a teacher or what one has learned. Suggested criteria are given for assessing learning, teaching, and the learning environment. These criteria are examples and can be modified to fit individual needs. Chapter 13 looks at the assessment of teaching and learning. Chapter 14 looks at the assessment of the learning environment and includes suggestions for managing hands-on materials and selecting appropriate mathematics and science activities.

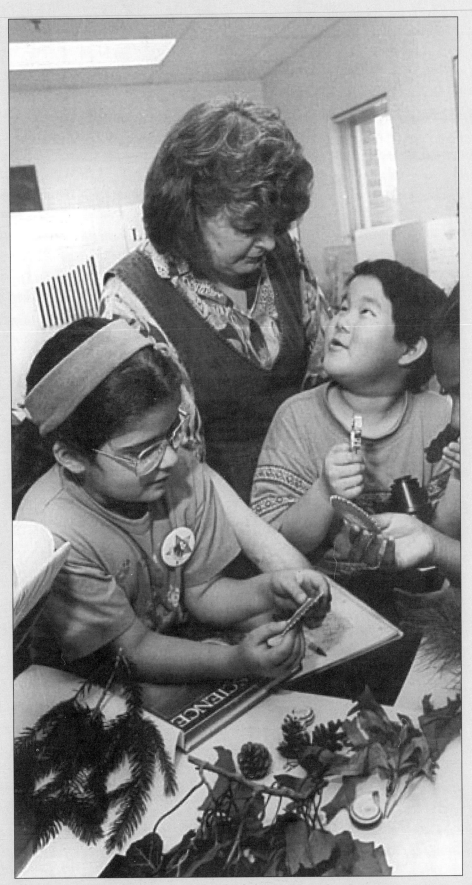

CHAPTER 13 | Assessing Teaching and Learning Through Inquiry

The virtues involved in not knowing are the ones that really count in the long run. What you do about what you don't know is, in the final analysis, what determines what you will ultimately know. . . .

The only difficulty is that teachers are rarely encouraged to do that—largely because standardized tests play such a powerful role in determining what teachers pay attention to. Standardized tests can never, even at their best, tell us anything other than whether a given fact, notion, or ability is already within a child's repertoire. As a result, teachers are encouraged to go for right answers, as often as possible, and whatever happens along the way is treated as incidental.

E. Duckworth, *The Having of Wonderful Ideas and Other Essays on Teaching and Learning*

JOURNEY PREPARATION

Reflective Questions

- What is the difference between assessment and evaluation?

- What is authentic assessment?

- What principles of learning mathematics and science do you now understand?

- Reflect on these principles. What are the implications for teaching and learning?

- What are ways to assess children's construction of mathematical and scientific ideas?

- What are appropriate teaching behaviors during hands-on mathematics and science activities?

- What are ways to objectively assess teaching behaviors during hands-on mathematics and science activities?

- What is the relationship between teaching and learning mathematics and science?

- What would lesson plans for inquiry teaching and learning look like?

Introduction

The activities in Chapters 10, 11, and 12 provide experiences for children to understand major mathematical and scientific concepts. These activities are rich in opportunities for collecting observable data that can be abstracted and internalized to form new understandings about the underlying concepts. The activities require minimal memorization and are open-ended to allow all children to learn from them. In other words, children can construct knowledge beginning at their own level of understanding. These activities are multicultural because they appeal to a wide range of interests, backgrounds, and experiences. This chapter addresses ways to assess teaching behaviors appropriate to such inquiry teaching and to assess what children learn from hands-on inquiry activities.

Assessing Teaching and Learning

Teaching and learning are mirror images and assessment helps to keep both of them in focus. Inquiry and standardized testing are incompatible. Standardized tests can be culturally biased and do not take into account individual differences in the development of learning. These tests compare children rather than looking at the growth of understanding in individual children. Standardized testing also tends to make teaching emphasize a narrow range of concepts to ensure that children will pass the tests. Not knowing and inquiry are compatible because we begin to ask questions that lead to real learning: What are children learning? What teaching behaviors support children's learning? What do children learn from experiences and activities? Answering these questions is crucial to assessment. They help teachers reflect on teaching and learning. Finding answers to these questions through problem solving provides many different possibilities for assessing learning. By using inquiry to determine what is learned we model inquiry used in science and mathematics.

The following principles of learning focus on assessment as it is discussed throughout this chapter. These principles are based on the ideas that were presented in Chapters 7, 8, and 9.

Principles of Learning

1. *Learning is self-regulated.* Human beings learn what they want and when they want to learn. What is learned depends on age, interests, and experiences. The causal links between what teachers do and what children learn are elusive; it is very difficult to link learning to teacher behaviors. There are too many variables that influence learning and often there is a lag between experiences and what is learned from them. The best we can do is provide a variety of rich learning experiences.

2. *Learning is a continual process.* Ideas are constructed and reconstructed through the collection of data, which are gathered through the senses while interacting with concrete objects.

3. *Learning takes time.* Children do not learn the concept of density, for example, from one single activity in the fifth grade on a Friday in January. The understanding of density occurs over time through a variety of hands-on experiences.

4. *Learning begins with the learner's viewpoint.* Often, children are unaware of their own viewpoints unless they are given opportunities to express them. Children must develop their own understanding before understanding the viewpoints of other children and adults.

5. *Learning is the internalization of actions with concrete objects.* Mental operations are constructed from this process. Ideas or relationships are abstracted from the objects. This is the prerequisite to formal thinking: abstracting ideas from ideas.

6. *Learning develops memory.* Memory is the reconstruction of content. Content is abstracted from action on objects. Content or knowledge is part of the framework created by mental operations. If knowledge is internalized, memory serves as a way to draw upon that knowledge.

7. *Learning concepts is developmental.* Individual children, regardless of their age, are at different levels of development of individual concepts. Concepts are broad, general ideas that change as the learner gathers additional information through experiences.

8. *Learning begins with perceptual ideas.* Perceptual ideas are often explained as misconceptions, but are real to children. Labeling their perceptions as misconceptions sends a message that their ideas are wrong. They are not wrong; they are just at a different level of development.

9. *Learning involves changing perceptual ideas.* Perceptual ideas are difficult to change. Children often ignore contradictory observable data and hold on to perceptual ideas. Maturation and experiences influence the change of ideas.

10. *Learning is influenced by perceptual ideas.* Children translate facts within existing perceptual frameworks. For example, Piaget (1979) relates a story about children who were told that clouds are vapor produced by heating and boiling water. However, these particular children concluded that clouds are produced in saucepans because the example discussed boiling water in a saucepan!

11. *Learning involves classifying and ordering objects.* "This ability to order things into likes and unlikes is, I think, the foundation of human thought" (Bronowski, 1978, p. 22). Mathematical operations develop from classifying and ordering objects. This encompasses comparing objects or groups of objects in quantitative terms.

12. *Learning involves the use of spatial structures.* Spatial structures are important for understanding measurement, time, speed, and the majority of science concepts.

The twelve principles stress the individual learner and the outcomes of learning that lead to understanding. They have implications for teaching. What a teacher does in terms of individual children's behaviors and experiences will be totally different from teaching every child the same thing through the transmission of knowledge.

Understanding the principles and implications behind the processes of teaching and learning mathematics and science provides a rationale, based on valid research, to guide teaching and children's learning. Otherwise teaching is reduced to transmission of information and learning to the memorization of facts. The principles of learning are inherent in human beings but have been ignored for the sake of making every child learn the same thing. This is an unrealistic expectation. The rationale for teaching and learning provides the foundation for the selection of appropriate teaching behaviors and activities as well as assessment strategies.

Implications for Teaching

1. Provide opportunities for children to explain what they learn.
2. Understanding of mathematical and scientific concepts occurs through a variety of concrete experiences and activities.
3. Provide a variety of experiences throughout the school years.
4. Provide each child with his or her own set of materials.
5. Allow children to work by themselves or in groups depending on their interest levels and the complexity of the tasks.
6. Use children's interests as foundations for developing a science and mathematics curriculum.
7. Focus the mathematics and science curriculum on the construction of concepts rather than memorization.
8. Emphasize the construction of in-depth understanding of a selection of concepts rather than trying to "cover" a wide range of concepts.
9. Understanding leads to achievement.
10. Create a classroom atmosphere that stimulates curiosity.

Table 13.1 summarizes the learning principles and their implications for teaching.

Definition of Assessment

Assessment, as opposed to evaluation, becomes the focus when inquiry is used for teaching and learning. Through inquiry, assessments are based on data, unlike evaluations, which are based on perceptions. Assessment goes below the surface yielding understanding while evaluation skims the surface yielding achievement. Interpretations of an evaluation such as "student does above-average work" can vary from teacher to teacher because interpretations are usually based on individual teacher perceptions. Standardized tests are attempts to make the evaluation of learning objective, but since it is difficult to standardize reasoning, most standardized tests are based on the ability to recall particular facts. A report by Wingert (1996) about the results of the Third International Mathematics and Science Study states that American eighth-grade math scores were lower than the world average. Wingert concludes that the reason is that teachers are still relying on textbooks and rote learning rather than helping children develop an understanding of broad principles.

Authentic assessment is based on the goal of collecting observable, concrete evidence and data to find out if learning is supported or is happening. For example, "the child was able to construct multiple ways to solve the problem" is a piece of data that provides evidence of understanding. Data can be gathered in many different ways, such as sampling students when it is not possible to assess every child. Not only are concrete data more authentic than paper and pencil tests but the data tell us more about individual children rather than groups of children. The following are excerpts of assessment standards for mathematics and science.

TABLE 13.1

**Matching Learning Principles
with Their Implications**

Learning	Implications
Self-regulated	Stimulate curiosity to stimulate interest.
	Allow children to work by themselves or in groups.
	Use children's interest as the context for choosing mathematics and science curricula.
Continual process	Emphasize in-depth learning rather than covering material.
Takes time	Offer a variety of different activities that explore the same concepts throughout the school years.
Begins with child's viewpoint	Allow children to explain what they understand.
Internalization of actions with concrete objects	Each child should have own set of objects.
Develops memory	Provide a variety of concrete experiences.
Concept formation is a developmental process	Provide a variety of concrete experiences.
Begins with perceptual ideas	Provide a variety of concrete experiences.
Involves changing perceptual ideas	Focus on construction of knowledge rather than memorization.
Influenced by perceptual ideas	Focus on construction of knowledge rather than memorization.
Involves classifying and ordering objects	Understanding leads to achievement.
Involves the use of spatial structures	Understanding leads to achievement.

As was mentioned before, assessment and inquiry go hand in hand because the process of assessment involves answering questions. Seven questions that encompass assessment of the major areas of teaching and learning will be discussed in terms of methods of collecting data:

1. What are appropriate teaching behaviors for inquiry?
2. What are appropriate student behaviors during inquiry?
3. What will students understand from inquiry learning?
4. What are appropriate learning processes during inquiry?
5. What are appropriate learning skills during inquiry?
6. What is the appropriate learning environment for inquiry?
7. What is the appropriate curriculum for inquiry?

All of these issues have an impact on learning, and answering the questions can provide evidence needed to know if it is occurring. Questions 1 through 4

TOUR GUIDE

National Council of Teachers of Mathematics (1989)
Standard 2: Multiple Sources of Information

Decisions concerning students' learning should be made on the basis of a convergence of information obtained from a variety of sources. These sources should encompass tasks that—

demand different kinds of mathematical thinking; present the same mathematical concept or procedure in different contexts, formats, and problem situations. (p. 196)

Standard 3: Appropriate Assessment Methods and Uses

Assessment methods and instruments should be selected on the basis of—

the type of information sought; the use to which the information will be put; the developmental level and maturity of the student. (p. 199)

Standard 4: Mathematical Power

The assessment of students' mathematical knowledge should yield information about their—

ability to apply their knowledge to solve problems within mathematics and in other disciplines; ability to use mathematical language to communicate ideas; ability to reason and analyze; knowledge and understanding of concepts and procedures; dispositions toward mathematics; understanding of the nature of mathematics; integration of these aspects of mathematical knowledge. (p. 205)

Standard 5: Problem Solving

The assessment of students' ability to use mathematics in solving problems should provide evidence that they can—

formulate problems; apply a variety of strategies to solve problems; solve problems; verify and interpret results. (p. 209)

Standard 6: Communication

The assessment of students' ability to communicate mathematics should provide evidence that they can—

express mathematical ideas by speaking, writing, demonstrating, and depicting them visually: understand, interpret, and evaluate mathematical ideas that are presented in written, oral, or visual forms; use mathematical vocabulary, notation, and structure to represent ideas, describe relationships, and model situations. (p. 214)

Standard 7: Reasoning

The assessment of students' ability to reason mathematically should provide evidence that they can—

use inductive reasoning to recognize patterns and form conjectures; use reasoning to develop plausible arguments for mathematical statements; use proportional and spatial reasoning to solve problems; use deductive reasoning to verify conclusions, judge the validity of arguments, and construct valid arguments; analyze situations to determine common properties and structures. (p. 219)

**TOUR GUIDE
(CONTINUED)**

Standard 8: Mathematical Concepts

The assessment of students' knowledge and understanding of mathematics should provide evidence that they can—

label, verbalize, and define concepts; identify and generate examples and nonexamples; use models, diagrams, and symbols to represent concepts; translate from one mode of representation to another; recognize the various meanings and interpretations of concepts; identify properties of a given concept and compare and contrast concepts. (p. 223)

Standard 9: Mathematical Procedures

The assessment of students' knowledge of procedures should provide evidence that they can—

recognize when a procedure is appropriate; reliably and efficiently execute procedures; verify the results of procedures empirically; recognize correct and incorrect procedures; generate new procedures and extend or modify familiar ones. (p. 228)

Standard 10: Mathematical Disposition

The assessment of students' mathematical disposition should seek information about their—

confidence in using mathematics to solve problems, to communicate ideas, and to reason; flexibility in exploring mathematical ideas and trying alternative methods in solving problems; willingness to persevere in mathematical tasks; interest, curiosity, and inventiveness in doing mathematics; inclination to monitor and reflect on their own thinking and performance; valuing of the application of mathematics to situations arising in other disciplines and everyday experiences; appreciation of the role of mathematics in our culture and its value as a tool and as a language. (p. 233)

National Research Council (1996) Teaching Standard C

Teachers engage in ongoing assessment of their teaching and of student learning. In doing this, teachers

- Use multiple methods and systematically gather data about student understanding and ability
- Analyze assessment data to guide teaching
- Guide students in self-assessment
- Use student data, observations of teaching, and interactions with colleagues to reflect on and improve teaching practice.
- Use student data, observations of teaching, interactions with colleagues to report student achievement and opportunities to learn to students, teachers, parents, policy makers, and the general public. (pp. 37–38)

Assessment Standard A

Assessment must be consistent with the decisions they are designed to inform.

■ Assessments are deliberately designed. Assessments have explicitly stated purposes.

■ The relationship between the decisions and the data is clear.

■ The procedures are internally consistent. (p. 78)

Assessment Standard B

Achievement and opportunity to learn science must be assessed.

■ Achievement data collected focus on the science content that is most important for students to learn.

■ Opportunity-to-learn data collected focus on the most powerful indicators.

■ Equal attention must be given to the assessment of opportunity to learn and to the assessment of student achievement. (p. 79)

Assessment Standard C

The technical quality of the data collected is well matched to the decisions and actions taken on the basis of their interpretation.

■ The feature that is claimed to be measured is actually measured.

■ Assessment tasks are authentic.

■ An individual student's performance is similar on two or more tasks that claim to measure the same aspect of student achievement.

■ Students have adequate opportunity to demonstrate their achievements.

■ Assessment tasks and methods of presenting them provide data that are sufficiently stable to lead to the same decisions if used at different times. (p. 83)

Assessment Standard D

Assessment practices must be fair.
Assessment tasks must be

■ reviewed for the use of stereotypes, for assumptions that reflect the perspectives or experiences of a particular group, for language that might be offensive to a particular group, and for other features that might distract students from the intended tasks.

■ appropriately modified to accommodate the needs of students with physical and learning disabilities, or limited English proficiency.

■ set in a variety of contexts, be engaging to students with different interests and experiences, and must not assume the perspective or experience of a particular gender, racial, or ethnic group.

Large-scale assessment must use statistical techniques to identify potential bias among groups. (p. 85)

> ### Assessment Standard E
>
> The inferences made from assessments about student achievement and opportunity to learn must be sound.
>
> - When making inferences from assessment data about student achievement and opportunity to learn science, explicit reference needs to be made to the assumptions on which the inferences are based. (p. 86)

envelop the actions and behaviors of teachers and students; questions 6 and 7 assess the environment and the curriculum. (The latter two questions will be addressed in Chapter 14.) Question 5 is the most important because the child's understanding should be the focus of teaching. Answers to the other questions also provide supporting evidence that learning is occurring even though it is difficult to link certain behaviors with learning.

The questions are addressed by providing ways to gather data to answer the questions. Assessing teaching behaviors, student behaviors and performances, the classroom environment, and the curriculum is easier than assessing student understanding because direct observable data can be collected. What we know about student learning is based on inferences because we cannot look directly into the brain to see what has been learned. Questioning is important for revealing what children understand. Remember the implications of the inference boxes for learning?

What Are Appropriate Teaching Behaviors for Inquiry?

REST STOP 13.1

Imagine walking into a hands-on mathematics and science classroom. What teaching behaviors would you expect to observe? Make a list of observable teaching behaviors.

For example, *giving directions* is an observable teaching behavior. Giving encouragement is not a teaching behavior because it is not directly observable. It is an inference based on particular behaviors exhibited by the teacher because "encouragement" can be defined or interpreted in different ways. Giving encouragement might be a smile or a pat on the back. It might be in the form of praise or other verbal acknowledgments.

Teachers will exhibit certain behaviors that parallel their philosophies of teaching. Some teachers believe in transmitting knowledge; others believe in facilitating learning. Teaching behaviors range along a continuum that reflects these two contrasting philosophies. The different philosophies can be described in terms of models. The following are four symbolic representations of teaching models (Foster and Pellens, 1989) that can be observed during the teaching of mathematics and science.

Model 1: Transmitting information:

$$T \longrightarrow S$$

Model 2: Transmitting information through hands-on activities:

$$T \longrightarrow S \longrightarrow O$$

Model 3: Guided learning through hands-on activities:

$$T \rightarrow S \rightleftharpoons O$$

Model 4: Integration of teacher actions with children's actions on objects:

$$T \rightleftharpoons S \rightleftharpoons O$$

T is the symbol for *teacher;* S is the symbol for *student;* O is the symbol for *objects.* The arrows indicate the direction of the interactions. Describe the philosophy that governs each model. Are your descriptions similar to the following?

Model 1: Teacher is the dispenser of knowledge. Students learn from other secondary sources such as textbooks. They take notes. Assessment is based on memorizing facts.

Model 2: Hands-on activities are part of the curriculum but teacher determines what is to be learned from the activities. The activities consist of a list of procedures children follow to arrive at specific answers.

Model 3: Hands-on activities are part of the curriculum. The hands-on activities allow children limited freedom to act upon the objects. Teacher focuses children on certain types of actions. However, teacher guides children toward specific outcomes by making suggestions and asking children specific questions. Children are guided through the discovery process.

Model 4: Hands-on activities are part of the curriculum. Children have freedom to act upon objects but must show respect for materials and other children. Teacher questions and makes suggestions determined by children's actions. Teacher allows students to arrive at different outcomes and conclusions. Questions and suggestions are posed to help students think through their problem-solving techniques.

Classroom Activity 13.1

Identifying Teaching Behaviors

DISCUSSION QUESTIONS

- What teaching behaviors are associated with each model?
- Which model supports the development of understanding?
- Which model is associated with the least number of teaching behaviors? What are those behaviors?
- Which model is associated with a wide range of teaching behaviors?
- Which model supports an environment of inquiry?
- Which model(s) support the facilitation of mathematics and science standards?

Classroom Activity 13.2

Matching Behaviors with Teaching Models

DISCUSSION QUESTIONS

- Which behaviors do you want to use in your classroom?
- Which model represents the type of teaching you want to practice?
- For those behaviors you chose, what percentage of time would you like to do them?

SCENIC VIEW 13.1

SLIC Assessment Instrument

This instrument (Shymansky, Penick, Kelsey, and Foster, 1976) was specifically designed to assess teaching behaviors during hands-on activities. (You may want to use this with graduate students only.) The following information can be gathered with the use of this instrument.

Frequency of the Behavior

How often does a particular behavior occur? A time period can be designated and teaching behaviors can be coded during that time. For example, observing three 10-minute time periods during an hour of hands-on activity will provide evidence of the kinds of teaching behaviors used.

Patterns of Behaviors

Coding the behaviors (listed below) will reveal patterns. For example, does the teacher provide more information than questions? Is the behavior of asking questions followed by the behavior of listening?

Number of Children Associated with the Behavior

It is important to assess the number of children involved in particular interactions. Hands-on science will be more individualized than whole group instruction. The number of students with whom the teacher interacts can be coded. Numbers from 1 to 9 indicate the number of students during interactions. *N* represents a number larger than 9.

Gender Interactions

Questions about gender bias can be answered by recording teacher interaction with children. Use F for female, M for male, and G for mixed groups. Thus questions such as the following can be answered: Does a teacher spend more time with one gender than the other?

Description of the Coding Instrument

The coding instrument consists of sheets of $8\frac{1}{2}'' \times 11''$ paper that are blocked into rows of cells. There are four blocks consisting of three rows. The first row is for recording the teaching behavior, the second row is for recording the size of the group, and the third row is for recording the gender of the students. A vertical column of three cells can be recorded in 3 seconds:

Teaching behavior	O
Number of students	N
Gender	M

The rows within a block represent 30 seconds of data because there are 10 cells across the page. The following illustration represents 30 seconds of data because it consists of 10 columns. One piece of paper contains four blocks or 2 minutes' worth of data. Thus, 10 minutes of data can be recorded on five sheets of paper. A template of an SLIC coding sheet is found in Appendix A.

O	D	D	D	Q	Q	L	L	L	Q
N	N	N	N	1	1	1	1	1	N
G	G	G	G	M	M	M	M	M	G

After some practice, you will probably memorize the letters for each behavior. You can anticipate that some behaviors will always follow others; for example, listening should follow questioning. You can also anticipate the size of the group for certain behaviors; thus, the teacher usually gives information to the whole class.

The SLIC assessment instrument furnishes observable data rather than inferences or judgments. The data can be used to determine whether to change teaching behaviors. Each type of teaching model above requires different teaching behaviors. The SLIC assessment provides a way to ensure that behaviors are appropriate for the model.

List of Teaching Behaviors

O = Observing children

D = Giving suggestions/directions

I = Giving information/explanations

F = Giving verbal praise/reinforcement

Q = Asking short-answer questions

X = Asking open-ended questions

L = Listening to children

A = Answering questions

P = Paraphrasing children's ideas or questions

K = Acknowledging children's ideas or answers

M = Working with materials

E = Demonstrating use of equipment

R = Reading

W = Writing

Explanation of Teaching Behaviors

The teacher behaviors above have been listed in a somewhat hierarchical fashion. "Observing" is listed at the top because interactions begin with observations and provide data on the teaching behaviors that should follow. Just as children act on objects to process knowledge, children are the objects of study for teachers. Children's behaviors are the source of knowledge about what is being learned from the activities. What is observed provides data about what behaviors should follow. Observing is very important to inquiry teaching.

The "giving" categories are grouped together after "observing." The "giving" (D, I, F) categories originate from the teacher. "Giving verbal praise/reinforcement" refers to the teacher saying things like "I like the fact that you are whispering." The "giving" categories require minimal interaction between teacher and students and typically involve groups of children rather than individuals. They are likely to occur more frequently than the other behaviors.

The "interacting" categories (Q, X, L, A, P, K) involve questioning, listening, and providing feedback to children and usually occur together in sequences. Short-answer questions (Q) require a student to respond with a yes or no answer based on recall. Open-ended questions (X) require a student to explain in his or her own words. The answer may be several sentences long. (Refer to Chapter 4 on questioning.) Teachers acknowledge children by responding with such stock phrases as "I see, I agree with you," and "I understand what you mean." A teacher can also acknowledge through body language such as nodding in agreement. "Acknowledging children's ideas or answers" (K) indicates a nonverbal response as well.

"Working with materials" (M) refers to the teacher manipulating objects. This might be trying to figure out why the batteries are not working or assisting students to put things together. An example of "demonstrating use of equipment" (E) is showing children how to use a microscope. The teacher is giving information to children by manipulating equipment. "Reading" (R) involves such examples as looking at children's written notes or data, reading a book such as a teacher's guide or student textbooks, or reading directions to self or to children. "Writing" (W) involves such things as taking notes about student learning or behaviors, and writing information or directions on the chalkboard or overhead projector.

The SLIC instrument can also be used to code behaviors while children are working at computers.

Classroom Activity 13.3

Discussing the Interpretation of the Data

INSTRUCTIONS

Refer back to the vertical column of three cells in Scenic View 13.1. Think about the data coded in those cells.

DISCUSSION QUESTIONS

- What do the data say about the pattern of teaching behaviors used?
- What do the data say about the number of students involved in interactions and their gender?
- Which teaching model appears to be represented? Explain.

Field Experience Activity 13.1

Collecting Data about Teaching Behaviors

INSTRUCTIONS

Use the SLIC assessment instrument to collect data about teaching behaviors.

1. Find a classroom teacher who will allow you to observe his or her teaching behaviors during mathematics and science classes.

2. Arrange to work with a small group of children. Have a classmate code your behaviors or videotape yourself and code your behaviors later.

3. Predict which behaviors the classroom teacher will use and which ones you plan to use. Record your predictions before collecting data. Your predictions can be expressed in percentages. For example, you might predict that you will observe the teacher give information (I) 80% and read (R) 20% of the time to the entire class.

4. After collecting and analyzing the data, answer the following question: Does the observed frequency match the expected frequency?

What Are Appropriate Student Behaviors During Inquiry?

Classroom Activity 13.4

Identifying Children's Behaviors During Hands-On Activities

INSTRUCTIONS

Make a list of student behaviors that might occur during mathematics and science activities. Discuss it with your peers. Review the teaching models above and match the listed student behaviors to each model.

What categories did you identify that are similar to teacher behaviors?

Table 13.2 lists 12 student behaviors. The table also indicates whether the behaviors are related to the lesson or not. The student behavior categories have the same definitions as the teaching categories in Scenic View 13.1. Categories 3–9 are interactions with the teacher or other students. Category 12 refers to students retrieving equipment or returning it where it belongs. Students may also walk over to talk or work with students in a different part of the room.

One might think that "boredom" should be listed as a student behavior. However, boredom is an inference or judgment based on certain behaviors, and these behaviors can be interpreted in several different ways. For example, a child resting her chin on her folded hands may be bored. On the other hand, she may be thinking through a problem. What is the best way to find out if a child is bored? Ask!

Use the chart located in Appendix B. Observe one student at a time. Make tally marks every 15 seconds in the appropriate behavior box. This shows frequency of behaviors but not a sequence of behavior patterns. The percentage of time for each behavior can be tabulated and analyzed to determine a child's level of engagement with the activities.

Which behaviors in the chart are associated with understanding concepts?

Examine the data in Table 13.2. Create a profile of the student's behaviors. Express the profile in percentages. What does the profile tell you about the student's behaviors? As a teacher, what actions might you take as a result of the data analysis?

Field Experience Activity 13.2

Collecting Data about Student Behaviors During Hands-On Activities

INSTRUCTIONS

Visit a classroom to observe student behaviors during mathematics and science lessons. Choose one child at a time and observe the child's behavior for a given period of time. Ten minutes per child should provide enough data to give a sense of the patterns of behavior exhibited. Observe another child at a different time during the activity session. You might want to observe a child at the beginning, another child during, and another child at the end of a hands-on activity session. This will provide data on three children. Appendix B gives a template for coding children's behaviors. Table 13.3 lists both teacher and student behaviors during hands-on activities to illustrate the relationships between what a teacher does and how children respond.

TABLE 13.2
Student Behaviors with Sample Observations

Student Behaviors	Lesson Related 15 seconds/tally (min.)	Total	Non–Lesson Related 15 seconds/tally (min.)	Total
1. Manipulating objects	ⵏ ⵏ ⵏ ⵏ	5		
2. Making observations	ⵏ ⵏ ⵏ	3.75		
3. Asking short-answer questions	ⵏ I	1.5		
4. Asking extended-thought questions				
5. Listening	ⵏ	1.25	ⵏ ⵏ IIII	3.5
6. Answering questions	ⵏ ⵏ II	3		
7. Giving explanations	ⵏ I	1.5		
8. Giving information	ⵏ III	2	ⵏ ⵏ	2.5
9. Demonstrating equipment	ⵏ ⵏ II	3		
10. Writing				
11. Reading			ⵏ I	3
12. Walking around				
	Total min.	21	Total min.	9

The corresponding student behaviors for the teacher's observing, reading, and writing behaviors are omitted. There are no direct correlations between these behaviors and how children might react since they do not necessarily involve direct interactions with children. However, teachers can anticipate the types of behaviors children are likely to display for each exhibited teacher behavior.

What Will Students Understand from Inquiry Learning?

Children's understanding of concepts may be difficult to assess since it is difficult to gather such data from direct observations. Children's understanding has to be assessed in different ways to make inferences about what they learned as valid as possible.

Interview Assessment

One-on-one verbal interviews are the best way to assess what children understand. Recall that the type of questions asked will elicit responses that indicate perceptual, factual, or conceptual understanding. Piaget's theory was

Teacher Behaviors	Student Behaviors
Observing	
Giving suggestions and directions	Listening Writing
Giving information and explanations	Listening Writing
Giving verbal praise and reinforcement	Listening
Asking short-answer questions	Answering questions
Asking open-ended questions	Answering questions
Listening to children	Answering questions Giving explanations Giving information Demonstrating equipment
Answering questions	Listening Writing
Paraphrasing children's ideas	Listening
Acknowledging children's ideas or answers	Listening
Working with materials	Observing
Demonstrating use of equipment	Listening Observing
Reading	
Writing	

developed by asking questions of individual children. Through one-on-one verbal interviews, the teacher can probe and clarify a child's responses. The questions can be rephrased so that the child can understand them. The questions can be tailored to individual children. Asking a whole class of children questions at the same time does not allow the teacher to give individual attention. The same can be said for giving children written questions. First, the child may have difficulty with the words in the questions. Second, the manner in which questions are phrased may not be comprehensible to the child. And finally, answers may not fully express what children understand. The limitation on interviewing children one by one is, of course, time.

To illustrate the value of individual interviews, consider the example of Piaget. He wanted to find out what children understand about the origin of the moon and sun, and about meteorological events such as rain, snow, and clouds (Piaget, 1979). Children's answers ranged from animism (describing these objects or events as living things), to artificialism (humans created the objects), to naturalism (natural events). "Rocks grow" is an example of animism. "The sun started with matches" is an example of artificialism. "Clouds come from smoke" is a natural event explanation. Through these interviews

Piaget found that children's ideas represent different levels of understanding. These three levels, animism, artificialism, and naturalism, indicate shifts from egocentric points of view based on perceptions. As children grow in understanding, they could provide explanations expressed in causal relationships or sequences of events. For example, "it snows when the temperature is cold enough." These different levels of understanding were revealed by probing the answers children gave. They were not derived from the first answer given by a child, which is the case with written tests.

Phillips (1996) provides interviews based on Piaget's research data. These interviews are excellent models for assessing understanding of mathematic and science concepts. The interviews provide opportunities to examine what children think about classification, seriation, time, topology, projections, Euclidean space, motion, speed, and measurement. In other words, are children using logic to explain a given concept? Since these are all related to the concrete operational stage, objects are used as part of this interview. Children are asked a series of questions that require yes or no answers or other factual answers such as the same, more, or less and are followed by "why" questions. The interviewer expresses actions with the objects and asks the child to explain the actions. "Why do you think so?" is asked to see if a child can give a logical reason. If the interviewer feels that a child might give a logical answer but is not expressing it, he or she can ask the question in other ways. This gives the child opportunities and time to gather thoughts and express them. The responses to the questions at various places in the interview determine the level of understanding. The responses are categorized to indicate how much of the interview children complete. The categories are indicators of their understanding. The information from the interviews can be used to determine what activities are needed for children in the classroom. The Piagetian interview model of asking probing questions can be used for assessing other concepts that involve logical thinking.

Piaget's conservation tasks, which involve number, weight, area, volume, and length, are examples of the interview model. The purpose of conservation tasks is to determine whether a child holds a particular mental concept constant regardless of perceptual changes. For example, the conservation of number task involves setting up rows of objects such as poker chips. The interviewer makes one row of chips and asks the child to make a row of chips that is exactly the same as the other row. If the child does that, the interviewer spreads out the chips in one row so that the space between them increases. This creates a perceptual difference between the two rows. The interviewer asks the child if there are more, less, or the same number of chips in each row. If the child says more or less, a logical reason cannot be given. If the child says "the same," the interviewer can continue with "why do you think so?" to see if the child will give a logical reason. In this particular interview, a logical reason is "because you have not taken away chips or added any chips." However, if the response is "they are the same," the interviewer will probe further because this response is only a description. This answer does not express logic. It merely describes an action without expressing any relationship between the way the chips are now and the way they were before. A logical reason expresses the relationship. Thus, the conservation of an idea implies that an idea has become internalized, no matter what is done to the objects perceptually. The idea is held constant because the child knows what the objects were like before the action was taken. These interviews help teachers to know if a child understands an idea at the perceptual (belief, opinion), factual (descriptive, quantitative), or conceptual (relationships) level.

Embedded Assessment

Embedded assessment (Foster and Heiting, 1994) refers to the idea that assessment is integrated into daily activities, as opposed to formal assessment prior to or after the learning experiences. This type of assessment does not require special equipment, time, and space, apart from the activities. Embedded assessment is a continuous process occurring during teaching but it requires creative methods of collecting data. The following are suggested guidelines when using embedded assessment.

1. ***Decide what is to be assessed by formulating questions.*** What information is needed to know if the hands-on activities are supporting learning? Which processes are children using? Which skills are they using? What behaviors are they using during the activity? What concepts are they learning? Since there are many factors to consider, focus the question on one particular factor. How will the data be used? To report grades? To adopt new activities? For example, you might want to know how children are using measurement as a process to decide whether prior activities were effective. This type of inquiry allows you to collect data over a period of time through sampling. On another occasion, you may want to know what they understand about measurement so you can discuss it in parent conferences. If the information is to be used for parent conferences, all children will have to be assessed.

2. ***Decide who will be assessed.*** Embedded assessment is very time consuming if the attempt is to assess everyone on a regular basis. An alternative would be to target a few children per day. Collect data over the span of a week during the activity. If there are 30 children, observational data would have to be collected for six children per day.

3. ***Decide the methodology for collecting data.*** Develop a format that allows you to collect data with the least amount of interference. Checklists and charts allow data collection through observation by requiring minimal information. A checklist might be a list of science and mathematics processes. Focus on a particular group of children and check the appropriate processes you observe children using. Charts can be created with key questions that will inform you about what children understand. Anticipate the type of answers children might give as part of a code for filling in the charts. "The bulbs get dimmer when more bulbs are added" might be a typical response. Place the initials of the children giving this response below the answer. Answers that were not anticipated will have to be written in the chart.

Anecdotal notes may have to be used when in-depth understanding of responses or behaviors is needed. Anecdotal notes can be recorded on index cards. Have a card for each child and select the cards for the children you want to observe each day.

Artifact Assessment

It is not always possible to collect data while working with children. However, there are ways to assess data after completion of activities. Take time during a break or after school to write or record mental notes about children's behaviors, questions, or your own teaching behaviors. Require children to keep records of their activities in journals or logs and compare your notes to theirs. Have young children make pictures or use simple words in their journals. Older children can organize their data in the form of tables and charts and give explanations. Journals and logs can be analyzed later. Audiotape or videotape children during activities. This allows you time to analyze student behaviors and understandings later. Many activities or units can end with products completed by children. These products can be the results of questions that they attempt to answer. This is a good way to find out whether children understand particular concepts. The following is an example of how a product might be analyzed for understanding.

Situation: Children have been classifying angles and shapes of a variety of quadrilaterals by making them with straws. The project requires children to use their knowledge about angles and shapes to construct bridges that will resist collapsing when weight is added to them.

The assessment: Create a rubric that reflects different levels of understanding angles, shapes, and strength for bridge building. A rubric is developed by establishing a set of criteria that describes different levels of understanding. The following is an example of a rubric based on perceptions, facts, and concepts at the different levels of understanding:

Level 1: The constructed bridge is built through trial and error efforts without applying principles learned about angles and shapes. (perceptual)

Level 2: The constructed bridge was developed from plans created from knowledge about angles and shapes. (factual)

Level 3: The bridge was constructed from plans. In addition, the builder can predict how much weight the bridge will hold before collapsing. The builder can also explain why the bridge collapses at a particular weight. (conceptual)

Information gathered through rubrics can be used to determine levels of understanding and whether more time or other activities are needed to explore the concept further.

The following are examples of questions that can help the teacher determine whether the child is using perceptual, factual, or conceptual knowledge:

1. Develop an egg container and see how high you can hold an egg in the container and drop it without breaking the egg.

2. What is the most weight a toothpick bridge can hold?

3. What is the tallest structure that can be made using drinking straws?

4. Can you make a geodesic dome from wooden dowels?

5. Can you make an electric quiz game about the human body?

6. How many bricks were used to construct the school building?

7. How many blades of grass are there on the school grounds?

8. Can you cook a hot dog using the heat from the sun?

9. What are some different ways to make a toy car move on a flat surface without pushing it by hand?

10. What are the odds of winning a lottery?

Computers can be used to facilitate finding solutions to these questions. Children can use software programs for organizing and analyzing data, especially if the data are complex.

Portfolio Assessment

A classroom teacher can be creative in collecting data to find out what children learn and understand. Using a variety of ways to collect data creates a portfolio of knowledge about each child. A portfolio includes samples of children's work from before the activities began through the completion of the activities. Thus, a portfolio can include data from interviews, data collected during activities, data collected from performance assessment, and data from artifacts. All these sources can be analyzed to reveal patterns of understanding about using processes and skills and understanding concepts.

Table 13.4 summarizes the ways to use assessment strategies to find out what children know about processes and skills, and their levels of conceptual understanding.

What Are Appropriate Learning Processes During Inquiry?

Processes, which were discussed in Chapters 4, 5, and 6, are more difficult to assess than skills or behaviors because they are not always clearly observable and are often integrated with each other. A child may be classifying and observing at the same time. However, processes are important since they are links to the development of mental operations and structures. Children's use of processes can be analyzed by developing rubrics or criteria as indicators of different levels of use. Foster and Heiting (1994) present a detailed description of levels of processes that children are likely to use. The following is an example of the different levels of the use of observing:

Level 1: Uses only one sense when others are required to successfully complete the investigation.

Level 2: Uses appropriate senses to gather data.

Level 3: Uses appropriate senses and includes appropriate technology to increase powers of observation.

The above examples of the different levels of use of observing is also representative of a rubric. Data about the use of processes can be gathered through observations, questions, and analysis of written works or projects. For example, a teacher might ask, "What do you see when you add the two colors together?" The degree to which children use any particular process can be an indicator of what they are learning from the activities. Processes can be assessed by setting up activity stations, but this type of assessment is more authentic if it is done while children are working on daily activities, i.e., embedded assessment. Writing down children's comments and actions while observing them provides data about their use of processes.

What Are Appropriate Learning Skills During Inquiry?

In science as in mathematics, there are certain technological instruments and tools that students need to know how to use if they are going to complete certain activities successfully. These may range from protractors, compasses, balance scales, microscopes, telescopes, and calculators to temperature and heat

TABLE 13.4
Summary of
Assessment Strategies

Assessment	Description	Strategies
Interviews	Formal assessment. Collect data about children's level of understanding for a given concept. Done before and after activities.	Questioning and probing individual children for verbal responses. Level of logic is determined.
Performance	Formal assessment. Skills and/or processes are analyzed before and after activities.	Individual stations with materials that children manipulate. Rubrics or criteria assess levels of performances.
Embedded	Informal assessment. Occurs during classroom activities. Skills, processes, and concepts are analyzed.	Collect anecdotal data from observing children's behaviors. Question their predictions, data, and explanations.
Artifacts	Formal asssessment. Analysis is done after completion of hands-on activities. Skills, processes, and concepts are analyzed.	Analyze such items as journals, logs, laboratory notes, products, audio and videotapes. Criteria used to analyze levels of understanding.
Portfolio	Formal assessment. Analysis of all data collected from assessment strategies used prior to and after classroom activities. Analysis of patterns in use and understanding of skills and processes, and concepts.	Create rubrics or criteria to analyze student work.

probes hooked up to computers. Thus, children's level of use and proficiency with technology may need to be assessed before beginning an activity that requires the use of technology. Besides assessing proficiency levels, assessment shows whether children can handle the technology safely and carefully.

Children's levels of performance or skills can be assessed through stations that require them to apply their knowledge. Each station consists of sets of directions for solving problems using the technology. The following are examples of questions to assess children's use of a compass, a protractor, and a triple beam balance:

Station 1: Using the compass, make the following angles: 90°, 45°, and 10°.

Station 2: Using the protractor, find the number of degrees for the angles in Figure 13.1.

Station 3: Using the triple beam balance, weigh the objects to the nearest gram.

FIGURE 13.1

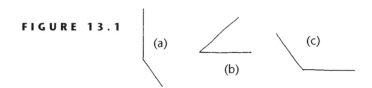

(a)

(b)

(c)

Guidelines for Developing Performance Assessment Items

1. ***Determine technologies to be assessed.*** They may be skills that children will use throughout the year or they may be required for specific activities. Both pre- and postassessments can be conducted to identify changes in knowledge. The pre-assessment can provide baseline data about children's understanding at the beginning of the year. Technology assessment should focus on manipulating materials to perform specific skills. For example, children can measure the temperature of water using a thermometer.

2. ***Write instructions for each assessment station on index cards.*** Ideally, there should be one station for each child. All children can participate at the same time. If the assessment is limited to certain types of skills or equipment is limited, some children can be engaged in the assessment while others work at another activity. The space of the classroom may limit the scope of the assessment. Stations can be set up in another area of the school and several teachers can use the same assessment.

3. ***Gather the necessary materials for each station.*** Each station should have enough material for one child.

4. ***Develop a rubric or criteria for acceptable levels of proficiency.*** Do this before administering the performance assessment. The following is an example for assessing the use of a compass.

Points	Criteria
3	No margin of error. The exact angle is made.
2	Plus or minus for one degree of error.
1	Plus or minus for more than one degree of error.
0	Unable to measure angle.

The total number of points a child accumulates determines whether he or she has enough proficiency to continue using the skill without further practice. For example, a teacher may decide that using a compass within one degree of error is sufficient to work with activities that require a compass.

5. ***Determine the number of minutes that each child is allowed to spend at a station.*** The minutes will have to be determined by the skills involved. Using a temperature probe connected to a computer may take twenty minutes; focusing a microscope may take only five minutes. If children are allowed to take as much time as they need, they may have to bring a book or something else to read or do while other children are finishing.

6. ***Give children instructions before beginning the assessment.*** Performance assessments must be very structured for children to complete each station in an orderly fashion. Before beginning the assessment, tell students the length of time they have at each station and the direction in which they

are to rotate from station to station. For example, if a child starts at station 3, she will end at station 2.

7. ***Provide a form for answering the questions.*** A form will help in assessing children's work. The form should include the number of the assessment item and a place to display answers or work. Remind students to write the correct number if they do not begin at station 1.

The above guidelines assume that all students will be assessed at a specific time. But an assessment can extend over a long period of time and students can perform the assessments whenever they have completed other tasks. Or one or two stations can be set up and one student at a time can work at a station after completing a reading assignment. The stations can be left in place for several days until all students have completed them.

Performance assessments are more appropriate for upper grades than lower grades for two reasons. First, the technology used in upper grades is more sophisticated, making it necessary to know each child's level of proficiency. Second, since this assessment is very structured, the different procedures may be difficult for young children to follow.

The disadvantages of using performance assessments are the time limits given for each station and the written directions. Children who have difficulty reading the directions will be limited in performing the assessment items.

Classroom Activity 13.5

Reflections on Implementation of Assessment Strategies

INSTRUCTIONS

Kamen (1996) describes an elementary school teacher's implementation of assessment strategies in her science class. Individually, read the case study data (pages 863–873) and their implications (pages 873–875).

DISCUSSION QUESTIONS

■ What are your thoughts about this teacher's experiences with authentic assessment?

■ What questions does it raise about implementing authentic assessment in your own classroom?

■ What are your thoughts about the implications of this study?

A Word about Lesson Plans

Developing and writing lesson plans can be beneficial for successful teaching. Lesson plans for teaching model 1, transmitting information, can be fairly straightforward and simple. For this model, lesson plans might state goals and objectives, page numbers of the book, necessary handouts, and how children will be evaluated. All children are doing the same thing, such as reading, taking notes, answering questions, and/or watching demonstrations. But what if you are using inquiry and individualizing instruction to accommodate different levels of development? Inquiry is "messy" because of the uncertainty of where children will go with their questions and investigations. This style of teaching is reflected in model 4. Children are doing different activities. Teaching is facilitating learning through questioning and interacting with children on an individual basis. Children are assessed in a variety of ways. Activities are open-ended and extend over long periods of time. Children are learning a variety of concepts or they are learning concepts in depth through a variety of activities. Teacher and children are very active.

It becomes difficult to write traditional lesson plans for individualized inquiry situations because of the wide range of individual responses to activities. Teaching behaviors will change on the spot depending on the experiments and the children's reactions. With this in mind, think of developing *facilitation plans* rather than lesson plans. Facilitation plans can minimize those unexpected events and organize the learning experience.

In addition to facilitation plans, unexpected events can be minimized by actually doing the activity yourself before using it with the children. This is not always possible and unanticipated events still can happen.

- What would you want to include in a lesson plan that would help you anticipate and organize the learning experience?

Use the inquiry approach to develop facilitation plans. The following are suggested questions that will help you develop appropriate facilitation plans:

- What background information do I need to know about the activity?
- What are possible concepts children will learn from the activity?
- What evidence will be used to find out what they are learning?
- What materials will children need for the activity?
- What procedures should be used for children to collect materials?
- What procedures should be used for children to put things away?
- Should children work by themselves or in groups?
- What teaching behaviors will facilitate learning for this particular activity?
- What do children need to know to begin the activity?
- What will children do during the activity?
- Are there additional classroom management rules that must be stated?
- Are there specific safety precautions children should know about?

By addressing questions such as these, you can create an organized learning environment and minimize the number of unexpected events. But no matter how much detail you put into plans, unexpected events still happen. Learning to deal with those events successfully takes experience. And sometimes those unexpected events can lead to meaningful learning. Many scientific and mathematical ideas were revealed through serendipitous events. In the first few years of teaching, maintain records of those unexpected events so that activities and experiences can be modified.

Summary

Research plays an important part in teaching. A focus on research improves teaching and provides data about student understanding. However, behavioral research is complex because human behavior is affected by many variables. The national science and mathematics standards call for creating teaching conditions that allow children to learn to construct and solve their own problems.

The process of collecting, analyzing, and applying data about teaching and learning makes educational change and implementing standards meaningful.

Knowledge is constructed through inquiry. Curiosity is just as important for teaching mathematics and science as it is for learning about mathematics and science. Without curiosity about teaching and how children learn, professional growth is minimal. Questioning is the driving force for learning. A child may ask, "Why do we have to learn this?" or a teacher may ask, "Why do I have to teach this?" Answers like, "You have to learn this to prepare you for next year," or "This has to be taught because it is in the curriculum guide." are based on beliefs and opinions. Opinions and beliefs can be changed into facts by collecting data. Changes based on valid data are credible. Parents and administrators are likely to support changes based on facts rather than on beliefs or opinions.

"Why don't the children like the math worksheets?" "Why is Johnny distracting others during science activities?" "Why don't children do better on the math tests?" Rather than searching for answers to these questions based on data, teachers often revert to stock answers based on beliefs: "Children are different today." "Johnny doesn't know how to work with his peers." "Children just don't study hard enough." Reverting to these answers is easier than collecting data. Making changes to improve student learning takes work and perseverance.

Choices are made in teaching. One choice is to maintain the status quo by allowing external forces such as parents, politicians, and other officials to make the decisions. Doing this ignores the questions and data that arise from teaching experience. The second choice is to pay attention to those questions and data and initiate change, which includes stating why the changes need to be made. Maintaining the status quo creates friction between teachers and administrators and teachers and students, because teachers focus on maintaining discipline and making children do things they may not want to do. In turn, children focus on pleasing teachers or resisting teacher demands. This friction causes teacher burnout and children mentally dropping out. The second choice is dynamic, allowing both teacher and children to grow intellectually, because an attempt is made to follow one's own internal learning guidance system, making teaching and learning a growth experience. Even though this second choice requires much work, it is much more rewarding than the first choice. Make inquiry a part of teaching and learning mathematics and science. The mathematics Standard 6, analysis of teaching and learning, provides an excellent summary of the second choice. This standard incorporates the same learning processes that children use to learn mathematics and science. Read the standard again to identify these learning processes. Assessment involves inquiry and problem solving. These ideas will also be discussed in Chapter 14, which examines ways to assess the curriculum and the learning environment.

> **Go back to the reflective questions at the beginning of the chapter and the answers you recorded in your journal.**
>
> **Add to or modify your answers based on what you learned from this chapter.**

TOUR GUIDE

> *National Council of Teachers of Mathematics (1991)*
> *Standard 6: Analysis of Teaching and Learning*
>
> The teacher of mathematics should engage in ongoing analysis of teaching and learning by—
>
> observing, listening to, and gathering other information about students to assess what they are learning; examine effects of the tasks, discourse, and learning environment on students' mathematical knowledge, skills, and dispositions, in order to ensure that every student is learning sound and significant mathematics and is developing a positive disposition toward mathematics; challenge and extend student ideas; adapt or change activity while teaching; make plans, both short and long range; describe and comment on each student's learning to parents and administrators, as well as to the students themselves. (p. 63)

Bibliography

Bronowski, J. (1978). *The common sense of science*. Cambridge, MA: Harvard University Press.

Duckworth, E. (1987). *The having of wonderful ideas and other essays on teaching and learning*. New York: Teachers College Press, Columbia University.

Foster, G., and Heiting, A. (1994). Embedded assessment. *Science and Children, 23*(2), 30–33.

Foster, G., and Pellens, S. (1989). At risk: A pedogenic illness? In J. Lakebrink (Ed.), *Children at risk* (pp. 198–215). Springfield, IL: Charles C Thomas.

Kamen, M. (1996). A teacher's implementation of authentic assessment in an elementary science classroom. *Journal of Research in Science Teaching, 33*(8), 859–877.

Phillips, D. (1996). *Structures of thinking: Concrete operations*. Dubuque, IA: Kendall/Hunt.

Piaget, J. (1979). *The child's conception of the world*. Totowa, NJ: Littlefield, Adams.

National Council of Teachers of Mathematics. (1989). *Curriculum and evaluation standards for school mathematics*. Reston, VA: Author.

National Council of Teachers of Mathematics. (1991). *Professional standards for teaching mathematics*. Reston, VA: Author.

National Research Council. (1996). *National science education standards*. Washington, DC: National Academy Press.

Shymansky, J., Penick, J., Kelsey, L., and Foster, G. (1976). *Science laboratory interactions categories (SLIC)*—Teacher, unpublished report. Iowa City, IA: University of Iowa.

Wingert, P. (1996, December 2). The sum of mediocrity. *Newsweek*, 96.

APPENDIX A *SLIC Coding Sheet Template*

Student Behaviors Coding Sheet Template

Student Behaviors	Lesson Related 15 seconds/tally (min.)	Total	Non–Lesson Related 15 seconds/tally (min.)	Total
1. Manipulating objects				
2. Making observations				
3. Asking short-answer questions				
4. Asking extended-thought questions				
5. Listening				
6. Answering questions				
7. Giving explanations				
8. Giving information				
9. Demonstrating equipment				
10. Writing				
11. Reading				
12. Walking around				
	Total min.		Total min.	

CHAPTER 14 | Assessing the Management of the Learning Environment and Curriculum Through Inquiry

Ideas such as light travelling through space, matter being conserved on the Earth as a sphere in space may be assumed to be a starting point in our teaching schemes yet they may not have been constructed in a meaningful way by pupils taking the science courses.

This suggests that in curriculum planning it is necessary not only to consider the structure of the subject but also to take into account the learners' ideas.

R. Driver, E. Guesne, and A. Tiberghien, *Children's Ideas in Science*

JOURNEY PREPARATION

Reflective Questions

- What is a curriculum?

- What determines a curriculum framework?

- What are the disadvantages and advantages of commercially prepared curricula as opposed to locally prepared curricula?

- What are appropriate ways to manage materials and equipment in the classroom?

- What would be the ideal learning environment for hands-on inquiry teaching and learning?

- How do you know what science and mathematics activities are appropriate for learning concepts?

- As a classroom teacher, what would you do to prepare to teach science and mathematics activities?

- What would lesson plans look like for inquiry teaching and learning?

Introduction

A curriculum is a framework for learning. Typically, a curriculum is bound by the content of the subject area used and articulated by goals and outcomes, background information, teaching, learning, and assessment strategies. The goals and outcomes of a curriculum should, in some fashion, reflect national, state, and community educational goals or expectations. Science curriculum is defined by major biological, earth, and physical science topics. Mathematics is defined by basic mathematical operations (addition, subtraction, division, and multiplication), parts to the whole (fractions, ratios, and percentages), geometry, and algebra.

The use of commercially prepared programs is becoming just as popular as using textbooks. Although sometimes more expensive than a single textbook, these programs provide units developed around science and mathematics topics or concepts. For example, units may be organized around the ideas of cycles, populations, electricity, or even general topics such as earth science or geometry. Teacher guides are included, usually bound in loose-leaf notebooks so that teachers can remove specific instructions and other materials for copying. The teacher guides may also include background information, goals and outcomes, and assessment strategies. Ideas for integration with other subject areas, especially mathematics and the expansion of topics to include S/T/S (science, technology, and society) issues may be provided. Some companies provide only teacher guides; other companies provide materials organized in boxes according to topics or concepts. These programs are developed as articulated units that span kindergarten through upper elementary grades. Thus, teachers do not have to spend time developing units with an articulation component or finding additional activities and materials. The curriculum boxes are labeled and designed to be displayed in the classroom and accessible by children. The main responsibility of the teacher is to learn the contents of the teacher guides and to execute the activities. In the long run, commercially prepared programs are time savers for teachers.

The disadvantages of adopting textbook and curriculum programs often outweigh the advantages, however. They belong to the "one size fits all" model. Teachers are asked to adopt teaching and instructional strategies that may or may not fit the needs of individual children. All children in the same classroom are taught the same concept using the same materials following the same directions. Even though the authors of the curriculum may warn teachers there are no right or wrong answers in science, the activities are still focused on observable, predetermined outcomes. If experiments yield unexpected outcomes, teachers are instructed to brainstorm with students to find out why this happened. These messages set up the wrong expectations of science. However, if activities are open-ended with many possible events occurring as opposed to one expected event, the focus is on looking at patterns through different events. Criteria for selecting appropriate activities for mathematics and science learning are discussed later in this chapter.

In many cases, teachers have to attend many inservice days to learn about materials before units can be fully implemented in the classroom. That is, they have to "learn the script" for the activities. Their scripts can include such things as giving directions for the activity, asking children particular questions, and defining words for the given concept. Without these inservices and "script practices," curriculum programs have been known to remain in storage because teachers have little ownership in them or enough experience to make the transition to a new program.

Many curriculum programs are expensive because of the cost of the curriculum guides, specially prepared materials, and storage containers. In some cases, individual components or materials of the programs are not sold separately. Materials that can be purchased locally at a much lower cost may not be an option.

Another disadvantage of using packaged curriculum programs and textbooks is the perception that all of what children should know, regardless of background, experience, and age, is found within those boundaries (textbook or box). For example, a teacher may say: "I have to teach about crayfish

Advantages	Disadvantages
Saves time in preparing units and activities.	Expensive.
Materials and equipment are organized.	Usually require extended inservice program to learn the curriculum structure and philosophy.
Programs are articulated between grade levels.	Limited entering points to meet individual children's needs.
All-inclusive: goals, objectives, assessments, data sheets, etc.	Teachers may "stick to the script" for security rather than adapting to individual needs.
	Focus of activities is on expected outcomes rather than causal relationships.
	All programs will not appeal to all teachers.

because they are part of the textbook or curriculum." Any alternatives are likely to be dismissed in spite of knowing that there are local animals better suited for study than crayfish.

Many textbooks and curriculum programs appear progressive because of all the materials, but they often ignore the learning differences between children. Commercially made programs, no matter how worthy their intentions, can create blinders that block the possibilities for multiple entering points to learning opportunities more suited for the children in a given classroom. Teachers who have little experience with hands-on science and mathematics find security within these boundaries of prepared curricula and never venture out to explore other possibilities. Table 14.1 summarizes the advantages and disadvantages of commercially prepared materials.

Classroom Activity 14.1

Analysis of Commercial Mathematics and Science Curricula

INSTRUCTIONS

Find three different sets of commercially prepared science and mathematics curriculum program guides. In groups of four to five students, analyze the content of the teacher guides. Each group can choose a different grade level. Make a Venn diagram such as the one illustrated in Figure 14.1. The Venn diagram creates areas to compare two of the programs at a time as well as all three programs. Write the name of the program on the line next to a circle. Compare the differences and similarities among the three programs by placing descriptors in the appropriate areas of the Venn diagram. Place characteristics that are unique to each program within the areas of the circles that do not intersect.

DISCUSSION QUESTIONS

- Discuss the similarities and differences of the programs. What do they have in common? What are the differences?

- What is unique in each program?

FIGURE 14.1

Program Name _____   Program Name _____

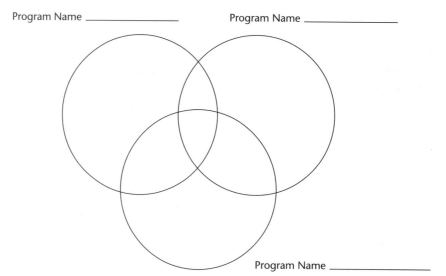

Program Name _____

- If you had to choose one of the programs, which would you choose?
- What are some of the disadvantages of the programs?
- What would you do to modify the programs?

As you glanced through these programs you might have noticed that the same idea can be presented in different ways. For example, activities related to volume may have different goals, outcomes, teaching strategies, and instructions. Nothing is written in stone regarding how a concept is taught or learned. This notion should give classroom teachers the freedom to modify activities to suit the learning styles of their classroom. The parameters of a curriculum should account for individual children's needs, interests, backgrounds, and intellect; the nature of learning; and the processes, skills, and concepts of mathematics and science.

Consider what the national standards for both mathematics and science say (page 353).

What common themes are found in both standards? These standards define the learning environment as all-encompassing. Learning occurs everywhere and opportunities for learning should not be limited by the contents of textbooks and curriculum guides. Our culture is diverse; many societal issues may be ignored if a curriculum is highly structured.

The Classroom Environment

The last two questions of the seven presented in Chapter 13 were not discussed in that chapter. These two questions will now be addressed.

What is the appropriate learning environment for inquiry?

The learning environment includes not only the classroom but also the school grounds, the neighborhood, zoos, museums, farms, and nature centers. The environmental activities presented in Chapter 3 are examples of learning situations for using resources beyond the classroom. But since the classroom is the primary environment for learning science, its physical layout should also be assessed. How should the furniture and materials be organized to create an

TOUR GUIDE

> *National Council of Teachers of Mathematics (1991)*
> *Standard 5: Learning Environment*
>
> The teacher of mathematics should create a learning environment that fosters the development of each student's mathematical power by—
> providing and structuring the time necessary to explore sound mathematics and grapple with significant ideas and problems; using the physical space and materials in ways that facilitate students' learning of mathematics; providing a context that encourages the development of mathematical skill and proficiency; respecting and valuing student ideas, ways of thinking, and mathematical dispositions;
> and by consistently expecting and encouraging students to
> —work independently or collaboratively to make sense of mathematics; take intellectual risks by raising questions and formulating conjectures; display a sense of mathematical competence by validating and supporting ideas with mathematical arguments. (p. 57)
>
> *National Research Council (1996)*
> *Teaching Standard D*
>
> Teachers of science design and manage learning environments that provide students with the time, space, and resources needed for learning science. In doing this, teachers
>
> - Structure the time available so that students are able to engage in extended investigations.
> - Create a setting for student work that is flexible and supportive of science inquiry.
> - Ensure a safe working environment.
> - Make the available science tools, materials, media, and technological resources accessible to students.
> - Identify and use resources outside the school.
> - Engage students in designing the learning environment. (p. 43)

environment conducive to learning? What can be done to the classroom to make it aesthetically pleasing? How will the materials be organized and managed when children are working on hands-on activities? What behaviors are acceptable during science and mathematics activities? The answers to these questions can help the teacher create an environment that allows children freedom to learn within secure, safe boundaries.

Classroom Activity 14.2   ***Ideal Environment***

INSTRUCTIONS

Think about the ideal classroom environment for teaching and learning mathematics and science. Make a list of what you would want to include to support learning mathematics and science. On paper, create an illustration of the environment that incorporates elements from the list. Be imaginative and creative. Your creation may be the classroom of the future!

FIGURE 14.2
Side view of buckets

Read Kohn's (1996) description of the ideal classroom for promoting understanding.

DISCUSSION QUESTIONS

■ How does Kohn's description compare with your thoughts about the ideal classroom?

■ What items does Kohn include that make sense to you?

Physical Attributes of the Classroom That Promote Learning

Discuss your lists and illustrations from Classroom Activity 14.2 with others in a small group. Compare your findings to the following suggestions for the ideal classroom.

Make Materials Accessible to Children

Children should be able to find materials on their own. If materials are hidden, children will depend on the teacher to find things, and a classroom teacher has enough to do without having to retrieve equipment for children. Label storage areas to identify the location of particular materials. When materials are openly displayed, make a visual check to see if all materials have been placed in their appropriate storage containers, and to determine what is missing. Materials can be stored in such items as five-gallon ice cream buckets, washtubs, clear plastic storage containers, and milk carton crates. The five-gallon ice cream buckets (see Figure 14.2), can be stacked pyramid style on their sides, and can be glued, taped, or stapled to each other. Children can see what is in each bucket and retrieve items easily. When space is not a problem, materials can be stored on tables, shelves, and countertops. Shelves can be made from bricks and wooden boards.

Items that are infrequently used can be stored in other places in the school and brought to the classroom at the appropriate times. These items can be stored in boxes, labeled according to contents, topics, units, or some other description. Visit schools that have hands-on mathematics and science programs to find out how they store and display materials.

Include Living Organisms in the Classroom

Besides being learning tools, plants add beauty to the learning environment. If a classroom has windows, place potted plants on the sills or near the light. They can also be hung from the ceiling. Children can make terrariums and herbariums from old aquariums. A piece of nonbreakable glass can be cut to fit over the opening of the terrarium or herbarium to keep animals and moisture inside. And of course, classrooms can include aquariums as well. You can arrange to have one child per day bring pets to school so classmates can see them. If there is an unused area of the school, it can be turned into a miniature zoo or greenhouse that the children maintain. Besides learning about plants and animals, children will learn responsibility by taking care of living things. It is important to remember, though, that not all animals and plants can survive in a classroom. Most wild animals are difficult to keep alive outside their natural environments. Some states restrict the species that can be collected. Be sure you know the restrictions before collecting them.

Have children create a science museum in the school. Each grade can be responsible for adding, modifying, or deleting activities on a rotating basis.

Display Student Projects

Projects can be displayed on tables and counters in classrooms or hallways. Projects can be suspended from ceilings, or shown in other, special areas of the school building.

Change Furniture Arrangements

Rather than keeping desks in straight rows, place them in different arrangements that are conducive to the activity taking place. Move some desks together when children work in groups and keep other desks separate for those who want to work by themselves. Provide an area of the room where children can sit together for group discussions. Set up special places in the room such as learning stations, reading areas, and exploration and experimenting areas.

Provide Multiple Activities for a Given Concept

Providing multiple activities for a given concept helps children choose activities that relate to their ability levels and interests. It also helps reduce the amount of materials needed to conduct activities. Giving each child a set of batteries and bulbs at the same time, for example, can be very expensive. Limit the number of children per activity. Children can rotate from one activity to the next. The time spent per activity can be determined by the interest levels of the children.

All of the activity's materials need not be made accessible immediately. Hold materials back. For example, if a child wants to work with Pattern Blocks, which often contain mirrors, give the child the set of blocks minus the mirrors. Provide the mirrors later after the child has had ample time to explore the shapes and patterns of the blocks. When children are beginning to study electricity, do not give them entire sets of batteries, wires, bulbs, and holders. Let them begin with one battery, one bulb, and one wire to see if they can light the bulb. Once this is accomplished, add additional bulbs, batteries, and wires. Gradually add materials as they are needed.

Provide Activity Learning Stations or Centers

A multiple activity classroom can be set up with learning centers for mathematics, science, and reading. An individual center consists of a focused activity with appropriate materials and instructions. The instructions should be clear enough that children can become engaged in the activity without depending on the teacher. Depending on the activity, children can work by themselves or together at a station. The stations are not replaced by new ones until all children have had the opportunity to work at them. Typically, stations are used for activities that are structured in directions and outcomes. For example, children do not need a list of instructions to work with Pattern Blocks or Geoblocks. However, if a crystal-making center is available, children will need specific directions to make the crystals.

Provide Resource Areas

Not all questions can be answered through hands-on activities nor can a teacher be expected to answer all of them. Provide plenty of resources that will help children find answers to their questions. Have a section of the room supplied with a variety of books, both fiction and nonfiction, related to mathematics and science. Nonfiction books on science and mathematics can be motivating for emerging readers or those who need more experience with reading. If you do not have enough books, libraries often provide classroom collections based on topics for prescribed periods of time. Ask parents and others in the community to donate books. For upper grades, computers and accessories, such as heat and temperature probes and motion detectors, can be valuable resources for finding answers to questions. Access to the Internet will also allow students to search for information that cannot be found in other classroom sources.

Use the Environment Surrounding the School

The environment surrounding the school is just as important to learning mathematics and science as is the classroom. The environment may include the school playground or extend to other areas of the community. The school playground can be used to create vegetable and flower gardens, wetland or prairie areas, and to plant trees. Often parents are willing to share their time and talent in school-related projects. Birdhouses and feeders can be placed on the school grounds so children can observe bird activities. If the area surrounding the school is big enough, develop a nature trail. Otherwise find out if there are places in the community to take nature hikes.

Identify and locate other community resources such as zoos, nature centers, museums, and science centers. Plan field trips to these sites or have professionals from these locations work with children at school. Some corporations welcome student observers. Scientists from these businesses may make themselves available to work with students on their science projects.

Table 14.2 summarizes many possibilities for providing a rich learning environment both within and outside the school. Not all of these possibilities may be feasible for a particular school, but they are presented as reminders to consider when the goal is to improve the learning environment with available resources. Many items for improving the inside learning environment can also be used to enrich learning that occurs at an outside learning site.

Inside Learning Environment	*Outside Learning Environment*
Multiple Seating Arrangements Children work ■ With desks separate or together ■ On floor ■ At tables **Multiple Furniture Styles** ■ Desks ■ Tables **Grow and Care for Live Plants and Animals** ■ Terrariums ■ Aquariums ■ Herbariums ■ Potted plants **Multiple Storage Areas** ■ Shelves, cupboards, and drawers ■ Bins, boxes, tubs, crates ■ Ice cream buckets ■ Clear plastic milk cartons and two-liter bottles **Visibility and Accessibility** ■ Labeled materials/equipment ■ Transparent storage containers **Technology Support** ■ Computers with Internet connections, word processing, laboratory accessories ■ Calculators ■ Rulers, compasses, protractors ■ Magnifying lenses, microscopes ■ Balances and scales ■ Graduated cylinders ■ Hot plates **Reading Resources** ■ Books ■ Magazines **Activity Learning Centers** ■ Materials ■ Instructions	**School Yard/Neighborhood** Locate or establish ■ Nature trails ■ Vegetable and flower gardens ■ At tables **Neighborhood/Cities** Locate or establish ■ Ponds, lakes, rivers, forests, deserts, and prairies as habitat sites ■ Nature trails **Towns and Cities** Find and use ■ Planetariums ■ Botanical gardens ■ Interactive museums ■ Farms ■ Orchards

Classroom Management

Children regularly use manipulatives and other equipment. These materials must be organized, maintained, and replaced. An inventory of materials should be made on a regular basis. The following suggestions will help with managing materials and the children who use them. The strategies you use will depend on the resources available to you.

Involve Students or Parents with Materials Management

Every child has to accept responsibility for retrieving materials, cleaning them, and putting them away. However, having assistance helps to ensure that children do put away the materials in the proper places. Assign students specific responsibilities, on a rotating basis, to help other classmates put things away. For example, one person from each group can make sure that everyone has put materials back in the proper place. This child can report to the teacher about the status of the materials before moving on to other activities. Children love the responsibility of helping the teacher. Involve them as much as possible in managing science and mathematics materials.

Another strategy is to put one type of equipment away at a time. Mini kits can be created, using plastic storage bags containing the necessary materials. Each bag may hold one set of materials for each child or for children working in pairs. Children put everything back into the bag and return it to the storage area. A visual check of the bags shows whether everything has been returned. A more structured strategy is to have all the children put each piece of equipment back into the storage bag at the same time. The teacher can hold up each piece of equipment and wait for the child to place it in the bag. This procedure continues until all equipment has been returned to the bags.

Another possibility is to ask the assistance of older students or children's parents to act as teacher aides and help with organizing, ordering and purchasing, repairing, and collecting materials for the classroom. If the budget is limited, parents can help find inexpensive materials solicited from other parents, local community organizations, or businesses. Aides can contact personnel at hospitals, garden shops, grocery stores, and/or fast-food stores to see if they have items to donate. For example, plastic coffee stirrers shaped like miniature spoons or spatulas make excellent measuring devices for working with dry household or kitchen ingredients.

Keep the Classroom Clean and Safe

Make cleanup accessible to children. If the room has no water source, store water in plastic washtubs or plastic buckets of various sizes. Cover surfaces with newspaper, plastic drop cloths, or plastic tablecloths, even old plastic shower curtains. Children can wear adults' old shirts or T-shirts as smocks. Children can work right on the floor on top of the tablecloth or shower curtain. In fact, it is a good idea to have children work on the floor when they are using manipulatives that can be easily knocked over or fall off their desks. In addition, give children trays to hold their materials. The trays act as containment areas and also help contain spills of liquids and powders.

Require children to work with small amounts of liquids and materials, especially those that consist of small or fine particles. Use small containers such as vials and coffee stirrers for mixing and measuring devices. When children carry water in large containers such as washtubs, instruct them to fill the tubs halfway to prevent splashing and spilling.

If possible, avoid using containers and other equipment made of glass. Have a special area of the classroom designated for the use of chemicals or burners and keep to a minimum the number of children who can be in the area. Have safety goggles available for children who work in these areas as well as a fire extinguisher and fire blanket. Make sure that children with long hair keep it tied back.

Analyze Work Spaces

When children work by themselves, space them throughout the room to reduce their interactions. When children are too close together, some will disrupt the learning process of others. Children working at desks that are in rows are more likely to talk with each other or bother each other's materials. The same is true of children sitting at tables. Place children back to back on the floor between chairs or desks. Turn desks so children are not facing each other. There are numerous arrangements that allow children their own working space with minimal disruptions from their peers. For young children working on the floor, draw an imaginary circle around each one and tell them that the circle is their own private space and they must stay within it. No child can enter another child's circle without permission from the teacher. Consider using hula hoops or clothesline ropes to physically mark the spaces.

Allow Group Work to Be Dynamic

As children mature, interaction with their peers is essential to learning. Just as children learn from action on objects, they also learn from action on the ideas of others. This was discussed in Chapter 3. Group work tends not to function properly unless each child has his or her own set of materials. Children who end up watching may disengage mentally from an activity. Their attention may then be drawn toward activities that are non–lesson related and disruptive to others.

Creating groups because equipment is minimal is good as long as each child is engaged in the activity and has the responsibility of completing the activity tasks. A successful working group becomes a cohesive unit. Groups develop individualized learning characteristics, making them unique in terms of interests, needs, and learning outcomes. If children are assigned to groups, however, cohesive bonding may be difficult to attain. Certain negative behavior characteristics may appear when children are placed in situations that are uncomfortable for them. Allowing children to choose and form their own groups or to work by themselves aids in reducing the number of social conflicts that may arise. Social conflicts generally have negative effects on learning; intellectual conflicts have positive effects.

Some educators may argue that children must learn to get along with each other. Children will learn to work and get along with each other if they have common interests and goals. Group work is effective when children can form their own groups based on mutual interests and needs. Many activities require more than one pair of hands for setup or involve solving complex questions or problems, which requires a collaborative effort. Problem solving may involve numerous activities such as writing, assembling materials, and researching.

The individuals in a group combine their talents to support the problem-solving process. The purpose of grouping during mathematics and science is to support intellectual development.

Behavior Management

Boredom, improper use of equipment, or disruptive behavior may be the results of disparate activities. Unsuitable behavior may also result from the lack of sufficient materials or too many directions to follow. Disruptive behaviors can be viewed as indicators of irrelevant activities rather than something wrong with children. Disruptive behavior may occur in spite of teachers' good intentions. There are too many variables affecting human behavior to develop a formula for preventing them. The best that can be done is to keep inappropriate behaviors to a minimum. It is important to work through activities before using them with children. This will tell a teacher what problems children may have with the activity. However, it is not always possible to do this. Go ahead and do the activity with children but be ready for unanticipated events. Alert children that the activity is new and solicit their patience if problems do arise.

Establish Rules and Consequences for Working with Hands-On Materials

Rules are important when working with manipulatives because they inform children about the boundaries for acceptable behavior. Children have much more freedom to walk around and to converse with others during hands-on science activities compared to the traditional ways of teaching. This section presents suggestions for managing classroom behaviors. *Keep the rules simple and minimal.* The more rules there are, the more difficult it is to enforce them or for children to remember them.

These two rules sum it up:

1. Work by yourself.
2. Use the materials and equipment only for learning purposes.

Any additional rules can be added as necessary. Post the rules where they can be seen by all, with an appropriate set of consequences for not following them. A consequence for rule 2 might be: Materials are put away and children work on a non–hands-on activity. Most children do not want to lose the right to work with manipulatives!

Consider the Noise Level

The noise level, of course, will be high when children are using manipulatives. A teacher has to decide how much noise can be tolerated, especially non-lesson-related noise. Children cannot be expected to remain on task for the entire time. The noise level tolerance may be defined by whether children and teacher have to raise their voices to be heard. When children spend too much time talking about non-lesson-related topics, it is a signal for the teacher to investigate what is occurring. A teacher has the right to inform children when they have reached noise-level tolerance. Say: "I cannot hear what Alicia is telling me. I want everyone to whisper when talking."

Make Children Aware of Their Behavior

Sometimes children are not aware that their actions are breaking the rules. If a child is using the materials inappropriately, ask the child what he is doing. Let him explain before passing judgment. If a rule has been broken, ask the child, "What does the rule say about the use of equipment?" He may have forgotten, misunderstood, or not have heard the rule. Another alternative is to give choices when a rule is broken. For example, say, "Either you work by yourself or you will have to do another assignment. What is your choice?" It is important to give responsibility to children for their own actions by making them aware of what they are doing and letting them make choices as to how they will behave. Usually, there are valid reasons for disruptive behavior. Assess the situation before deciding what action to take.

Help Children Choose Activities

Children will choose activities that interest them. Discipline problems arise when all children must do the exact same activity. You can give them choices of different activities on the same topic or different activities on different topics. Tell them they will all eventually have an opportunity to work with all activities. If children still lose interest, the responsibility is theirs. The teacher can ask: "Why did you choose the activity?" This gives the child an opportunity to explain and the teacher to offer suggestions to maintain the child's interest. In contrast, teachers who assign activities often expend inordinate amounts of energy finding ways to motivate children to stay on task. But choices often lead to internal motivation and rewards because children are driven by curiosity and interest. When children learn something because of their own motivation, the learning is meaningful, which is a reward in itself. Real learning and teaching take place.

Facilitate Learning

Fact finding and looking for solutions to disruptive behavior are characteristic of teachers who facilitate learning. This is much more rewarding than having to develop generic reward systems for good behavior. A facilitator helps the learner think when interest appears to wane. When the child feels she has exhausted all the possibilities of working with an activity, the teacher as facilitator should be willing to help her with alternative choices. A child-centered focus helps children to become independent learners; a teacher-centered focus makes children depend on someone else in order to learn. Treffinger (1978) confirms that when children are evaluated their curiosity and inquiry are inhibited, which in turn ensures undue dependency on the teacher.

Exploration of a few concepts in depth is more important to learning than covering a large amount of content. Unfortunately, students are accustomed to fragmented learning dictated by schedules. It may take some time to help youngsters learn to stay on task and explore options for longer periods of time. Do not despair.

Offer Appropriate Praise

Some children resent another child receiving praise. The child receiving praise may feel embarrassed for being singled out. The child may feel pressure either to side with peers or to side with the teacher. If the child sides with other children, they will likely avoid interacting with the teacher. If the child sides with the teacher, peers are likely to avoid contact with him.

Praise and positive reinforcement are appropriate if you want children to follow specific rules of behavior or learn specific things. They are effective if you want children to remain at their work stations. "Mark, I appreciate you working at your station." "Susie, thank you for carrying the balance with two hands." In learning situations, praise and positive reinforcement often become ways to manipulate children to do things they are not interested in doing. Lepper, Keavney, and Drake (1996, p. 24) say: "Thus, extrinsic rewards may often signal an attempt by some external agent to control the individual's actions, and may therefore lead the individual to view his or her engagement in the rewarded activity as extrinsically, rather than as intrinsically, motivated."

Most children want to please adults. However, the most meaningful reward children can receive is to learn something on their own or solve a problem by themselves. Their self-confidence rises. Activities that are interesting and challenging act as motivators for a child's success. Children who feel they are valued as individuals will not need external rewards and reinforcement.

Classroom Activity 14.3

Reflections about Praise and Positive Reinforcement

INSTRUCTIONS

Take a few minutes to think about your experiences with praise and positive reinforcement given by a teacher during your elementary mathematics and science classes.

DISCUSSION QUESTIONS

- What kinds of rewards did the teacher use?
- What kinds of experiences were rewarded?
- Did the rewards help you to learn?
- What feelings did you have when other children received rewards?
- What feelings did you have when you received rewards and other children did not?
- Think about experiences that were internally rewarding. What were they like? What feelings did you have?
- Read and discuss the article by Brandt (1995), focusing on this quote:

  Instead we need to examine the task itself, the content of the curriculum, to see how it can be made more engaging. Regardless of what we do about it, though, one of the most thoroughly researched findings in social psychology is that the more you reward someone for doing something, the less interest that person will tend to have in whatever he or she was rewarded to do. (p. 14)

Positive Reinforcement and Recognition

Give children recognition in the following ways and they will build self-confidence in learning.

Listen to Children and Their Ideas

Listening to children validates that what they say is important. Children know you are listening if you paraphrase. Paraphrasing is responding by reiterating what the child has said. Children also know a teacher is listening if their answers or observations are taken seriously. Driver, Guesne, and Tiberghien (1991) say opportunities should be provided for students to make their own ideas explicit if conceptual learning is to occur. Your acceptance can be expressed by a mere nod of the head or by discussing ideas with the child.

Allow Children Enough Time to Answer Questions

Often, the teacher does not allow enough time for responses and calls on someone else. This happens when teachers have a predetermined answer in mind. Allow children time to think through their answers by waiting or rephrasing the question. Waiting for an answer demonstrates interest. Ask open-ended questions that allow children to express their own ideas. This relieves children from trying to give the "right" answer. It allows them to express themselves and what they know rather than to respond with what they think the teacher wants to hear. Driver, Guesne, and Tiberghien (1991) state: "In whatever way the new ideas are introduced individual pupils still have to make them meaningful to themselves: just because someone is told something does not mean they understand it in the way intended" (p. 200). Refer back to Chapter 4 about the processes of questioning.

Give Praise for Appropriate Behaviors

Certain behaviors are expected and children should receive feedback when they do act appropriately. For example, you may want to praise everyone for using the microscopes properly. This informs them of your expectations and levels of tolerance. Real learning is rewarded internally. Make praising behaviors genuine. Tell children specifically what you like about their behaviors. Tell the whole class when everyone follows the rules for appropriate behavior. Public praise can place children in an awkward position. Give praise privately by writing notes or speaking to a child alone. Be honest about what you like or do not like about what the child has done, rather than using praise to manipulate. Always focus on the child's needs and interests. By addressing these needs through genuine interest and sensible solutions you will keep discipline problems to a minimum.

Table 14.3 summarizes ways to manage materials and behaviors.

Developing the Curriculum

What is the appropriate curriculum for inquiry?

Chapter 7 was devoted to how children learn mathematics and science based on Piaget's theory of intellectual development. A set of criteria for selecting appropriate concepts or topics that support the development of students' intelligence will be described here. From kindergarten through eighth grade, all mathematical operations should be learned through manipulating objects before moving to the symbolic level. The emphasis on concrete objects is espe-

Materials	*Behaviors*
Give children responsibility to: ■ Retrieve and return materials ■ Assist other children ■ Count pieces ■ Inventory missing or broken pieces	Praise behaviors and skills: ■ Give specific feedback ■ State in behavioral terms Avoid praising learning: ■ Stifles creativity ■ Narrows children's thinking Replace praise with: ■ Listening ■ Paraphrasing
Coordinate repair and replacement: ■ Systematic inventory of materials ■ Request consumable items from parents—common household items, recyclable containers	Guidelines for establishing rules: ■ Viewed as framework to enhance learning ■ Maintain minimum number of rules ■ Focus on expected behaviors ■ Consequences used when rules are ignored ■ Place behavior responsibilities on children
Seek assistance from teenagers and parents	Give children responsibility: ■ To choose activities ■ To work individually or in groups
Cover work areas to minimize cleanup	Children use only relevant materials
Provide each child with own materials	Children know teacher's tolerance levels
Maximize classroom space for work	Activity directions are minimized

cially important to primary grade children because this is foundational learning, constructing knowledge that creates a framework for abstract thinking. These first experiences should begin with free exploration. This includes the construction of mental operations such as addition, subtraction, multiplication, division, and geometrical relationships. Expressing relationships between numbers by using ratios, proportions, percentages, and algebraic expressions should also be learned through the use of concrete objects. Graphs are symbolic representations of relationships. As children mature and gain experience learning mathematics through concrete operations, they can begin to use symbolic representations for algebraic expressions. Mathematical symbolic representations are appropriate for quantifying scientific relationships created through data collection and analysis. Science provides the context for the application of mathematics. Thus, measurement becomes an important tool for science. The free exploration of developing nonstandard units of measurement should be emphasized in the primary grades; standard units can be emphasized in the upper grades.

Understanding science concepts at the symbolic level is much more difficult for elementary school children. Scientists express concepts symbolically because they are shorthand expressions but children need a great deal of experience and intellectual development to use the symbols successfully. Chemical formulas and equations are far removed from concrete experiences because to successfully balance chemical equations, the learner has to understand chemical characteristics at the atomic level. Concepts such as Boyle's law, electrical resistance and power, gravitational pull, speed, light, and sound express actions that are not directly visible. Thus, symbols are used in science to represent complex abstract ideas that are typically beyond the intellectual levels of children at the elementary level.

Selecting science concepts as the contextual frameworks for learning classification and relations, spatial relations, and measurement becomes difficult. There are no specific science concepts that children need to know to progress from grade to grade. For example, learning about electricity is not essential for learning about sound. Learning about insects is not essential to learning about plants. Overall, it is hoped that children do develop an understanding of major science concepts but one concept does not necessarily precede or follow another. In contrast, understanding the concept of numbers is essential for addition and subtraction. Addition and subtraction are needed to understand multiplication and division. Selecting a sequence of mathematical concepts is much more appropriate than selecting a sequence of scientific concepts.

Field Experience Activity 14.1

Teacher Interviews

INSTRUCTIONS

Make an appointment to meet with several elementary teachers. Ask them about their science curriculum and why specific concepts were chosen to be taught. Before questioning the teachers, discuss in a group what kinds of answers they are likely to give.

DISCUSSION QUESTIONS

■ What are the various ways of selecting science topics?

■ What is the most common way to select science topics?

In addition to using concrete objects, select science topics by considering children's interests. Create questionnaires to find out what children want to learn. Give them a list of topics and have them circle the ones that interest them. Use the "I wonder about . . ." activity described in Chapter 4. Questionnaires can be given for several consecutive years to see if there is a trend toward certain topics. Some topics may be of interest to children year after year; others may be deleted, added, or modified.

Think about the science topics that interested you as a child. What science learning experiences were meaningful to you? What were the science concepts that were taught? Ask children if they want to explore the same topics. Using topics that create a comfort level for you can be a springboard for implementing other topics. Both sets of standards for mathematics and science also give suggestions and guidelines for selecting topics.

The concepts in Table 14.4 are recommended for elementary schools because they can be explored through hands-on activities that tap into children's interests. The focus should be on the characteristics of the concepts rather than on symbolic representations (formulas) developed from the characteristics. These concepts should be revisited throughout the elementary school years.

TABLE 14.4
Observable Ideas

Physical Science	Earth Science	Biological Science
Balancing objects	Observable weather	Plant/animal behaviors
Motion	Soil composition	Properties of liquids
Behavior of electricity	Shadows	Plant/animal structures
Behavior of sound	Erosion	Classification
Friction		Growing plants and animals
Behavior of light/color		Interactions of populations
Behavior of magnets		Behavior of populations
Chemical properties		

TABLE 14.5
Ideas Based on
Indirect Observations

Physical Science	Earth Science	Biological Science
Kinetic/potential energy	Plate tectonics	Genetics
Atomic models and structures	Barometric pressure	Food chains
Chemical formulas	Earthquakes/volcanoes	Food webs
Light waves	Planet composition	Ecology
Heat waves	Star composition	Photosynthesis
Radio waves	Earth's composition	Osmosis
Theory of electricity		
Ultraviolet waves		

Table 14.5 gives examples of science concepts that are difficult to explore through hands-on activities.

Compare the two tables. Table 14.4 contains ideas or concepts that children can explore through their senses and through interactions with objects. Data are collected directly through the action on objects. The ideas or concepts in Table 14.5 must be studied either at the molecular and subatomic level or on a grand scale. Take a few minutes to pick one of these ideas and try to explain it to someone else. How do you know what you know? Probably what you know about the idea was explained to you from books, teachers, or other secondary sources. Data were collected from indirect observations to create models of explanation. Remember: *Elementary school children learn best when they can see and touch what is happening.*

Yes, we can model plate tectonics, genetics, and the theory of electricity, but where do children get the information to create the models? Not from firsthand data but from other sources. Children may have fun creating a model, but what are they really learning? A common way to teach about vol-

TABLE 14.6
Mathematics and
Science Units Matrix

Mathematics (Proportions) Science (Motion)	A. Comparing Same Units	B. Equivalent Fractions	C. Percentages
1. Forces			
2. Friction			
3. Speed			

canoes is to mix vinegar and baking soda in a cone and watch the reaction, but this is far from what actually happens. Volcanic activity is very complicated. Or children can pretend to be lions eating antelopes eating grass, to represent a food chain, but other animals eat antelopes as well. Predator and prey relationships are complex. Food chains or food webs cannot be directly observed; they are mental representations of predator and prey relationships. What do children really understand when these concepts are reduced to such simple activities? Do these activities represent inquiry and problem solving or are they just "concrete" ways of transmitting information? *Hands-on activities that rely on understanding secondary knowledge are more likely to perpetuate misconceptions than hands-on activities that generate firsthand knowledge.* Shamos (1995) says:

> It is wrong to assume, for example, that some understanding of the concept of energy, or even how energy is transformed from one form to another, makes one truly literate on the subject of energy, for without appreciation of the overarching conceptual scheme of conservation of energy, the students and particularly the teachers are left with a substantial void in their perceptions of what science is about. (p. 139)

Before assuming that all science concepts can be taught through hands-on activities, consider what children will understand. Will they remember having fun? Is the activity just another way to memorize facts? Does the activity actually represent the phenomenon or is it so simplified that it has little meaning? The purpose of any mathematics or science hands-on activity should be to develop understanding and reasoning.

Throughout this book, parallels have been drawn about teaching and learning science and mathematics, but the following are suggestions for integrating mathematics and science concepts. Francis and Underhill (1996) suggest choosing one science and one mathematics topic and breaking them down into components. A matrix is created to incorporate the components. Table 14.6 is an illustration of integrating selected science and mathematics ideas.

In this case the mathematics components are placed along the horizontal cells (A–C) and the science components along the vertical cells (1–3). For example, motion might be the science concept. Three components of motion could be forces, friction, and speed. The mathematics unit might be proportions and the components could be comparing same units, equivalent fractions, and percentages. Each cell becomes a combination of the mathematics and science components and determines the type of activities required to learn these concepts.

Classroom Activity 14.4　　*Integrate Mathematics and Science Units*

INSTRUCTIONS

Read the article by Francis and Underhill (1996). As a group, select a science concept from the National Science Education Standards (National Research Council, 1996) and a mathematics concept from the Mathematics Educational Standards (National Council of Teachers of Mathematics, 1989). Create a matrix using the Francis and Underhill (1996) model.

DISCUSSION QUESTIONS

▪ What questions were raised as you selected components?

▪ What activities would you suggest for each component?

Choosing, Selecting, and Adapting Activities

There are many science and mathematics activity resource books available for selection of activities. These resource books can be found in teacher stores, at conferences and conventions, in libraries, and from the National Science Teachers Association and the National Council of Teachers of Mathematics. Volumes of activities can be found on the World Wide Web. Remember, not all hands-on activities promote understanding and reasoning. The following criteria are useful in selecting appropriate hands-on activities (Phillips, 1995):

1. The activity must have *objects* for manipulation.

    Objects are those things required to build relationships based on classification, ordering, and spatial relations. A child can manipulate objects and observe them from different angles and viewpoints. Videos, computer images, book and magazine pictures, drawings, and photographs do not fit these criteria and should be used as a resource to supplement learning. For example, trying to classify animals from photographs or pictures is intellectually limiting. The actual size of the animal is misrepresented and only one view is presented. Touching and observing animals are extremely important for understanding the characteristics of animals. Doing mathematical computations with books, worksheets, calculators, or computers without manipulating objects is jumping to the abstract without experiencing the concrete.

2. Each child should have his or her own set of *objects*.

    Children need their own set of objects to reduce the number of interruptions in thinking. Children who have to share materials will lose concentration if they have to obtain materials from other children. Conflicts will erupt and children will disengage if they have to wait or observe others do the activities.

3. The activity goal is to find *relationships*.

    Logic is based on finding relationships. Understanding occurs through cause and effect relationships.

4. The activity must provide *diverse possibilities* for finding relationships.

    The more options of working with materials, the more likely the activity will be appropriate for a diverse range of interests, intellectual levels, and experiences.

5. The activity must have *multiple entering points.*

   Activities that have options will appeal to a wide range of children. For example, children can begin working with Pattern Blocks by building, making patterns, classifying pieces, or creating new shapes.

6. The activity must have *minimal directions.*

   This criterion is related to the two preceding criteria. Activities that allow children to become independently engaged without the teacher's assistance will reduce the number of management problems. A litany of written or verbal instructions make children depend on the teacher for assistance. Verbal instructions are likely to be forgotten or misinterpreted. Written instructions handicap those children who have difficulty reading. Learning mathematics and science should not be totally dependent on children's ability to read or listen. Children who wait for the teacher's help with directions lose interest in activities and find other interesting activities, usually non-lesson-related.

7. Relationships must be clearly *observable* from action on objects.

   Observable means that relationships can be abstracted from touching, looking, hearing, smelling, or tasting. If the relationships are clearly observable, both student and teacher can rely on the objects as the source of information. Both have the same frame of reference. If there is disagreement with the observation, further investigations can be done. The content originates from the objects. Knowledge background is needed if the emphasis is on memorizing secondary information inferred from the action on objects. For example, the theories of electricity are based on inferences, not direct observations. Naturally, one would have to read about the theories of electricity if that information is to be passed on to children.

The more criteria the activities meet, the more they will appeal to children. Many activities can be modified to meet most of these criteria.

Classroom Activity 14.5 | ***Critique Curriculum Materials***

INSTRUCTIONS

Select four to five science activities from a textbook, curriculum program, or science activity resource book. Identify the concepts associated with the activity. Use the form given in Table 14.7 to assess each activity. A template is provided in Appendix A for copying.

Discuss your findings in a small group discussion. Select one or two activities that were assessed and discuss how they might be modified to meet the criteria given above, if they do not already do so. Use the following format to show the modifications:

- Name of activity
- Materials
- Instructions
- Teacher background information (if needed)
- Questions and suggestions to extend the activity

T A B L E   1 4 . 7
Assessing Activities
According to Criteria for
Selecting Activities

Activity name _____   Science concept _____

Criteria for Selecting Activities	Yes	No	Explanation
Objects for manipulation			
Own set of materials			
Goal is to find patterns and relationships			
Diverse possibilities for finding relationships			
Multiple entering points			
Minimal directions			
Observable relationships			

T A B L E   1 4 . 8
Mathematic and/or Scientific
Relationships and Their
Connection to the Activities

Describe Relationships	Directly Connected to Observable Data			Indirectly Connected to Observable Data		
	Yes	No	Explanation	Yes	No	Explanation

| *Classroom Activity 14.6* | *Assessing Activities for Learning Potential* |

INSTRUCTIONS

Assess at least five different activities from the books you selected in Classroom Activity 14.5. Use Table 14.8 for the assessment. A template of Table 14.8 can be found in Appendix B.

DISCUSSION QUESTIONS

- What kinds of relationships seem to be prevalent among the activities?
- What conclusions do you reach about the activities found in the examined books?

Sources for Science and Mathematics Activities

- Major book publishing companies
- Mathematics and science material supply companies
- National Science Teachers Association
- National Council of Teachers of Mathematics
- *Science and Children* journal
- *The Mathematics Teacher* journal

Book publishing and material supply companies have these resources available at conferences and conventions as well as in catalogues.

Sources for Materials

- Mathematics and science supply companies
- Local stores such as general and ethnic grocery stores, drugstores, hardware stores, craft stores, electrical supply stores, toy stores, garden stores

Sources for Curriculum Topics and Concepts

- National Science Education Standards
- National Mathematics Standards publications
- Local, regional, and national conferences and conventions sponsored by the National Science Teachers Association and the National Council of Teachers of Mathematics
- Project 2061 Curriculum Guide

A Word about Technology

At the beginning of this journey, we discussed living in an age of technological communications. Our ability to communicate over the Internet provides an abundance of instant information. The use of technology in the classroom has not been explicitly addressed in this journey because of the constant changes in this area, not only in information but also in the variety of ways to communicate and the new technologies. For example, hypercards and interactive videodisks can be used to create assessment portfolios. There are literally hundreds of Web sites (a few samples are given in Appendix C) for finding science and mathematics activities as well as instructional tools. However, they must be carefully chosen, using the criteria for selecting appropriate activities and instructional tools such as those given in this chapter.

Web sites come and go. Technology requires constant updating and determining how it fits in with inquiry learning. There is a danger that technology will be used to substitute for textbooks and perpetuate the memorization of facts. On the other hand, technology also opens up the possibilities of communicating with scientists, teachers, and other children across the world. Above all, there is no substitute for understanding fundamental mathematical and scientific concepts through hands-on, concrete activities. Technology provides enrichment experiences to support them.

Summary

The driving force for the selection of mathematics and science curriculum content should be based on helping children understand concepts in depth rather than to "cover" them. Thus, the number of concepts may be reduced and revisited year after year but through a variety of different activities. Research has shown that learning fundamental mathematics and science concepts is developmental; concrete experiences must come before abstract concepts. Individual interests and needs also influence what children learn. The experiences must allow for these differences and a variety of activities for the same concepts must be presented.

By adopting an inquiry attitude toward teaching mathematics and science, one is not only modeling science and mathematics, but also providing continuous feedback about the teaching and learning processes. This attitude encompasses collecting data for making decisions. This firsthand data will verify or contradict a teacher's own beliefs and the research found in the literature. The process of focusing on individual children's needs and asking "why" provides the foundation for structuring a dynamic relationship between teaching and learning mathematics and science. Learning to teach by constructing knowledge just as children construct knowledge will keep the teaching process exciting year after year.

Continue asking questions about teaching and learning. Continue learning about mathematics and science teaching by reading professional journals and attending conferences and workshops. Talk to your colleagues and share ideas. Above all, look inside yourself to reflect on what you do as a teacher. Ask yourself: Do I do these things because I am facilitating the natural learning process or because of tradition? Do these things reflect the natural learning process or are they merely procedures for memorizing concepts? Continually collect data about yourself as a teacher and the children as learners. Use the data to shape your teaching behaviors and the learning environment.

> **Go back to the reflective questions at the beginning of the chapter and the answers you recorded in your journal.**
>
> **Add to or modify your answers based on what you learned from this chapter.**

Template to Assess Activities Using the Criteria for Selecting Activities

Activity name _____   *Science concept* _____

Criteria for Selecting Activities	Yes	No	Explanation
Objects for manipulation			
Own set of materials			
Goal is to find patterns and relationships			
Diverse possibilities for finding relationships			
Multiple entering points			
Minimal directions			
Observable relationships			

APPENDIX B

Template to Assess Activities for Mathematic and/or Scientific Relationships and Their Connection to Direct Observations

Activity name _____   *Identified concepts* _____

Describe Relationships	Directly Connected to Observable Data			Indirectly Connected to Observable Data		
	Yes	No	Explanation	Yes	No	Explanation

APPENDIX C

Mathematics and Science Curriculum Guides

Mathematics Concepts Guides

- Barratta-Lorton, R. (1977). *Mathematics—A way of thinking.* Menlo Park, CA: Addison Wesley.
- National Council of Teachers of Mathematics. (1991). *Curriculum and evaluation standards for school mathematics.* Reston, VA: Author.
- K–8
  - Kindergarten Book—Addenda Series, Grades K–6
  - First Grade Book—Addenda Series, Grades K–6
  - Second Grade Book—Addenda Series, Grades K–6
  - Third Grade Book—Addenda Series, Grades K–6
  - Fourth Grade Book—Addenda Series, Grades K–6
  - Fifth Grade Book—Addenda Series, Grades K–6
  - Geometry in the Middle Grades—Addenda Series, Grades 5–8
  - Patterns and Functions—Addenda Series, Grades 5–8
- Phillips, D. G., and Phillips, D. R. (1991). *Developing logical thinking in children: The developmental activities program* (4th ed.). Coralville, IA: Insights Educational Materials and Consulting.

Science Concepts Guides

- American Association for the Advancement of Science. (1993). *Benchmarks for science literacy: Project 2061*. New York: Oxford University Press.

- American Association for the Advancement of Science. (1990). *Project 2061: Science for all Americans*. New York: Oxford University Press.

World Wide Web Sites

- The Clearinghouse of Subject Oriented Internet Resources Guides—http://www.clearinghouse.net

- New Tools for Teaching—http://ccat.sas.upenn.edu/teachdemo

- UnCover—http://www/carl.org. telnet://pac.carl.org

- NLightN—http://www.nlightn.com

- Library of Congress—gopher://marvel.loc.gov or http:www.loc.gov

- Hytelnet via telnet://laguna.epcc.edu

- gopher://liberty.us.wlu.edu

- http://www.einet.net/hytelnet/HYTELNET.html

- University of Michigan via gopher://joeboy.micros.umn.edu

- University of Texas—http://www.lib.utexas.edu/libs/pcl/etest.html

- World Wide Web Virtual Library—http://www.w3.org/hypertext/datasource/bySubject/overview.html

- ERIC Database—http://gopher.ericse.ohio-state.edu/

- Nesen Lesson Plans and Activities—http://nesen.unl.edu/activities/

- Activity Search from Houghton Mifflin—http://www.hmco.com/hmco/school/search/activity2.html

- World in Motion—http://www.schoolnet.ca/math_sco/phys/worldinmotion/

- JPL Learning Link—http://learn.jpl.nasa.gov/lessons.htm

- Bad Science—http://www.ems.psu.edu/~fraser/BadScience.html

- Recurring Science Misconceptions in K–6 Textbooks—http://www.eskimo.com/~billb/miscon/miscon4.html

Bibliography

Brandt, R. (1995). Punished by rewards? A conversation with Alfie Kohn. *Educational Leadership, 53*(1), 13–16.

Driver, R., Guesne, E., and Tiberghien, A. (Eds.). (1991). *Children's ideas in science*. Philadelphia, PA: Open University Press.

Francis, R., and Underhill, R. (1996). A procedure for integrating math and science units. *School Science and Mathematics, 96*(3), 114–119.

Kohn, A. (1996). What to look for in a classroom. *Educational Leadership, 54*(1), 54–55.

Lepper, M., Keavney, M., and Drake, M. (1996). Intrinsic motivation and extrinsic rewards: A commentary on Cameron and Pierce's meta-analysis. *Review of Educational Research, 66*(1), 5–32.

National Council of Teachers of Mathematics. (1989). *Curriculum and evaluation standards for school mathematics*. Reston, VA: Author.

National Council of Teachers of Mathematics. (1991). *Professional standards for teaching mathematics*. Reston, VA: Author.

National Research Council. (1996). *National science education standards.* Washington, DC: National Academy Press.

Phillips, D. (1995). *Sciencing: Towards logical thinking.* Dubuque, IA: Kendall/Hunt.

Shamos, M. (1995). *The myth of scientific literacy.* Brunswick, NJ: Rutgers University Press.

Treffinger, D. (1978). Guidelines for encouraging independence and self-direction among gifted students. *Journal of Creative Behavior, 12*(1), 14–20.

Index